Modern Critical Views

African American
   Poets: Wheatley-
   Tolson
African American
   Poets: Hayden-
   Dove
Edward Albee
American and
   Canadian Women
   Poets, 1930–present
American Women
   Poets, 1650–1950
Maya Angelou
Asian-American
   Writers
Margaret Atwood
Jane Austen
James Baldwin
Honoré de Balzac
Samuel Beckett
Saul Bellow
The Bible
William Blake
Jorge Luis Borges
Ray Bradbury
The Brontës
Gwendolyn Brooks
Elizabeth Barrett
   Browning
Robert Browning
Italo Calvino
Albert Camus
Truman Capote
Lewis Carroll
Willa Cather
Cervantes
Geoffrey Chaucer
Anton Chekhov
Kate Chopin
Agatha Christie
Samuel Taylor
   Coleridge
Joseph Conrad

Contemporary Poets
Stephen Crane
Dante
Daniel Defoe
Don DeLillo
Charles Dickens
Emily Dickinson
John Donne and the
   17th-Century Poets
Fyodor Dostoevsky
W.E.B. DuBois
George Eliot
T. S. Eliot
Ralph Ellison
Ralph Waldo Emerson
William Faulkner
F. Scott Fitzgerald
Sigmund Freud
Robert Frost
Johann Wolfgang
   von Goethe
George Gordon, Lord
   Byron
Graham Greene
Thomas Hardy
Nathaniel Hawthorne
Ernest Hemingway
Hermann Hesse
Hispanic-American
   Writers
Homer
Langston Hughes
Zora Neale Hurston
Aldous Huxley
Henrik Ibsen
John Irving
Henry James
James Joyce
Franz Kafka
John Keats
Jamaica Kincaid
Stephen King
Rudyard Kipling

Milan Kundera
D. H. Lawrence
Doris Lessing
Ursula K. Le Guin
Sinclair Lewis
Norman Mailer
Bernard Malamud
Christopher Marlowe
Gabriel García
   Márquez
Cormac McCarthy
Carson McCullers
Herman Melville
Arthur Miller
John Milton
Molière
Toni Morrison
Native-American
   Writers
Joyce Carol Oates
Flannery O'Connor
Eugene O'Neill
George Orwell
Octavio Paz
Sylvia Plath
Edgar Allan Poe
Katherine Anne
   Porter
Thomas Pynchon
Philip Roth
Salman Rushdie
J. D. Salinger
Jean-Paul Sartre
William Shakespeare:
   Histories and
   Poems
William Shakespeare:
   Romances
William Shakespeare:
   The Comedies
William Shakespeare:
   The Tragedies
George Bernard Shaw

Modern Critical Views

Mary Wollstonecraft
   Shelley
Percy Bysshe Shelley
Alexander
   Solzhenitsyn
Sophocles
John Steinbeck
Tom Stoppard
Jonathan Swift
Amy Tan
Alfred, Lord Tennyson

Henry David Thoreau
J. R. R. Tolkien
Leo Tolstoy
Ivan Turgenev
Mark Twain
John Updike
Kurt Vonnegut
Derek Walcott
Alice Walker
Robert Penn Warren
Eudora Welty

Edith Wharton
Walt Whitman
Oscar Wilde
Tennessee Williams
Thomas Wolfe
Tom Wolfe
Virginia Woolf
William Wordsworth
Richard Wright
William Butler Yeats

Modern Critical Views

AFRICAN-AMERICAN POETS
ROBERT HAYDEN through RITA DOVE

Edited and with an introduction by
Harold Bloom
Sterling Professor of the Humanities
Yale University

CHELSEA HOUSE PUBLISHERS
Philadelphia

10 9 8 7 6 5 4 3 2 1

Library of Congress Cataloging-in-Publication Data

African-American Poets: Robert Hayden through Rita Dove / edited and
with an introduction by Harold Bloom.
    p. cm. — (Bloom's modern critical views)
Includes bibliographical references and index.
  ISBN 0-7910-7396-3
  1. American poetry—African American authors—History and criticism.
2. American poetry—20th century—History and criticism. 3. African
Americans—Intellectual life—20th century. 4. African Americans in
literature. I. Bloom, Harold. II. Series. PS310.N4A35 2003

811'.509896073—dc21

                                                      2003002038

Chelsea House Publishers
1974 Sproul Road, Suite 400
Broomall, PA 19008-0914

http://www.chelseahouse.com

Contributing Editor: Janyce Marson

Cover Design by Takeshi Takahashi

Layout by EJB Publishing Services.

Contents

Editor's Note   vii

Introduction   1
    Harold Bloom

Robert Hayden (1913–1980)
Answering "The Waste Land": Robert Hayden and
    the Rise of the African American Poetic Sequence   5
    Brian Conniff
Calling the Names and Centering the Call
    in Robert Hayden's *American Journal*   35
    Ronald Walcott

Gwendolyn Brooks (1917–2000)
The Satisfactions of What's Difficult in
    Gwendolyn Brooks's Poetry   49
    Brooke Kenton Horvath

Amiri Baraka (LeRoi Jones) (1934–)
"All is Permitted": The Poetry
    of LeRoi Jones/Amiri Baraka   61
    W. D. E. Andrews

Maya Angelou (1928–)
Maya Angelou: Self and a Song of Freedom
    in the Southern Tradition   85
    Carole E. Neubauer

Derek Walcott (1930–)
An Empire of Poetry   113
    Sidney Burris
Aspects of Alienation in the Poetry of Derek Walcott   131
    Yvonne Ochillo

Jay Wright (1935–)
Jay Wright: *Transfigurations: Collected Poems*   145
    Steven Meyer
Decolonizing the Spirits: History and Storytelling
    in Jay Wright's *Soothsayers and Omens*   151
    C. K. Doreski

Lucille Clifton (1936–)
The Poetics of Matrilineage: Mothers and
    Daughters in the Poetry of African American   179
    Women, 1965–1985
    Fabian Clements Worsham

Michael S. Harper (1938–)
"Close Roads": The Friendship Songs
    of Michael S. Harper   193
    John F. Callahan

Ishmael Reed (1938–)
The Artist as Prophet, Priest and Gunslinger:
    Ishmael Reed's *Cowboy in the Boat of Ra*   205
    Shamoon Zamir

Rita Dove (1952–)
Rita Dove's Shakespeares   245
    Peter Erickson

Works by the Poets   261

Works about the Poets   267

Biographical Notes   273

Contributors   285

Acknowledgments   289

Index   291

Editor's Note

My Introduction considers the achievement of four strong poets, Robert Hayden, Derek Walcott, Jay Wright—the African-American poet whose work has most deeply affected me, and Thylias Moss (not covered in this volume).

Robert Hayden, a poet of great eminence, receives two considerations, the first from Brian Conniff, who sees Hayden as answering the poetic challenge of T. S. Eliot and the second, an overview of Hayden's *American Journal* by Ronald Walcott.

Brooke Kenton Horvath makes a passionate defense of the late Gwendolyn Brooks, while the perpetual revolutionary, Amiri Baraka, is celebrated by W. D. E. Andrews.

Maya Angelou, most popular of poets, is returned to her Southern roots by Carole E. Neubauer.

Derek Walcott, West Indian Nobel Prize Winner, is seen by Sidney Burris as replacing the British Empire by one of poetry, while Yvonne Ochillo conversely emphasizes profound alienation in Walcott.

Stephen Meyer presents an admirable overview of *Transformations*, Jay Wright's collected poems, after which C.K. Doreski gives a fine account of the poet's historical obsessions.

Fabian Clements Worsham finds in Lucille Clifton "the poetics of matrilineage," while John F. Callahan commends the friendship songs of Michael S. Harper.

The flamboyant Ishmael Reed is presented by Shamoon Zamir, after which Peter Erickson analyzes Rita Dove's relation to literary tradition.

Introduction

I will write here only briefly about four vital poets: Robert Hayden, Derek Walcott, Jay Wright, and Thylias Moss. This is not to evade my authentic admiration for aspects of the work of Gwendolyn Brooks, Michael Harper, Ishmael Reed, Yusef Komunyakaa, Rita Dove and others. Several admirable poets, including Carl Phillips and Elizabeth Alexander, are not here because substantial critical writing upon them remains to be published.

1

Robert Hayden was a major poet, who was schooled by W.H. Auden, a teacher's legacy still evident in poems as distinguished as "The Islands":

> Always this waking dream of palmtrees,
> magic flowers—of sensual joys
> like treasures brought up from the sea.
>
> Always this longing, this nostalgia
> for tropic islands we
> have never known and yet recall.
>
> We look for ease upon these islands named
> to honor holiness; in their chromatic
> torpor catch our breath.
>
> Scorn greets us with promises of rum,
> hostility welcomes us to bargain sales.
> We make friends with Flamboyant trees.

I hear Auden, at his most persuasive in: "We look for ease upon those islands we / have never known and yet recall." But Hayden's authentic agon was with Hart Crane, whose high rhetoric of vision underlies the astonishing "Middle Passage" and "Runagate Runagate," which achieve a Sublime that only Jay Wright among Hayden's followers was able to attain:

> Shuttles in the rocking loom of history,
> the dark ships move, the dark ships move,
> their bright ironical names
> like jests of kindness on a murderer's mouth;
> plough through thrashing glister toward
> fata morgana's lucent melting shore,
> weave toward New World littorals that are
> mirage and myth and actual shore.

Hart Crane would have loved this opening octave of "Middle Passage," III. Hayden, already fully formed in "Middle Passage" and "Runagate," reached his ecstatic originality in chants like "Bone-Flower Elegy," with its fierce conclusion:

> I have wept for you many times
> I whisper but shrink from the arms
> that would embrace me
> and trading water reach
> arched portals opening on a desert
> groves of enormous nameless flowers
> twist up from firegold sand
> skull flowers flowers of sawtooth bone
> their leaves and petals interlock
> caging me for you beastangel
> raging toward me
> angelbeast shining come
> to rend me and redeem

In this dream-vision, the dead beloved is invoked with triumphant ambivalences, and with a sadomasochistic exultation that scares me with its intensity. Robert Hayden was so strong a poet that the wounds he inflicts tend to endure.

2

The West Indian poet Derek Walcott, a Nobel laureate, also started from
Auden, but like Hayden's attachment to Hart Crane's mode, Walcott became
most himself when he explored his affinity to Wallace Stevens, as here in the
majestic poem, "The Bounty":

> The mango trees serenely rust when they are in flower,
> nobody knows the name for that voluble cedar
> whose bell-flowers fall, the pomme-arac purples its floor.
>
> The blue hills in late afternoon always look sadder.
> The country night waiting to come in outside the door;
> the firefly keeps striking matches, and the hillside fumes
>
> with a bluish signal of charcoal, then the smoke burns
> into a larger question, one that forms and unforms,
> then loses itself in a cloud, till the question returns.

But again like Hayden, Walcott does not wear a second-hand suit of
clothes (as did such celebrated modern American poets as Archibald
MacLeish, John Peale Bishop, and Robert Lowell). Walcottt's highest
rhetoric is neither Audenesque nor Stevensian, but very much his own:

> I tracked them where they led across the street
> to the bright side, entering the wax-
> sealed smell of neon, human heat,
> some all-night diner with its wise-guy cook,
> his stub thumb in my bowl of stew, and one
> man's pulped and beaten face, its look
> acknowledging all that, white-dark outside,
> was possible: some beast prowling the block,
> something fur-clotted, running wild
> beyond the boundary of will. Outside,
> more snow had fallen. My heart charred.
> I longed for darkness, evil that was warm.
> Walking, I'd stop and turn. What had I heard
> wheezing behind my heel with whitening breath?
> Nothing. Sixth Avenue yawned wet and wide.
> The night was white. There was nowhere to hide.

3

I want only to make a brief but large estimate of Wright's achievement, now fully available in his *Transfigurations: Collected Poems* (2000). I have reread, studied, and taught Wright for decades, and I find him comparable to the great masters of the Sublime mode: Hölderlin, Hart Crane, Luis Cernuda, Paul Celan. Like them, Jay Wright is a difficult and demanding poet, and again, with them, he is a permanent poet.

4

Thylias Moss, still in her mid-forties, is a poet who perpetually delights and astonishes me, with a wit comparable to that of the Canadian poet Anne Carson. Her hallucinatory force is difficult to describe, her originality being so enormous. Here is the second verse-paragraph of her "The Undertaker's Daughter Feels Neglect":

> It's been years since the mailman came, years
> since I woke in the middle of the night
> thinking a party was going on downstairs,
> thinking my father was a magician
> and all those scantily clad women his assistants,
> wondering why no one could hear me,
> why I was made to disappear permanently in the box.
> I seldom wake at all anymore.

The grisly delight of this is infectious: read the poem aloud to someone else. To be the daughter of an undertaker-magician who specializes in beautiful female—shall we say assistants or shall we say corpses?—ought not to be a hilarious fate, but Thylias Moss renders it so. Her wit and invention being supreme, I will venture no prophecies upon her poems to come.

BRIAN CONNIFF

Answering "The Waste Land": Robert Hayden and the Rise of the African American Poetic Sequence

April of 1966 was one of the most eventful and paradoxical months in the history of twentieth-century American poetry. At the Third World Festival of Negro Arts in Dakar, Senegal, Robert Hayden's *A Ballad of Remembrance* was awarded "the *Grand Prix*" as "the best" recent volume of Anglophone poetry (qtd. by Pool 43). In at least some international literary circles, the prestige of this award roughly matched its Olympic title. The first such event to be held on "independent African soil," the Festival was sponsored by Léopold Sédar Senghor in conjunction with UNESCO and the *Société Africaine de Culture* and was attended by over 10,000 people from thirty-seven nations (Vaillant 323).[1] The other finalists in the poetry competition were Derek Walcott's *In a Green Night* and Christopher Okigbo's *Limits*. Langston Hughes was one of the judges. Also in attendance were Aimé Césaire, Léon Damas, Alioune Diop, Yevgeny Yevtoshenko, and Duke Ellington. André Malraux, then French Minister of Culture, seems to have captured the prevailing spirit when he praised the Festival as an indication that Senghor's cultural program was about to shape "the destiny of a continent" (qtd. by Vaillant 323).

For Hayden, though, the *Grand Prix* was wildly unexpected. He had not yet published a book with a commercial or university press in the United States, and he was still teaching fifteen hours each semester as an associate

From *African American Review* 33, no. 3. © 1999 by Brian Conniff.

professor in the English department at Fisk University. Even the *Grand Prix* itself, when it first arrived, seemed to do him as much harm as good.[2]

In fact, within a few days, while his poetry was being praised in Senegal as the centerpiece of international négritude, back home in Nashville Hayden was being attacked as the scapegoat of choice for a new generation of African American poets.[3] At Fisk's First Black Writers' Conference, a group of writers and students, led by Melvin Tolson, assailed Hayden as the stooge of exploitive capitalists and, all in all, a traitor to his race. For the most part, Tolson and his supporters endorsed the "Black Cultural Nationalism" of Ron Karenga, with its declarations that "all art must reflect and support the Black Revolution" and that "any art that does not discuss and contribute to the revolution is invalid" (33). Hayden's crime was that he refused to be labeled a "Negro poet." From the beginning of the conference, and much to the dismay of most of his audience, he insisted that he should be considered, instead, "a poet who happens to be Negro" (Llorens 60).[4] When he reiterated his position at a panel discussion—which also included Tolson, Arna Bontemps, and Margaret Walker—the advocates of Black Cultural Nationalism reacted as though they had come face to face with the Enemy. Tolson's response was perhaps most characteristic. Among other things, he declared that, "when a man writes, he tells me which way he went in society." "I'm a black poet," he continued, "an African-American poet, a Negro poet. I'm no accident—and I don't give a tinker's damn what you think" (qtd. in Llorens 62–63).[5] One member of the audience even accused Hayden of contributing to the "delusion" of the "young black people" studying at Fisk (64). In the following months, students on the Fisk campus—almost all of whom, as Hayden was well aware, were from backgrounds more privileged than his own—continued to refer to him as an "Uncle Tom" or an "Oreo," believing that he should use the prestige granted by the *Grand Prix* to authorize and advance their political positions (Hatcher 38).

I begin with these events for three reasons. First of all, it is in these few days that studies of Hayden almost inevitably find their critical center—and, unfortunately, Hayden's defining moment.[6] From a conventionally biographical perspective, this focus might seem reasonable. In the years immediately following the Third World Festival of Negro Arts, Hayden was granted a brief flurry of academic and otherwise official interest. From 1967 to 1969, he was offered a couple of visiting professorships, a permanent position at the University of Louisville, a recording at the Library of Congress, and finally the position at the University of Michigan that he would accept and then occupy for the rest of his life (Williams 32). Nonetheless, it is safe to say that by the end of the 1960s, soon after the *Grand Prix* and his auspicious association with the négritude movement, and at least until very recently, Hayden would regain and retain his status as "one of the most underrated and unrecognized poets in America" (Lester 4).[7] This neglect is largely the result of a collective choice—usually implicit but nonetheless clear—that academic critics have made in their descriptions of Hayden's career. Hayden's poetry has rarely been considered in terms of its rich affiliations with the work of major international poets—including Walcott, Okigbo, and Césaire, among many others—as suggested at the Third World Festival. And his poetry has never been seriously considered— at least by mainstream critics—in relation to the major works by younger African American poets who have found it a rich resource and an inspiration.[8] Rather, his poetry has been viewed—by his detractors and most of his supporters—as somehow determined by his one-line answer to the "Negro question," as it was framed by his opponents at the Fisk Conference. For Tolson and the younger writers of the emerging Black Arts Movement, Hayden eventually came to be viewed as a poet of some ability—and some minor historical significance—whose work is irreparably limited and dated because, in their view, it was not sufficiently concerned with issues of race. Even Arna Bontemps, who was often sympathetic with Hayden's work, would conclude after the Fisk Conference that Hayden "doesn't really like that Negro thing" (qtd. in Llorens 61). For a handful of more conservative critics and editors, Hayden's poetry has also maintained a kind of marginal interest—and, ironically, for much the same reason. For instance, in the influential *Norton Anthology of Modern Poetry*, Richard Ellmann and Robert O'Clair begin their introduction to Hayden's poetry by stating that Hayden "did not subscribe to any esthetic of Black poetry." They describe his poetry in terms of his interest in the work of Countée Cullen, Carl Sandburg, Edna St. Vincent Millay, and "the English classics" (863), and then include a selection of Hayden's poetry that would seem to suggest, to a reader unfamiliar with his career, that he must have been trying to write a kind of race-free poetry. In either case, Hayden's critical reception has served, more than anything, to obscure and diminish his most formidable accomplishments.

Second, when viewed in the context of the history of American poetry over the past thirty years, the events of April, 1966, point to an even more striking neglect. Recent criticism has remained oblivious to one of the most remarkable developments in contemporary literature: the rise, in part out of Hayden's poetry, of the African American poetic sequence. Because of their particular moment in history, I think, the conferences in Dakar and Nashville were bound to have mixed legacies. Despite the notable absence of the more politically "radical" American writers, the Third World Festival of Negro Arts did help make the rich history of négritude known beyond the cultural centers of Paris and Dakar.[9] At the same time, as a formative moment in the American debate over a "black aesthetic," bringing together a number of still neglected writers on the verge of academic awareness—if not legitimacy— Fisk's First Black Writers' Conference helped expand the audience of such poets as Margaret Walker and Amiri Baraka, among others, and the Second Conference of 1967 would generally be recognized as the impetus for Gwendolyn Brooks's movement toward African poetic forms and what has been called a "new Black consciousness" (Melhem 154). Nonetheless, the universalizing grandeur with which Hayden was praised, on the one hand, and the vehemence with which he was attacked, on the other, suggest that the two conferences, like most events that end up being reconstructed as defining moments, obscured just about as much as they revealed. After all, the often contentious politics surrounding the emerging post-colonial African and Caribbean literature—still loosely grouped at the Dakar conference under the title "négritude"—was just about as foreign to Hayden's sensibilities as the cultural politics of the Fisk Conference.[10] A Baha'i by faith, Hayden was committed to "the affirmation of independent investigation of the truth" and to abstinence from partisan politics of any kind (Hatcher 68–69). Beginning just about a decade later, however, American poets would be better prepared to draw directly from the legacy of Hayden's poetry—at once individualistic and engaged, local and international, highly crafted and improvisational. Clearly conscious of Hayden's example, in recent years such poets as Michael S. Harper, Jay Wright, and Brenda Marie Osbey have been writing highly ambitious poetic sequences, firmly grounded in history, that invoke distinctly heterogeneous heritages with a wide range of formal experimentation.

Third, if the events of April, 1966, are located in the context of a more extensive literary history, Hayden becomes an even more significant figure. His career spans a crucial period, from the early 1940s through the early 1970s, and his poetry eventually plays a major role in the emergence and development of what I have come to call "post-traditional" poetry. This poetry is largely informed by its authors' paradoxical stance toward literary tradition. The post-traditional poet is certainly conscious—in fact, often intensely conscious—of tradition. At the same time, though, he or she manages, in one way or another, to view any distinctly literary tradition as historically contingent. Most often, the post-traditional poet uses this sense of contingency to construct from disparate sources a personal heritage— provisionally, heterogeneously, willfully—in order to address some perceived historical crisis or, especially in recent years, some immediate social need.

Post-traditional poetry has its most conspicuous origins in the mid-1920s, when, just about simultaneously, the leading canonizers of high modernism began to take radical measures to address what seemed to them a profound schism between their most revered traditions and their peculiar historical interpretations of post-War Europe. At this time, writing in Venice, Ezra Pound began to juxtapose paradisal visions with Dante's *Inferno* and Major Douglas's economics. At the same time, in London, T. S. Eliot, recently established as a cultural icon, began his second "career" as poetry editor at Faber and Gwyer, redefining himself as a "reactionary" man of letters in what was in effect an elaborate attempt to counterbalance his own philosophical uncertainty with a millennial vision of Christian culture. Meanwhile, in Ireland, William Butler Yeats set out on his first deliberate effort to distance himself from his early romantic nationalism—a truly strange journey, by way of a highly personal reclamation of an Anglo-Irish heritage, that would eventually lead him, in the last days of his life, to the striking embrace of common humanity in "The Circus Animal's Desertion" and "Cuchulain Comforted."

By the middle of their careers, these poets were writing as though tradition—as they knew it—was about to come to an end, under the assault of a debased and debasing culture. They cultivated their notions of historical crisis in ways that resulted not only in reactionary cultural politics but also, eventually, in an understanding that, if the sense of literary culture they so cherished could be threatened and even destroyed by the forces of history, then any canon, indeed any culture, might be considered radically contingent.

Of course, at least since the Bollingen Prize controversy of 1949, the efforts of later poets and critics to come to terms with this legacy—especially its disturbing mixture of poetic innovation and reactionary politics, its vast international influence and intense Eurocentrism—has amounted to a kind of collective anxiety attack. By now, though, I think it has become clear that these often embarrassing ancestors have contributed largely—and, politically speaking, despite themselves—to the rise of a post-traditional poetry that has been growing, at least since the mid-1980s, more explicitly heterogenous and more international, both in its sources and its influence, in such works as Adrienne Rich's *Your Native Land, Your Life* (1986), Seamus Heaney's *Station Island* (1983), and Derek Walcott's *Omeros* (1990). Considered more broadly, a distinctly post-traditional stance has become increasingly apparent in the linguistic heterogeneity of contemporary Irish poets like Nuala ni Dhomhnaill and Medbh McGuckian, in the communal heritage evident in the prison poetry and autobiographical writing of Jimmy Santiago Baca, and in the remarkable emergence of contemporary poetry by American Indians. For these later poets, any approximation of a tradition—any communal or even personal heritage—is conceived pragmatically, as one instrument among many others with which they can engage a world that is at once overwhelmingly various and desperately in need.

In this essay, I will focus primarily on Hayden's "Middle Passage," the long early poem that would remain his most significant contribution to the development of post-traditional poetry. In "Middle Passage," he developed an experimental poetics that could examine racism, directly and specifically, by telling an episode of its history in a number of contending voices. Even at this early point in his career, Hayden was able to challenge the modernists' sense of social crisis and give voice to his personal doubts about modernism's moral limitations—in terms that would not even be suggested at the conferences at Dakar and Fisk. In this sense, "Middle Passage" is crucial to any reconsideration of Hayden's career. It anticipates his later "Negro history" poems, including "Runagate Runagate," "The Ballad of Nat Turner," and "Frederick Douglass." It also anticipates a number of Hayden's poems in widely varied historical contexts—most notably "A Ballad of Remembrance," "Night, Death, Mississippi," "Belsen, Day of Liberation," "El-Hajj Malix El-Shabazz," and the important later sequence "Words in the Mourning Time"—in which he explores, often in brutal detail, the psychology and consequences of racism and xenophobia. Throughout this poetry, as William Meredith has put it, "there is scarcely a line of his which is not identifiable as an experience of Black America" (vi).

ELIOTIC INTONATIONS

For American poets of Hayden's generation, the development of a post-traditional poetry almost inevitably involved some kind of direct confrontation with received modernism. Hayden was certainly no exception. Beginning his career in the early 1940s, he was conspicuously aware of the previous generation's legacy, particularly as it was perceived in the academy. In this view, a few designated "masterpieces," the most conspicuous of which was "The Waste Land," tended to appear as the culmination—both in the sense of the highest attainment and in the sense of the end—of a predominantly English tradition. The post-traditional impulses in the work of the established modernists—Yeats's provisional reconstructions of his own heritage in his final poems, for instance, or the philosophical and linguistic uncertainty of Eliot's "Little Gidding"—were not yet recognized, or had not yet appeared.

Hayden's confrontation with this legacy can be seen in two contrary tendencies of his critical writing. On the one hand, he was prone to monumentalize Eliot's work—as would most academics of his time—by locating it at the end of the Great Tradition. In an overview of "Twentieth

Century American Poetry" written for a 1973 textbook entitled *The United States in Literature*, he begins with a surprisingly conventional narrative account of modern poetry in which he acknowledges "the supremacy of Auden and Eliot" in the 1940s and then finds his conclusion in a description of "The Lovesong of J. Alfred Prufrock" and "The Waste Land" as expressions of "the spiritual emptiness of industrialized civilization" (*Collected Prose* 45–49). On the other hand, having been raised in Detroit's Paradise Valley, Hayden was also unusually aware, for an academic of his time, of the persistence of folk culture, jazz, and popular song throughout modern poetry. So even in his textbook account he mentions, along the way, the influence of these populist forces on the work of Edward Arlington Robinson, Robert Frost, Carl Sandburg, Edgar Lee Masters, and the writers of the Harlem Renaissance—among many others.

Only on rare occasions in his critical writing could Hayden put aside this characteristic ambivalence—and, in doing so, move beyond the positions of both the "academicians and purists" and the Black Cultural Nationalists. Near the end of his career, in an address to the Library of Congress, he was finally able to articulate a more nuanced and culturally grounded understanding of "poetry as a medium, an instrument for social and political change":

> Poetry does make something happen, for it changes sensibility. In the early stages of a culture it helps to crystallize the language and is a repository for value, belief, ideals. The Griot in African tribes keeps names and legends and pride alive. Among the Eskimos the shaman or medicine man is a poet. In ancient Ireland and Wales the bard was a preserver of the culture. (*Collected Prose* 11)

From a perspective with this range of cultural and historical reference, the conventional academic canon of the mid-century—which usually seemed, with Eliot in his place, so complete—suddenly appears temporary, limited, and relatively inconsequential. So, in the same passage, Hayden is able to reconsider poetic tradition in terms that are personal, pragmatic, provisional, and moral:

> A point to consider: What would I as a poet do if my people were rounded up like the Jewish people in Germany under the Nazis? Claude McKay's sonnet "If We Must Die"; the poems of the Greek poet Yannis Ritsos that were recited and sung by men and women fighting in the streets for the freedom of their country; Pablo Neruda, William Butler Yeats, Emily Sachs, Muriel

Rukeyser, Gwendolyn Brooks, Walt Whitman; they stand out as poets even if you dislike their politics. To be a poet, it seems to me, is to care passionately about justice and one's fellow human beings. (11)

In this construction of a living poetic heritage, Hayden no longer sees tradition as a "line of development," leading toward an inevitable poetic conclusion. He is arranging writers, in heterogeneous combinations, to address a particular historical problem with a poetic vision of justice and compassion. One irony in Hayden's situation is that, obvious political differences aside, this general method of overcoming the canon of the day is something he shared not only with a number of his contemporaries but also, in a way he himself never recognized, with the canonized modernists themselves. Like Yeats, Pound, and Eliot—especially in the later stages of their careers—Hayden's most basic tendency was to reconstruct a standard canon and, at the same time, to locate himself outside this canon in a way that highlighted its limitations and, ultimately, its historical contingency. In this sense, his method was similar to that of philosophers like Nietzsche and Heidegger, as Richard Rorty has described it, when they redescribed their predecessors in terms of a tradition that seemed, in some sense, to have reached its end. Canon construction then became a strategy for dealing with "*the* problem of ironist theory ... the problem of how to overcome authority without claiming authority" (105). In this sense, at least from the mid-1920s on, each of the major modernists eventually came to see himself as Hayden saw Eliot: at the end of the English poetic tradition; as, in some manner of speaking, the last poet.

For those of us who have entered the academy well after the rise of post-modern theory, I think it is difficult to appreciate just how common, and at times overwhelming the monumentalizing view of Eliot was in the 1940s. Overcoming "The Waste Land" was a problem Hayden shared with such different poets as H.D. when she wrote her *Trilogy*, William Carlos Williams when he wrote the first four books of *Paterson*, and even Charles Olson, early in the next decade, when he began *The Maximus Poems*. As these poets progressed through the 1940s and 1950s, they were not worried, as their predecessors had been, that tradition, as they knew it, was about to end, and that therefore there might no longer be anything of significance to write; rather, they were driven, and at times practically inebriated, by a sense of freedom they associated with the end of tradition, in the conventional academic sense of the term. That is why, just when literary criticism was being established in an unprecedented state of institutional security and influence within the academy, and mainstream critics were settling on a totalizing view of poetic tradition, a number of American poets were undertaking some of the most ambitiously experimental work of the century.

That is also the reason that, no matter how monumental high modernist poetics might have seemed to be when Hayden began his career, his confrontation with "The Waste Land" should not be construed as the kind of agonistic struggle against "belatedness" imagined by Harold Bloom in books like *The Anxiety of Influence, A Map of Misreading,* and *Agon.* Hayden's revision of Eliot's poetics was far more conscious and strategic than Bloom's Freudian mythology would allow, and more engaged with history than Bloom's metaphysics and his preoccupation with private irony have ever permitted him to recognize. In the writing of his poetry, Hayden understood from the start that all acts of literary influence, and most of all those involving any kind of "alternative" tradition, take place in a world in which power is distributed unequally.[11] As Edward Said has written of narrative literature in relation to European imperialism, even the most essentialist accounts of influence always retain, in some form, traces of the relationship between master and disciple, even master and slave (191).

In "Middle Passage," Hayden's revisionist strategy is calculated most of all to challenge Eliot's poetics by drawing upon historical sources alien to Eliot's social world. He originally meant to use this poem as the opening piece in a volume to be entitled *The Black Spear,* in which he would attempt to "correct the misconceptions, and to destroy some of the stereotypes and clichés which surrounded Negro history" (*Prose* 162). Though Hayden never finished *The Black Spear,* an early manuscript version, without "Middle Passage," won the Hopwood Prize for creative writing in 1942 when he was a graduate student at the University of Michigan, and many of the poems later appeared, extensively revised, in the fifth section of his *Selected Poems* of 1966.

Several critics have discussed the significance of "Middle Passage" to Hayden's career-long effort to incorporate revisionist history into his poetry.[12] At the same time, however, most of the critics who have noticed the connections between Hayden's poetry and Eliot's have assumed that Hayden was, at least in matters of poetics, little more than a dutiful disciple, learning matters of technique from the master, and in some cases imitating him directly.[13]

In fact, the only readers who seem to have understood the kind and degree of confrontation involved in Hayden's reading of Eliot are those younger poets who have turned to Hayden's poetry as a resource for continuing innovation. For instance, in a letter to Hayden, Michael S. Harper has described his poetry as "a real testament" to "complexity and historical consciousness" (in Nicholas 995). Elsewhere, in a reminiscence written on the occasion of Hayden's death, Harper has referred to "Middle Passage" as, in part, an "answer" to "The Waste Land"—that is, a poetic and historical challenge rather than a reverent echo. Harper recognizes that Hayden tried, through his knowledge of diverse poetic traditions, to move "beyond many of the experiments steeped in conscious modernism" (184). According to Harper, "Middle Passage" recalls "the schizoid past's brutalities" in order to confront Eliot's poetry with "a broad and pungent social reality" (184). Along similar lines Jay Wright has written that "Middle Passage" alters Eliot's famous claim that a poet's fundamental responsibility is to language—and at the same time answers the criticism of many of Hayden's "younger contemporaries"—by demonstrating that "a language has a history and a relationship to other languages" that is more complex, and far more political, than Eliot ever imagined ("Desire's" 18). To these poets, Hayden's view of Anglo-American modernism is much like that of Houston Baker in *Modernism and the Harlem Renaissance*. Even though such iconic figures as Eliot and Joyce and Pound confronted the "changed condition of humankind" in the early twentieth century with "seriousness and sincerity," to use Baker's words, they also "mightily restricted the province of what constituted the tumbling of the towers, and they remained eternally self-conscious of their own pessimistic 'becomings'" (4).

As he worked on the manuscript of *The Black Spear* in New York City during the summer vacation of 1941, Hayden immersed himself in the various histories, journals, notebooks, and ships' logs related to the slave trade in the Schomburg collection (*Prose* 170–71). Most significantly, at least for "Middle Passage," he also read the account of an 1839 slave mutiny on a schooner named the *Amistad* in Muriel Rukeyser's remarkable biography of the theoretical chemist Willard Gibbs. Gibbs' father Josiah was, for most of his life, a retiring professor of theology and sacred literature at Yale; in his more daring moments, he was an amateur practitioner of the new German philology. But when a group of slaves who had seized control of the *Amistad* mysteriously appeared on Long Island, only to be thrown in jail, the elder Gibbs came to their aid, teaching them some English and finding translators for their legal defense among the African laborers in the ports of New York. He also seized the opportunity to begin a study of Mendi grammar.

Still, Hayden could not effectively use his research to answer "The Waste Land" until he had established a critical understanding of Eliot's poetics. At the end of the summer of 1941, he returned to Michigan, where he continued his research and enrolled in a course taught by W. H. Auden. Under the influence of Auden's teaching, Hayden's understanding of modern poetry, and Eliot in particular, was caught in an intellectual landslide. Auden still spoke of Eliot as a close friend, and regarded him as the leading arbiter of current literary taste, but he was also in the midst of a prolonged, difficult moral questioning of his own earlier poetry. Most of all, in 1941, Auden was struggling to reconcile his early leftist politics with his recent reading of modern theology, especially the Christian realism of Reinhold Niebuhr—often deliberately obscuring his earlier positions but still subjecting his poetry to the questions of conscience raised by the rise of Naziism, the fall of the Spanish Republic, and the ongoing war in Europe. Auden's understanding of Christianity was significantly different from Eliot's increasingly millennial vision of a homogeneous Christian culture and before long, most notably in *For the Time Being* (1942), he would reject Eliot's peculiar fusion of social crisis and reactionary ideology.

Auden's efforts to remake himself as a Christian intellectual led him to challenge the very idea of a stable literary canon. A couple of years before Hayden met him, in his "New Year Letter," Auden had satirized the prevailing concept of literary influence, the idea that anyone who dares to write poetry must face "interrogation" by "The grand constructions of the dead" (163). Dismissing this kind of purely literary anxiety, Auden had claimed for the poet a radical freedom to reshape the canon in order to serve immediate social needs, moral imperatives, and even personal whims:

> Each one, so liberal is the law,
> May choose whom he appears before,
> Pick any influential ghost
> From those whom he admires most.
>   (164)

By the time Hayden came along, Auden's method of teaching involved an apparently endless rearrangement of texts in constellations that were provisional, deliberately unconventional, and often downright playful. Another of Auden's students at Michigan, Donald Pearce, has described Auden's teaching at this time as driven by a "sense of verbal text as interdisciplinary conflux, or event ... of convergent-and-explosive text" (157). Tossed into one of Auden's textual "confluxes," Eliot's works could never appear as sacred, or as secure, as they were so often made out to be: For instance, in the reading list for Auden's course in the fall of 1941, Eliot's essays and *Family Reunion* appear alongside more than two dozen other books, including Kierkegaard's *Fear and Trembling*, Nietzsche's *The Case of Wagner*, and Rimbaud's *Season in Hell* (Miller 27).

As eccentric as they must have seemed to many of his poor students, Auden's exercises in textual convergence were motivated by a developing sense of moral purpose. Mostly through his reading of Niebuhr,

Kierkegaard, and Charles Williams, Auden had recently come to believe that the individual is far more capable of moral action than any larger social group can ever be. Primarily for this reason, the undermining and reconstruction of an authorized tradition was more than just the individual poet's prerogative. At the very least, it was a moral responsibility. At best, it could be a religious vocation. Before long, all of these revisionary forces—the "Negro history," the understanding of tradition as an array of cultural fragments provisionally constructed by an individual writer, the commitment to canon reconstruction as a moral imperative—would provide Hayden with his own means of answering "The Waste Land." Though "Middle Passage" was not finished in time for the Hopwood contest, *The Black Spear* manuscript did include a preliminary response to Eliot. This poem is far less impressive than "Middle Passage," but it does suggest just how quickly and systematically Hayden was developing his own revisionary poetics. "Schizophrenia" is a superficially Eliotic poem in two voices, each of which speaks a refrain with variations. The first voice recalls the "heap of broken images" from "The Waste Land" and its nearly exhausted anguish in the face of cultural and spiritual disintegration:

> We were trying to harvest the fragments
> of our scattered spirits,
> but it was the blitzkrieg's year,
> and the bombs were falling. (185)

"The blitzkrieg's year" is the most obvious among many symptoms of a culture so fragmented, so far beyond any hope of repair, that it seems to have come to the end of its history. The war continues, somehow, beyond human agency, yet, at the same time, it is all too ordinary, something like the weather. The second voice in "Schizophrenia" supplies the predictable metaphoric connection between this cultural catastrophe and personal insanity. For this second voice, the falling bombs are little more than background noise for a series of private nightmares: "I saw a man in a cracked gold mirror / and a man in surrealist streets"; "I saw a pale girl, savage of eye, / fondling a headless doll"; and so on.[14] Like a conspicuously modernist Parsifal, the narrator has set out on a quest of some significance, apparently, but he is unable to figure out where he should go or what he should do: "One of these tasks is mine, / and the other is mine, / but which is mine they won't tell me" (185). Needless to say, it is never clear just who "they" might be, these unhelpful shades. But that hardly seems to matter, either, since, as it turns out, within a few lines, both of the poem's speakers discover that they are locked up "in padded cells."

Poetically, the most basic problem with "Schizophrenia" is that its two voices sound far too much alike to answer each other—let alone anyone else—in any very meaningful way. Even if they are meant to be spoken by the same person, they could hardly support any respectable diagnosis of schizophrenia—perhaps clinical depression, or echolalia, or some such thing, but not schizophrenia. And, more importantly, these voices seem to be far too distant from recognizable events for "the blitzkrieg's year" to have any historical resonance, even in a time of war. Both voices echo Eliot's diction, syntax, rhythms, and repetitive phrasing, almost to the point of parody, but never to any discernable purpose.

Still, at this early point in Hayden's career, I think this little experiment proved to be very valuable: He learned that he could not answer Eliotic despair, in any very useful way, with his own rendition of Eliotic despair. By doing Eliot in two very similar voices—voices that just about any reader of poetry in the 1940s would find familiar—he discovered that all this preoccupation with the "tumbling towers" of some universalized. Western culture, the "split shards / of the major illusion," could be patently self-indulgent. In "Schizophrenia," the speakers' vaguely nostalgic longing to recover the "shattered spirit" of the past only hides their mutual impulse to turn the harshest realities of the ongoing war, the falling bombs, into an analogue for some vaguely personal anxiety, just as "The Waste Land's" compulsive allusion and nervous voices tend to obscure the social conditions of post-World War I London.

"MIDDLE PASSAGE"

For all "Schizophrenia's" shortcomings—Hayden would never include it in any of his published collections—the poem's half-hearted experiment in Eliotic voices soon developed into a more pointed and far more powerful response. In "Middle Passage," Hayden once again explored the theme of cultural "schizophrenia," but this time within the historical context provided by his research on the slave trade. This historical material gave him the means by which he could abandon the kind of psychological posturing—the inevitable blending of dreams and consciousness, self and other, world war and private neurosis—Eliot's poetry had helped make fashionable.

"Middle Passage's" most significant element of "social reality," as Harper would put it, was provided primarily by Rukeyser's account of the strange series of events set in motion by the *Amistad* mutiny. When the mutiny occurred, the *Amistad* held fifty-three Africans who had been part of a much larger group, probably captured in one of the local wars fought, in those days, primarily for the acquisition of slaves. They had already been dealt by traders in Sierra Leone, sent under a Portuguese flag to the thriving market in Havana, bought by two Spaniards named Ruiz and Montez, placed in irons, and shipped off once again, this time to Guanaja, the main port of Principe. Their capture and transportation violated the decree of Spain of 1817—and, for that matter, "all the treaties then in existence" among European countries and the United States (Rukeyser 16). Until the fourth night after the *Amistad*'s departure from Havana, their crossing was much like countless others on the middle passage. Hayden makes this point by constructing the poem's main narrative so that it emerges in the midst of fragments drawn from assorted accounts of earlier journeys. In this way, he is able to tell the story of the *Amistad* against a background of sickness, madness, fire, rape, and other cruelties:

> "Deponeth further sayeth *The Bella J.*
> left the Guinea Coast
> with cargo of five hundred blacks and odd
> for the barracoons of Florida:
>
> "That there was hardly room 'tween-decks for half
> the sweltering cattle stowed spoon-fashioned there;
> that some went mad of thirst and tore their flesh
> and sucked the blood:
>
> "That Crew and Captain lusted with the comeliest
> of the savage girls kept naked in the cabins." (49–50)

On that fourth night, however, the *Amistad*'s journey took an unusual turn. After just about all of the ship's crew had gone to sleep, having spent much of the day battling a storm, the slaves managed to get hold of machetes being sent along to cut sugar cane in the New World. Led by a man named Cinquez—"a powerful young rice planter, a powerful leader" (Rukeyser 18)—they quickly seized control of the ship, killing the captain and the cook, who had threatened them throughout their journey. Then, because they believed they would need experienced sailors to navigate back home, they decided to spare the lives of Montez, Ruiz, and a cabin boy who had helped them as a translator.

This decision backfired. For sixty-three days Montez and Ruiz managed to delay their return, guiding the ship east by day and then turning northwest by night when they knew their captors would be unable to judge their direction. Zigzagging across the Atlantic in this way, the *Amistad* soon became the subject of local legend, with reports in the American press of a "phantom ship" following a route so incomprehensible that it must be driven by ghosts. When the *Amistad* finally landed at Montauk, Long Island, the Africans were thrown in the county jail. Accordingly, in "Middle Passage" it is Montez and Ruiz, suddenly set free, who tell this part of the story:

>   It sickens me
>   to think of what I saw, of how these apes
>   threw overboard the butchered bodies of
>   our men, true Christians all, like so
>   much jetsam.
>   Enough, enough. The rest is quickly told:
>   Cinquez was forced to spare the two of us
>   you see to steer the ship to Africa,
>   and we like phantoms doomed to rove
>   the sea
>   voyaged east by day and west by night,
>   deceiving them, hoping for rescue,
>   prisoners on our own vessel, till
>   at length we drifted to the shores of this
>   your land, America, where we were
>   freed
>   from our unspeakable misery. (53)

The story of the *Amistad* provided Hayden with a narrative framework within which he could include accounts of cruelty, from various sources, that make "The Waste Land's" sense of "horror" seem timid and self-indulgent. But what would turn out to be just as important—at least for Hayden's development as a poet—was Rukeyser's less dramatic account of the series of trials and political maneuvers that began once the *Amistad* had landed on Montauk. This portion of the Gibbs biography, along with courtroom testimony by Montez and Ruiz published a hundred years earlier in John Barber's *A History of the Amistad Captives*, provided Hayden with a vision of a less personal, more historically grounded kind of "schizophrenia": the assorted moral duplicities in mainstream American culture that sustained the slave trade. In these accounts, he discovered a labyrinth of hypocrisy and rationalization so intricate that, to account for it with any degree of accuracy, he needed to master a more complex and ironic interplay of contending voices.

When the *Amistad* slaves landed on Long Island, they were surprised to discover that their arrival in a "free state" did not mean they would be set free. Of course, they "claimed freedom, charging Ruiz and Montez with assault, battery, and false imprisonment" (Rukeyser 36–37). And, for their part, Montez and Ruiz claimed possession of the *Amistad* and its passengers.

Strangely, though, they were not the only ones to make such a claim. Led by a Captain Green, who lived down the road, a group of Long Islanders also "claimed salvage on the vessel, the cargo, and the slaves" (37) on the grounds that they had been the first to speak to Cinquez and his men when they had come ashore looking for water. Still another claim was made by a certain Lieutenant Gedney, who, having seen the *Amistad* approaching Montauk, thinking it must have been a pirate ship, and hoping for an opportunity to revive his languishing career, had ordered his own crew to follow. Meanwhile, the Spanish Minister, with the support of the pro-slavery press in the United States, claimed the ship and its "cargo" for Spain, arguing that the trials should be held in Cuba since "a 'trial and execution' in Connecticut was not as good" (37). Not to be outdone in a matter of patriotic duty, the local District Attorney "claimed that the Africans should be held, according to the 1819 Act, subject to the pleasure of the President" (37). Secretary of State John Forsyth and Attorney General Felix Grundy intervened, trying to keep the proceedings within federal jurisdiction so that they might be able to turn the slaves and cargo over to "persons designated" by the Spanish Minister. Even President Van Buren considered getting involved—he too was inclined to return the ship and the slaves to Spain—until he realized that he lacked an extradition treaty.

All things considered, it is hardly surprising that, in Hayden's account, Montez and Ruiz are perplexed. Most of all, they have trouble understanding how some Americans—especially the members of the anti-slavery movement who sponsored the Africans' defense—fail to recognize their right to what they consider their own property. When Hayden gives them a chance to speak for themselves, they focus their astonishment primarily on John Quincy Adams, who has taken up the cause of the Amistad slaves and will eventually argue for their freedom in their final appeal before the Supreme Court. When the events of the poem take place, Adams is seventy-three years old and returning to court after a thirty-two-year hiatus. Even by his own account, he is not in very good shape, with "a shaking hand, a darkening eye, a drowsy brain, and with all of my faculties dropping from me one by one, as the teeth are dropping from my head" (qtd. in Rukeyser 46). To the Spanish slavers, he seems to have been transported from the Roman Empire, rhetorically extravagant and oblivious to the practical demands of their very modern business:

> We find it paradoxical indeed
> that you whose wealth, whose tree of liberty

are rooted in the labor of your slaves
should suffer the august John Quincy Adams
to speak with so much passion of the right
of chattel slaves to kill their lawful masters
and with his Roman rhetoric weave a hero's
garland for Cinquez. I tell you that
we are determined to return to Cuba
with our slaves and there see justice done. Cinquez—
or let us say "the Prince"—Cinquez shall die. (53)

Ironically, it is with this slaver's speech that "Middle Passage" enters a maze of moral contradictions: between the law of New York and the broader political interests of the federal government; between the "Christian" slave traders, whose legacy of violence and lust has been documented throughout the poem, and the so-called "apes" who have spared their lives; between the slaves' perception of the United States, during the journey, as "mirage and myth" and these strangely "civilized" events that occur once the ship reaches the "actual shore" (51); between the talk of liberty in the free states and the roots" of this liberty in slave labor; between the familiar language of Montez and Ruiz, confident in its sense of a culture shared with educated Americans, and the increasing isolation of the poem's main narrative voice, as it traces the history of "dark ships" that move like "Shuttles in the rocking loom of history" (51).

Within this narrative framework, Hayden uses his historical sources to turn Eliot's own poetics against his restricted vision of cultural decline. In "Middle Passage" Hayden makes use of "The Waste Land's" abrupt shifts between multiple voices, its cryptic quotations, its central symbols of fire and water, its references to the sea as the site of transformation, and its mythical hero who must journey through the land of the dead in order to restore a vital society. He even includes a bitter variation on Eliot's variations on Shakespeare. The two passages from *The Tempest* used by Eliot-Ariel's song, "Full fathom five thy father lies," and Ferdinand's lament for his missing father—are displaced from Prospero's magic island, compressed, and relocated in the hold of a slave ship:

Deep in the festering hold thy father lies,
the corpse of mercy rots with him,
rats eat love's rotten gelid eyes. (51)

By establishing this doubly ironic relationship among his poem, "The Waste Land," and the Shakespearean "original," Hayden undermines the cultural nostalgia that Eliot characteristically imposes upon such passages: the search among the ruins for a once-coherent civilization, the pained intimations of moral decline, the longing almost beyond hope for some reconstruction of the fragmented past that might bring spiritual redemption. To put it another way, in Hayden's allusions, the passages from earlier texts do not appear as a bulwark against the ruinous forces of modernity, they, too, have been transformed so that they carry the indelible marks of history in their imagery and even in their music. After "Middle Passage's" accounts of, among other things, opthalamia, starvation, death by fire, and live people fed to sharks, "The Waste Land's" method of allusion seems painfully literary.

This is the most important difference between "Middle Passage" and "Schizophrenia." In "Middle Passage," Hayden appropriates Eliot's poetics with this distinct purpose—and, in doing so, he develops a morally engaged, pragmatic poetics that would eventually align his work with the post-traditional poetry of a younger generation. Most fundamentally, his answer to "The Waste Land" demonstrates just how Eliot's poem struggles toward moral condemnation, without being able to establish any convincing or consistent moral ground. In this way, Hayden is able to exploit a radical philosophical uncertainty that is one of the pervasive features of Eliot's poetry but is typically obscured by Eliot's later pronouncements on culture and religion. At the center of "The Waste Land's" moral universe, as Eliot and others have noted, is the vision of Tiresias, old and blind, "throbbing between two lives." According to Eliot's famous notes, Tiresias is "the most important personage in the poem, uniting all the rest" (50):

> I Tiresias, old man with wrinkled dugs
> Perceived the scene, and foretold the rest—
> I too awaited the expected guest
> He, the young man carbuncular, arrives,
> A small house agent's clerk, with one bold stare,
> One of the low on whom assurance sits
> As a silk hat on a Bradford millionaire. (38)

Of course, Tiresias's vision turns out to be the most famous—and discouraging—seduction in twentieth-century poetry:

> Flushed and decided, he assaults at once;
> Exploring hands encounter no defence;
> His vanity requires no response,
> And makes a welcome of indifference.
> (And I Tiresias have foresuffered all

Enacted on this same divan or bed;
I who have sat by Thebes below the wall
And walked among the lowest of the dead.) (39)

With its shifts between vatic proclamation and mock-heroic deflation, this passage brings "The Waste Land's" method of allusion close to that of English neoclassical satire, with its characteristic manner of exposing contemporary pretensions by holding them up to the standards of an idealized past that is deceptively made to seem available by the imitation of conventional poetic form. But as Ezra Pound understood, I think, in some of his revisions of Eliot's typescript, such a method is fundamentally irreconcilable with either the poem's sense of irreparable fragmentation or its striving to give voice to distinctly modern anxieties. On the other hand, without the ironies generated by its classical and neoclassical allusions, this passage would suggest that Eliot's vision of Western civilization's impending doom must somehow wrench its moral authority from a voyeuristic commentary on an uninspired sexual fling—as if sexual boredom were the end of the world.

In "Middle Passage," Hayden places a reply to Tiresias's vision at his poem's center, both spacially and thematically. For Hayden, the heart of darkness resides in the speech of an anonymous slave trader who, in the course of twenty prosperous years, has come to view his work, from its basic sources to its net profits, as an ordinary business. Loosely based on Theodore Canot's account of his own career in his *Adventures of an African Slaver*, it is a passage that, I imagine, must have been noticed by the judges at the Senegal conference, given their tendency to view both literature and racism in the context of colonialism:

Aye, lad, and I have seen those factories,
Gambia, Rio Pongo, Calabar;
have watched the artful mongos baiting traps
of war wherein the victor and the vanquished

Were caught as prizes for our barracoons.
Have seen the nigger kings whose vanity
and greed turned wild black hides of Fellatah,
Mandingo, lbo, Kru to gold for us.

And there was one—King Anthracite we named him—
fetish face beneath French parasols
of brass and orange velvet, impudent mouth
whose cups were carven skulls of enemies:

He'd honor us with drum and feast and conjo
and palm-oil-glistening wenches deft with love,
and for tin crowns that shone with paste,
red calico and German-silver trinkets

would have the drums talk war and send
his warriors to burn the sleeping villages
and kill the sick and old and lead the young
in coffles to our factories. (50–51)

By placing this speech at the center of "Middle Passage," Hayden also develops the strategy of moral implication he uses when Montez and Ruiz contrast Adams's rhetoric to the economic realities of slavery in America.[15] By including this particular slaver's voice, he is able to widen his net of implication: The speech is effective precisely because it seems so familiar, the words of a man who has simply been carried along in a job that leads him to everyone from local rulers like "King Anthracite" to "factory" workers at the barracoons to lawyers in New York.

Passages like this one suggest that Hayden's rejection of Black Cultural Nationalism, almost twenty-five years later, was primarily determined by the already formidable achievement of his own poetry. He would never be a "Negro poet," if that meant—as it certainly seemed to mean to his audience at the Fisk Conference—that he could not mimic for his own purposes the voices of lynchers and common slavers. He would never be a Negro poet, if that meant he could not use such impersonations to implicate, among many others, the African kings whose vanity and greed were so necessary to the slave trade, especially in its early years when white men rarely entered Africa's interior. And he would never be a Negro poet, if that meant he could not give full voice to historical characters like Montez and Ruiz in order to account, accurately and with sufficient moral complexity, for the contending political and social forces at work when the Amistad captives finally landed in New York.

But even more fundamentally, in his work of the early 1940s Hayden sets out to restore to poetry the sense of contingency by which a particular historical moment—say, for instance, a mutiny aboard a Spanish slave ship— appears vividly uncertain and, for that reason, at that moment, human action is potentially prophetic.[16] The fragmentary narrative in the final lines of "The Waste Land" depends, more than any other passage of the poem, upon the myth of Parsifal, in various incarnations, searching for the Chapel Perilous in his quest to restore, and reconnect, the natural and social orders. "The Waste Land's" other more or less religious allusions—most notably the vision of the disciples on the road to Emmaus and the ritualistic ending of the Upanishads—are more than anything else variations on this theme. This overarching mythic structure and the poem's dominant narrative voice imply that these apparent fragments are ultimately unified in the refuge of a collective unconscious—or some such half-concealed repository of cultural memory and meaning—where they dwell, in their more complete forms, beyond the changes and challenges of history. In this way, Eliot strains poetic metaphysics just about, but not quite, to the point of breaking. Or, to put it another way, in *The Waste Land* Eliot stops just on the verge of the post-traditional.

On the other hand, by rescuing Cinquez from obscurity—by returning him, through poetry, to living history—Hayden asserts the possibility that an unlikely individual, even after one of the most convoluted journeys through the middle passage and the American courts, can act in a manner that "transfigures many lives." In the end, despite the eloquence of Montez and Ruiz—and the many others who claimed to own him—Cinquez did not die for his part in the mutiny. Somehow, Adams managed to revive his long-neglected skills as a litigator, and the Supreme Court ultimately ruled that Cinquez should be released to the missionary society for transportation back to Sierra Leone—along with those other slaves who had managed to survive their journey, imprisonment, and legal odyssey. By ending "Middle Passage" with a poetic account of Cinquez's survival, Hayden transforms "The Waste Land's" theme of transformation. He replaces "mirage and myth" with historical revision and continuance. Even more important, in contrast to Eliot's nostalgia for a stable tradition, supported by an equally stable social order, Hayden ends with a prophetic voice capable of resurrecting the suppressed past in, and beyond, the present:

> The deep immortal human wish,
> the timeless will:
>
>> Cinquez its deathless primaveral image,
>> life that transfigures; many lives.
>
> Voyage through death
>> to life upon these shores. (55)

And so, a "deep immortal human wish" finds expression in the poetic image—but what is most important is that the poem does not end there. The couplet at the center of this concluding passage balances two visions of Cinquez: For an instant, he is equally a figure within the poem and an individual living in an historical moment. But the sequencing of the couplet's two lines, like the larger movement of this passage, suggests that the poetic image aspires to the status of an individual life, which can transfigure many other lives through prophetic action. The poem and the historical life invest each other with meaning, in a common world, for "life upon these shores."

HAYDEN AND THE CONTEMPORARY AFRICAN AMERICAN POETIC SEQUENCE

Of all the consequences of the literary politics of April, 1966, probably the strangest is that Hayden's poetry—with its radical contingency, historical detail, moral complexity, and formal experimentation—would be so persistently ignored or undervalued by scholars and critics. This neglect can be interpreted within a number of contexts: for instance, the conflict between the cultural politics of New Criticism, in the years of its greatest domination in elite universities, and the Black Arts Movement, as it shaped one generation's discussion of African American poetry; or the recent ascendency of African American novelists like Alice Walker and Toni Morrison; or the declining status of contemporary poetry within the academy over the past forty years or so, with the tendency to relegate poetry to creative writing programs; or the increasing influence of theories that seem to be more readily proven by narrative fiction and, in some cases, popular culture.

But none of these contexts really does much to lessen the irony, or the larger significance, of Hayden's situation. Just as critical approaches more sympathetic to history and issues of race have gained academic acceptance and influence, African American poets have produced a body of work that is, I think, unprecedented in the degree to which it adapts innovative poetics to address historical and racial issues. Yet the criticism has remained virtually oblivious to the poetry. Hayden himself anticipated this problem when he said, in one way or another, any number of times, that discussions of "race and poetry" always seem to turn into discussions of "race."

So, for the most part, it has been left to a younger generation of African American poets to claim and continue Hayden's legacy. These poets have generally begun their careers with a clear recognition of the limitations of both Black Cultural Nationalism, with its tendency toward the kind of rigid political proscription that led to Tolson's denunciation of Hayden, and New Critical aestheticism, with its tendency to ignore race altogether and treat Hayden as a kind of minor formalist. At the same time, these poets have recovered some of the more useful affinities between African American poetry and international négritude that were merely suggested by the conference in Dakar.

Most of all, these more recent poets have drawn from the approach to historical poetry that Hayden began to develop in "Middle Passage." By demonstrating that literary tradition—like history itself, as it is actually being lived—is radically contingent, Hayden made it easier for younger poets to view any given tradition as provisional, even improvisational. To put it in the more familiar terms of literary history, these poets have extended many of the poetic experiments of modernism while historicizing the modernists' sense of historical crisis—that is, the peculiar dread of impending chaos and social disruption, the barbarians-at-the-gates mentality, that so often characterizes the later canon formations of Yeats, Eliot, and Pound.

For instance, in his sequence "Debridement" Michael S. Harper extends Hayden's experiments in multiple voices and historical disjunctions. Using a prosody derived in part from jazz, "Debridement" comments upon a more recent but equally "schizoid" episode of the recent past: the Vietnam War, in which the poem's main character inadvertently wins a Medal of Honor, and the years immediately following, in which he returns to the projects, only to be berated by "militants," then shot and killed by a white store manager who is frightened to see "a car filled with blacks" parked in his neighborhood (*Images of Kin* 110). Shifting, often with the syncopation of a Charlie Parker solo, between Cambodia, the Projects, and the hospital where its main character dies, "Debridement" depends upon a sense of history in which the past remains oddly alive in the present, and in which it seems that poetry—in particular, a distinctly post-traditional poetry—can provide the resources necessary to bring this past to judgment in a manner that serves the needs of the present.

Hayden's legacy also endures in the poetic sequences of Brenda Marie Osbey, with their multiple voices, disjunctive narratives, and heterogeneous cultural traditions. In works like "Ceremony for Minneconjoux," *In These Houses*, and most of all the book-length narrative poem *Desperate Circumstances, Dangerous Women*, Osbey's féfé women recreate a local history of New Orleans' Tremé district in heterogeneous voices rich with the rhythms of island songs, okono drums, hoodoo chants, and "root ends / against tamborines" (*Ceremony* 6). Fittingly, Osbey begins the final sequence of *In These Houses* with a tribute to Hayden, a variation on his poem "O Daedalus, Fly Away Home." In this poem, Hayden adopts a popular legend from Georgia Sea Island: "It was believed there were certain Africans who, after being brought here as slaves, flew back to Africa. They had magic power and, as I say in the poem, they could just spread their arms and fly away" (*Collected Prose* 174). Drawing from the personal reminiscences of former slaves, Hayden recounts these legends in a kind of juba, accompanied by "coonskin drum and jubilee banjo":

Do you remember Africa?

O cleave the air and fly away home

My gran, he flew back to Africa,
just spread his arms and
flew away home.

Drifting night in the windy pines;
night is a laughing, night is a longing.
Pretty Malinda, come to me. (*Collected Prose* 174)

Osbey's tribute recalls not only Hayden's "Daedelus" but also the end of
"Middle Passage":

amid all the laughter
i manage to fly away home
have yet to perish
in the sea. (*Houses* 33)

In her poetry, as in Hayden's, legend functions as both local history and
living literature. A "tradition" of this kind is not something preserved by the
purifiers of language against the corrupting influences of common culture—
whether within the boundaries established by the range of allusion and other
restrictive gestures of modernist poetics or within the institutional practices
of the academy. A "tradition" of this kind is woven by the individual poet
from the strands of assorted heritages still alive within her community. It still
serves immediate purposes. It is a means of survival. It seems to me that
Hayden's legacy is apparent in similar ways in Melvin Dixon's "Tour Guide:
La Maison des Esclaves," Yusef Komunyakaa's "Blues Chant Hoodoo Revival,"
Elizabeth Alexander's "The Venus Hottentot," and perhaps most
significantly Jay Wright's *Dimensions of History* and *The Double Invention of
Komo*. One way of looking at these works would be to say that they are part
of one of the richest—and least appreciated—"traditions" in modern
American literature, a "tradition" that undoubtably includes Hayden as a
shaping and presiding presence.[17] It is also certainly true that all of these
works draw, in one way or another, from what Robert Stepto has called, in a
discussion of Wright's poetry, "the tangle of black traditions binding the
Americas to West Africa" (x).
    But in remarkable ways all of these works point to a more fundamental
lesson that should be drawn from the strange events of April, 1966, from

Hayden's calculated response to Eliot's poetics—and from the kind of reconsideration of Hayden's career that I am advocating. Terms like *tradition* and *influence* can only be applied to this poetry in a manner that is self-conscious and ironic, if at all, for the poetry is so highly attuned to historical, social, cultural, and moral disjunctions that it never pretends to resolve, through direct appropriation of an established poetic *convention*, any injustice or hypocrisy that remains unresolved in the society at large. Instead, this poetry uses improvisation and linguistic heterogeneity as a means of constantly redescribing, and cultivating, human complexity and dignity.

So I think it would be more accurate and more useful to say that this poetry—which might be called, rather loosely, the contemporary African American poetic sequence—builds on Hayden's legacy by constantly renegotiating relationships between contending traditions and contending social orders. Each of these poets reconstructs, at will, a heritage that is at once personal and historically grounded, continuous and progressively hybrid, in order to serve immediate social need. To put it another way, for more than fifty years now, Hayden's work has been one of the most persistent forces moving poetry in the direction of the post-traditional.

NOTES

1. Clearly, the significance of the Festival's location was not lost on its organizers or its participants. The first Festival had been held in 1956 at the Sorbonne—as Vaillant notes, "the center of French scholarship"—and the second in 1959 in Rome, "The Capital of Christian Europe" (322).

2. As Fetrow points out, it was the *Grand Prix*, more than any previous attention to Hayden's work, that seems to have inspired the four reviews of his *Selected Poems* in the fall of 1966. The *Selected Poems* was the first American publication of one of Hayden's books since 1948 (24–25).

3. Rosey Pool, a member of the "Grand Jury" for Hayden's *Grand Prix* and for many years the leading advocate of his poetry, proclaimed that "At Dakar the words 'Negro' and 'Negritude,' Negro-ness, took on new meaning and dignity" (42–43). She also used the example of Hayden to invest "négritude," in particular, with unusually extended, personal, and religious overtones: "In light half-nightmare and half-vision he speaks of the face of Baha'u'llah, prophet of the Baha'i faith, in whose eyes Hayden sees the suffering of the men and women who died at Dachau and Buchenwald for their specific *Negritude*" (43). In his

keynote address at the Fisk Conference, Saunders Redding was more upbeat: He drew loud applause by referring to "négritude" as a "relatively inexplicable mystique" (Llorens 55).

4. In the introduction to their recent anthology *Every Shut Eye Ain't Asleep*, Michael S. Harper and Anthony Walton suggest that the very similar question "is a poet first a poet, or first a black?" is "an underlying, if often unspoken, theme of African American poetry since 1945" (1). It is also worth noting that Hayden's position at the Fisk Conference was certainly nothing new, echoing W.E.B. Du Bois's *Souls of Black Folk*, the conclusion of Langston Hughes's "The Negro Artist and the Racial Mountain," and several earlier arguments within the négritude movement. Like many recent literary critics—including the Marxists Raymond Williams, Fredric Jameson, and Terry Eagleton—Hayden thought that some recognition of "culture's limited but significant autonomy within its own sphere" (Graff 155) was true to his own experience and, more importantly, one key to any effective position for poetry within a movement for social change.

5. More than a decade later, in his 1978 address at the Library of Congress, Hayden would respond to this particular comment. At one point in a dialogue between "the Poet" and "the Inquisitor" (a figure "more like Chekhov's Black Monk than anything else"), the Poet rebukes his adversary with the phrase "As if you give a tinker's damn about poetry" (*Collected Prose* 4, 15).

6. The three book-length studies of Hayden, each of which begins with a biographical overview and then proceeds to critical analysis of his poetry, are typical in this regard, though they vary in their estimation of the degree to which the events of 1966 would ultimately shape Hayden's career. Fred M. Fetrow accurately describes the changes in Hayden's critical reception following the International Prize and the Fisk Conference. Pontheolla Williams uses Hayden's response to the conference—his rejection of Black Nationalism and his continued determination not to be bound by any kind of "Black Aesthetic"—as the central message of her "Biographical Sketch" and as the recurrent theme of her critical analysis. John Hatcher entitles his chapter on Hayden's life in the 1960s "The Crucial Years" and begins the critical portion of his book with an attempt to focus Hayden's career by accounting for his response to "The Problem of a 'Black Aesthetic.'"

7. Interestingly, Julius Lester, a former student of Hayden's at Fisk, attributes Hayden's relative obscurity to his refusal to affiliate not just with Black Cultural Nationalism but with any "school" or "movement" or "cause." "Both races," Lester concludes, "think the black writer is a

priest, offering absolution to whites or leading blacks to the holy wars" (5).

8. The notable exception is Robert Stepto, who considers Hayden, Michael Harper, and Jay Wright as three poets who develop "post-modernist expressions" anticipated by the ending of Ralph Ellison's *Invisible Man* ("After Modernism" 471). Also, in his "Introduction" to the *Selected Poems of Jay Wright*, Stepto suggests that, "from the view of literary history," Hayden's "Middle Passage" might be "the poem behind Wright's art," since it anticipates Wrights attention to "the tangle of black traditions binding the Americas to West Africa" (x). In his "Afterword" to the same volume, Harold Bloom echoes Stepto's observation but with, as in all of his writing, a less historically grounded sense of traditions (194–95).

9. Vaillant mentions that there were rumors at the Dakar conference that "black American radicals had been denied entrance" (323).

10. A general idea of the academic consensus on the dimensions of négritude, at about the time of the Dakar conference, is provided by Lilyan Kesteloot's rather conservative survey, described in chapters 21 and 22 of her *Black Writers in French: A Literary History of Négritude* (298–332).

11. An important early document, in this regard, is Hayden's 1948 "manifesto" for the Counterpoise Series, a series for which he also edited several books of poetry and fiction (*Collected Prose* 41–42).

12. See the essays by Kutzinski, Davis, and Wright.

13. Of Hayden's critics, Williams is the most aware of the many similarities between "Middle Passage" and "The Waste Land," but her commentary assumes throughout that Hayden is borrowing various elements of "technique"—especially "the technique of fragmentation" (79)—from Eliot, without ever suggesting that Hayden saw any limitations in Eliot's poem or its social implications. Hatcher does not consider Eliot in his reading of "Middle Passage," but in the later stages of his study he, too, repeatedly refers to Eliot as a kind of exemplary model. Davis, in his seminal essay, merely mentions that Hayden's echo of Ariel's song had a "precedent" in "The Waste Land" (258).

14. This merger in Eliot's early poetry of philosophical solipsism and psychosis, which often leads to the collapse of cultural criticism into the psychic projections of the poem's speaker, has become much clearer with the recent publication of Eliot's early manuscripts in *Inventions of the March Hare*, edited by Christopher Flicks. In a previously unpublished passage from an early draft of "The Lovesong of J. Alfred

Prufrock," for instance, Prufrock nearly exhausts himself in an effort to get to the window of his room. Once there, he listens to his "Madness singing," or perhaps he witnesses the end of the world (43).

15. Hayden uses a similar strategy in "Night, Death, Mississippi," in which a later episode in American racism is described through the voice of one of its villains—an old man who, as his son is out taking part in a lynching, looks back with a nearly sexual excitement to the times when he too could join in the torture and killing.

16. For a discussion of some of the possible relationships between an understanding of historical contingency and the ability "to achieve certain moral consequences in light of effective strategies and tactics," see Cornel West's criticism of Richard Rorty in *The American Evasion of Philosophy: A Genealogy of Pragmatism* (209). Like West, I am trying to draw upon some of the implications of Rorty's neopragmatism while avoiding Rorty's tendency, seen most obviously in his recent *Language, Contingency, Solidarity*, to collapse contingency—of language, of self, of community—into mere arbitrariness.

17. This sense of a contemporary African American poetic tradition overlaps with that of *Every Shut Eye Ain't Asleep*, in which Harper and Walton view Hayden's "work and career" as "a kind of signpost in sensibility" (3) and begin their anthology with a selection of his poetry. *Every Shut Eye Ain't Asleep* takes its title from one in a series of "words and phrases remembered from childhood and youth" that Hayden once collected as "part of the design of a new series of poems." The fuller version is "Every shut-eye ain't sleep and every goodbye ain't gone" (*Collected Prose* 22).

WORKS CITED

Auden, W. H. *Collected Poems*. Ed. Edward Mendelson. New York: Random, 1976.

Baker, Houston. *Modernism and the Harlem Renaissance*. Chicago: U of Chicago P, 1987.

Barber, John Warner. *A History of the Amistad Captives*. 1840. New York: Arno P, 1969.

Bloom, Harold. "Afterword." Wright, *Selected Poems* 194–97.

Canot, Theodore. *The Adventures of an African Slaver*. 1854. New York: Dover, 1969.

Davis, Charles T. "Robert Hayden's Use of History." *Black is the Color of the Cosmos*. Ed. Henry Louis Gates. Washington: Howard UP, 1989. 253–68.

Eliot, T. S. *The Waste Land and Other Poems*. New York: Harcourt, 1962.

Ellmann, Richard, and Robert O'Clair, eds. *The Norton Anthology of Modern Poetry*. New York: Norton, 1988.

Fetrow, Fred M. *Robert Hayden*. Boston: Twayne, 1984.

Graff, Gerald. *Beyond the Culture Wars*. New York: Norton, 1992.

Harper, Michael S. *Images of Kin: New and Selected Poems*. Urbana: U of Illinois P, 1977.

———. "Remembering Robert Hayden." *Michigan Quarterly Review* 21.1 (1982): 182–88.

———, and Anthony Walton, eds. *Every Shut Eye Ain't Asleep: An Anthology of Poetry by African Americans Since 1945*. Boston: Little, Brown, 1994.

Hatcher, John. *From the Auroral Darkness: The Life and Poetry of Robert Hayden*. Oxford: George Ronald, 1984.

Hayden, Robert. *Collected Poems*. Ed. Frederick Glaysher. New York: Liveright, 1985.

———. *Collected Prose*. Ed. Frederick Glaysher. Ann Arbor: U of Michigan P, 1984.

———. "Schizophrenia." "Robert Hayden in the 1940's." By Reginald Gibbons. *TriQuarterly* 62 (1985): 185–86.

Karenga, Ron. "Black Cultural Nationalism." *The Black Aesthetic*. Ed. Addison Gayle, Jr. New York: Doubleday, 1971. 32–38.

Kesteloot, Lilyan. *Black Writers in French: A Literary History of Negritude*. Trans. Ellen Conroy Kennedy. Philadelphia: Temple UP, 1974.

Kutzinski, Vera M. "Changing Permanences: Historical and Literary Revisionism in Robert Hayden's 'Middle Passage.'" *Callaloo* 9.1 (1986): 171–83.

Lester, Julius. "Words in the Mourning Time." *New York Times Book Review* 24 Jan. 1971: 4+.

Llorens, David. "Writers Converge at Fisk University." *Negro Digest* 15 (June 1966): 54-68.

Melhem, D. H. *Gwendolyn Brooks: Poetry and the Heroic Voice*. Lexington: UP of Kentucky, 1987.

Meredith, William. "Foreword." Hayden, *Collected Prose* v–vii.

Miller, Charles. *Auden: An American Friendship*. New York: Paragon, 1989.

Nicholas, Xavier. "Robert Hayden & Michael S. Harper: A Literary Friendship." *Callaloo* 17 (1994): 976–1016.

Osbey, Brenda Marie. *Ceremony for Minneconjoux*. Lexington: Callaloo, 1983.

———. *In These Houses*. Middletown: Wesleyan UP, 1988.

Pearce, Donald. "Fortunate Fall: W. H. Auden at Michigan." *W. H. Auden: The Far Interior*. Ed. Alan Bold. Totowa: Barnes & Noble, 1985.129–57.

Pool, Rosey. "Robert Hayden: Poet Laureate." *Negro Digest* 15 (June 1966): 39–43.

Rorty, Richard. *Contingency, Irony, Solidarity*. New York: Cambridge UP, 1989.

Rukeyser, Muriel. *William Gibbs: American Genius*. New York: Doubleday, 1942,

Said, Edward. *Culture and Imperialism*. New York: Knopf, 1993.

Stepto, Robert B. "After Modernism, After Hibernation: Michael Harper, Robert Hayden, and Jay Wright." *Chant of Saints*. Ed. Michael S. Harper and Stepto. Urbana: U of Illinois P, 1979. 470–85.

———. "Introduction." Wright, *Selected Poems* ix–xv.

Vaillant, Janet G. *Black, French, and African: a Life of Leopold Sedar Senghor*. Cambridge: Harvard UP, 1990.

West, Cornel. *The American Evasion of Philosophy: A Genealogy of Pragmatism*. Madison: U of Wisconsin P, 1989.

Williams, Pontheolla T. *Robert Hayden: A Critical Analysis of His Poetry*. Urbana: U of Illinois P, 1987.

Wright, Jay. "Desire's Design, Vision's Resonance: Black Poetry's Ritual and Historical Voice." *Callaloo* 10.1 (1987): 13–28.

———. *Selected Poems of Jay Wright*. Ed. Robert B. Stepto. Princeton: Princeton UP, 1987.

RONALD WALCOTT

Calling the Names and Centering the Call in Robert Hayden's American Journal

Robert Hayden (1913–1980) spent much of the last decade of his life in failing health. His always-poor vision was made worse by cataracts; he suffered contusions in a car accident, and he underwent treatment for cancer. Professionally, however, the nineteen seventies were very kind to Hayden. He co-edited two anthologies of American literature, served as a staff member of the Breadloaf Writers Conference, held guest positions at a number of universities, became a fellow of the American Academy of Poets for his distinguished poetic achievement, and was appointed Consultant in Poetry at the Library of Congress. In addition, although never prolific, he had four volumes of poetry come into print: *Words in the Mourning Time* (1970), *The Night-Blooming Cereus* (1972), *Angle of Ascent* (1975), and *American Journal* (1978), which was nominated for a National Book Award. When he submitted to his publisher the poems that would appear in *American Journal*, Hayden used the occasion of the volume to reaffirm his most personal concerns and values and to give shape, one last time, to a vision which sought, like "the beauty of what's hard-bitten" in "Locus," to "flourish in despite, on thorny meagerness," and, in flourishing to twist "into grace."[1]

Slightly more than half of the entries in *American Journal* fall comfortably onto a single page, with the rest ranging from two to eight pages

From *CLA Journal*, vol. XLIII, no. 3 (March 2000). © 2000 by *CLA Journal*.

(the 132-line "Elegies for Paradise Valley"). The poetry is arranged in symmetrical stanzas whose lines, although metrically fairly loose, follow consistent patterns, with stanza structures that are individual adaptations of traditional forms. Even in the freer arrangements of the song-chant in "from The SNOW LAMP" and the telegraphic paragraphs of "[American Journal]," the verse is tightly controlled. Instead of full rhyme, Hayden uses occasional half-rhyme, assonance, consonance, and repeated lines and phrases. The fragmental four-, five-, and six-line stanzas, which he favors, seem to fit together perfectly like a puzzle, and the most visually arresting poems are those in which ingenuity of design reinforces sound and meaning in unexpectedly "right" ways, for example, "Homage to Paul Robeson," in which the judgment of the final sentence is confirmed by the diamond-hard quality of the work's five lines:

> Call him deluded, say that he
> was dupe and by half-truths betrayed.
> I speak him fair in death,
> remembering the power of his
> compassionate art. All else fades.
>
> (*Collected Poems* 157)

Another example is the sinuous structure of "Bone-Flower Elegy" (185), which approximates the "sensual movements" of "a naked corpse turning" on a coffin-bed spied in the "icy nonlight" of dream, the twisting of "nameless flowers," the shrinking of the poet from arms of death, and the "interlocking" of leaves and petals. A third example is "from The SNOW LAMP," about Peary's expedition in 1909 and the reaction to Matthew Henson, co-discoverer of the North Pole and considered by the Eskimos to be one of their own "returning" to the fold. Renamed and remembered in legend, the poem tells us, Henson forever travels "toward Furthest North / where all / meridians end." The shape of the lines and their placement on the page, however, show us the mythical journey into "Demonic dark" and

> Across lunar wastes of wind and snow
> Yeti's tract
>   chimera's land
> horizonless
>   as outer space
> through ice-rock sea
> and valley
>   (palm tree

fossils locked
in paleocrystic ice)
through darkness dire
as though God slept
in clutch of nightmare....

(*Collected Poems* 188, lines 1–13)

On display here are a painstaking, loving sense of form and a frequently impressive verbal technique. As Julius Lester has noted, Hayden's language is so precise and his lines so tightly compressed as to be unbearable.[2]

Hayden has been called a poet of remembrance with a "symbolist bent for mysticism and the occult," but Michael Harper points out that he was most of all a consummate storyteller,[3] and the poems in *American Journal* bear him out. They are written in a fairly straightforward descriptive or narrative style, their firm structural logic unclouded by the messy emotion which Hayden's personal reserve led him to see as narcissistic indulgence. Asked by John O'Brien whether it was not true that his poetry had an impersonal tone because he seemed to be removed from his work even when it was obviously about something that had happened to him, Hayden acknowledged that he was "unwilling, even unable, to reveal" himself directly in his work, and instead preferred to speak "on the slant," by donning a mask or assuming a persona.[4]

Indirection, disguises, and acting are wherever we look: in the armour and "mirrormasks" of "Astronauts" (190), in the "vulture masks" of presences that "play scenes of erotic violence / on a scaffold stage" in "Bone-Flower Elegy" (185), in the mind of the English chimney sweep who wonders whether Phillis Wheatley is not wearing a mask of soot (147); in the "gilt and scarlet" body of the tattooed man whose "gargoyle kisses," appalling "jungle arms" and spectacularly colored breast make of him a "grotesque outsider" (160); in the "gaudy otherness" of the gypsies Hayden recalls from his Detroit youth in "Elegies for Paradise Valley," who are "aliens among the alien" and yet, distressingly, "like us like us" (163); and in the assumed identities and mimicry of the space-traveling alien whose "[American Journal]" tries to describe "that some thing essence / quiddity i cannot penetrate or name" precisely because "this baffling / multi people" seem themselves to be wearing masks—"imprecise and strangering distinctions" of pigmentation and costume and mores—removed and replaced so often that they change "even as i / examine" (192).[5]

Deliberately distancing himself from his material, Hayden is drawn to similarly removed figures, those "baroque" outsiders, pariahs and losers in whom he was more interested, so he said, than he was in abstract and philosophical ideas.[6] Kindred spirits, their alienation objectifies his own and offers a unique vantage point from which to watch the play of light on character and culture. The estranged and the marginal, by virtue of their presence, confound society's premises and expectations and belie familiar answers to fundamental questions: what the self is and how it comes to be, to what extent identity is chosen or imposed, fashioned or accepted, to what extent comradeship and compassion are possible in "an evil time," and whether history is an illusionist's "soulscape" living out its "lengthy dying" ("Locus") or "process, major means whereby, / oh dreadfully, our humanness must be achieved" ("Words in the Mourning Time" 90).

"I gaze at you," Hayden's tattooed man says in the first line of his self-titled dramatic monologue (16–62). He gazes and longs to declare his love, to touch and hold another close, to "break through" and free himself "from servitude / I willed." But he frightens and makes people avert their faces, especially her for whom "he would endure caustic acids, / keenest knives." His "unnaturalness," however, serves a purpose: it "assures them they / are natural, they indeed belong." Repelling "union," the tattooed man belongs only to himself—that self the subject of a debate of long-standing at which the melodrama of flesh and ink only hints. He is a lifer in The Hole, but by whose choice, that of "evil circumstance" or his own? Did he "seek / in strangeness strange abiding-place," or was "bizarrity" thrust upon him who was "born alien" and is "homeless everywhere"? Did he choose, "having no other choice?" Do the answers matter? He thinks not: We select one among countless possible lives, as he wears this tattoo and not that, and, paradoxically, having "no other choice," we then experience the "pride" not of difference but of definition and the "servitude" of self-will. Besides, "the agonies of metamorphosis"—the price of identity—are so great that "I cannot / (will not?) change. / It is too late / for any / but death. / I am I."

One question lingers. If by some act of imagination he were to accommodate the conception of self of her who is "love's own," "would I not find / you altered then?" Who, in that event, would assure them that "they indeed belong"? Who, then, would become the grotesque but indispensable outsider? Just to raise the question is to glimpse the chaos against which the self is conceived along with the allure of at least some boundaries. His alien status his true home, he forgoes yet another metamorphosis, even a fanciful one.[7] Like O'Connor's Parker[8] and Kafka's hunger artist, Hayden's tattooed man is a solitary, discomfiting reminder that the artist does not choose to deny himself ordinary, untransformed experience; it simply does not nourish him.

The uncaring world revealed in the monologue determines identity and worth on the basis of appearance and a "normal" range of behavior.

Following his illustrious predecessors, Hayden insists that humanity is a matter of consciousness, not convention, and is achieved not by physical but by intellectual and moral action. By reconciling himself to difference—"I am I"—the tattooed man affirms his humanity and calls into question "yours."[9]

So extreme is his disaffection and so penetrating his gaze that the tattooed man does not require the confirmation of self that the scarred young lifters do in "The Prisoners" (159), the dispossessed whose plea the poet senses, the "plea / of men denied: Believe us human / like yourselves, who but for Grace...." But equally troubling in its way is the presence of the "noted stranger" in "The Rag Man" (158), "who long since / (the story goes) rejected all / that we risk chills and fever and cold / hearts to keep." Wordlessly disdaining all that others hold dear as well as their presence and "brief concern," the rag man cannot be defined by negation, existing in reaches of mind where everyday interests are meaningless. Looking at one who does not take them seriously enough to look back, the poem's "we" wonders, "Who is he really, the Rag Man?" The question is perhaps even more fundamental than those raised in "The Tattooed Man," for at least there "bizarrity" alerted one and all to the outer limits of the "natural." But here, "Who is he really?" has no answer that believably addresses the more pressing issue of who we are really. Facing the mysterious other, those walking by respond with condescending charity and the desire "to get shut of the sight of him."

Depictions of baroque figures, both historical and fictional, have inspired much of Hayden's best work. In *Selected Poems* (1966), there were Nat Turner, Harriet Tubman, and Frederick Douglass, of course, but also Sue Ellen Westerfield, a fugitive "whose only dangerous hidingplace / was love" with a white man (13); the religious charlatan of "Witch Doctor," "dancing, dancing, ensorcelled and aloof, / the fervid juba of God as lover, healer, / conjurer. And of himself as God" (35); the quadroon mermaids, Afro angels, black saints, Zulu king and gun-metal priestess of "A Ballad of Remembrance" (27); the ragged boys of "Market" (23), and the tippling ironists of "The Rabbi" (9). At the start of the decade, *Words in the Mourning Time* featured Aunt Jemima of the Ocean Waves, a sideshow mammy embarrassing to the speaker, who eventually realizes that as a self-aware and self-distancing manipulator of images and "notions" of racial identity, she is closer to Cellini than to the carnival, a "voluptuous imago" in one of her incarnations, "floating in the wake / of slave-ships on fantastic seas" (72); Mystery Boy, whom "Puzzle faces in the dying elms" sometimes "hiss and spit at" and who hears, "like the loudening of his heart / the name he never can he never can repeat" (68); the addicted denizen of "Soledad," lying "in the blinded room / chainsmoking, cradled by drugs, by jazz," who "hides on the dark side of the moon, / takes refuge in a stained-glass cell, / flies to a clockless country of crystal" (71); and Malcolm X, Martin Luther King, Jr., and Robert Kennedy, assassinated, Hayden implies, for being men outside their time.

What is most striking about *American Journal* in this regard is simply the number and authority of such portraits; they comprise a gallery of the dispossessed and the denied, the duped and the deluded, the imprisoned and the alien, the homeless and the martyred, the failed and the diseased, the divided and the desperate. Of the twenty-three poems in the volume, only in three is there no outsider as the focus of concern, and even with these one is not certain. It is, after all, rather difficult to go much further "out" than the "land's end" of "The Point" (181) and the moonscape of "Astronauts"; moreover, in "Zinnias" (182), the "hardy elan" of the flowers still would make one "scarcely present / bouquets of them / to Nureyev / or Leontyne Price"!

In the poetry of his sixties, it is clear, the center shifts for Hayden, his gaze become so encompassing that there no longer is an outside, in any useful sense. Like the diarist of "[American Journal]," the poet recognizes that most of us are outsiders, uncertain of "what or who" we are, stumbling about making "extravagant claims" about our importance and identity, and seeking a reassurance from the past that we cannot find in the present. In "Elegies for Paradise Valley" (163–70), the poet himself returns to the past "of all our dead" in search of the communal sources of his nature and his art; that these sources neither account for his secret desires nor explain his art underscores how little reassurance and hope of "union" the past actually offers.

"Elegies" characteristically opens with the young Hayden looking from his bedroom window onto the alley below as a junkie dead from an overdose is taken away, and looking, too, at a policeman who in turn looks at "our kind" with hatred "glistening like tears" in his eyes. Childhood "no time of starched / and ironed innocence," elders, grifters, the sinful and the saved, his mother, aunt, uncle, the local restaurant owner and many more gather 'round to shelter him as best they can from "alley stench," maggots, rats fighting in walls, Gypsies whose children "all got lice in their hair," early disaster and the ever-present hatred of "our kind." Years later, it is "our neighbors" that "materialize before the eye / of memory," and he realizes that to sing their song he must "Let vanished rooms, let dead streets tell."

They tell him what he knew even as a child "precocious in the ways of guilt / and secret pain," which is that there is no protection. His beloved Uncle Crip, who laughs and dances with him "to Jellyroll / Morton's brimstone piano" and passes on lore, is himself murdered and laid "among

floral pieces / in the front room where / the Christmas tree had stood."
Almost certainly dead also are "Tump, the defeated artist, for meals or booze
/ daubing with quarrelsome reds, disconsolate blues," shell-shocked Stump,
"clowning for us in parodies of war," Christopher, "sad queen of night," Ray,
"who cursing crossed the color line," dopefiend Mel, and mad Miss Alice,
"who ate from garbage cans." And "of all our dead," it is Madam Artelia,
fortuneteller and spiritualist, who most clearly comes to mind; it is she to
whom his aunt and mother turn when Crip dies and through whom Crip
says, "Dying's not death," and "Happy yes I am happy here."

But it is not a story of death that the poet needs to tell. Death and dying
were a part of it, but so were love and sin and mystery, and to tell that story
he must call the names of the missing and unaccounted: Tump and Stump
and Christopher and Ray and Mel and Miss Alice; Belle the classy dresser,
stagestruck Nora, fast Iola, snuffdipping Lucy, Hattie and Melissabelle, Jim
and Good Old Boy, Les the Huntsman and Tough Kid Chocolate, dapper
Jess and gentle Brother Davis. In calling their names, he magically brings
them once more before the eye of memory and peoples vanished rooms and
dead streets.

A recollection not of "our kind" hated by the police or the "gaudy
other" studied by sociologists, this is memory without regret. Come to praise
as well as to mourn and, most of all, to make poetry of it all, Hayden offers
portraits so finely observed, so vivid and so varied that they become a
panorama of individuals working, dreaming, gambling, serving their country,
preparing for success, fashioning styles of dress and art, involving themselves
in schemes and calamities, and, as happens, dying. Their lives and his poetry
everywhere informed by rhythms and sounds heard in church, at the Palace,
on Lucy's guitar, and on the victrola, these men and women are a real
community attempting to provide succor and sanctuary for their young and
no more able to do so than one day he will be. Shining forth now, though, is
not the vulnerability of one generation but the saving attempt of another.
For this is a portrait of survival and becoming. The elegy begins with the
poet's looking at a corpse, and it ends with his looking at himself in youth—
"the devil's own rag babydoll"—precocious in the ways of guilty sexuality,
furtive, mindful of the power of words and eyes glistening with hatred, yet
determined to thrive and, always, loved. So he calls the names, listens to the
dead, and captures the moment of telling in his art.

He is not the only guide in this place of shadows and spirit, however.
In the poem-within-a-poem which is section IV of "Elegies," Madam Artelia,
"part Seminole and confidant" of the dead, also calls the names, speaks for
the departed and is charged with the prophetic task. A product of diverse
peoples (African and Indian), religions (Christianity and Buddhism), and

styles, she lays her hands in blessing on the head of the poet-to-be, crosses
over—"Dying's not death"—and knows the power of inner vision to intensify
seeing. Her art of inspired telling in which past and present meet and in
meeting renew and transform each other, her submission to the
requirements of solitary thought and unobstructed seeing, her ritual-like
service to community, and her use of eclectic influences—these are all
animating principles of Hayden's poetry. That such a self-conscious
statement of aesthetic philosophy would be made in a work presumably
about memory as incantation does not surprise. For a poet who was certain
that the past is always involved in the present and the present in the past, the
seasons of a life comment on one another in ways both privileged and
consequential, as do the levels of meaning in art or as did his own childhood
and maturity.[10]

Writing plays, poems, and stories, the young Hayden "fled / to safety
in the danger zones / Tom Swift and Kubla Khan traversed," as later he
would be waylaid and empowered by the "rainbow darkness" of art and
religion ("Theme and Variation" 45). In his fourth decade, however, Hayden
learned that "my name was not my name," and with the loss of his name the
foundation of his identity was badly shaken. Having been told by "the old
ones" that they had adopted him, it was not until after their deaths, as he
recounts in "Names" (171), that he discovered no adoption had taken place
and that he was neither Asa Sheffey Bundy nor Robert Earl Hayden: he
didn't exist, "at least / not legally, the lawyer said." Stripped of language's
capacity to create what it names, he felt "deserted, mocked," "lied to," and
wondered whether he was "ghost, double, alter ego then?" He was struck, as
never before, by how removed his life was from the center of what he took
to be common experience and by how essential words are, especially words
that can reclaim the center. Only as years pass does it occur to him that lack
of affiliation and assurance is the common experience and that he has
occupied the center all along.

"The Year of the Child" (179) records the naming of Hayden's
grandchild and the hopes for the future embodied by those names: Michael,
"an archangel's name— / and great poet's," and Ahman, "hero of peace";
talismans, the grandfather prays, that may "invoke divine / magic to protect
/ as we cannot, / in a world that is / no place for a child." In "The Islands"
(183), friends look forward to vacationing on "islands named / to honor
holiness." Instead, they are met with disdain and outright hostility. But the
names which honor holiness work their magic: Scarlet hibiscus are brought
to them by the cleaning woman, herself "called alien" by the islanders and
supposedly full of "raucous anger," and the "patina'd cliches" of historical
evil, of which the poet has grown tired, miraculously abandon "their long

pursuit." And when he goes behind steel doors in "The Prisoners" (159) to read his work, he shares "reprieving Hidden Words / revealed by the Godlike imprisoned / One whose crime was truth." His poems, a young lifer tells him, are *true*. "It's like you been there, brother, been there."

The words which inspire hope, deflect scorn, and grant reprieve are, Hayden never forgets, the same words the writer works with as he searches for those methods that give form to vision. But like so much else in *American Journal*, in which there is "paradox on paradox," it is not that simple. The marvellous portrait of the slave insurrectionist whose soul goes "marching on" is a case in point.

"John Brown" (149–55) revolves around the fury of The Word: The Word that makes "pikes guns / swords" and instructs followers to "Arm the slaves / seize their masters / kill only if you must." The Word that serves as a grindstone upon which those Doing the Lord's work sharpen their sabres. And The Word that Brown gives is blessing "the Chosen, who in the name / of justice killed" at his command. Other words name Brown, among them "De Old Man" and "Ossawatomie," the latter a region in Kansas where Brown became a leader of anti-slavery guerillas whom he led on a nighttime raid on a pro-slavery settlement at Pottawatomie Creek, in which five men were dragged out of their cabins and hacked to death; a name which conjures up fearful images. Another of his names is never uttered, not even here, although "Shall we not say he died / for us?"

It is, moreover, the inadequacy of language in the instant of "dying / becoming" which the poem brings home. Before the "blinding enigmas" of truth and one man's "colossal" vision, words lose their compass, their capacity to see what they name, and once they do, the difference between prophecy and delusion as between the charge to do the Lord's work and the command at Harper's Ferry to "kill / only if you must" fades in "bloody light," with language the servant of contradiction: If Brown is a Jehovah holding an axe in his "loving wrathful hand"; if one who "slew no man" is for all time "aureoled in violence," "loved feared hated"; and if death is urged to breathe life into abolition's cause, then has righteousness become "angelic evil" or "demonic good"?

In these circumstances, the task of the poet as custodian of the language is not prophetic but reconstructive: to make words mean again. In the final lines, "mordant images," "vibrant stainedglass colors," and "elemental shapes," not easy analyses, try to make sense of character, "what we know of him / know yet fail to understand," for only in the "ardent interplay" of a poet's ways of knowing and the "symmetry" of an outsized life can a transforming moment of American history, and its agent, be recovered.

Another quintessentially American figure, hers also a life with a certain symmetry and an appreciation of "God's ways," is the subject and persona of the first poem in *American Journal*. "A Letter from Phillis Wheatley" (147) is a meditation of sorts on the vagaries of fate and identity. Writing to her sister, Wheatley recalls her first ocean voyage, "[d]estined" and long ago; of its horrors, in understated fashion, she yet has "some remembrance" and considers the irony of her second voyage, this one to England and accompanied by "dear Nathaniel," to read her "latest Elegies." Acclaimed by all as "True Poetess, albeit once a slave," she nevertheless dines "apart like captive Royalty." Still, when the possibility arises of being presented at court—like Pocahantas, she imagines—her first thought is that, as a patriot, she must decline the honor.

With occasional murmurings of Yankee Pedlar and Cannibal Mockingbird in the background, the stay makes clear that "there / is no Eden without its Serpent," not even in Idyllic England, and it reinforces her sense of black and American identity in that while she is from Africa, she cannot answer questions about a land she barely recalls. For better or worse, she is an American, and never more so than when the chimney sweep asks whether she too is a 'sweep what with her soot-blackened face! The exchange is, as she terms it, droll, and more. She is what she is, cut off from one people and at home with another but an outsider, however gifted, even with them and everywhere, and such she will remain. However, she will not allow the intractable nature of race to prevent her from finding amusement when and where she can, nor alter her faith in God. Like another remembrancer and wearer of masks, she will hone her craft and hold "back tears, as is my wont." Of such things is character made.

The nation's character is the focus of the title poem which closes *American Journal*; it also is in the form of a letter, this one by an interplanetary voyager to himself, in which he records his difficulty in preparing a report to be submitted to "The Counselors" on the American people. The Americans are so vital, inventive, and paradoxical that their essence eludes him; "some constant amid the variables defies analysis and imitation," and he wonders whether his report will be found wanting. Energy, violence, delusion, ignorance, the "strangering distinctions by which they live [and] by which they justify their cruelties to one another"—all this he sees. Living among them, he also sees the "night mare facts" they cannot escape from but try, as well as their self-importance and insecurity, fear and mistrust of freedom, obsession with history and need to "play at the carnage whereby" they "achieved identity." That they are "a divided / people seeking reassurance from a past few under / stand and many scorn" he does not doubt. But what they are beyond the noise, the barbarous confusion, the evasions and the unceasing change he does not know. Nonetheless he is both repelled by and attracted to them.

To be sure, the report suggests that the bewilderment the alien experiences when looking at us is the very same bewilderment we feel when looking at ourselves; hence the fearful fascination with the past and difference and self-worth. That "fact [and] fantasy are never twice the same" and that this is a landscape of "dream like vistas" as well as nightmare facts— these are what make American experience so fluid, "an organism that changes even as i examine it," and the attempts of Americans at self-definition so "imprecise" and driven.

Framing the volume, "A Letter from Phillis Wheatley" and "[American Journal]" are set in territory Hayden has charted ever since the "'prentice pieces" he wrote as a graduate student at the University of Michigan. The alien's perspective in both poems has been this writer's characteristic angle of vision, and the poems detailing and shaping his findings, letters back from a place as far away as the mirror. What distinguishes the two entries is their poignancy and century-spanning scope. More typical, although equally fine, have been more modest efforts like the poem entitled "Letter," which effectively centers *American Journal*.

Addressing one who has before saved him from "fierce current jagged with debris," the poet acknowledges that he is desperate still, entering old age, "the elegy time," in which there is a sense of shores receding. What "rends" his spirit, though, is the lifelong conundrum of identity that has "nurtured and tormented" him and, in his torment, caused him to lash out at one who is "yet compassionate." Having at last managed to accept himself as he is, his letter announces, he will now accept others as they are, and especially "will no longer ask for more / than you have freely given me or can give" (174). Compassion that has been freely given despite desperation, despite confusion, despite the risk of pain, is of the utmost importance to Hayden, the one value in his work as in his life that transcends paradox.

In the nocturnal mood of "A Letter from Phillis Wheatley," the haunting images of "John Brown," the Where are they now? of "Elegies for Paradise Valley," the receding shores of "Letter," and the knowledge of the poet's terminal illness throughout, the tone of *American Journal* is elegiac indeed. Nor is it just the tone which is somber. The concern with the "sometimes night mare facts" of the "american dream" and the great social problems cited in "The Year of the Child," "Killing the Calves" (178) and the title poem—this concern is sharp-edged and unsentimental. Furthermore, in "As My Blood Was Drawn," Hayden asks of the "World I have loved / and lovingly hated, / is it your evil / that has invaded / my body's world?" As his cancer was "put to the knife," "the People of Baha / were savaged were slain; /

skeletons were gleaning / famine fields ... innocents were sacrificed ... exiles
drowned ... [and] spreading oilslicks / burned the seas" (176).

Hayden, however, is the poet who gave us the "Voyage through death /
to life upon these shores" in "Middle Passage" (48) and the "flourishing in
despite" of "Locus," who observed in "The Tattooed Man" that "All art is
pain / suffered and outlived," and who saw courage and community in
"Elegies for Paradise Valley" as timeless as hope. In "Ice Storm," too, when
he asks of God whether he is less to Him than the moonstruck trees outside,
he knows that those trees, "as in winters past, / will survive their burdening,
/ broken thrive" (175). And "[American Journal]" does not end until mention
is made of the Americans' elan vital; only *then* does the alien find that he has
no name for the unnameable.

In *American Journal* and other works of the 'seventies Hayden
rethought the meaning of the center, with the figure of the outsider replaced
by that of the internal exile, an individual cut off emotionally, spiritually, and
imaginatively from a self and a society collapsing under the weight of their
own contradictions, and with "alienation" become too weak a word to
describe the various blindnesses and obsessions which pass for ordinary
experience of life. Somehow, though, Hayden never doubted that a light
flickered amid the "dead-of-night sorrows." In an early work, "Theme and
Variation" (45), it was the light of "an imminence / that turns to curiosa" all
that one knows; in "Stars" (134) it was the light of paradox by which one
thrives, and in "John Brown," it was the torchlight of the poet's imagination
revealing a vision in which "nothing human is foreign."[11] Sustained by the
light, Hayden affirmed the "bravura persistence" of nature and faith and love
and creativity. And he called the names, the names of his youth and his
ancestors[12] and the names of agents of historical change and those like
Dunbar, Wheatley and Robeson, whose compassionate art speaks to the
center and to the margins. Some mysteries Hayden hoped would remain
mysteries.[13] His art, however, should not be one of them. Often enough,
Robert Hayden was a first-rate poet, and *American Journal* is very fine
indeed.

NOTES

1.   Robert Hayden, *Collected Poems*, ed. Frederick Glaysher (New York:
     Liveright, 1985) 76. Hereafter cited in the text.

2.   Julius Lester, *Falling Pieces of the Broken Sky* (New York: Little, Brown,
     1990), 13.

3.   Michael S. Harper, "Remembering Robert E. Hayden," *Chant of Saints*,
     ed. Michael S. Harper and Robert B. Stepto (Urbana: U of Illinois P,
     1979) 231.

4. John O'Brien, *Interviews with Black Writers* (New York: Liveright, 1973) 115–16. Also, see Robert Hayden, "From The Life: Some Remembrances," *Collected Prose*, ed. Frederick Glaysher (Ann Arbor: U of Michigan P, 1984) 17–27.

5. Maurice J. O'Sullivan explores the "call of illusion" and tactical masquerade in Hayden's early work in terms of the example of Dunbar, hailed in *American Journal* as "elder brother" (156): "The Mask of Allusion in Robert Hayden's 'The Diver,'" *CLA Journal* 17 (1973): 85–72. See also Fred M. Fetrow, "Minority Reporting and Psychic Distancing in the Poetry of Robert Hayden," *CLA Journal* 33 (1989): 117–29.

6. O'Brien 112.

7. In "The Poet and His Art: A Conversation," Hayden told Paul McCluskey that his favorite paradox was "No place is home for me, therefore every place is home." See *How I Write / 1* (New York: Harcourt, 1972) 203.

8. Flannery O'Connor, "Parker's Back," *Norton Anthology of Short Fiction*, ed. R. V. Cassill (New York: Norton, 1986) 1148–65.

9. For a different view of "The Tattooed Man," see Pontheolla Williams, *Robert Hayden: A Critical Analysis of His Poetry* (Urbana: U of Illinois P, 1987) 173–74.

10. O'Brien 119.

11. *Collected Prose* 114.

12. See "Beginnings," from *Angle of Ascent*, in *Collected Poems* 125.

13 O'Brien 112.

BROOKE KENTON HORVATH

The Satisfactions of What's Difficult in Gwendolyn Brooks's Poetry

Gwendolyn Brooks has been both praised and condemned for her often mandarin style. Thus David Littlejohn, writing in 1966, could acknowledge her craft—"she exercises, customarily," he wrote, "a greater degree of artistic control than any other American Negro writer"—but not, finally, the results of that craftsmanship. "In many of her early poems," Littlejohn felt,

> Mrs. Brooks appears only to pretend to talk of things and of people; her real love is words. The inlay work of words, the *precieux* sonics, the lapidary insets of jeweled images (like those of Gerard Manley Hopkins) can, in excess, squeeze out life and impact altogether, and all but give the lie to the passions professed in the verbs.[1]

For other critics, the real bone of contention has been the fact that, despite her efforts to forge a black aesthetic, Brooks has practiced a poetics indebted as much to T. S. Eliot as to Langston Hughes (though brought to bear on black subject matter). This white style/black content debate can be heard clearly in Houston A. Baker's *Singers of Daybreak*: "Mrs. Brooks," says Baker, "writes tense, complex, rhythmic verse that contains the metaphysical complexities of John Donne and the word magic of Apollinaire, Pound, and

From *American Literature* 62, no. 4 (1990). © 1990 by Duke University Press.

Eliot." Yet this style is employed "to explicate the condition of the black American trapped behind a veil that separates him from the white world. What one seems to have is 'white' style and 'black' content—two warring ideals in one dark body."[2]

Both of these issues are complex. Behind the former—the emotional effectiveness of the poet's meticulous "inlay work of words"—lies in part the vexed question of modernism, which under the aegis of T. S. Eliot has been responsible, according to Christopher Clausen, for "the decline in the American poetic audience" and "the disappearance of poetry as a major cultural force."[3] Behind the latter—the problem of a "proper" aesthetic for a poet wrestling with an artistic double consciousness—stands the still-troubled assessment of, say, Phillis Wheatley and Paul Laurence Dunbar as well as more recent poets as diverse as Melvin Tolson and the Armageddon school of the Sixties.[4] In the pages that follow, I would like to add to this discussion of the appropriateness of Brooks's "tense, complex" early style as it relates to black concerns and, more centrally here, as it does or does not justify itself at its most elliptical apart from racial considerations. I intend to do this by examining in some detail one poem notable initially for its opacity: "'Do Not Be Afraid of No,'" which constitutes section nine of the "Notes from the Childhood and Girlhood" sequence in *Annie Allen*, Brooks's Pulitzer Prize-winning collection of 1949.[5]

A succinct example of Brooks's complexity at its most revealing/concealing, "'Do Not Be Afraid of No'" has received little close attention. Those critics who have commented upon the poem do so only briefly and with the intention of explaining its problematic place within the larger work of which it is a part. Thus, Charles Israel suggests that the poem reveals some of the "moral and ethical lessons of Annie's youth"; D. H. Melhem offers two paragraphs arguing that the poem constitutes Annie's motto," her refusal "to emulate her mother's submission"; and Harry B. Shaw reads the poem as equating "the high life with death" and admonishing Annie not to choose prostitution as the only alternative to "the death of no life," a reading that finds parallels between "'Do Not Be Afraid of No'" and other poems such as "Gang Girls" and "Big Bessie Throws Her Son into the Street."[6] If none of these readings confronts fully the interpretive difficulties introduced by the poem's appearance as part of *Annie Allen*—for instance, determining who is offering Annie this advice (the answer will affect one's assessment of the wisdom of that advice and its impact upon Annie) or establishing the connection between the advice offered in the poem's opening lines and the remainder of the poem (for surely the response to this initial advice cannot be credited to even the most precocious young girl, as the poet's use of the third-person pronoun indicates)—this is not the greatest cause for disappointment.[7] Rather, what one feels most is the lack of any extended analysis of the poem that would account not only for its "meaning" but also for the poet's stylistic choices and for the relation of both message and style to Brooks's concerns as a black female poet. I suggest that such a close reading reveals a style not merely justified by the poem's content but essential if readers are to *experience* (rather than simply be told) the truth the poem embodies.

"'Do Not Be Afraid of No'" begins straightforwardly enough by reiterating the advice of its title in two lines enclosed by quotation marks and concluded by a colon, which suggests that what follows will be a gloss upon this advice, the development of an argument in support of this thesis.

> "Do not be afraid of no,
> Who has so far so very far to go":

"Do not be afraid [to say] no" seems simple advice; indeed, now that "Just say no" has become the lamest sort of response to social problems, Brooks's opening lines may seem not so much simple as simple-minded (they will prove to be neither). But certain problems arise even here: Who is speaking and to whom? Are these lines something the poet has been told or read (hence the quotation marks)? One can of course fall back upon the response that these lines are spoken by someone to Annie (although I don't find this wholly clarifying for reasons such as those sketched above), but here I am suggesting that for "Annie" one might—for the duration of the poem— substitute "any young (black) girl" or, more generally, "anyone"—and here it is useful to recall George Kent's observation that in *Annie Allen* one advantage of the poetic form is to "move experiences immediately into symbols broader than the person serving as subject."[8] But further, to whom or what does the "who" of line two refer: to "no," its grammatical antecedent (in which case, why "who" instead of "which"?), or to the addressee—Annie aside, the choices would seem to be the poem's readers, self-reflexively the poet, or some unknown third party—who has "so far so very far to go"? And "to go" where? In life? One can be no more precise than that for now. These questions, however, are only mildly vexing because one presumes they will be answered (they won't be) in language similarly direct (it won't be but will tend toward greater confusion before somewhat clarifying itself).

Stanza two acknowledges that saying "no" is never easy:

> New caution to occur
> To one whose inner scream set her to cede, for
>   softer lapping and smooth fur!

As noted above, the opening lines appear in quotation marks possibly to suggest they contain received wisdom the perspicacity of which the poet intends to ponder. For one thing, she knows that saying "yes" means reaching agreement, solving a problem, accepting a plan, a truth, a life mate: "yes" is at least superficially positive, resolves that often unsettling uncertainty and probable antagonism "no" involves; "no" leaves one in suspense, in suspension, dissatisfied, perhaps closed off from comforts and companions. To say "no" to something is not, after all, necessarily to say "yes" to something else.

But through stanza two (and beyond), what exactly is at issue remains terribly amorphous. The reader, aware of who has written the poem and the historical circumstances surrounding its composition, might conclude that Brooks has something racial to denounce but is couching that denunciation in self-protectively cryptic language. But what? Is the poem an example of what Gary Smith has labelled Brooks's "remarkably consistent" identification of "white racism and its pervasive socio-economic effects" on the black community?[9] If so, how so? Or perhaps the poem is not primarily racial but speaks of some political, economic, or ideological crisis on the international scene? Or perhaps this is a prototypical instance of confessional poetry that speaks of larger concerns only as they impinge upon the private psyche? If Clara Claiborne Park is correct in reading *Annie Allen* as "a varied and inventive sequence of poems evoking a poor black woman's progress from exquisite illusion to the recognition of a harder yet more satisfying reality," and if one recalls Brooks's early poetic successes (encouraged by a mother who "intended her to be 'the *lady* Paul Laurence Dunbar'") within the white world of poetry and subsequent break in the late Sixties with that world in favor of poetry intent on speaking to African Americans of their concerns and in their language, then the poem might well be read as offering an elliptical rejection of poetic success in white literary terms (as either the black T. S. Eliot or the "lady" Paul Laurence Dunbar).[10] Such a reading is possible, but without seeking extratextual aid one cannot say "yes" to any of these possibilities—and so the poem is already teaching the reader the wisdom of the provisional "no."

At any rate, the advice of stanza one is a "new caution" to one predisposed to saying "yes," a new word of warning whose wisdom has occurred to the poet. The "she" of line four may refer to Everywoman, but the advice is pertinent to anyone—that is, to all of us—whose heart cries out to accede, to surrender by conceding and so avoid unpleasantness and secure comfort, that "softer lapping and smooth fur!" This last phrase is a wonderfully odd and unexpected evocation of pseudo-desiderata that, in conjunction with "set her to cede" (which recalls the cliché "gone to seed"), suggests that "yes" buys the reader something that leaves her less than human. And here one recalls John Updike's remark that "a person who has what he wants"—or thinks he has—"ceases to be a person," is "just an animal with clothes on," as Brooks's images of lapping and fur imply.[11] But perhaps at this point the poem now seems more feminist than racial, the combination of the feminine pronoun and the sensual, vaguely sexual imagery suggesting that women ought not sell out by acquiescing to marriage or a subordinate position in a relationship—although this is, obviously, as conjectural as those racial/political/autobiographical concerns hypothesized earlier. Whatever surrender is to be avoided, the exclamation point registers the poet's shock that such capitulation could even be considered for the tawdry prizes it would win one.

Stanzas three and four analyze and thereby judge the kind of person who could so easily acquiesce as well as the shortsightedness of such a maneuver:

> Whose esoteric need
> Was merely to avoid the nettle, to not-bleed.

> Stupid, like a street
> That beats into a dead end and dies there, with nothing left
>   to reprimand or meet.

Such an individual's need is "esoteric," not in the sense of being understandable only to a few (the poet has implicitly—through her avoidance of greater specificity—acknowledged the universality of the desire to avoid pain and to seek pleasure) but in the sense of being "difficult to understand," of being "not publicly disclosed."[12] To seek merely to "not-bleed," to sell one's birthright for a mess of ease, is finally difficult to fathom and rarely the reason offered publicly to explain one's ceding. For instance, to return (for illustrative purposes only) to the possibility of the poem offering us a feminist commentary upon marriage: a bride's "I do" does not normally confess to a desire "merely to avoid the nettle" but rather professes acceptance of a noble calling, honorable commitments.

However, as the reader moves into stanza four, "yes" becomes more than demeaning; it is also "stupid": a dead end where one dies. The "no" that typically may seem pure denial now becomes by contrast the means of opening one to possibility, of keeping one in motion and alive in a world where, yes, there still exists the chance of severe censure but also of further experiences to encounter, to undergo (for the experience "no" makes possible never loses here its sense of trial). And beyond the multiple apposite senses of "meet," one may also recall that "reprimand" derives from *reprimere*, "to repress": in death those fears "yes" repressed will indeed be at an end. In the context of the poem, "yes" becomes a denial of life, "no" implicitly its affirmation. Brooks is here advocating an invigorating sort of denial not unlike that "No! in thunder" Melville spoke of and which Leslie Fiedler has argued underlies all first-rate literature.[13] For now, the redefinition of "yes" and "no" these lines are effecting is perhaps best suggested by reference to Melville's famous letter to Hawthorne in which he observes that "All men who say *yes*, lie; and all men who say *no*,—why, they are in the happy condition of judicious, unincumbered travellers in Europe; they cross the frontiers into Eternity with nothing but a carpetbag—that is to say Ego. Whereas those *yes*-gentry, they travel with heaps of baggage, and damn them! they will never get through the Custom House."[14] But again, if the reader is unwilling to assent to these remarks, she is learning Brooks's lesson.

Stanzas five and six elaborate and complicate the yea-sayer's increasingly dismal situation through images and syntax themselves increasingly elaborate and complex.

> And like a candle fixed
> Against dismay and countershine of mixed
>
> Wild moon and sun. And like
> A flying furniture, or bird with lattice wing; or gaunt thing,
>
> a-stammer down nightmare neon peopled with
> condor, hawk, and shrike.

These lines are difficult to negotiate in part because the key to understanding Brooks's symbolic candle is buried—like the implications of "yes," whose consequences now seem a nightmare deferred—midway through a grammatical fragment (the poem's third so far, each hinting at the level of sentence structure at the incompleteness of the yes-man or yes-woman, at his or her inability to entertain a complete thought on what consent signifies). The key is "wild" and is underscored by the "flying furniture" of line twelve: in the face of present reality, "yes" is no more than a candle in the wild winds of dismay that will send one's (domestic) ease flying like tables and chairs in a tornado.

Stanza six's imagery is apocalyptic ("countershine of mixed // Wild moon and sun"), Bosch-like ("A flying furniture, or bird with lattice wing," this last a hopeless image of impossible flight), and violent with the predatory horror of nightmarish phantasm. At this point in the poem, the reader has been sucked deep into the maelstrom of the once-benign "yes." The language has reached fever pitch with its invocation of a neon-lit landscape "peopled" by condor, hawk, and shrike (also known, tellingly, as the butcherbird) across which "stammers" a "gaunt *thing*"—perhaps the yes-victim, perhaps her assassin.

So that the point will not be lost, the poet recapitulates bluntly in stanza seven. Earlier, such a direct, unambiguous assertion could have passed as so much lame rhetoric, but now it strides forth as stark summation:

> To say yes is to die
> A lot or a little. The dead wear capably their wry
>
> Enameled emblems. They smell.
> But that and that they do not altogether yell is all that we
>   know well.

The reader has heard before—in the final line of stanza two—the exasperated sarcasm that reappears with "a little." This modifier is neither a crumb thrown to one's desire for mitigation nor a means of toning down the poem's rhetorical frenzy. Rather, it implies that yes-people have but a small transition to make from nominal living to quiet, smelly death, a condition they wear "capably," their headstones no doubt bearing affirmative "enameled" (protective possibly, but probably merely decorative) "emblems."

The case against "yes" complete, the poem moves explicitly into its advocacy of "no":

> It is brave to be involved,
> To be not fearful to be unresolved.
>
> Her new wish was to smile
> When answers took no airships, walked a while.

Nay-saying, as observed before, is not to be perceived as resolution, as a negative means (otherwise similar to "yes") of closing the books. It is instead a way of bravely remaining "involved" while vitally "unresolved." "No" engenders life and keeps that life in conceivably uncomfortable but nonetheless healthy motion. Although the specific concerns being addressed remain undefined even at poem's end, its final lines suggest that those answers to which allegiance may one day be pledged will come, but they must be worked for and may be some time in arriving (they walk; they do not fly). This hope, this promise of resolution has, one notices, been present throughout the poem. In line two, for instance, the reader realizes that "so very far" was actually not a feeble attempt to intensify the initial "so far"; rather, "so far" was qualifying "so very far" in the sense of "at the moment." Thus the sense of line two is not primarily that "no" has "very very far to go" but that, although it does have a long way to go, every day, every line, will find "no" closer to its goal. And after all, the poem is written in rhyming couplets manifesting consonance (a correspondence of sound implying agreement, harmony, accord), although line lengths and rhythm vary wildly, postponing for varying lengths of time that consonance (a consonance most readily apparent in those most regular couplets devoted to the virtues of "no"). Here, then, at the level of sound, rhythm, and structure, the poem bodies forth its message that agreement will come (though necessarily delayed) but must not be sought prematurely or expected as a matter of (strict metrical) course.

The poem's final images are clear and positive, sparkling with hope, cheer, courage, and newness (just as they introduce a new tone into the poem). They also highlight what should be obvious by now: "no" is safer than "yes," just as walking is (whatever airlines may say) safer than flying (with the walking nay-sayer contrasted with the dead yea-sayer and dead-end streets where motion comes to an end, while the airships, associated with the yea-sayer's wish for trouble-free rapid transit, recall the flying furniture of the poem's horrific sixth stanza).

The complexity of "'Do Not Be Afraid of No'" is, then, aesthetically justified because the poem teaches at every level of itself the need to remain actively engaged (as one must be involved with it) yet wary of reaching closure (as one must be when confronted by a poem that refuses too quickly to relinquish its meaning). No image easily elicits the reader's consent, which must anyway await one's understanding of each part in relation to the whole, just as one must assess any extratextual consent in relation to its effect on one's life as a whole. Similarly, the poem's terribly precise vagueness is likewise justified insofar as it leaves the poem open to speak to anyone confronted by any situation where a preemptive assent seems the path of least resistance (a message as intensely relevant for blacks in 1949 as it ever was before or after this date). Just as does Brooks's famous sonnet "First fight. Then fiddle," "'Do Not Be Afraid of No'" places stylistic resistance at the center of her message concerning the need for resistance at the social/political level. And if "'Do Not Be Afraid of No'" is still worlds away from the directness of, say, "We Real Cool," Brooks might be seen in this early poem to be considering already that stylistic maneuver Park discovers in the much later "In the Mecca" (1968), wherein the critic finds Brooks "los[ing] faith in the kind of music she had loved and was so well qualified to sing" but which "blacks now found unusable."[15]

At the poem's end, as I have noted, whatever it was—social issue, personal concern, aesthetic challenge—that planted the seed of the poem in Brooks's mind ("set her to cede") remains as indefinite as it was when we began. We can ask, Does she wish to urge "no" upon blacks too willing to accept token adjustments of the status quo? Or does she desire to tell women not to surrender their dreams too easily? Or to tell readers not to dismiss her work too quickly? Does she wish to say "no" to a poetic style already proving itself unsatisfactory? All would be provocative messages—and Brooks allows us to entertain each of them—but I see no special textual support for any of them.

"'Do Not Be Afraid of No'" works hard at keeping the reader involved with it by making her feel she has not yet fully gotten into it, leaving open a multiplicity of interpretive possibilities by neither sanctioning nor precluding any of them. And if this assessment is accurate, the poem reveals as well the wisdom of Brooks's strategy as the vehicle for black (social/political) content, for she knows, as do we all, that America will, alas, always provide situations demanding rejection but tempting us to acquiesce either because we grow exhausted and resigned or because the carrot on the stick is lusciously attractive. And beyond the circumference of these concerns, and to return to Melville by way of Fiedler, Brooks knows the aesthetic correctness of the "no! in thunder," a denial not circumscribed completely by events of the moment any more than "'Do Not Be Afraid of No'" is delimited by its appearance originally as part of *Annie Allen*. As the engaged, topical poetry of the early Nikki Giovanni or of Don L. Lee (Haki Madhubuti) suggests, the easy "no"—to racism, poverty, whatever—can make finally for limited art.[16] Alternatively, "'Do Not Be Afraid of No'"— which might now be seen working metapoetically—offers instead a timeless "no," a "no" applicable in any circumstance that tempts anyone with the desire to acquiesce. Thus, Brooks offers a poem that is both timely and timeless, which is, after all, one definition of a classic.

Indeed, logically, no ready consent to the poem's message is possible even after lengthy explication, for to say "yes" to "'Do Not Be Afraid of No'" is to imply one has possibly misread it. On the other hand, to say "no" to the poem is, willy-nilly, to act upon the poem's advice, hence to concur with the wisdom of that advice, suggesting once again that the lesson has been lost upon one. In this logical conundrum the reader is left, nettled by interpretive possibilities no gloss can smooth but that serve to keep the game and so the poem alive. The poem's difficulties are, in this sense, both its content and its style, which is as it should be, for such are the ends, and the satisfactions, of Gwendolyn Brooks's craft.

Notes

1. *Black on White: A Critical Survey of Writing by American Negroes* (1966; rpt. New York: Viking-Compass, 1969), pp. 89, 90.

2. *Singers of Daybreak: Studies in Black American Literature* (Washington: Howard Univ. Press, 1974), p. 43.

3. "The Decline of Anglo-American Poetry," *Virginia Quarterly*, 54 (1978), 74.

4. Other issues are equally at stake, issues extending beyond poetry proper and suggested by remarks such as Littlejohn's contention that Brooks is "far more a poet than a Negro," p. 89, and Dan Jaffe's observation that "the label 'black poetry' cheapens the achievement of Gwendolyn Brooks" ("Gwendolyn Brooks: An Appreciation from the White Suburbs," in *The Black American Writer*, ed. C. W. E. Bigsby [DeLand: Everett/Edwards, 1969], II, 92). On Brooks's poetics and her desire to produce work espousing a black aesthetic, see Norris B. Clark, "Gwendolyn Brooks and a Black Aesthetic," in *A Life Distilled: Gwendolyn Brooks, Her Poetry and Fiction*, ed. Maria K. Mootry and Gary Smith (Urbana: Univ. of Illinois Press, 1987), pp. 81–99; and Clara Claiborne Park, "First Fight, Then Fiddle," *The Nation*, 26 September 1987, pp. 308–12. For Brooks's comments on this matter, see Martha H. Brown and Marilyn Zorn, "GLR Interview: Gwendolyn Brooks," *Great Lakes Review*, 6, No. 1 (1979), 48–55.

5. *Annie Allen* (New York: Harper, 1949), pp. 12–13.

6. Charles Israel, "Gwendolyn Brooks," in *American Poets Since World War II, Part 1. A–K (Dictionary of Literary Biography, Vol. 5)*, ed. Donald J. Greiner (Detroit: Gale, 1980), p. 101; D. H. Melhem, *Gwendolyn Brooks: Poetry and the Heroic Voice* (Lexington: Univ. Press of Kentucky, 1987), p. 60; and Harry B. Shaw, *Gwendolyn Brooks* (Boston: Twayne, 1980), pp. 71–72, 108–09.

7. As a "note" on Annie's childhood and girlhood, "'Do Not Be Afraid of No'" is not alone in bearing a puzzling relation to the sequence and to the book as a whole; cf. "'Pygmies Are Pygmies Still, Though Percht on Alps,'" *Annie Allen*, p. 14.

8. "Gwendolyn Brooks' Poetic Realism: A Developmental Survey," in *Black Women Writers (1950–1980): A Critical Evaluation*, ed. Mari Evans (New York: Doubleday, 1984), p. 92. Kent's observation is echoed elsewhere: see Blyden Jackson and Louis D. Rubin, Jr., *Black Poetry in America* (Baton Rouge: Louisiana State Univ. Press, 1974), pp. 81–85; Jackson and Rubin argue, with particular reference to *Annie Allen*, that Brooks's method is constantly to subordinate matters of sex or race to universal insights.

9. "Gwendolyn Brooks's *A Street in Bronzeville*, the Harlem Renaissance and the Mythologies of Black Women," *MELUS*, 10, No. 3 (1983), p. 45.

10. Park, "Fight First, Then Fiddle," p. 308.

11. "One Big Interview," in *Picked-Up Pieces* (Greenwich, Conn.: Fawcett, 1975), p. 485.

12. *American Heritage Dictionary*, New College Ed., 1979.

13. On the reasons why both "yes" and the easy "no" make for poor art, see Leslie Fiedler, "No! In Thunder," in *No! In Thunder* (Boston: Beacon, 1960), pp. 1–18.

14. Letter to Nathaniel Hawthorne, 16 (?) April 1851, in *The Portable Melville*, ed. Jay Leyda (New York: Viking, 1952), p. 428.

15. "Fight First, Then Fiddle," pp. 311, 310.

16. This assessment is admittedly a matter of personal taste. Brooks herself is clearly—and particularly after 1967—not averse to writing just such poetry, as *In the Mecca* and critical favorites such as "We Real Cool" indicate. Again, I would direct the interested reader to Park, Clark, and Brown and Zorn.

W. D. E. ANDREWS

"All Is Permitted": The Poetry of LeRoi Jones/Amiri Baraka

No one man can personalize the course of history, but in periods of intense radical awareness and social confrontation some individuals may appear to embody the complex forces of historical becoming. LeRoi Jones was such a child of his times. From his middle-class Newark origins to a life-style of Greenwich Village hipsterism, through ethnic discovery and self-renewal to a self-styled black revolutionary priesthood, his career has followed a logic related both to internal psychological imperatives and to external changes in American society.

Following his military discharge in 1957, Jones moved to New York to begin his literary career among the Greenwich Village Beats. Originating in San Francisco, the Beat Movement was riding high on waves of publicity in the fifties. It represented an expression of defiance flung in the face of middle-class American conformism and materialism; it was a reaction against apathy, against the compromises of respectability, against the shibboleths of the social mainstream. The Beats proposed a cult of amorality, hedonism, and general irresponsibility; in their quest for expanded consciousness and psychedelic experience they had recourse to pot, jazz, Zen, and other exotic mysteries. Norman Mailer's term *the white Negro*[1] was a reference to the hipster's mystique of the outsider. For the first time in American literary and social history, the black man's traditionally alienated position in American

From *Southwest Review* 67, no. 2 (1982 Spring). © 1982 by Southern Methodist University Press.

society conferred upon him a privileged status in bohemian circles. No black writer before Jones had achieved the American Dream of racial assimilation so effortlessly. Jones joined Kerouac, Ginsberg, Ray Bremser, Frank O'Hara, Joel Oppenheimer, Gilbert Sorrentino, and other angry young men in nightclubs and coffeehouses like Le Metro to declaim his poetry to the beat of jazz accompaniment.

Though nearly all the so-called Beat Poets were well educated and, for all their self-advertised primitivism and "naturalness," capable of a complex, allusive, "learned" poetry from time to time, one of their central claims was to represent an alternative expression to the formalism and conservatism of the academy. Theirs tended to be an exacerbated poetry of revolt and revenge against the craziness of a self-contradictory, self-destructive "square" world. Their stance contained no reformist intent: it was informed by disillusionment, by consuming hates and fears that permitted no hope for a better order of things. They devoted themselves, not to the orthodox poetic practice of attempting to create order out of disorder, but to reflecting the disorder itself. Confusion and exasperation are registered in a typically rhapsodic, frantic style, the distortions of a nightmare world reflected in a welter of crowded fragments. But while the Beat Movement had, undoubtedly, more sociological than literary interest, it did provide an important impetus to the emergence of numerous little magazines and presses which offered new writers who found themselves at odds with the academic establishment a vehicle for publication.

It was not long till Jones himself had earned a reputation as an editor as well as a poet of the Beat Generation. The first issue of his new magazine bearing the Dadaist title *Yugen* appeared in Spring 1958 and struggled through eight issues until 1962. The overt intention to resurrect the quality and tenor of Robert Creeley's *Black Mountain Review* was unmistakable in Jones's concentration on the work of writers associated with the earlier magazine: Ginsberg, Corso, Snyder, Orlovsky, Loewinsohn, Kerouac, McClure, Wieners, Marshall, Oppenheimer, and, of course, Olson and Creeley. While still involved with *Yugen*, Jones began to diversify his editorial activities. In 1958 he founded Totem Press and in 1961, along with Diane di Prima, he started *The Floating Bear*, one of the first mimeographed newsletters designed to provide a cheap and rapid outlet for poems, short stories, and notes. Also during the early 1960s he was taking an increasing interest in *Kulchur* (the title of the magazine probably deriving from Olson's preferred spelling of the word). Many *Yugen* contributors also used *Kulchur* as an outlet.

Up to 1960, Jones's poetry had appeared in little magazines such as the *Naked Ear*, *Combustion*, *Penny Poems*, *White Dove Review*, *Evergreen Review*,

Provincetown Review, Beat East Coast, Nomad, Signal, Niagara Frontier Review, The Seasons, and *Set,* as well as in established periodicals like *Poetry,* the *Nation, Massachusetts Review, Yale Literary Review,* and the *Village Voice.* Curiously, little of his own best work appears in *Yugen.* The inclusion of seven of his poems in Donald Allen's *Anthology of New American Poetry 1945–1960* meant that now Jones was given a much wider circulation than ever before and could enjoy the prestige of being placed beside such well-known names as Duncan, Creeley, Olson, Levertov, Ginsberg, Corso, and Ferlinghetti. Allen had divided his anthology of "poets of the avant-garde" into five distinct groups: the Black Mountain group, the San Francisco Renaissance, the Beat Generation, the New York poets, and a catchall group which "has no geographical definition" and "includes younger poets who have been associated with and in some cases influenced by the leading writers of the preceding groups, but who have evolved their own original styles and new conceptions of poetry." Jones is slotted into this last category.

Then, in 1960, Totem collaborated with Corinth Books to bring out a total of ten books of poetry, among which was Jones's first collection, *Preface to a Twenty Thousand Volume Suicide Note,* published in 1961. Three years later, in August, 1964, Grove Press produced his second volume of poetry, *The Dead Lecturer,* most of the poems in which had appeared in periodicals in 1962 and 1963. This early poetry may be used to place Jones with those artists who constituted a special caste at the margin of society, an avant-garde marked by aggressive defensiveness, extreme self-consciousness, prophetic inclination, the stigmata of alienation, and intransigent individualism.

Jones's "Statement on Poetics" in Allen's anthology is a useful introduction to his early poetry. Here he lists those writers who, he feels, have most strongly shaped his attitudes and techniques: "For me, Lorca, Williams, Pound and Charles Olson have had the greatest influence. Eliot, earlier.... And there are so many young wizards around now doing great things that everybody calling himself poet can learn from ... Whalen, Snyder, McClure, O'Hara, Loewinsohn, Wieners, Creeley, Ginsberg." A cursory view of Jones's poems is enough to confirm these (white) influences.

Following Williams, all really ambitious young American experimenters were seeking to evolve a thoroughly emancipated American verse. In his Statement, Jones reacts strongly against the orthodoxy that had prevailed in American poetry since the twenties, and which may be said to reveal itself in an academic orientation, a predilection for a poetry of symmetry, intellect, irony, and wit, a tendency toward traditional metrics and the metaphysical and symbolist poetics of Eliot and the New Critics. Jones denounces these rigidities: "Accentual verse, the regular metric of rumbling iambics, is dry as slivers of sand. Nothing happens in that frame anymore.

We can get nothing from England. And the diluted formalism of the academy (the formal culture of the U.S.) is anaemic and fraught with incompetence and unreality." One is reminded of Williams's vigorous attack (in his Prologue to *Kora in Hell*) on the international school of modernism as led by Eliot and Pound, for its "parodies of the middle ages, Dante and Langue D'Oc ... as the best in U.S. poetry." Like Williams before him, Jones rejects Eliot's sense of the continuity of English and American poetry, the assumption that the American poet functions as a part of the English tradition. Williams's comment (in *The Autobiography*) that "it is in the newness of a live speech that the line exists undiscovered" is echoed in Jones's elevation of experience above civilization and his emphasis on the resources of the indigenous language. Jones shares the preoccupation which, more than anything else, characterizes the modernist—the preoccupation with the need for continual renovation of the language; and the question is not just a technical one, but a moral one also. Jones calls for a reappraisal of the art of poetry as practiced in America because he feels it has become "literary" in the sense of "unreal," no longer responsive to present actuality. What he advocates is a readjustment of social and poetic strategies to the pressures of the poet's own most authentic experience.

The Jonesian aesthetic is ultimately synthetic, one in which nothing is beyond consideration. In *New American Poetry* he is quoted as saying: "MY POETRY is whatever I think I am.... I CAN BE ANYTHING I CAN. I make a poetry with what I feel is useful & can be saved out of all the garbage of our lives." Refurbishing Williams's dictum, "no ideas but in things," Jones pursues his plea for untrammeled imagination and expression: "What I see, am touched by (CAN HEAR) ... wives, gardens, jobs, cement yards where cats pee, all my interminable artifacts.... ALL are a poetry, & nothing moves (with any grace) pried apart from these things. There cannot be closet poetry." He wishes to oppose the abstracting pressures of the contemporary wasteland with the full weight of whatever in his own life seems concretely worth saving, and the peculiar strenuousness of Jones's poetry lies in his continually despairing recognition of the inevitable failure of his effort to transmute into valid wisdom the fragments of experience which he both hoards and flees. In *Preface to a Twenty Volume Suicide Note* he writes:

> Asked to be special, & alive in the mornings, if they are green /
> & I am still alive, (& green) hovering above all the things I /
> seem to want to be apart of (curious smells, the high-noon idea / of life
> ... a crowded train station where they broadcast a slice, / just one
> green slice, of some glamourous person's life). / & I cant even
> isolate my pleasures. All the things I can talk about / mean nothing
> to me.

Of particular interest is Jones's declared refusal to write self-consciously as a Negro. When asked in a 1960 interview if there was in his work "the sense of 'being a Negro' that occurs, say, in the poetry of Langston Hughes," Jones replied:

> That's not the way I write poetry. I'm fully conscious all the time that I am an American Negro, because it's part of my life. But I know also if I want to say, "I see a bus full of people," I don't have to say, "I am a Negro seeing a bus full of people." I would deal with it when it has to do directly with the poem, and not as a kind of broad generalisation that doesn't have much to do with a lot of young writers today who are Negroes.... It's always been a separate section of writing that wasn't quite up to the level of the other writing ... but it's a new generation now, and people are beset by other kinds of ideas that don't have much to do with sociology *per se*."[2]

Thus it is the intense subjectivity of Jones's early poetry which impresses itself upon us. He concentrates, not on the problems of social life, not on ideas, but on a narrow world of personal experience and feeling ("the quiet delicacy of my sadness") in which there is no forward and no backward, but only a timeless, directionless "existence." He belongs to that generation of poets which has lost all power to understand itself, which has no standards, no security, no simple acquiescence, to whom the decorums of the past no longer count for very much in determining present reality. He strives to turn poetry, through a release of imaginative energy, into an intuitive act of discovery. It is here that one can perceive Jones's affinity with another well-publicized school of American poets: those advocates of the "new imagination" and the "new surrealism" who wrote for Robert Bly's "Sixties Press"—James Dickey, Louis Simpson, James Wright. Jones's poetry evinces a similar concern with dramatizing the "deep image" which proceeds from the unconscious. There is only human consciousness striving to rebuild new worlds out of its own creativity—not to reflect the visible, but to make visible—to create the very grounds of being, through a revolution of sensibility and style.

Jones's poetry all too often demonstrates the obvious dangers in such an enterprise: the devotion to an inner world of perception and feeling tends to generate a cult of arbitrariness. Much of the early poetry is therefore impenetrably self-indulgent; transitions are often too fractionally or too arbitrarily achieved, and Jones is overready to expose himself to accidents— though these are sometimes exciting—of free association. The humane anarchism often seems to stop only a little short of total breakdown, as if anything less were narrowly self-defensive, the derangement of motive and power an attempt to reflect within the poem what is being suffered. The released subconscious, when it severs completely the Image from all referential burdens, is doomed to generality, eccentricity, or triviality. Composed of fluid, heightened sensations, Jones's poems never yield themselves readily to conceptual analysis. But in the best of them the correspondences that are revealed may seem extravagant, yet operate dynamically from a center of deep emotional involvement and are, therefore, finally verifiable and coherent. Because Jones relies so heavily on tone for his effects, it is impossible to do justice to his poetry by quoting fragments. I give, therefore, "The Turncoat" in full, as an example of the kind of exquisiteness he only rarely achieves:

> The steel fibrous slant & ribboned glint
> of water. The Sea. Even my secret speech is moist
> with it. When I am alone & brooding, locked in
> with dull memories & self hate, & the terrible disorder
> of a young man.
>
> I move slowly. My cape spread stiff & pressing cautiously
> in the first night wind off the Hudson. I glide down
> onto my own roof, peering in at the pitiful shadow of myself.
> How can it mean anything? The stop & spout, the
> wind's dumb shift. Creak of the house & wet smells
> coming in. Night forms on my left. The blind still
> up to admit a sun that no longer exists. Sea move.
>
> I dream long bays & towers ... & soft steps,on moist sand.
> I become them, sometimes. Pure flight. Pure fantasy. Lean.

The verse in its rhythms and diction recognizes the actual world, but holds against it a longing for perfection. Jones voices an impulse to turn away, to forget, to seek an essence, a streamlined definition in his own special kind of dream. The poem is, quite frankly, a piece of enchantment; the rhythm is a potent spell. Jones is exploiting the fairy-tale stratum of experience, playing upon reminiscences of Nosferatu and Superman. But though it is a poem of withdrawal that recaptures the child's mentality, it is spare, hard and sinewy, and in tone firmly sardonic, expressing the bitterness and disillusion of one who has struggled and been defeated. It is idiomatic and has the run of free speech, but bare. The critical self-awareness saves it from sentimental evasion, from being anemic, romantic reverie; Jones achieves a difficult and delicate sincerity, a subtle poise. There is a deliberate muting of the poetic voice, a diminished ambition, an unwillingness to risk a language that would engage our imaginative energies or dare approach a level of emotion absent from the poet's own experience. Instead, the distinctive tonalities of Jones's verse register impulses on the verge of remaining unconscious. The longer, more expansive poems (say, "Look for you Yesterday, Here you Come Today," "Hymn for Lanie Poo," "The Clearing," "The Death of Nick Charles," "Betancourt," "From an Almanac," and "Roi's New Blues") exploit more elaborately (though not necessarily more successfully) a structure reflective of the mind in unfixed contemplation. These poems are composed of a questioning, querulous rendering of conversation and commonplace observation; of juxtaposed scenes and images, remembered words and gestures, contrasting rhythms and states of mind, perceptions crowded, immediately and directly, one upon the other. It is a subject matter drawn from the common, everyday heritage of the urban adventurer, among the elements of which conspicuously figure jazz, the comic strips, radio, and the movies. The intention is to be shockingly "primitive." In "In Memory of Radio," for example, Jones writes:

> Who has ever stopped to think of the divinity of Lamont Cranston?
> (Only Jack Kerouac, that I know of: & me.
> The rest of you probably had on WCBS and Kate Smith,
> Or something equally unattractive.)
> . . . .
> Saturday mornings we listened to *Red Lantern* & his undersea folk.
> At 11, *Let's Pretend* / & we did / & I, the poet, still do, Thank God!

Rhythm is the great enacting agency in Jones's poetry—not the pattern rhythm of the lines, but the invoked rhythm of his personal sensibility unviolated by ideas, beating mutually in the thought and feeling and syllable of the whole poem. It is this pervasive, fermenting, synergical influence that can re-create, can lift and deliver into actuality, the diverse experiences of life lived. The model of the Beats was often alleged to be jazz (Ginsberg, quoted in Jones's *Blues People*, described Kerouac's writing as "bop prosody"): in seeking to capture a "black feeling," to capture the rhythms and phrasings of black music, the Beats were doing what Langston Hughes had done a generation earlier; they were, in fact, approaching through empathy with the black experience some of the very same considerations that writers like Hughes, and now Jones, could approach from the inside.

Jones's experiment involved a radical departure from the demands of an agreed metrical voice. He relates his "measure" to the dictates of his pulse and breath-rate, in the effort to make the metrical movement a direct expression of perception, of the movement of consciousness, rather than, as in other approaches, the mold into which experience is cast. In seeking to capture the vitality and rhythm of the living, spoken language, Jones's poems demand to be read aloud. The eccentric typography is an attempt at a notation which will render the precise modulations of tempo and inflection, the nuances of mind and voice. As meaning inheres in experience and not paraphrase, it cannot be relayed in a less bodily, a more explanatory language.

Jones's idiom not only astounds traditional metrical preconceptions, it also disturbs the agreed shape of English syntax in a way which implies tentativeness or bewilderment in the approach to experience, as if restlessness is the sign of sentience. The syntax becomes elliptical, volatile; complicated pyramids of periods are dismantled into the single elements of independent clauses; commas are lost and brackets left unclosed. He continues the revolt against the structures and tactics of earlier poetry in order to articulate daringly new areas of being. The expectation of formal unity, order, and coherence implies an intellectual and emotional, indeed a philosophic, composure. It assumes that the artist stands above his material, able to control it. But Jones presents dilemmas. He offers his struggle with them as the substance of his testimony; and whatever unity his poems possess comes from the emotional rhythm, the thrust toward completion of that struggle. Sincerity becomes a virtue in itself, regardless of whether it can lead to truth or whether truth can be found. In overthrowing traditional proprieties and self-containment of culture, he seeks to evolve a form of absolute personal speech, a poetry deprived of ceremony and stripped to personal revelation.

In his Statement on Poetics he fights for this new expression against an accepted poetic that was rational, orderly, conventionalized, cerebral, and, through the influence of the New Critics, somewhat codified:

> I *must* be completely free to do just what I want ... "All is permitted." ... There cannot be anything I must *fit* the poem into. Everything must be made to fit into the poem. There must not be any preconceived notion or *design* for what the poem *ought* to be. "Who knows what a poem ought to sound like? Until it's thar." Says Charles Olson ... & I follow closely with that. I'm not interested in writing sonnets, sestinas or anything ... only poems. If the poem his got to be a sonnet (unlikely tho) or whatever, it'll certainly let me know. The only "recognizable tradition" a poet

needs to follow is himself ... & with that, say, all those things out
of tradition he can use, adapt, work over, into something for
himself. To broaden his *own* voice with.

All this is, as Jones says, a reassertion of Olson's advocacy of an "open" poetic
form determined by the dynamics of the subject matter. The title of Jones's
Statement—"How You Sound?"—is a quotation from the older poet, whose
revolutionary theory of organic form (contained in the famous essay on
"projective verse" or "composition by field" first published in 1950) was
reprinted by Jones's Totem Press in 1959.

There is always the tendency for Jones's poems—in their broken
polyrhythmic music, the accumulation of inconclusive evidence, the series of
images jerkily strung together in a short-winded discontinuity that
sometimes borders on telegraphese—to slip into blurred and wispy dream-
spinning. The kind of open form in which he specialized is capable of a
pleasing range of effects, but the preoccupation with technique can lead him
to break his line rather unnaturally against the syntax and cadences of
ordinary speech. At times his metric strikes one as staccato whimsy more
than anything else (see the "From an Almanac" poems quoted below): one
feels that his brittle, elusive lines of free verse have yielded too easily, and the
sense of a firm medium—half-forbidding, half-pliant—is lost.

The best poems are those where he has managed to unite the extremes
of incantation and meaning, the language of unconscious thought and the
received language of poetry. The voice is a specific recognizable voice; at the
same time it sheds personality and becomes simply the voice of a man
speaking; it is divested of all that is confessional and autobiographical to
speak, not of particular pain, but of general subjective life; it becomes numb,
neutral, universal, a transparency through which we penetrate directly to the
state of being or feeling. Jones does not aim to impress with his eloquence:
his poetry is not an art of words, but an art of which the words are the
diaphanous medium.

In his early poetry Jones may well appear to be concerning himself with
a legend about his own demise—even the titles of his two books would seem
to indicate as much. But there is a growing awareness of the need for an
opposed and urgent kind of poetry, one which could free him from
confinement in his own temperament, one in which his rebellious vigor could
appropriate society and politics. What we find, then, is a developing social
consciousness, an increasing racial involvement, a crystallizing concept of
blackness. "Let my poems be a graph / of me," he says in *The Dead Lecturer*.

The early Statement makes it clear that at the beginning of his career
he was more eager to align himself with the New American Writing than

with Black American Writing. Only one of his dedications in *Preface* is to a black person—his daughter, Kellie. The others are to Ginsberg, Snyder, Wieners, McClure, Olson, and Rubi Betancourt (a woman he met during his 1960 visit to Cuba). The book is dedicated to his (white) wife, Hettie. In these early poems, the Jonesian mythos does not develop along insistently political or racial lines; instead, the contemporary *angst* is more generally registered as being of metaphysical rather than moral origin. And yet, one can see how the sense of displacement and dispossession in these poems has an obviously special relevance to the American black man.

One of the first of Jones's poems to appear in print was a tribute to Lorca, entitled "Lines to Garcia Lorca," which was published in the first issue of *Yugen*. It is a useful starting point in tracing Jones's development.

> Climin up the mountain, Chilrun
> Didn't come here for to stay.
> If I'm ever gonna see you agin,
> It'll be on the judgment day.
> —Negro Spiritual

Send soldiers again to kill you, Garcia.
Send them to quell my escape. These things mean nothing.
You are dying, again, Garcia. This is all I remember.
Send soldiers again, Garcia. Hail Mary,
Holy mother.
Pray for me.

I live near a mountain, green mirror
Of burning paths and a low sun to measure my growing by.
There is a wind that repeats a bird's name and near his
Cage is a poem, and a small boy herding
Cattle with diamonds
In their mouths.

Mandolins grow on the highslopes
And orange robed monks collect songs
Just beyond the last line of fruit trees.
Naked girls pretend they are butterflies,
And a deer tells stories to the twilight.

Garcia, where is my bible?
I want to read those myths again.

No answer.
But way off, quite close to the daylight,
I hear his voice, and he is laughing, laughing
Like a Spanish guitar.

"At the time I got hold of Lorca," Jones has said, "I was very much influenced by Eliot, and reading Lorca helped to bring me out of my 'Eliot period' and break that shell—not so much *Poet in New York*, which is the more surreal verse, but the early *Gipsy Ballads*—that kind of feeling and exoticism."[3] Jones responded readily to the legend of Lorca as a spontaneous, childlike poet, whose art sprang like magic from institutions which defy analysis; an inspired primitive, singing of the exotic myths and mores of his un-European Andalusian tribe. Jones's early poems display a similar preoccupation with themes of frustration, loss, and death; there is a similar lightheartedness playing over the somber depths of some of them. Like Lorca he has no qualms about puzzling the reader with mysterious images and symbols bearing highly personal connotations. As Lorca claimed the gypsies would understand his poems, so Jones may also be seen to abandon the useful fiction of the common reader and demand the devotions of a cult.

Jones's poem also demonstrates a feeling for the political legend of Lorca, as a poet cut down in his prime by fascist barbarism. At the beginning of his poem, Jones explicitly identifies with the fate of the gentle Spanish poet who embodied the humanistic, democratic spirit and, by opening with an epigraph from a Negro spiritual and closing on notes from a Spanish guitar, links the suffering of his own people to that of the victims of Spanish oppression. Yet the dynamic of Jones's poem is not sociological: rather, Jones impresses by the sheer elegiac power of his lyricism. The influence of Lorca's Spanish romanticism is deeply embedded in Jones's tribute—in the synthesis of violence and beauty, the incantatory language, the sensuous colorful imagery, and the religious exoticism.

Eliot's influence is also clearly in evidence, in the way feeling is not expressed but, in typical modernist fashion, scientifically evoked by the objective correlative. The interior confusion of the persona to whom "These things mean nothing" recalls Prufrock's dilemma, while the addendum to the first stanza echoes the litany in *Ash Wednesday*. That Eliot should remain one of the most important and pervasive influences on the early work of a young experimentalist is, of course, not remarkable: Eliot deeply affected the whole course of modern poetry by introducing new ways of expressing spiritual predicaments, new possibilities of feeling and subject matter, and by initiating a revolution in the language of poetry.

In Jones's series of jazz-poems, "From an Almanac," the rhythms, images, and theme of Eliot's poems of the *Waste Land* period are strongly evoked:

> Respect the season
> and dance to the rattle
> of its bones.
>   The flesh
> hung
> from trees. Blown
> down. A cold
> music. A colder
> hand, will grip
> you. Your bare
> soul. (Where is the soul's place. What is
> its
> nature?) Winter rattles
> like the throat
> of the hanged man.
> . . . .
> This bizness, of dancing, how
> can it suit us? Old men, naked
> sterile women.
>   (Our time,
> a cruel one. Our souls warmth
> left out. Little match children
> dance
> against the weather.
>   )The soul's
> warmth
> is how
> shall I say
> it,
>   Its own. A place
> of warmth, for children
> wd dance there,
>   if they cd. If they
> left their brittle selves behind (our time's
> a cruel one.
>   Children
> of winter. (I cross myself

like religion
>   Children
of a cruel time. (the wind
stirs the bones
& they drag clumsily
thru the cold.)
>   These children
are older
than their worlds. and
cannot dance.

Like Eliot, Jones offers a double picture—a cross section of a tortured mind
and the image of an arid world. Jones's attempt to communicate states of
feeling entails a similar avoidance of plain statement and finality of definition
in favor of intimations that approximate the "indefiniteness" of music. There
is a similar rapid flow of apparently unrelated sensations and images and
discordant metaphors in the effort to render an emotional response; a similar
flat, exhausted rhythmic movement which, as Williams said of Eliot's, evinces
a concern "with the line as it is modulated by a kind of half-alive speech."

While none of Jones's effects is as elaborately subtle as Eliot's, his
poems go considerably farther in reflecting nervous disintegration. Eliot's
vision in *The Waste Land* may be a despairing one, but the *Four Quartets*
demonstrate that his ultimate faith survives. In Jones's Almanac poems,
however, there is no resolution. The winds are cutting, the people are
infertile, words are at the mercy of the "clown gods," the hanged man is
"Swung/against our windows," the children are aged. "From wrong to wrong
the exasperated spirit / Proceeds, unless restored by that refining fire /
Where you must move in measure, like a dancer," writes Eliot in "Little
Gidding." But Jones's season is endless winter, the only warmth is the soul,
isolated and uninspirited. Where Eliot affirms "A dignified and commodious
sacrament" ("East Coker," 1), concretized in the image of dancing, Jones's
children "cannot dance."

Time and again, Jones returns to the theme of disorder: in "Vice" he
refers to the "Mosaic of disorder I owe but cannot recognize"; the disorder
of the seasons in the Almanac poems is taken up in "the intricate disorder of
the seasons" in "Way Out West"; in the jazz-poem for Billy Holiday,
"Bridge," "the chords / of your disorder meddle with your would be
disguises"; in "The Turncoat," he speaks of the "dull memories & self hate,
& the terrible disorder / of a young man"; and in "Roi's New Blues," the
forces of redemption that would rescue him from a winter that "locked us
in," are epitomized in an image which combines the horsemen of the

apocalypse and a band of western samurai: "Coldness will be / stamped out, when those gray horsemen / with sunny faces / ride thru our town. O, God / we've waited for them. Stood / for, years with our eyes full / of a violent wind."

The comic strip heroes of Jones's youth exert a powerful fascination since they are types of the existential hero who is both man of action and man of understanding, capable of restoring order through the power of his own extraordinary personality. Hence, such figures from the sharp-edged world of pop culture as Lamont Cranston, Green Lantern, the Shadow, and the Lone Ranger, join Eliot's hanged man as potential embodiments of an order Jones struggles to affirm: "Heh, heh, heh, / Who knows what evil lurks in the hearts of men? The Shadow knows. / O, yes he does / O, yes he does. / An evil word it is, / This love." The suspicion of doubt carried in the insistent repetition here becomes explicit in the line from "Look for You Yesterday, Here You Come Today": "THERE *MUST* BE A LONE RANGER!!!" This poem ends on an image of loss and disintegration, an uneasy sense of racial complication:

> My silver bullets all gone
> My black mask trampled in the dust
>
> & Tonto way off in the hills
> moaning like Bessie Smith.

In "The New Sheriff" he intimates that if there is no Lone Ranger, he may have to assume that social role himself. But though the call to action is insistent, Jones is not ready to commit himself: there is something in him "so cruel, so / silent," that "It hesitates / to sit on the grass / with the young white virgins." One of the last poems in *The Dead Lecturer*, "Green Lantern's Solo," elaborates the internal tensions, the self-questioning which makes individual action in the real world impossible: "What man unremoved from his meat's source, can continue / To believe totally in himself?" Only the ignorant, like "our leaders," or the "completely devious / who are our lovers. No man except a charlatan / could be called 'Teacher'." The individual continually seeks a supernatural sanction for his actions: "Who cannot but yearn / for the One Mind, or Right, or call it some God." The same desire is expressed in "A Poem for Willie Best," where Jones says he is treating of "no God / but what is given. Give me / Something more / than what is here." But in "A Poem for Democrats," it is clear that Eliot's God is dead: the hanged man merges with Phlebas the Phoenician merchant to share a death by drowning at the hands of a contemporary Roman soldier—the Mafia: "Drowned love / hanged man, swung, cement on his feet."

The Dead Lecturer reflects a growing belief in the necessity for action and an increasing preoccupation with the political scene. "The Politics of rich painters," "A Poem for Democrats," "SHORT SPEECH TO MY FRIENDS," and "Political Poem" are among the best poems in this vein. The Statue of Liberty is figured as "the french whore / who wades slowly in the narrows, waving her burnt out / torch"; the "pity of democracy" is that "we must sit here / and listen to how he made his money." The much-valued affluence of America and the complacency that goes with it fill the poet with disgust: "Luxury, then, is a way of / being ignorant, comfortably / An approach to the open market of least information." Five poems (written in obvious imitation of Yeats's "Crazy Jane" series) are centered around "Crow Jane," a heroine of blues ballads who is the archetypal temptress. Like Lula in *Dutchman*, "Crow Jane" is a symbol of America, seducing "Young gigolo's / of the 3rd estate" into believing that she has great wealth to offer them. The poet, once entranced by her himself, now warns others of her siren-call: "Crow Jane In High Society" looks for "Openings / where she can lay all / this greasy talk / on somebody. Me, once. Now / I am her teller."

Yet the moral impulses that lead the poet to believe in action also render him unfit for action. There is the continual awareness that he can act with full power only if he commands, for his followers and himself, an implicit belief in the meaningfulness of the human scene, in the integrity of his own motives. But in *The Dead Lecturer*, the poet's personality is never a coherent, definable, well-structured entity; it is a psychic battlefield, an insoluble puzzle, the occasion for a flow of atomized perceptions and sensations. It is in the more private lyrics of lost love in *The Dead Lecturer* that this dislocation is most directly articulated. Jones is to be seen struggling to affirm an identity which would enable him to transcend the world and achieve love. Here he addresses a departing lover:

> I am what I think I am. You are what
> I think you are. The world is the
> one thing, that will not move. It is
> made of stone, round, and very ugly.

He longs for wholeness and love, the possibility of connecting with even the anonymous reader:

> And let me once, create myself.
> And let you, whoever
> sits now breathing on my words
> create a self of your own. One
> that will love me.

But the self seems unresolvably problematic:

> When they say, "It is Roi
> Who is dead?" I wonder
> Who will they mean?

The black man's historically ambivalent position in American society compounds the crisis of identity. The classic articulation of this cultural schizophrenia is W. E. B. Du Bois's, made over fifty years earlier in *The Souls of Black Folk*:

> The Negro is a sort of seventh son, born with a veil, and gifted with second-sight in this American world—a world which yields him no true self-consciousness, but only lets him see himself through the revelation of the other world. It is a peculiar sensation, this double-consciousness, this sense of always looking at one's self through the eyes of others, of measuring one's soul by the tape of a world that looks on in amused contempt and pity. One ever feels his two-ness—an American, a Negro; two souls, two thoughts, two unreconciled strivings; two warring ideals in one dark body, whose dogged strength alone keeps it from being torn asunder.

Jones's increasing awareness of the social and racial matrix of selfhood leads him to a point where he rejects the world of the white liberal intelligentsia, to make of the "poor" and the "black' the absolute theme and necessity of his art:

> /The perversity
> of separation, isolation
> after so many years trying to enter their kingdoms,
> now they suffer in tears, these others, saxophones whining
> through the wooden doors of their less thin gracious homes.
> The poor have become our creators. The black. The thoroughly
> ignorant.
> Let the combination of morality
> and inhumanity
> begin.

This proclamation signals Jones's wish to enter the arena of history: as artist, he will assume social responsibility, a commitment to his people. Calling for

"A political art," he writes, "I am deaf and blind and lost and will not sing again your quiet / verse. I have lost / even the art of poetry." Torn between two cultures, he is willing to experiment with blackness, yet "frightened / that the flame of my sickness / will burn off my face. And leave / the bones, my stewed black skull, an empty cage of failure."

Still, most of the poems in *The Dead Lecturer* which deal with specifically racial themes may be described as "quiet verse." In the tribute to Willie Best, a black actor whose Hollywood name was Sleep 'n' eat, Jones echoes Dunbar in treating the tragedy of the black man who must always be "a renegade / behind the mask." He remembers his own ancestors with more sadness than bitterness or anger:

> That force is lost
> which shaped me, spent
> in its image, battered, an old brown thing
> swept off the streets,
> where it sucked its
> gentle living.

The history of slavery is evoked in hushed, lyrical tones:

> The story is a long one. Why
> I am here like this. Why you
> should listen, now, so late, and
> weary at the night. Its
> heavy rain
> pushing
> the grass flat.

There are, however, two poems on *The Dead Lecturer* which stand out from all the rest as a premonition of things to come from Jones—the two "Black Dada Nihilismus" poems. They demonstrate the new combination of "morality and inhumanity." He begins by rejecting utterly the Christian God: "God, if they bring him / bleeding, I would not / forgive, or even call him / black dada nihilismus." Likewise the civilization of the Christian West is damned for its history of conquest and exploitation:

> Trismegistus, have
> them, in their transmutation, from stone
> to bleeding pearl, from lead to burning
> looting, dead Moctezuma, find the West.

In the even more brutally forceful second poem, Jones speaks longingly of "A cult of death, / need of the simple striking arm under / the streetlamp. The cutters, from under / their rented earth. Come up, black dada nihilismus. Rape the white girls / Rape / their fathers. Cut the mother's throats / Black dada nihilismus, choke my friends." What animates the kingdoms of the West is "money, God, power, / a moral code, so cruel / it destroyed Byzantium, Tenochtitlan, Commanch." Only "the murders we intend / against his lost white children," Jones asserts, will ever make the black man whole. The new heroes are "tambo, willie best, dubois, patrice, mantan, the bronze buckaroos ... tom russ, l'overture, vesey, beau jack."

In these poems the value of sensation and shock is suddenly inflated as Jones abandons himself to a paroxysm of wish fulfillment. The iconoclastic "craziness" of the hipster becomes the "black madness" of the racial anarchist. The poems are, certainly, purgative outbursts of an agony of pent-up fury and frustration, the unleashing of a dark and brutal energy. But they are more than mere revenge-fantasies and go beyond mere nihilism. The language of fragments, violence, and exasperation registers a despair of human history. Jones is searching the darkness of a terrible freedom for a new principle of order—a new God and a more humane moral code; and he is searching still for a style which could give poetic shape to a seething mass of sensations, of randomness and ugliness.

To examine Jones's further development as a poet, it is necessary to turn to his next major collection, *Black Magic: Collected Poetry 1961–1967*, published in 1969. There are three sections: *Sabotage* (1961–1963), *Target Study* (1963–1965), and *Black Art* (1965–1966). The dating and grouping of these sections seem somewhat arbitrary. None of the poems in *Sabotage* appeared in print until 1964 or 1965, and it would seem logical that poems written as early as 1961 would have been included in *The Dead Lecturer*. The obvious explanation for these apparent discrepancies is that Jones was trying to compensate for the lack of racial material in his early work by assigning negritudinous and revolutionary poems in *Black Magic* dates prior to 1964. It is probably safe to assume that most of *Black Magic* was written after publication of *The Dead Lecturer*.

All of Jones's work after 1964 is devoted to exorcism of the evil white spirits that had possessed him and continued to bedevil his people. The rejection of the Judeo-Christian God already begun in the early poetry is intensified to sneering contempt. In "The Black Man is Making New Gods," Eliot's hanged man is reviled as a ridiculous imitation of black suffering: "The Fag's Death / they give us on a cross. To Worship. Our dead selves / in disguise. They give us / to worship / a dead jew / and not ourselves ... The empty jew / betrays us, as he does / hanging stupidly / from a cross, in an oven, the pantomime / of our torture." Jones's loss of faith in the Christian God, in the existential heroes of his comic-book youth ("THE SHADOW IS DEAD"), in the old values, leads to the call for a destruction of the old order. His poems, he tells us now, are "less passive ... less uselessly literary."

One of the first poems in *Black Magic*, "A Poem Some People Will Have to Understand," opens with a call for the machine gunners to step forward. "Black People" speaks of robbery, taking what is needed, dancing in the streets, turning things upside down: "We must make our own / World, man, our own world, and we can not do this unless the white man / is dead." Jones demands "magic," the "black magic" of his titles: "The magic words are UP against the wall mother / fucker this is a stick up!" The obscenity is an integral part of Jones's strategy of inversion.

The poem is a call to action in which there are no ambiguities, no hesitations. Jones has moved from the heroism of consciousness (available only in defeat) to the heroic act (even though it is vicious, bloody, and revengeful). Before passing a two-and-a-half-year prison sentence on Jones in 1968 for illegal possession of arms during the Newark riots of 1967, the presiding Judge Kapp offered the following observations on the poem, which he had felt compelled to read to the court: it was, he said, "a diabolical prescription to commit murder and to steal and plunder ... causing one to suspect that you were a participant in formulating a plot to ignite the spark ... to burn the city of Newark! ... It is my considered opinion that you are sick and require medical attention."[4] It is not hard to see why the judge should have felt threatened and outraged by this poem: what is less obvious is how such writing, ostensibly serving the cause of black Nation-Building, could help to effect the expansion and raising of black consciousness which Jones elsewhere calls for. It can hardly be called a poem about black people freeing themselves, about what Jones refers to in another poem as "future goodness." It is, in fact, a vision of the Newark riots, and Jones himself was under no illusions that what was looted was likely to be what was needed. His contempt for what can be stolen from white stores is registered in another poem: "Those Things. These refrigerators, stoves / automobiles, airships, let us return to the reality of the spirit / to how our black ancestors predicted life should be, from the / mind and the heart, our souls like gigantic kites sweep across / the heavens, let us follow them, with our trembling love for the world."

Clearly, the vision of "Black People" has nothing to do with the ultimate promise of black revolution, with the ideals of militant negritude. But it does express what Jones considers to be a necessary part of the painstaking and violent exorcism of whiteness. "Evil" has a positive function: "We are / in love with the virtue of evil." Jones may be seen to encourage an apocalyptic vandalism because it represents a shattering of the spell of the white man. "Black People" is a delirious vision of black people defying the hallowed absolutes of the white man's morality and law, of black people transforming themselves from passive victims into agents of a fearful destruction. Jones writes from a readiness to "soil his hands" in the pursuit of long-term moral and political aims. His conception of revolution puts historical and sociological realities before ethics. But, ultimately, revolution *is* a moral and spiritual project: "The will to be in tune / the depth of god / the will of wills thunder and rain / silence throws light and decision / to be in / tune / with / God ... to be alone with the God of creation the / holy nuance / in all beings. / Is the melody, and rhythm / of / the dancing / shit / itself."

The remarkable reorientation of Jones's energies which produced the later poems involved a trimming down of his mind—in his own terms, an "exorcism" of whiteness. The vague, indefinable despair of the early work finds, in the later poems, a source, a sufficient cause in the enormities of white injustice. The plain looking at self, the never complete assessment of the personal reality, has its limits. The "double consciousness" is painfully troubling, proves ultimately to be unendurable:

> Read this line
> young colored or white and know I felt the twist of dividing
> memory. Blood spoiled in the air, caked and anonymous.

With all dispassion spent (in *Preface* he refers to himself as "me / incapable of a simple straightforward / anger"), he craves the reassurance of system, the excitement of action.

The stance of principled subjectivity that Jones adopts in the early work requires the most remarkable heroism, the heroism of patience. The early poems enact a drama of doubt, but commitment to the problematic— especially for the black writer—is very hard to sustain. Like other writers of an activist temperament—Yeats and Pound on the right; Brecht, Malraux, and Gide on the left—Jones succumbed to the glamour of ideology, and embarked on an authoritarian adventure by turning to daily politics, championing an insurgent revolution. He attempts to escape from suffering to energizing, from angst to indignation. For Jones, indignation was not just stirring and exalting; it would appear to have been a psychic aid to survival. It concentrates energies on the rigors of combat. It is a unifier of emotions, curing the painful divergency of feeling present in states of high self-awareness. It is the unquestioning, unquestionable assertion of one's own rectitude. For Jones, revolutionary nationalism was invigorating, defining, even life-giving; through it he found distraction from, and quasi therapy for, inner turmoil. All his resources are directed against the enemy; hence energies of mind and passion are turned away from examining self. Militant action is an affirmation of virile passion, a means by which the anguish of isolation, the sense of futility and despair, can be transcended. Individuality is to be achieved through self-possession in involvement and action in a collective historical situation. By committing himself in action, he seeks to escape his solitude and join his fellow black men in assuming the suffering and responsibility of a racial destiny.

One cannot avoid the sense that Jones's espousal of militant negritude served personal ends as well as public ones. Certainly he is, in a substantial way, constituted and defined in racial terms through his championing of revolutionary nationalism; he is absorbed in that collectivity of actions toward the goal of Black Power. But he is also partly to be seen (in the light of his early work) as a heroic parasite who cherishes his individuality, wanting others to recognize it, and yet seeks to escape his isolation in action. By relating his life to a political cause he attempts to intensify it and justify it. He is fully conscious of his situation and analyzes his sense of guilt and inadequacy in a self-accusatory manner.

In "An Explanation of the Work," included in *Black Magic*, Jones disassociates himself from his early work and the sterile ideology from which it sprang:

> You notice the preoccupation with death, suicide in the early works. Always my own, caught up in the deathurge of this twisted society. The work a cloud of abstraction and disjointedness, that was just whiteness. European influence etc. just as the concept of hopelessness and despair, from the dead minds and dying morality of Europe.

A new aesthetic emerges to embody the new modes of perception. It is powerfully expressed in "Black Art":

> ... We want "poems that kill."
> Assassin poems, Poems that shoot
> guns. Poems that wrestle cops into alleys
> and take their weapons leaving them dead
> with tongues pulled out and sent to Ireland.

The poem implies confidence in the political efficacy of art. Art itself becomes a social act. In stressing the strictly utilitarian function of black art, Jones seeks to explode the view of art as involving a "distancing" of reality, a certain abstraction and remoteness from the very material with which it deals. Art is to become a "weapon" in the war against the white enemy; and war is the opposite of the "complicated" and the "self-contradictory." In vigorous flight from division, Jones prefers the crusade against the tangible, visible enemy; he moves from concern with states of being, which have no fixed center but their common origin in the depths of one man's mind, to confronting external problems. Such a project demands only vigorous, unreflective action; troubling introspection is replaced by the exhilaration of polemics.

While there is still a considerable number of free-form reflective lyrics in *Black Magic*, the most notable feature of this collection is Jones's development of a hortatory, highly oratorical style. As he says in one poem, "I'm here now, LeRoi, who tried to say something long for you. Keep it. / Forget me, or what I say, but not the tone, and exit image." The style relies heavily on hyperbole, repetition, incantation, and other devices that have a strong, visceral appeal. Such writing shares with the early, intensely personal work a rejection of poetry as a crystalline expression of idea or experience. The early poems, which represent a kind of insult to "good literature" and a break with academic standards, come closer to "intuitions," wherein discursive and logical language is replaced with invocatory, repetitive, and digressive structures. But in cultivating an oral poetry, Jones does not admit us into the poet's emotional privacy. There is no time for personal revelation or reflection, only for public declarations and revolutionary assertions. The language is even more insistently black, deriving from black speech and black music, from the techniques and timbres of the sermon and other forms of oratory—the dozens, the rap, the signifying, the folktale, the voodoo curse, the neo-African chant; the spirituals, the shouts, jubilees, gospel songs, field cries, black popular songs, and jazz. "A Poem for Black Hearts," Jones's tribute to Malcolm X, is a fine example of the new, public voice:

> For all of him, and all of yourself, look up,
> black man, quit stuttering and shuffling, look up,
> black man, quit whining and stooping, for all of him,
> For Great Malcolm a prince of the earth, let nothing in us rest
> until we avenge ourselves for his death.

Jones is reaching out to an audience that is not a reading public, which has little time for such things as poetry in the conventional sense. The later poems often have a rough-and-ready quality that results from Jones's assumption that they will not be studied or analyzed. They are essentially dramatic. He explores the possibilities of uniting poetry with music and drama, of the poet as public performer, and of the poem as public gesture.

In the early work, the poet, adrift in a hateful world, feels gutted or dead, is driven to attempt a mad engagement with the external world ("Black Dada Nihilismus"). It is a poetry of severity written on the very edge of crisis. Unable to support the full consequences of his perceptions, in flight from the engulfing nightmare, he oversimplifies life into an arena of polar opposites: blackness becomes the source of all heroism, vitality, humane virtue, and spirituality; whiteness of all horror and stupidity. As well as man of action, Jones becomes "soothsayer"—a priest, a black magician, an Imam. Moving beyond the diabolical inversion of white values, he seeks to discover for black people the secret mysteries of negritude. He is less often the conscious observer expressing ideas on political, social, and cultural affairs than the visionary poet seeking to define blackness as a transcendental, spiritual state. The deepening mysticism (his poems, he says, become "self-consciously spiritual and stronger") is animated by the same hip, underground avant-garde sensibility of the early poetry, though now the imagination is continually pressed into overstatement, expression into the fierce, rhetorical lyricism of a "long-breath singer" (in contrast to the halting, tentative telegraphese of the early poetry), as he strains toward the fever of eloquence. The vision involves the revenge of the imagination on the hated "real" world and is, ultimately, as intensely personal as that which informs the early poems. The later work still demands a cult following: it is not the "average" black American who might be expected to respond enthusiastically to Jones's revolutionary vision and voice, but an elite of black nationalist insiders. The direction of the poetry is still inward, but it operates from a basis in private myth that cannot admit too much reality, for that would involve the imagination too deeply in contradiction and trammel the gesture. The sense of self reflected in the later poems is coordinated and related in ways that depend on a high degree of selection. It is a chosen self, an imagined self, a mythic, metaphorical entity, the dialectics of which are governed by its black collective significance. Jones offers his people dreams of innocence—the last, desperate refuge in this confused and fumbling world:

> When I die, the consciousness I carry I will to
> black people. May they pick me apart and take
> the useful parts, the sweet meat of my feelings.
> And leave the bitter bullshit rotten white parts alone.

NOTES

1.   Norman Mailer, "The White Negro," in *Protest: The Beat Generation and the Angry Young Men*, ed. Gene Feldman and Max Gartenberg (London, 1958), p. 291.

2.   "LeRoi Jones," in David Ossman, comp., *The Sullen Art: Interviews with Modern American Poets* (New York, 1963), p. 81.

3.   Quoted in Ossman, *The Sullen Art*, p. 80.

4.   Stephen Schneck, "LeRoi Jones or, Poetics & Policemen or, Trying Heart, Bleeding Heart," *Ramparts*, June 29, 1968, p. 16.

CAROLE E. NEUBAUER

Maya Angelou: Self and a Song of Freedom in the Southern Tradition

W ithin the last fifteen years, Maya Angelou has become one of the best-known black writers in the United States. Her reputation rests firmly on her prolific career as an autobiographer, poet, dancer-singer, actress, producer, director, scriptwriter, political activist, and editor. Throughout her life, she has identified with the South, and she calls Stamps, Arkansas, where she spent ten years of her childhood, her home.

Maya Angelou was born Marguerite Annie Johnson on 4 April 1928 in St. Louis to Vivian Baxter and Bailey Johnson, a civilian dietitian for the U.S. Navy. At age three, when her parents' marriage ended in divorce, she was sent, along with her brother, Bailey, from Long Beach to Stamps to be cared for by their paternal grandmother, Mrs. Annie Henderson. During the next ten years, a time of severe economic depression and intense racial bigotry in the South, she spent nearly all of her time either in school, at the daily meetings of the Colored Methodist Episcopal Church, or at her grandmother's general merchandise store. In 1940, she graduated with top honors from the Lafayette County Training School and soon thereafter returned to her mother, who lived in the San Francisco-Oakland area at that time. There she continued her education at George Washington High School under the direction of her beloved Miss Kirwin. At the same time, she attended evening classes at the California Labor School, where she received

From *Southern Women Writers: The New Generation*, edited by Tonette Bond Inge. © 1990 by The University of Alabama Press.

a scholarship to study drama and dance. A few weeks after she received her high school diploma, she gave birth to her son, Guy Bailey Johnson.

Her career as a professional entertainer began on the West Coast, where she performed as a dancer-singer at the Purple Onion in the early 1950s. While working in this popular cabaret, she was spotted by members of the *Porgy and Bess* cast and invited to audition for the chorus. Upon her return from the play's 1954–55 tour of Europe and Africa, she continued to perform at nightclubs throughout the United States, acquiring valuable experience that would eventually lead her into new avenues of professional work.

In 1959, Angelou and her son moved to New York, where she soon joined the Harlem Writers Guild at the invitation of John Killens. Together with Godfrey Cambridge, she produced, directed, and starred in *Cabaret for Freedom* to raise funds for the Southern Christian Leadership Conference. Following the close of the highly successful show, she accepted the position of Northern coordinator for the SCLC at the request of Dr. Martin Luther King, Jr.

Her work in theater landed her the role of the White Queen in Genet's *The Blacks*, directed by Gene Frankel at St. Mark's Playhouse. For this production, she joined a cast of stars—Roscoe Lee Brown, Godfrey Cambridge, James Earl Jones, and Cicely Tyson. In 1974, she adapted Sophocles' *Ajax* for its premiere at the Mark Taper Forum in Los Angeles. Original screenplays to her credit include the film version of *Georgia, Georgia* and the television productions of *I Know Why the Caged Bird Sings* and *The Sisters*. She also authored and produced a television series on African traditions inherent in American culture and played the role of Kunte Kinte's grandmother in *Roots*. For PBS programming, she served as a guest interviewer on *Assignment America* and most recently appeared in a special series on creativity hosted by Bill Moyers, which featured a return visit to Stamps.

Among her other honors, Maya Angelou was appointed to the Commission of International Women's Year by former President Carter. In 1975, *Ladies' Home Journal* named her Woman of the Year in communications. A trustee of the American Film Institute, she is also one of the few women members of the Directors Guild. In recent years, she has received more than a dozen honorary degrees, including one from the University of Arkansas located near her childhood home. Fluent in seven languages, she has worked as the editor of the *Arab Observer* in Cairo and the *African Review* in Ghana. In December 1981, Angelou accepted a lifetime appointment as the first Reynolds Professor of American Studies at Wake Forest University in Winston-Salem, where she lectures on literature and popular culture. In 1983, Women in Communications presented her with the Matrix Award in the field of books.

Her personal life has been anything but smooth. As a young mother, Angelou had to endure painful periods of separation from her son while she worked at more than one job to support them. Often her ventures into show business would take her far from home, and she would put Guy in the care of her mother or baby-sitters. When she was twenty-one years old, she married Tosh Angelos, a sailor of Greek-American ancestry, but their marriage ended after three years. While working in New York, she met and later married Vusumzi Make, a black South African activist who traveled extensively raising money to end apartheid. They divided their time between New York and Cairo, but after a few years their marriage deteriorated. In 1973, Angelou married Paul du Feu, a carpenter and construction worker she had met in London. They lived together on the West Coast during most of their seven-year marriage.

SOUTHERN ROOTS AND LITERARY REPUTATION

Although she is rarely called a regional writer, Maya Angelou is frequently identified with the new generation of Southern writers. She has always called the South her home, and recently, after much deliberation, she settled in North Carolina, ending an absence of more than thirty years. Her autobiographies and poetry are rich with references to her childhood home in Arkansas and to the South in general. For Angelou, as for many black American writers, the South has become a powerfully evocative metaphor for the history of racial bigotry and social inequality, for brutal inhumanity and final failure. Yet the South also represents a life-affirming force energized by a somewhat spiritual bond to the land itself. It is a region where generations of black families have sacrificed their brightest dreams for a better future; yet it is here that ties to forebears whose very blood has nourished the soil are most vibrant and resilient. Stamps, Arkansas, in the 1930s was not a place where a black child could grow up freely or reach her full intellectual and social potential, but the town was nevertheless the home of Angelou's grandmother, who came to stand for all the courage and stability she ever knew as a child.

Her literary reputation is based on the publication of five volumes of autobiography (*I Know Why the Caged Bird Sings, Gather Together in My Name, Singin' and Swingin' and Gettin' Merry Like Christmas, The Heart of a Woman*, and *All God's Children Need Traveling Shoes*) and five volumes of poetry (*Just Give Me a Cool Drink of Water 'fore I Diiie, Oh Pray My Wings Are*

Gonna Fit Me Well, And Still I Rise, Shaker, Why Don't You Sing? and *Now Sheba Sings the Song*). In the twenty years of her publishing history, she has developed a rapport with her audiences who await each new work as a continuation of an ongoing dialogue with the author. Beginning with *Caged Bird* in 1970, her works have received wide critical acclaim and have been praised for reaching universal truths while examining the complicated life of one individual. The broad appeal of her autobiographies and poetry is evidenced in the numerous college anthologies that include portions of her work and in the popularity of the television adaptation of *Caged Bird*. In years to come, Angelou's voice, already recognized as one of the most original and versatile, will be measured by the standards of great American writers of our time.

AUTOBIOGRAPHY

In her first volume of autobiography, *I Know Why the Caged Bird Sings* (1970), Maya Angelou calls displacement the most important loss in her childhood, because she is separated from her mother and father at age three and never fully regains a sense of security and belonging. Her displacement from her family is not only an emotional handicap but is compounded by an equally unsettling sense of racial and geographic displacement. Her parents frequently move Angelou and her brother, Bailey, from St. Louis to Arkansas to the West Coast. As young children in Stamps in the 1930s, racial prejudice severely limits their lives. With the first pages, she sums up this demoralizing period of alienation: "If growing up is painful for the Southern Black girl, being aware of her displacement is the rust on the razor that threatens the throat" (*CB*, 3). The pain of her continual rejection comes not only from the displacement itself, but even more poignantly, from the child's acute understanding of prejudice. A smooth, clean razor would be enough of a threat, but a rusty, jagged one leaves no doubt in the victim's mind.

In *Caged Bird*, Angelou recounts many explosive incidents of the racial discrimination she experienced as a child. In the 1930s, Stamps was a fully segregated town. Marguerite and Bailey, however, are welcomed by a grandmother who is not only devoted to them but, as owner of the Wm. Johnson General Merchandise Store, is highly successful and independent. Momma is their most constant source of love and strength. "I saw only her power and strength. She was taller than any woman in my personal world, and her hands were so large they could span my head from ear to ear" (*CB*, 38). As powerful as her grandmother's presence seems to Marguerite, Momma uses her strength solely to guide and protect her family but not to confront the white community directly. Momma's resilient power usually reassures Marguerite, but one of the child's most difficult lessons teaches her that racial prejudice in Stamps can effectively circumscribe and even defeat her grandmother's protective influence.

In fact, it is only in the autobiographical narrative that Momma's personality begins to loom larger than life and provides Angelou's memories of childhood with a sense of personal dignity and meaning. On one occasion, for example, Momma takes Marguerite to the local dentist to be treated for a severe toothache. The dentist, who is ironically named Lincoln, refuses to treat the child, even though he is indebted to Momma for a loan she extended to him during the depression: "'Annie, my policy is I'd rather stick my hand in a dog's mouth than in a nigger's.'" As a silent witness to this scene, Marguerite suffers not only from the pain of her two decayed teeth, which have been reduced to tiny enamel bits by the avenging "Angel of the candy counter," but also from the utter humiliation of the dentist's bigotry as well: "It seemed terribly unfair to have a toothache and a headache and have to bear at the same time the heavy burden of Blackness" (CB, 159–60).

In an alternate version of the confrontation, which Angelou deliberately fantasizes and then italicizes to emphasize its invention, Momma asks Marguerite to wait for her outside the dentist's office. As the door closes, the frightened child imagines her grandmother becoming "ten feet tall with eight-foot arms." Without mincing words, Momma instructs Lincoln to "'leave Stamps by sundown'" and "'never again practice dentistry'": "'When you get settled in your next place, you will be a vegetarian caring for dogs with the mange, cats with the cholera and cows with the epizootic. Is that clear?'" (CB, 162). The poetic justice in Momma's superhuman power is perfect; the racist dentist who refused to treat her ailing granddaughter will in the future be restricted to treating the dogs he prefers to "niggers." After a trip to the black dentist in Texarkana, Momma and Marguerite return to Stamps, where we learn the "real" version of the story by overhearing a conversation between Momma and Uncle Willie. In spite of her prodigious powers, all that Momma accomplishes in Dr. Lincoln's office is to demand ten dollars as unpaid interest on the loan to pay for their bus trip to Texarkana.

In the child's imagined version, fantasy comes into play as the recounted scene ventures into the unreal or the impossible. Momma becomes a sort of superwoman of enormous proportions ("ten feet tall with eight-foot arms") and comes to the helpless child's rescue. In this alternate vision, Angelou switches to fantasy to suggest the depth of the child's humiliation and the residue of pain even after her two bad teeth have been pulled. Fantasy, finally, is used to demonstrate the undiminished strength of the character of Momma. Summarizing the complete anecdote, Angelou attests, "I preferred, much preferred, my version." Carefully selected elements of fiction and fantasy in the scene involving Dr. Lincoln and her childhood hero, Momma, partially compensate for the racial displacement that she experiences as a child.

When Angelou is thirteen, she and Bailey leave the repressive atmosphere of Stamps to join their mother. During these years, she continues to took for a place in life that will dissolve her sense of displacement. By the time she and Bailey are in their early teens, they have criss-crossed the western half of the country traveling between their parents' separate homes and their grandmother's in Stamps. Her sense of geographic displacement alone would be enough to upset any child's security, since the life-styles of her father in southern California and her mother in St. Louis and later in San Francisco represent worlds completely different and even foreign to the pace of life in the rural South. Each time the children move, a different set of relatives or another of their parents' lovers greets them, and they never feel a part of a stable family group, except when they are in Stamps at the general store with Momma and Uncle Willie.

Once settled in San Francisco in the early 1940s, Angelou enrolls at George Washington High School and the California Labor School, where she studies dance and drama in evening classes. She excels in both schools, and her teachers quickly recognize her intelligence and talent. Later she breaks the color barrier by becoming the first black female conductor on the San Francisco streetcars. Just months before her high school graduation, she engages in a onetime sexual encounter to prove her sexuality to herself and becomes pregnant. *Caged Bird*, however, ends on a note of awakening with the birth of her son and the beginning of a significant measure of strength and confidence in her ability to succeed and find her place in life. As autobiographer, Angelou uses the theme of displacement to unify the first volume of her life story as well as to suggest her long-term determination to create security and permanency in her life.

Between the conclusion of *Caged Bird* and the beginning of Angelou's second volume of autobiography, *Gather Together in My Name* (1974), there is virtually no break in the narrative. As the first ends with the birth of her son, the second starts when Guy is only a few months old, As a whole, *Gather Together* tells the story of his first three years and focuses on a young single mother's struggle to achieve respect, love, and a sense of self-worth. Her battle to win financial independence and the devotion of a faithful man could hardly have been easy in the years immediately following World War II, when racial discrimination, unemployment, and McCarthyism were all on the rise. In spite of her initial optimism, which is, incidentally, shared by many members of the postwar black community who fervently believed that "race prejudice was dead. A mistake made by a young country. Something to be forgiven as an unpleasant act committed by an intoxicated friend" (*GT*, 2), Angelou soon realizes that her dreams for a better America are still too fragile to survive. But worst of all is the burden of guilt that rests on the shoulders of the seventeen-year-old mother who desperately believes that she must assume full adult responsibility. Fortunately, her mother encourages her to set high goals, to maintain her sense of dignity and self-worth, and to work hard to succeed. Her mother's words come back to her throughout her life: "Anything worth doing is worth doing well" (*GT*, 81), and "be the best of anything you get into" (*GT*, 24).

Like many young women who came of age in the postwar era, Angelou easily imagines herself moving into a life modeled on *Good Housekeeping* and *Better Homes and Gardens*. She describes herself as both a "product of Hollywood upbringing" and her own "romanticism" and continually envisions herself smoothly slipping into the role guaranteed by popular culture. Whenever she meets a man who might potentially fulfill her dream, she anticipates the enviable comfort of "settling down." The scenario is always the same: "I would always wear pretty aprons and my son would play in the Little League. My husband would come home (he looked like Curly) and smoke his pipe in the den as I made cookies for the Scouts meeting" (*GT*, 127–28), or "We would live quietly in a pretty little house and I'd have another child, a girl, and the two children (whom he'd love equally) would climb over his knees and I would make three layer caramel cakes in my electric kitchen until they went off to college" (*GT*, 120). These glamorous dreams, of course, never quite materialize, but Angelou maintains a hopeful outlook and a determination to support and protect herself and her infant son. Her primary motivation during these early years of motherhood is to spare her son the insecurity and rejection she faced as a child. During these years, Angelou even works as an absentee madam and a prostitute, in hopes of achieving a regular family life and easing her unabiding sense of guilt over not being able to provide herself and her son with financial and familial security.

Yet Angelou understands that the hurdles she has to cross on her road to success are often higher than those set by her own expectations and standards of performance. Although she spends the first years of her son's life in California, both in the Bay Area and in San Diego, she often faces racial discrimination reminiscent of her childhood experiences in the South. At one point in *Gather Together*, when she suspects that her thriving business as a madam of a two-prostitute house will soon be uncovered by the police, Angelou returns to Stamps with her son, hoping to find the same comfort and protection she had known as a child. Specifically, she seeks her grandmother's "protective embrace" and her "courage" as well as the "shield of anonymity," but she soon realizes that the South is not ready to welcome her and that she has "outgrown" its "childhood protection." The five years she has spent in school and working in California have broadened her horizons and convinced her of her right to be accepted on the basis of her character and intelligence. But the South to which she returns is unchanged: "The town was halved by railroad tracks, the swift Red River and racial prejudice, ..." and "above all, the atmosphere was pressed down with the smell of old fears, and hates, and guilt" (GT, 61–63).

Not long after her arrival in Stamps, Angelou comes face to face with the double standards of racial discrimination during an unpleasant confrontation with a salesclerk in the white-owned general merchandise store. Although she attempts to explain to her grandmother why she refused to accept the clerk's humiliating insults, Momma warns her that her "principles" are all too flimsy a protection against the unrestrained contempt of bigotry: "'You think 'cause you've been to California these crazy people won't kill you? You think them lunatic cracker boys won't try to catch you in the road and violate you? You think because of your all-fired principle some of the men won't feel like putting their white sheets on and riding over here to stir up trouble? You do, you're wrong'" (GT, 78–79). That same day, her grandmother sends her back to California where she and her son are somewhat more distanced from the lingering hatred of the South. Not until the filming of a segment for Bill Moyers's PBS series on creativity thirty years later does Angelou return to her childhood home.

Upon her return to the Bay Area and to her mother's home, she is more determined than ever to achieve independence and win the respect of others. Leaving her son in the care of baby-sitters, she works long hours first as a dancer and entertainer and then as a short-order cook in Stockton. But as is often the case, the reality of her situation falls far below her ideal, and Angelou eventually turns to marijuana as a temporary consolation: "The pot had been important when I was alone and lonely, when my present was dull and the future uncertain" (GT, 131). During this period, she also falls in love with an older man who is a professional gambler supported by prostitution. When his luck fails him, Angelou agrees to help him pay his debt by becoming a prostitute herself. She makes this sacrifice fully believing that after her man has regained his financial security, he will marry her and provide her with the fulfillment of her romantic dream. Rationalizing her decision, she compares prostitution to marriage: "There are married women who are more whorish than a street prostitute because they have sold their bodies for marriage licenses, and there are some women who sleep with men for money who have great integrity because they are doing it for a purpose"

(*GT*, 135). But once again her dreams are disappointed, and she finds herself on her own at the end.

The second volume of her autobiography ends just before she decides to settle down with a man she pictures as an "ideal husband," who is in fact a heroin addict and gambler. Before it is too late, Angelou learns that she is on the verge of embracing disaster and defeat. At the end, she regains her innocence through the lessons of a compassionate drug addict: "I had walked the precipice and seen it all; and at the critical moment, one man's generosity pushed me safely away from the edge.... I had given a promise and found my innocence. I swore I'd never lose it again" (*GT*, 181). With these words, ready to accept the challenge of life anew, Angelou brings the second volume of her life story to a close. In *Gather Together in My Name*, a title inspired by the Gospel of Matthew (18:20), she asks her family and readers to gather around her and bear witness to her past.

The third volume of Maya Angelou's autobiography, *Singin' and Swingin' and Gettin' Merry Like Christmas* (1976) concentrates on the early years of her career as a professional dancer and singer, her related experience with racial prejudice, and with the guilt suffered through separation from her young son. During her childhood, her love for music grows through her almost daily attendance at the Colored Methodist Episcopal Church in Stamps and through her dance classes in California. Music in fact is her closest companion and source of moral support during her first few months back in the San Francisco area. She calls music her "refuge" during this period of her life and welcomes its protective embrace, into which she could "crawl into the spaces between the notes and curl [her] back to loneliness" (*SS*, 1). Without losing any time, she secures a job in sales and inventory at the Melrose Record Shop on Fillmore, which at the time served as a meeting place for musicians and music lovers of all description. In addition to earning enough money to quit her two previous jobs and bring her son home from the baby-sitter's in the evenings and on Sundays, Angelou also gains valuable exposure to the newest releases in blues and jazz and to an expansive circle of eccentric people.

Her sales position at the record shop is her first step into the world of entertainment. Her hours behind the cashier counter studying catalogs and helping customers make their selections bring her an easy familiarity with the newest stars and songs. Relying on her dance lessons and her trusted memory of popular lyrics, she later auditions for a position as a dancer at the Garden of Allah, where she is eventually hired as the first black show girl. Unlike the three white women who are also featured in the nightly show, Angelou is not required to strip but rather earns her audience's attention on the basis of her dance routines alone. All of the dancers, however, are instructed to supplement their regular salary by selling B-grade drinks and bottles of champagne on commission to interested customers. At first reluctant to put herself at the mercy of fawning, flirtatious spectators, she soon learns to sell more drinks than any of the others, simply by giving away the house secret on the composition of the ginger ale and Seven-Up cocktails and the details of the commission scale. But her success evokes the jealousy of the other women, and soon her first venture into professional entertainment comes to an end.

Through contacts established during her work at the Garden of Allah, Angelou auditions for an opening at the Purple Onion, a North Beach cabaret where she soon replaces Jorie Remus and shares the nightly bill with Phyllis Diller. After lessons with her drama coach, Lloyd Clark, who, incidentally, is responsible for coining her stage name, Maya Angelou, she polishes her style as an interpretative dancer and perfects a series of calypso songs that eventually comprise her regular act at the cabaret. Although the audience at the Purple Onion has never been entertained by a performer like Angelou, she quickly becomes extremely popular and gains much wider exposure than she did as a dancer at the Garden of Allah. Many professional stars and talent scouts, visiting San Francisco from New York and Chicago, drop in at the Purple Onion and some eventually invite her to audition for their shows. In 1954, for example, Leonard Sillman brought his Broadway hit *New Faces of 1953* to the Bay Area. When she learns through friends that Sillman needed a replacement for Eartha Kitt, who would be leaving for an engagement in Las Vegas, she jumps at the chance to work with a cast of talented performers. Even though she is invited to join the show, the management at the Purple Onion refuses to release her from her contract. Her first real show business break, therefore, does not come until after she goes to New York to try out for a new Broadway show called *House of Flowers*, starring Pearl Bailey and directed by Saint Subber. While there she is unexpectedly asked to join the company of *Porgy and Bess* in the role of Ruby, just as the troupe is finishing up its engagement in Montreal and embarking on its first European tour. She accepts, thereby launching her international career as a dancer-singer.

As her professional career in entertainment develops, Angelou worries about her responsibility to care for her young son and provide him with a secure family life. In *Singin' and Swingin'*, she continues to trace her pursuit of romantic ideals in the face of loneliness and disappointment. While working in the Melrose Record Shop, she meets Tosh Angelos, a sailor of Greek-American heritage, and later marries him. Her first impression of marriage could not have been more idealistic:

> At last I was a housewife, legally a member of that enviable tribe
> of consumers whom security made fat as butter and who under no
> circumstances considered living by bread alone, because their
> husbands brought home the bacon. I had a son, a father for him,
> a husband and a pretty home for us to live in. My life began to
> resemble a Good Housekeeping advertisement. I cooked well-
> balanced meals and molded fabulous jello desserts. My floors
> were dangerous with daily applications of wax and our furniture
> slick with polish. (SS, 26)

Unfortunately, after a year, Tosh and she begin to argue and recognize that
their different attitudes stand in the way of true compatibility and trust. Her
"Eden"-like homelife and "cocoon of safety" begin to smother her sense of
integrity and independence. In her autobiography, she describes this difficult
period as a time in which she felt a "sense of loss," which "suffused [her] until
[she] was suffocating within the vapors" (SS, 37). When their marriage ends,
Angelou again looks for a way to give her young child a stable home and a
permanent sense of family security. Understandably, her son temporarily
distrusts her and wonders whether she will stop loving him and leave him
behind to be cared for by others.

Before she marries Tosh, she seriously questions the nature of
interracial marriage and is advised by others, including her mother, to
examine the relationship carefully. Throughout *Singin' and Swingin'*, she
studies her attitude toward white people and explains her growing familiarity
with their life-styles and their acceptance of her as an equal within the world
of entertainment. When she first meets her future Greek-American husband,
she suspects that her racial heritage precludes the possibility of any kind of
permanent relationship. Her Southern childhood is too close, too vibrant in
her memory: "I would never forget the slavery tales, or my Southern past,
where all whites, including the poor and ignorant, had the right to speak
rudely to and even physically abuse any Negro they met. I knew the ugliness
of white prejudice" (SS, 23). Although she discounts her suspicion in her
dealings with Tosh Angelos, her deeply rooted fears stay close to the surface
as she comes to associate with a large number of white artists and
entertainers during her career as a dancer: "I knew you could never tell about
white people. Negroes had survived centuries of inhuman treatment and
retained their humanity by hoping for the best from their pale-skinned
oppressors but at the same time being prepared for the worst" (SS, 104).
Later, during her role as Ruby in *Porgy and Bess*, which played throughout
Europe, the Middle East, and North Africa, she observes the double
standards of white people who readily accept black Americans in Europe,

because they are fascinated by their exotic foreignness, but who are equally quick to discriminate against other people of color. In North Africa, she witnesses yet another version of racial bigotry in the way members of the Arab elite mistreat their African servants, "not realizing that auction blocks and whipping posts were too recent in our history for us [black Americans] to be comfortable around slavish servants" (*SS*, 210).

While in Rome, Angelou decides to cut short her engagement with *Porgy and Bess*, not because she has witnessed the complexities of racial prejudice but rather because she realizes that her son has suffered during her extended absence. Throughout her European tour, she carries the burden of guilt, which comes to characterize her early years of motherhood. Although she recognizes the pattern of abandonment emerging in her son's life as it had in her own, she often sees no alternative than to accept a job and, with it, the pain of separation. Finally, upon learning that her son has developed a severe and seemingly untreatable rash in her absence, she decides to return to San Francisco. Once there, she assumes full responsibility for "ruining [her] beautiful son by neglect" and for the "devastation to his mind and body" (*SS*, 233). Shortly after her return, Guy recovers, and together they reach a new level of trust and mutual dependence based on the understanding that their separation is now over for good. *Singin' and Swingin'* comes to a close as mother and son settle into a Hawaiian beach resort where she has just opened a new engagement at a nightclub. She achieves a longed for peace of mind as she comes to treasure her "wonderful, dependently independent son" (*SS*, 242).

In *The Heart of a Woman* (1980), the fourth in the autobiographical series, Maya Angelou continues the account of her son's youth and, in the process, repeatedly returns to the story of her childhood. The references to her childhood serve partly to create a textual link for readers who might be unfamiliar with the earlier volumes and partly to emphasize the suggestive similarities between her childhood and her son's. Her overwhelming sense of displacement and instability is, ironically, her son's burden too. In a brief flashback in the second chapter, she reminds us of the displacement that characterized her youth and links this aspect of her past with her son's present attitude. When Guy is fourteen, Angelou decides to move to New York. She does not bring Guy to the East until she has found a place for them to live, and when he arrives after a one-month separation, he initially resists her attempts to make a new home for them:

> The air between us [Angelou and Guy] was burdened with his aloof scorn. I understood him too well.
> When I was three my parents divorced in Long Beach, California, and sent me and my four-year-old brother,

unescorted, to our paternal grandmother. We wore wrist tags which informed anyone concerned that we were Marguerite and Bailey Johnson, en route to Mrs. Annie Henderson in Stamps, Arkansas.

Except for disastrous and mercifully brief encounters with each of them when I was seven, we didn't see our parents again until I was thirteen. (*HW*, 34–35)

From this and similar encounters with Guy, Angelou learns that the continual displacement of her own childhood is something she cannot prevent from recurring in her son's life.

In New York, Angelou begins to work as the Northern coordinator of the Southern Christian Leadership Conference and devotes most of her time to raising funds, boosting membership, and organizing volunteer labor, both in the office and in the neighborhoods. Throughout *Heart of a Woman*, she expands her own narrative by including anecdotes about well-known entertainers and political figures. Her account of a visit with Martin Luther King, Jr., at her SCLC office is just one example of this autobiographical technique. When Dr. King pays his first visit to the New York office during her tenure, she does not have advance notice of his presence and rushes into her office one day after lunch to find him sitting at her desk. They begin to talk about her background and eventually focus their comments on her brother, Bailey:

"Come on, take your seat back and tell me about yourself."
... When I mentioned my brother Bailey, he asked what he was doing now.
The question stopped me. He was friendly and understanding, but if I told him my brother was in prison, I couldn't be sure how long his understanding would last. I could lose my job. Even more important, I might lose his respect. Birds of a feather and all that, but I took a chance and told him Bailey was in Sing Sing.
He dropped his head and looked at his hands.
"I understand. Disappointment drives our young men to some desperate lengths." Sympathy and sadness kept his voice low. "That's why we must fight and win. We must save the Baileys of the world. And Maya, never stop loving him. Never give up on him. Never deny him. And remember, he is freer than those who hold him behind bars." (*HW*, 92–93)

Angelou appreciates King's sympathy and of course shares his hope that their work will make the world more fair and free. She recognizes the undeniable

effects of displacement on Bailey's life and fervently hopes that her own son
will be spared any further humiliation and rejection.

From time to time, Angelou sees marriage as the answer to her own
sense of dislocation and fully envisions a perfect future with various
prospective husbands. While in New York, she meets Vusumzi Make, a black
South African freedom fighter, and imagines that he will provide her with the
same domestic security she had hoped would develop from other
relationships: "I was getting a husband, and a part of that gift was having
someone to share responsibility and guilt" (HW, 131). Yet her hopes are even
more idealistic than usual, inasmuch as she imagines herself participating in
the liberation of South Africa as Vus Make's wife: "With my courage added
to his own, he would succeed in bringing the ignominious white rule in
South Africa to an end. If I didn't already have the qualities he needed, then
I would just develop them. Infatuation made me believe in my ability to
create myself into my lover's desire" (HW, 123). In reality, Angelou is only
willing to go so far in re-creating herself to meet her husband's desires and is
all too soon frustrated with her role as Make's wife. He does not want her to
work but is unable on his own to support his expensive tastes as well as his
family. They are evicted from their New York apartment just before they
leave for Egypt and soon face similar problems in Cairo. Their marriage
dissolves after some months, despite Angelou's efforts to contribute to their
financial assets by working as editor of the Arab Observer. In Heart of a
Woman, she underscores the illusory nature of her fantasy about marriage to
show how her perspective has shifted over the years and how much
understanding she has gained about life in general. Re-creating these
fantasies in her autobiography is a subtle form of truth telling and a way to
present hard-earned insights about her life to her readers.

A second type of fantasy in Heart of a Woman is borne out in reality
rather than in illusion, as is the case with her expectations of marriage. One
of the most important uses of the second kind of fantasy involves a sequence
that demonstrates how much she fears for Guy's safety throughout his youth.
A few days after mother and son arrive in Accra, where they move when her
marriage with Vus Make deteriorates, some friends invite them to a picnic.
Although his mother declines, Guy immediately accepts the invitation in a
show of independence. On the way home from the day's outing, her son is
seriously injured in an automobile accident. Even though he has had very
little experience driving, his intoxicated host asks Guy to drive. When their
return is delayed, Angelou is terrified by her recurring fear for Guy's safety.
Later, in the Korle Bu emergency ward, her familiar fantasy about harm
endangering her son's life moves to the level of reality, as she relates the
vulnerability she feels in her role as mother with full responsibility for the

well-being of her only child. In a new country, estranged from her husband and with no immediate prospects for employment, she possesses very little control over her life or her son's safety. After the accident in Ghana, Guy is not only fighting for independence from his mother but also for life itself. The conclusion of *Heart of a Woman*, nevertheless, announces a new beginning for Angelou and hope for her future relationship with Guy.

Her most recent autobiography, *All God's Children Need Traveling Shoes* (1986), has swept Angelou to new heights of critical and popular acclaim. Her life story resumes exactly where it ended chronologically and geographically in *The Heart of a Woman*, with Guy's recovery from his automobile accident in Accra. Although only portions of two earlier volumes of her autobiographical narrative occur in Africa, her latest addition to the series takes place almost exclusively in Ghana. In *All God's Children Need Traveling Shoes*, however, Angelou focuses primarily on the story of her and many other black Americans' attempts in the early 1960s to return to the ancestral home in Africa. As in her four previous autobiographies, she explores the theme of displacement and the difficulties involved in creating a home for oneself, one's family, and one's people.

In choosing to live in Ghana following the deterioration of her marriage to Vus Make, Angelou hopes to find a place where she and her son can make a home for themselves, free at last from the racial bigotry she has faced throughout the United States, Europe, and parts of the Middle East. While Guy is recuperating from his injuries, she carefully evaluates her assets and concludes that since his birth, her only home has been wherever she and her son are together: "we had been each other's home and center for seventeen years. He could die if he wanted to and go off to wherever dead folks go, but I, I would be left without a home" (*TS*, 5). Her initial expectations, therefore, for feeling at ease and settling down in West Africa are, understandably, considerable: "We had come home, and if home was not what we had expected, never mind, our need for belonging allowed us to ignore the obvious and to create real places or even illusory places, befitting our imagination" (*TS*, 19). Unfortunately, the Ghanian people do not readily accept Angelou, her son, and most of the black American community in Accra, and they unexpectedly find themselves isolated and often ignored.

Taken as a whole, *All God's Children Need Traveling Shoes* recounts the sequence of events that gradually brings the autobiographer closer to an understanding and eventually to an acceptance of the seemingly unbreachable distance between the Ghanians and the black American expatriates. Within the first few weeks of her stay in Ghana, Angelou suspects that she has mistakenly followed the misdirected footsteps of other black Americans who "had not come home, but had left one familiar place of painful memory for another strange place with none" (*TS*, 40). In time, she understands that their alienation is most likely based on the fact that they, unlike the Ghanians, are the descendants of African slaves, who painfully bear the knowledge that "'not all slaves were stolen, nor were all slave dealers European'" (*TS*, 47). No one in the expatriate group can feel fully at ease in Africa as long as they carry the haunting suspicion that "African slavery stemmed mostly from tribal exploitation" (*TS*, 48) and not solely from European colonial imperialism.

Angelou, nevertheless, perseveres; she eventually settles into lasting friendships with both Americans and Africans and finds work through her talents as a journalist and a performer. With her professional and personal contacts, she meets many African political activists, as well as diplomats and artists from around the world. These acquaintances, in addition to a brief tour in Berlin and Venice with the original St. Mark's Playhouse company of Genet's *The Blacks*, enlarge Angelou's perspective on racial complexities and help her locate a place in Africa where she can live, albeit temporarily, at peace.

In *All God's Children Need Traveling Shoes*, Angelou continually reminds the reader that the quest for a place to call home is virtually endemic to the human condition. During her time in Ghana, she comes to understand that the search is seldom successful, regardless of the political or social circumstances involved. Toward the end of her personal narrative, Angelou sums up her conclusions about the struggle to find or create a home: "If the heart of Africa still remained allusive, my search for it had brought me closer to understanding myself and other human beings. The ache for home lives in all of us, the safe place where we can go as we are and not be questioned" (*TS*, 196). In a 1984 interview conducted during the period when she was completing an earlier draft of *All Gods Children Need Traveling Shoes*, Angelou voices the same illuminating insight:

NEUBAUER: How far will the fifth volume go?

ANGELOU: Actually, it's a new kind. It's really quite a new voice. I'm looking at the black American resident, me and the other black American residents in Ghana, and trying to see all the magic of the eternal quest of human beings to go home again. That is maybe what life is anyway. To return to the Creator. All of that naivete, the innocence of trying to. That awful rowing towards God, whatever it is. Whether it's to return to your village or the lover you lost or the youth that some people want to return to or the beauty that some want to return to.

NEUBAUER: Writing autobiography frequently involves this quest to return to the past, to the home. Sometimes, if the home can't be found, if it can't be located again, then that home or that love or that family, whatever has been lost, is recreated or invented.

ANGELOU: Yes, of course. That's it! That's what I'm seeing in this trek back to Africa. That in so many cases that idealized home of course is non-existent. In so many cases some black Americans created it on the spot. On the spot. And I did too. Created something, looked, seemed like what we have idealized very far from reality.

Whatever vision of home Angelou creates for herself and her son in Ghana, she discovers a heightened sense of self-awareness and independence. By the end of her stay in West Africa, she has a renewed image of herself as a woman, lover, mother, writer, performer, and political activist. In her state of fortified strength, she decides to leave Africa and return to the country of her birth, however disturbing the memories of slavery and the reality of racial hatred. In fact, Angelou ends her sojourn in foreign lands to commit herself to Malcolm X's struggle for racial equality and social justice in the United States, by planning to work as an office coordinator for the Organization of Afro-American Unity. She has finally freed herself from the illusion of claiming an ancestral home in Africa. Ironically perhaps, with the writing of *All God's Children Need Traveling Shoes* and the brilliant clarity of the autobiographical present, "this trek back to Africa," Maya Angelou also decides to return to the South, and for the first time since her youth, make her home there. Although she has learned that "the idealized home of course is non-existent," she leaves her readers to suspect that her traveling shoes are never really out of sight; if nothing else, we will soon find ourselves following her paths of autobiographical discovery once again.

POETRY

Most of the thirty-eight poems in Maya Angelou's *Just Give Me a Cool Drink of Water 'fore I Diiie* (1971) appeared several years earlier in a collection called *The Poetry of Maya Angelou*, published by Hirt Music. Among these are some of her best known pieces, such as "Miss Scarlett, Mr. Rhett and Other Latter Day Saints" and "Harlem Hopscotch." The volume is divided into two parts; the first deals with love, its joy and inevitable sorrow, and the second with the trials of the black race. Taken as a whole, the poems cover a wide range of settings from Harlem streets to Southern churches to abandoned African coasts. These poems contain a certain power, which stems from the strong metric control that finds its way into the terse lines characteristic of her poetry. Not a word is wasted, not a beat lost. Angelou's poetic voice speaks with a sure confidence that dares return to even the most painful memories to capture the first signs of loss or hate.

The first twenty poems of *Cool Drink* describe the whole gamut of love, from the first moment of passionate discovery to the first suspicion of painful loss. One poem, in fact, is entitled "The Gamut" and in its sonnet form moves from "velvet soft" dawn when "my true love approaches" to the "deathly quiet" of night when "my true love is leaving" (*CD*, 5). Two poems, "To a Husband" and "After," however, celebrate the joyous fulfillment of love. In the first, Angelou suggests that her husband is a symbol of African strength and beauty and that through his almost majestic presence she can sense the former riches of the exploited continent. To capture his vibrant spirit, she retreats to Africa's original splendor and conjures up images as ancient as "Pharaoh's tomb":

> You're Africa to me
> At brightest dawn.
> The congo's green and
> Copper's brackish hue ...

In this one man, she sees the vital strength of an entire race: "A continent to build / With Black Man's brawn" (*CD*, 15). His sacrifice, reminiscent of generations of unacknowledged labor, inspires her love and her commitment to the African cause. "After" also speaks of the love between woman and man but is far more tender and passionate. The scene is the lovers' bed when "no sound falls / from the moaning sky" and "no scowl wrinkles / the evening pool." Here, as in "To a Husband," love is seen as strong and sustaining, even jubilant in its harmonious union, its peaceful calm. Even "the stars lean down / A stony brilliance" in recognition of their love (*CD*, 18). And yet there is a certain absent emptiness in the quiet that hints of future loss.

In the second section, Angelou turns her attention to the lives of black people in America from the time of slavery to the rebellious 1960s. Her themes deal broadly with the painful anguish suffered by blacks forced into submission, with guilt over accepting too much, and with protest and basic survival.

"No No No No" is a poem about the rejection of American myths that promise justice for all but only guarantee freedom for a few. The powerfully cadenced stanzas in turn decry the immorality of American involvement in Vietnam,

> while crackling babies
> in napalm coats
> stretch mouths to receive
> burning tears ...

as well as the insincere invitation of the Statue of Liberty, which welcomes immigrants who crossed "over the sinuous cemetery / of my many brothers," and the inadequate apologies offered by white liberals. The first stanza ends with the refrain that titles the complete collection of poems, "JUST GIVE ME A COOL DRINK OF WATER 'FORE I DIIIE." In the second half of the poem, the speaker identifies with those who suffered humiliation

> on the back porches
> of forever
> in the kitchens and fields
> of rejections

and boldly cautions that the dreams and hopes of a better tomorrow have vanished (*CD*, 40–43). Even pity, the last defense against inhumanity, is spent.

Two poems that embody the poet's confident determination that conditions must improve for the black race are "Times-Square-Shoeshine Composition" and "Harlem Hopscotch." Both ring with a lively, invincible beat that carries defeated figures into at least momentary triumph. "Times-Square" tells the story of a shoeshine man who claims to be an unequaled master at his trade. He cleans and shines shoes to a vibrant rhythm that sustains his spirit in spite of humiliating circumstances. When a would-be customer offers him twenty-five cents instead of the requested thirty-five cents, the shoeshine man refuses the job and flatly renounces the insulting attempt to minimize the value of his trade. Fully appreciating his own expertise, the vendor proudly instructs his potential Times Square patron to give his measly quarter to his daughter, sister, or mamma, for they clearly need it more than he does. Denying the charge that he is a "greedy bigot," the shoeshine man simply admits that he is a striving "capitalist," trying to be successful in a city owned by the superrich.

Moving uptown, "Harlem Hopscotch" celebrates the sheer strength necessary for survival. The rhythm of this powerful poem echoes the beat of feet, first hopping, then suspended in air, and finally landing in the appropriate square. To live in a world measured by such blunt announcements as "food is gone" and "the rent is due," people need to be extremely energetic and resilient. Compounding the pressures of hunger, poverty, and unemployment is the racial bigotry that consistently discriminates against people of color. Life itself has become a brutal game of hopscotch, a series of desperate yet hopeful leaps, landing but never pausing long: "In the air, now both feet down. / Since you black, don't stick around." Yet in the final analysis, the words that bring the poem and the complete collection to a close triumphantly announce the poet's victory: "Both feet flat, the game is done. / They think I lost. I think I won" (*CD*, 50). These poems in their sensitive treatment of both love and black identity are the poet's own defense against the incredible odds in the game of life.

Within four years of the publication of *Just Give Me a Cool Drink 'fore I Diiie*, Maya Angelou completed a second volume of poetry, *Oh Pray My Wings Are Gonna Fit Me Well* (1975). By the time of its release, her reputation as a poet who transforms much of the pain and disappointment of life into lively verse had been established. During the 1970s, her reading public grew accustomed to seeing her poems printed in *Cosmopolitan*. Angelou had become recognized not only as a spokesperson for blacks and women, but also for all people who are committed to raising the moral standards of living in the United States. The poems collected in *My Wings*, indeed, appear at the end of the Vietnam era and in some important ways exceed the scope of her first volume. Many question traditional American values and urge people to make an honest appraisal of the demoralizing rift between the ideal and the real. Along with poems about love and the oppression of black people, the poet adds several that directly challenge Americans to reexamine their lives and to strive to reach the potential richness that has been compromised by self-interest since the beginnings of the country.

One of the most moving poems in *My Wings* is entitled "Alone," in which carefully measured verses describe the general alienation of people in the twentieth century. "Alone" is not directed at any one particular sector of society but rather is focused on the human condition in general. No one, the poet cautions, can live in this world alone. This message punctuates the end of the three major stanzas and also serves as a separate refrain between each and at the close of the poem:

> Alone, all alone
> Nobody, but nobody
> Can make it out here alone.

Angelou begins by looking within herself and discovering that her soul is without a home. Moving from an inward glimpse to an outward sweep, she recognizes that even millionaires suffer from this modern malaise and live lonely lives with "hearts of stone." Finally, she warns her readers to listen carefully and change the direction of their lives:

> Storm clouds are gathering
> The wind is gonna blow
> The race of man is suffering. (*MW*, 70)

For its own survival, the human race must break down barriers and rescue one another from loneliness. The only cure, the poet predicts, is to acknowledge common interests and work toward common goals.

A poem entitled "America" is no less penetrating in its account of the country's problems. Again Angelou pleads with the American people to "discover this country" and realize its full potential. In its two-hundred-year history, "the gold of her promise / has never been mined." The promise of justice for all has not been kept and in spite of "her crops of abundance / the fruit and the grain," many citizens live below the poverty line and never have enough food to feed their families. Similarly, racial bigotry has denied generations of Americans their full dignity and natural rights, while depriving them of the opportunity to contribute freely to the nation's strength. At the close of the poem, Angelou calls for the end of "legends untrue," which are perpetrated through history to "entrap" America's children (*MW*, 78–79). The only hope for the country is to discard these false myths once and for all and to guarantee that all people benefit from democratic principles.

In one poem, "Southeast Arkansia," the poet shifts her attention from the general condition of humanity to the plight of black people in America. The setting of this tightly structured poem is the locale where Angelou spent most of her childhood. At the end of the three stanzas, she poses a question concerning the responsibility and guilt involved in the exploitation of the slaves. Presumably, the white men most immediately involved have never answered for their inhumane treatment of "bartered flesh and broken bones." The poet doubts that they have ever even paused to "ponder" or "wonder" about their proclivity to value profit more than human life (*MW*, 99).

Any discussion of *My Wings* that did not address the poems written about the nature of love would be necessarily incomplete. The entire volume is dedicated to Paul du Feu, Angelou's husband from 1973 to 1980. One very brief poem, "Passing Time," speaks of a love that is finely balanced and delicately counterpoised. This love stretches over time, blanketing both the beginning and end of a day: "Your skin like dawn / Mine like dusk" (*MW*,

62). Together is reached a certain harmony that carries the lovers through the day, perfectly complementing each other's spirit. Equally economical in form is the poem "Greyday," which in nine short lines compares a lonely lover to Christ. While she is separated from her man, "the day hangs heavy / loose and grey." The woman feels as if she is wearing "a crown of thorns" and "a shirt of hair." Alone, she suffers in her solitude and mourns that

> No one knows
> my lonely heart
> when we're apart. (*MW*, 64)

Such is love in the world of *My Wings*; when all is going well, love sustains and inspires, but when love fades, loneliness and pain have free rein.

As the title of Maya Angelou's third volume of poetry, *And Still I Rise* (1978), suggests, this collection contains a hopeful determination to rise above discouraging defeat. These poems are inspired and spoken by a confident voice of strength that recognizes its own power and will no longer be pushed into passivity. The book consists of thirty-two poems, which are divided into three sections, "Touch Me, Life, Not Softly," "Traveling," and "And Still I Rise." Two poems, "Phenomenal Woman" and "Just for a Time" appeared in *Cosmopolitan* in 1978. Taken as a whole, this series of poems covers a broader range of subjects than the earlier two volumes and shifts smoothly from issues such as springtime and aging to sexual awakening, drug addiction, and Christian salvation. The familiar themes of love and its inevitable loneliness and the oppressive climate of the South are still central concerns. But even more striking than the poet's careful treatment of these subjects is her attention to the nature of woman and the importance of family.

One of the best poems in this collection is "Phenomenal Woman," which captures the essence of womanhood and at the same time describes the many talents of the poet herself. As is characteristic of Angelou's poetic style, the lines are terse and forcefully, albeit irregularly, rhymed. The words themselves are short, often monosyllabic, and collectively create an even, provocative rhythm that resounds with underlying confidence. In four different stanzas, a woman explains her special graces that make her stand out in a crowd and attract the attention of both men and women, although she is not, by her own admission, "cut or built to suit a fashion model's size." One by one, she enumerates her gifts, from "the span of my hips" to "the curl of my lips," from "the flash of my teeth" to "the joy in my feet." Yet her attraction is not purely physical; men seek her for her "inner mystery," "the grace of [her] style," and "the need for [her] care." Together each alluring part adds up to a phenomenal woman who need not "bow" her head but can walk tall with a quiet pride that beckons those in her presence (*IR*, 121–23).

Similar to "Phenomenal Woman" in its economical form, strong rhyme scheme, and forceful rhythm is "Woman Work." The two poems also bear a thematic resemblance in their praise of woman's vitality. Although "Woman Work" does not concern the physical appeal of woman, as "Phenomenal Woman" does, it delivers a corresponding litany of the endless cycle of chores in a woman's typical day. In the first stanza, the long list unravels itself in forcefully rhymed couplets:

> I've got the children to tend
> The clothes to mend
> The floor to mop
> The food to shop
> Then the chicken to fry
> Then baby to dry.

Following the complete category of tasks, the poet adds four shorter stanzas, which reveal the source of woman's strength. This woman claims the sunshine, rain, and dew as well as storms, wind, and snow as her own. The dew cools her brow, the wind lifts her "across the sky," the snow covers her "with white / Cold icy kisses," all bringing her rest and eventually the strength to continue (*IR*, 144–45). For her, there is no other source of solace and consolation than nature and its powerful elements.

In two poems, "Willie" and "Kin," Angelou turns her attention from woman to her family. "Willie" tells the story of her paternal uncle, with whom she and her brother, Bailey, lived during their childhood in Stamps, Arkansas. This man, although "crippled and limping, always walking lame," knows the secret of survival. For years, he suffers humiliation and loneliness, both as a result of his physical affliction and his color. Yet from him, the child learns about the hidden richness of life and later follows his example to overcome seemingly insurmountable hardships. Willie's undying message echoes throughout the poem: "I may cry and I will die, / But my spirit is the soul of every spring" and "my spirit is the surge of open seas." Although he cannot personally change the inhumane way people treat their brothers and sisters, Willie's spirit will always be around; for, as he says, "I am the time," and his inspiration lives on beyond him (*IR*, 141–42).

As in "Willie," the setting of "Kin" is the South, particularly Arkansas, and the subject is family. This powerful poem is dedicated to Bailey and is based on the painful separation of brother and sister during their adult years. As children, Marguerite and Bailey were constant companions and buffered each other somewhat from the continual awareness of what it meant to grow up black in the South. Then, she writes, "We were entwined in red rings / Of blood and loneliness...." Now, distanced by time and Bailey's involvement with drugs, the poet is left

> ... to force strangers
> Into brother molds, exacting
> Taxations they never
> Owed or could pay.

Meanwhile, her brother slips further and further away and fights

> ... to die, thinking
> In destruction lies the seed
> Of birth....

Although she cannot reach him in his "regions of terror," Angelou sinks through memory to "silent walks in Southern woods" and an "Arkansas twilight" and is willing to concede that her brother "may be right" (*IR*, 149–50).

But ultimately, the poet challenges her readers to fight against the insipid invitation of destruction and death. Throughout *And Still I Rise*, the strong, steady rhythm of her poetic voice beckons whoever will listen to transcend beyond the level of demoralizing defeat and to grasp life on its own terms. The single strongest affirmation of life is the title poem, "And Still I Rise." In the face of "bitter, twisted lies," "hatefulness," and "history's shame," the poet promises not to surrender. Silently, she absorbs the power of the sun and moon and becomes a "black ocean, leaping and wide, / Welling and swelling I hear in the tide." Her inner resources, "oil wells," "gold mines," and "diamonds," nourish her strength and sustain her courage. Her spirit will soar as she transforms "the gifts that my ancestors gave" into poetry, and herself into "the dream and the hope of the slave" (*IR*, 154–55). Through all of her verse, Angelou reaches out to touch the lives of others and to offer them hope and confidence in place of humiliation and despair.

Her fourth volume of verse, *Shaker, Why Don't You Sing?* (1983), is dedicated to her son, Guy Johnson, and her grandson, Colin Ashanti Murphy Johnson. As do her three previous collections of poems, *Shaker* celebrates the power to struggle against lost love, defeated dreams, and threatened freedom, and to survive. Her poetic voice resonates with the control and confidence that have become characteristic of Angelou's work in general and of her determination that "life loves the person who dares to live it." The vibrant tone of these poems moves gracefully from the promise of potential strength to the humor of light satire, at all times bearing witness to a spirit that soars and sings in spite of repeated disappointment. Perhaps even more than in her earlier poems, Angelou forcefully captures the loneliness of love and the sacrifice of slavery without surrendering to defeat or despair.

More than half of the twenty-eight poems in *Shaker* concern the subject of love between woman and man, and of these, most deal with the pain, loss, and loneliness that typically characterize unrequited love. In many of these poems, a woman awakens at sunrise, with or without her lover by her side, wondering how much longer their dying relationship will limp along before its failure will be openly acknowledged. An underlying issue in these poignant poems about love is deception—not so much the intricate fabrication of lies to cover up infidelity but rather the unvoiced acquiescence to fading and failing love. In "The Lie," for example, a woman protects herself from humiliation when her lover threatens to leave her by holding back her anger and pretending to be unmoved, even eager to see her man go:

> I hold curses, in my mouth,
> which could flood your path, sear
> bottomless chasms in your road.

Deception is her only defense:

> I keep, behind my lips,
> invectives capable of tearing
> the septum from your
> nostrils and the skin from your back. (*SW*, 33)

Similarly, in the very brief poem "Prelude to a Parting," a woman lying in bed beside her lover senses the imminent end when he draws away from her touch. Yet neither will acknowledge "the tacit fact" or face the "awful fear of losing," knowing, as they do without speaking, that nothing will "cause / a fleeing love / to stay" (*SW*, 25).

Not all of the love poems in this collection suggest deception or dishonesty, but most describe the seemingly inevitable loss of love. The title poem, "Shaker, Why Don't You Sing?," belongs to this second group. A woman, "evicted from sleep's mute palace" and lying awake alone in bed, remembers the "perfect harmonies" and the "insistent / rhythm" of a lost love. Her life fills with silence now that love has withdrawn its music, its "chanteys" that "hummed / [her] life alive." Now she rests "somewhere / between the unsung notes of night" and passionately asks love to return its song to her life: "O Shaker, why don't you sing?" (*SW*, 42–43). This mournful apostrophe to love serves as a refrain in an unsung song and, in its second utterance, brings the poem to a close unanswered.

The same determined voice comes through in a number of other poems that relate unabiding anguish over the oppression of the black race. Several of these poems deal specifically with the inhumane treatment of the slaves in the South. "A Georgia Song," for example, in its beautifully lyrical cadences, recalls the unforgotten memories of slavery, which linger like "odors of Southern cities" and the "great green / Smell of fresh sweat. / In Southern fields." Angelou deftly recounts the "ancient / Wrongs" and describes a South broken by injustice and sorrow. Now, "dusty / Flags droop their unbearable / Sadness." Yet the poet calls for a new dream to rise up from the rich soil of Georgia and replace the "liquid notes of / Sorrow songs" with "a new song. A song / Of Southern peace" (*SW*, 8–10). Although the memories of "ancient / Wrongs" can never be forgotten, the poem invites a renewal of Southern dreams and peace.

Perhaps the most powerful poem in this collection is "Caged Bird," which inevitably brings Angelou's audience full circle with her best-known autobiography, *I Know Why the Caged Bird Sings*. This poem tells the story of a free bird and a caged bird. The free bird floats leisurely on "trade winds soft through the sighing trees" and even "dares to claim the sky," He feeds on "fat worms waiting on a dawn-bright lawn" and soars to "name the sky his own." Unlike his unbound brother, the caged bird leads a life of confinement that sorely inhibits his need to fly and sing. Trapped by the unyielding bars of his cage, the bird can only lift his voice in protest against his imprisonment and the "grave of dreams" on which he perches. Appearing both in the middle and end of the poem, this stanza serves as a dual refrain:

> The caged bird sings
> with a fearful trill
> of things unknown
> but longed for still
> and his tune is heard
> on the distant hill
> for the caged bird
> sings of freedom. (*SW*, 16–17)

Although he sings of "things unknown," the bird's song of freedom is heard even as far as the "distant hill." His song is his protest, his only alternative to submission and entrapment. Angelou knows why the caged bird and all oppressed beings must sing. Her poems in *Shaker, Why Don't You Sing?* imply that as long as such melodies are sung and heard, hope and strength will overcome defeated dreams.

At the end of *All God's Children Need Traveling Shoes*, Angelou hints at her association with Tom Feelings, a young black American artist who lived in Ghana during the early 1960s. Angelou cites Malcolm X's introduction of this newcomer to the black American expatriate community: "'A young painter named Tom Feelings is coming to Ghana. Do everything you can for him. I am counting on you'" (*HW*, 193). By introducing Feelings at the conclusion of her latest autobiography, she subtly sets the scene for her most recent publication, *Now Sheba Sings the Song* (1987), a single poem, illustrated by eighty-two of Feelings's drawings of black women, sketched throughout the world over a period of twenty-five years. Together the poem and the sepia-toned drawings royally celebrate the universal majesty of the black woman. In his introduction to the book, Feelings credits Angelou as the "someone who shared a similar experience [with the women he drew], someone who traveled, opened up, took in, and mentally recorded everything observed. And most important of all, it [his collaborator] had to be someone whose *center* is woman" (*NS*, 6). Angelou's poem, in turn, glorifies the spiritual, physical, emotional, and intellectual powers of black women or what Feelings calls "Africa's beauty, strength, and dignity [which are] wherever the Black woman is" (*NS*, 6). Angelou affirms the black woman's "love of good and God and Life" (*NS*, 48) and beckons "he who is daring and brave" (*NS*, 54) to meet the open challenge of the radiant Queen of Sheba. Maya Angelou's songs, like Sheba's, testify to the creative powers inherent in the works of today's Southern women writers.

MAYA ANGELOU BIBLIOGRAPHY

Autobiographies

I Know Why the Caged Bird Sings. New York: Random House, 1970; Bantam, 1971 (paper).

Gather Together in My Name. New York: Random House, 1974; Bantam, 1975 (paper).

Singin' and Swingin' and Gettin' Merry Like Christmas. New York: Random House, 1976; Bantam, 1977 (paper).

The Heart of a Woman. New York: Random House, 1981; Bantam, 1982 (paper).

All God's Children Need Traveling Shoes. New York: Random House, 1986; Bantam, 1987 (paper).

Poetry

Just Give Me a Cool Drink of Water 'fore I Diiie. New York: Random House, 1971; Bantam, 1973 (paper).

Oh Pray My Wings Are Gonna Fit Me Well. New York: Random House, 1975; Bantam, 1977 (paper).

And Still I Rise. New York: Random House, 1978; Bantam, 1980 (paper).

Shaker, Why Don't You Sing? New York: Random House, 1983.

Now Sheba Sings the Song. Illustrated by Tom Feelings. New York: Dutton / Dial, 1987.

Interviews

"The AFI-Aspen Conference." *American Film* 5 (July / August 1980): 57–64.

Benson, C. "Out of the Cage and Still Singing: Interview with Maya Angelou." *Writers Digest,* January 1975, 18–19.

"The Black Scholar Interviews: Maya Angelou." *Black Scholar* 8, no. 4 (January / February 1977): 44–53.

Elliot, Jeffrey M. "Author Maya Angelou Raps." *Sepia* 26 (October 1977): 22–27.

———. "Maya Angelou: In Search of Self." *Negro History Bulletin* 40 (1979): 694–95.

"Maya Angelou: Interview." *Harper's Bazaar,* November 1972, 124.

Neubauer, Carol E. "An Interview with Maya Angelou." *Massachusetts Review* 28, no. 2 (1987): 286–92.

Oliver, Stephanie Stokes. "Maya Angelou: The Heart of a Woman." *Essence* 14 (May 1983): 112–14.

Paterson, Judith. "Interview: Maya Angelou." *Vogue* 172 (September 1982): 416–17, 420, 422.

Tate, Claudia. "Maya Angelou." In *Black Women Writers at Work,* I–II. New York: Continuum, 1983.

Weston, Carol, and Caroline Seebohm. "Talks with Two Singular Women." *House and Garden* 153 (November 1981): 128–29, 190, 192.

Bibliographical Guide

Cameron, Dee Birch. "A Maya Angelou Bibliography." *Bulletin of Bibliography* 36 (1979): 50–52.

SIDNEY BURRIS

An Empire of Poetry

Adam Smith, the eighteenth-century political economist best known for his treatise *The Wealth of Nations*, described in "Essay on Colonies" the peculiar problem that confronted Christopher Columbus as he sailed into the uncharted territories that would become known as the West Indies. These lush, heavily forested islands bore little resemblance to the Eastern world that Marco Polo had described, but Columbus persevered in his illusion, confident that he had made landfall in the vicinity of the Ganges river. Eventually Columbus realized that Oriental wealth had eluded him; but he could not elude Isabella. Attempting to satisfy his Queen, Columbus faced a problem of marketing and advertising, one of the earliest instances of the socio-cultural practice that dominates our own century. Over two hundred years ago Smith precisely described its Columbian appearance:

> But the countries which Columbus discovered either in this or in any of his subsequent voyages, had no resemblance to those which he had gone in quest of.... It was of importance to Columbus, however, that the countries which he had discovered, whatever they were, should be represented to the court of Spain as of very great consequence; and, in what constitutes the real riches of every country, the animal and vegetable productions of

From *The Southern Review* 27, no. 3. © 1991 by Sidney Burris.

the soil, there was at that time nothing which could well justify
such a representation of them.

Faced with an intractable dilemma, Columbus was forced to characterize the
island culture in the most alluring terms that he could conjure, terms that
neatly, prophetically encapsulate the informing structure of colonialist
thought: "They [the islanders] exhibit great affection to all," Columbus
wrote, "and always give much for little, content with very little or nothing in
return." According to Columbus' rhetoric of profit, these islands offered
good prospects for a sound investment.
 Derek Walcott's sprawling new poem, *Omeros*, attempts to provide for
his Caribbean homeland the definitive strengths and comforts of a national
narrative, and it is keenly aware of the ways in which the Columbian
perspective survives in the late twentieth century. Part of the poem's
herculean ambition lies in its effort to counter the fragmentary
representations encouraged by the colonial vision and emblematized briefly
but pointedly throughout the poem by the camera, that simplifying tool of
the tourist who comes to capture on film, as the saying goes, the exotic
images that have been judiciously disseminated to titillate his Columbian
wanderlust. The first tercet of the poem, in fact, finds Philoctete; one of the
main characters, smiling for the tourists, "who try taking / his soul eras," and
as the poem closes, Achille, another of its main characters, is raging "at being
misunderstood / by a camera."
 Imperial culture in the West Indies, which Walcott does not consider
an entirely pernicious one, practices an art of deception that can be
psychologically debilitating to its subjects, and it is a deception as old as
Columbus. Determined, often deceived by the argumentative strategies,
even the visual imagery, of colonial promotion, village life occasionally
fashions itself around this authorized narration, accepting in the process an
imposed history. In his essay "What the Twilight Says: An Overture"
(included in the 1970 collection *Dream on Monkey Mountain and Other Plays*),
Walcott addresses this problem:

> Every state sees its image in those forms which have the mass
> appeal of sport, seasonal and amateurish. Stamped on that image
> is the old colonial grimace of the laughing nigger, steelbandsman,
> carnival masker, calypsonian and limbo dancer. These popular
> artists are trapped in the State's concept of the folk form, for they
> preserve the colonial demeanour and threaten nothing.

Speaking of one of the villages in which much of the poem takes place,
Walcott develops this idea in *Omeros*, writing that the village "had become a

souvenir / of itself," a degrading accommodation that ultimately sanctions a subliteracy deemed quaint and a poverty deemed exotic, or photogenic":

... Its life adjusted to the lenses

of cameras that, perniciously elegiac,
took shots of passing things—Seven Seas and the dog
in the pharmacy's shade, every comic mistake
of spelling, like *In God We Troust* on a pirogue,
BLUE GENES, ARTLANTIC CITY, NO GABBAGE DUMPED HERE.
The village imitated the hotel brochure

with photogenic poverty, with atmosphere.

Walcott's poem immediately takes its place among those richly tessellated works of colonialism whose sense of cultural solidity is shot through with an array of diverse allegiances. But notes of severe skepticism and weariness now and again pervade the narrative, and even though they are largely resolved by the exuberant historiography that continuously engages the poet, they never entirely vanish from his score. The muscular persuasion of Walcott's line—overwhelming, exhausting—aptly reenacts, whenever it chooses to do so, the baroque *ennui* of island life.

A portion of the fundamental structure of this historiography derives from the two classical epics popularly attributed to Homer. In "What the Twilight Says," Walcott stated categorically that the writers of his generation were "assimilators" and that they "knew the literature of Empires, Greek, Roman, British, through their essential classics." Walcott, who grew up on St. Lucia, received a sound colonial education, and in interviews he has expressed his gratitude to the system that carried this literature to a small island in the Caribbean. Commentators on *Omeros*, then, will understandably busy themselves in tracking down the Homeric parallels in Walcott's poem—after Joyce, there are many practiced hands waiting in the wings—but this seems a particularly ill-fated approach because part of the poem's task, its attempt to recreate the original authenticity of Walcott's Caribbean culture, lies in its deliberate deflation of analogy.

Central to much contemporary Irish poetry, for example, the analogical imagination searches for similitude in the historical events that have given rise to other political structures in other countries, hoping to find there a conceptual basis for its own response to its own dilemma. Walcott, on the other hand, often sets up an obvious parallel between one of his characters and its Homeric equivalent only to punctuate it with a kind of slapstick disregard—a Joycean technique—as when Machaon, who heals Philoctete's wound in the *Odyssey*, becomes Ma Kilman, who heals Philoctete's ulcerous wound in *Omeros*. Or in Book Seven, the last book of the poem, the narrator cavalierly confesses to Omeros that he never read the *Odyssey* "all the way through." Finally, the narrator's ultimate pronouncement on Helen, who stands at the center of the narrative, arrives late in the poem and encapsulates the most trenchant commentary on the enticing but frustrating, even fruitless business of tracking down the Homeric parallel:

> ... Names are not oars
>
> that have to be laid side by side, nor are legends;
> slowly the foaming clouds have forgotten ours.
> You were never in Troy, and, between two Helens,
>
> yours is here and alive; their classic features
> were turned into silhouettes from the lightning bolt
> of a glance. These Helens are different creatures,
>
> one marble, one ebony. One unknots a belt
> of yellow cotton slowly from her shelving waist,
> one a cord of purple wool, the other one takes
>
> a bracelet of white cowries from a narrow wrist;
> one lies in a room with olive-eyed mosaics,
> another in a beach shack with its straw mattress....

Here is Walcott's deft revision of what Eliot identified as the "mythic method" in his review of Joyce's *Ulysses* (the work that in all likelihood will emerge as the most generous sponsor of *Omeros*). Instead of advocating the contemporaneity of mythic structures, thereby establishing the linear clarities of a tradition, Walcott gradually reveals the failure of such structures to represent adequately the multifarious tensions of his own culture, thereby establishing its sovereign integrity. The most persuasive approach to Walcott's mythic method would find, particularly in Helen, the gradual sloughing of the Homeric associations until, in the case of Helen, for example, she stands at the end of the poem, a figure, fully Caribbean, of ebony.

Walcott's deepest organizational structures, both formal and conceptual, lie buried in his developing sense of the theater, and like Yeats before him, his poetry and plays participate in a fecund network of cross-fertilization. Walcott published his first collection of verse in 1948, and, two years later, *Cry for a Leader*, one of his earliest dramatic pieces—there is still some question concerning the bibliography—was produced in St. Lucia. Since that time over thirty plays have been staged, and Walcott continues his involvement in the dramatic arts, a genre whose engaged social function Walcott acknowledged when he established the Trinidad Theatre Workshop in 1959. In "What the Twilight Says," Walcott speaks to the two ingredients that informed his colonial boyhood, two perspectives that, when combined, lead directly to the world of the theater:

> Colonials, we began with this malarial enervation: that nothing could ever be built among these rotting shacks, barefooted backyards and moulting shingles; that being poor, we already had the theater of our lives.... In that simple schizophrenic boyhood one could lead two lives: the interior life of poetry, the outward life of action and dialect.

Action and dialect balanced by a sustaining poetic sensibility, provided Walcott with the basis for his notion of a Caribbean theater that would legitimate the life and language of his people, and *Omeros* represents an elaborate extension of this project.

Over twenty-five characters, each varying considerably in importance, appear throughout this poem comprising seven books, sixty-four chapters, and roughly eight thousand lines. Achille and Philoctete, two fishermen, occupy the foreground of the narrative with Hector, another fisherman who abandoned his career to become a taxi driver and who "paid the penalty of giving up the sea" by losing his life in a wreck; the English Empire is represented by Major Dennis Plunkett, who fought with Montgomery's Eighth Army in North Africa and who, when we first meet him, is drinking a Guinness and wiping away "the rime of gold foam freckling his pensioned mustache / with a surf-curling tongue." His wife, Maud, is Irish in the old style, "framed forever in the last century," and her association with Glendalough in County Wicklow further connects her, as does her Christian name, with the Gonne family (Iseult lived at Laragh, a few miles away) and with Yeats's lyric "Stream and Sun at Glendalough." And Helen heavily influences the lives of these five characters, even when she is not present in the narrative; brooding over the events, giving them their particular cast and hue, she becomes the tutelary spirit of her home, "selling herself like the island, without any pain."

The poem tracks these characters through their daily lives, sometimes hinting at their varied relationships, sometimes describing baldly the arc of each biography. Monologues are unimportant to Walcott, unless we consider

the narrator's voice monologic, because the essence of his technique involves
the steady revelation of character through dialogue with other characters,
real or imagined, and this is a technique fundamental of course to
dramaturgy. But even dialogue for Walcott is fraught with social and
historical implication. The linguistic fragmentation of the Caribbean islands,
caused by the various colonizers imposing their native languages, has in turn
created the kind of cultural *insularismo* that has led each island group to
become, as David Lowenthal has argued in *Social and Cultural Pluralism in the
Caribbean*, "a museum in which archaic distinctions [are] preserved."
Walcott's verse marshals these fencing energies effectively, as in the
following passage when the narrator meets Major Plunkett in the bank soon
after Maud's funeral. The passage cries out to be staged:

> "Our wanderer's home, is he?"
>   I said: "For a while, sir,"
> too crisply, mentally snapping to attention,
> thumbs along trousers' seam, picking up his accent
>
> from a khaki order.
>   "Been travellin' a bit, what?"
> I forgot the melody of my own accent,
> but I knew I'd caught him, and he knew he'd been
>   caught,
>
> caught out in the class-war. It stirred my contempt.
> He knew the "what" was a farce, I knew it was not
> officer-quality, a strutting R.S.M.,
>
> Regimental Sarn't Major Plunkett, Retired.
> Not real colonial gentry, but spoke like
> them from the height of his pig farm, but I felt as tired
>
> as he looked. Still, he'd led us in Kipling's requiem.
> "Been doin' a spot of writing meself. Research."
> The "meself" his accommodation.

The deeply ceremonial nature of this confrontation, reminiscent of the
"tundish" episode in Joyce's *A Portrait of the Artist as a Young Man*, derives its
definitive energy from the spoken language's ability to demarcate cultural
hierarchies and political allegiances, and Walcott's insistence on situating
these verbal exchanges within heavily plotted contexts aligns one

predominant strain of this poem's structure with the renovative Caribbean theater that has engaged him for years.

Walcott's deepest hopes for the artistic enfranchisement of his community are bound up in his concept of a local theater that gradually assumes international acceptance. "The future of West Indian militancy," he wrote in "What the Twilight Says," "lies in art." These are large claims, but not unrealistic ones as long as the stage continues to define itself as resistive, as continually aligned against an indigenous diffidence that arises from the native inhabitants who are uncertain about their abilities to participate in the grand ritual of theater: "there was in the sullen ambition of the West Indian actor a fear that he lacked proper weapons, that his voice, colour and body were no match for the civilised concepts of theater." Walcott's new poem, with its deep fund of history inflected through its melodious and regional song, deploys in great abundance an array of proper weapons.

But the consoling grace of theater lies in the simple reconciliation of the falling curtain, in the sense that the social environment of the stage has reached its purposeful conclusion. However revolutionary the intention of the play, the last word of the last scene of the last act envisions more than an audience, it imagines a community, and it is from this deeply felt resolution that some of the most stirring scenes of *Omeros* derive. In Book Two, Plunkett and Achille, each moving through their radically different social spheres, pause to look at the night sky. The discursive dimension of language requires, of course, that we view these episodes sequentially, but Walcott has typically conceived the two vignettes dramatically, as if they took place on a split stage. As in the first scene of the fourth act in *Othello* where the Moor is allowed to overhear Cassio and Iago, with both parties in plain view of the audience, and with each party unaware of the other, so Plunkett "counted the stars / like buttons through the orchids," while Achille in another part of the village is viewing the same sky:

> From night-fishing he knew the necessary ones,
> the one that sparkled at dusk, and at dawn, the other.
>
> All in a night's work he saw them simply as twins.
> He knew others but would not call them by their given
> names, forcing a silvery web to link their designs,
>
> neither the Bear nor the Plough, to him there was heaven
> and earth and the sea, but Ursa or Plunkett Major,
> or the Archer aiming? He tried but could not distinguish

their pattern, nor call one Venus, nor even find the
pierced holes of Pisces, the dots named for the Fish;
he knew them as stars, they fitted his own design.

Although the divisive histories that stand behind these two misaligned
characters have resigned them to their hierarchical positions in Caribbean
culture, their passing engagement with the constellations, their beguiling
ignorance of their astronomical names, briefly unites them in their vision.
Theatrically conceived, such moments never entirely assuage the conflicts—
linguistic, social, political—that Walcott addresses in this poem, but they do
assert the prominence of the Caribbean's locale, its overwhelming
environment. It is in this alone that Walcott often locates, perhaps
paradoxically, much of the trenchant interrogation that sustains this national
narrative. In Chapter XXII, Walcott finds for Plunkett a peculiar attraction,
"something unexpected," in the colonial experience, and it adumbrates the
final words of the poem where the sea, like the two opposing histories
represented by the Major and Achille, is "still going on":

... The Plunketts quietly continued,

parades continued, cricket resumed, and the white feathers
of the proconsul's pith-helmet, and the brass and red
of the fire engines. Everything that was once theirs

was given to us now to ruin it as we chose,
but in the bugle of twilight also, something unexpected.
A government that made no difference to Philoctete,

to Achille. That did not buy a bottle of white kerosene
from Ma Kilman, a dusk that had no historical regret
for the fishermen beating mackerel into their seine,

only for Plunkett, in the pale orange glow of the wharf
reddening the vendors' mangoes, alchemizing the bananas
near the coal market, this town he had come to love.

Plunkett has become absorbed by the diurnal rhythms of life on the island,
but even more than his absorption, he relishes the colonizer's freedom, the
oddly liberating sense of displacement that strengthens him whenever he
realizes that he has fallen in love with a town whose welfare he can, if the
need arises, safely disregard. Now and again, uneasy truces are worked out in

Walcott's poem between the native inhabitants of the island and the governing class, but these are truces whose terms have historically misrepresented the magnificent biographies of islanders like Achille, Philoctete, and Helen. Recording the evidence to correct such a misrepresentation is one of the most fundamental purposes of *Omeros*, and in this endeavor Walcott has succeeded wildly, providing for his region a deeply assimilative work that immediately becomes essential to further assessments of the Caribbean literary tradition.

Seamus Heaney's new volume of verse, *Selected Poems: 1966–1987*, resonates with the same sort of regional authority—although differently inflected—that distinguishes Walcott's new poem. His selection, his implicit judgment of his own corpus, represents one of his most sustained acts of criticism to date, and his preservation in this collection of the early parish vision where he is king of banks and stones and every blooming thing tills the ground for the later, more cosmopolitan vision where, as Walcott has observed, Heaney has begun to use "the abstract noun as a whole territory." From the specificity of "Death of a Naturalist" to the allusive abstractions of "The Mud Vision," Heaney's selection showcases those poems where the inscrutable detail is forced to give up its secret, to reveal its larger significance. This technique, fundamental to Heaney's art, has yielded diverse and memorable results, but it is essential to realize that Heaney is attempting to loosen what he has called the "tight gag of place," and this strategy commands a myriad of perspectives, ranging from the affectionate whimsicality of "Anahorish" to the sustained keening of "Station Island." Heaney's is a poetry of intoned implication, and his insistent search for the means to manage this narrative method has indelibly, though often subtly, shaped his career.

The early verse has sustained the severest casualties. Gone from *Death of a Naturalist* (1966) are "The Early Purges," the poem that caused a national brouhaha when it was set for an examination in Ireland, complete with its salty phrase, "the scraggy, wee shits." "At a Potato Digging," heavily indebted to Kavanagh's "The Great Hunger," has been excluded, as has both "Trout," with its Hughesian evocation of tooth and claw, and "Churning Day," a rambunctious gathering of monosyllables that heralded the arrival of a poet listening to an old yet inventive metronome. The title pieces for the next two volumes, *Door into the Dark* (1969) and *Wintering Out* (1972), do not appear in this collection, but "Digging," the poem of epigraphic prominence in Heaney's career is where, one hopes, it ever shall be—at the head of the collection.

Heaney has salvaged only seven poems from each of the first two books, and those chosen strive to present a balance between what one of his earliest reviewers called his "mud-caked fingers" and the less provincially focused poems that seem now most valuable for their clairvoyant sense of Heaney's highly original achievement in *North* (1975). Heaney's carefully trained awareness of the natural metaphor, an awareness exercised, for example, in a poem like "Blackberry-Picking," is offset by the more ingrained sensibility that infuses a poem like "Relic of Memory" or "Bogland," poems where the poetic appropriation of an entire landscape begins to take on the coherence and strength of an ideology. Yet these represent the two strains of Heaney's art, the one insisting on the circumspect vision of the anecdote, the other on the broader, more adaptable wisdom of the parable, and they are entwined together throughout the volume.

In his third collection, *Wintering Out*, Heaney has been more generous with his admissions—there are thirteen poems here—but he has not been indiscriminate, and in this spartan environment "The Tollund Man" stands in highest relief, pointing inexorably toward the austere accomplishment of *North*. In "Exposure," the closing lyric of that volume, Heaney is living in the Republic, having abdicated his role as the poet of Northern Ireland who dared to live in Northern Ireland, and he has depicted himself in that poem as an "inner émigré ... escaped from the massacre." But this perspective of the domestic exile makes its first appearance in the closing section of "The Tollund Man":

> Something of his sad freedom
> As he rode the tumbril
> Should come to me, driving,
> Saying the names
>
> Tollund, Grauballe, Nebelgard,
> Watching the pointing hands
> Of country people,
> Not knowing their tongue...
>
> Out there in Jutland
> In the old man-killing parishes
> I will feel lost,
> Unhappy and at home.

Several poems in the original volume of *Wintering Out* softened the hard edges of alienation that riddle the final section of "The Tollund Man," but Heaney has excluded these often satisfied pieces—"Shore Woman" is a good example—and has chosen instead to point up his most dramatic line of development, the line that will culminate in the abstract and parablelike engagements of *The Haw Lantern* (1987).

Much has been made of Heaney's political sympathies, particularly of the ways in which they have engendered his own Irish *ars Poetica*. Typically, the early work has been less amenable to such bluntly political analysis, and the poetry from *North* and beyond more susceptible to it. Heaney's illuminating selections will do much to remedy this simplicity, suggesting the kind of persistent focus that shifts and sharpens according to the subjects traversed. Recently Heaney has addressed in his essays various topics that bear directly on our understanding of his sense of political literature, and they have been gathered together in his most recent collection of prose, *The Government of the Tongue* (1989). Of special importance is "The Impact of Translation," an essay that originally appeared in the *Yale Review* and addressed several issues worth considering when reading Heaney's selected edition.

Heaney argued in that essay that the translation of verse into English from the Eastern European countries has excited, as he wrote in the *Yale Review* version, "two main lines of reaction which might be characterized as 'envy' and 'identification.'" By "envy," Heaney means, as he explains later, a "kind of admiration" for those poets of the Soviet Union and Warsaw Pact countries who have suffered or died for the prosecution of their art. But he sees other, more substantial changes taking place:

> What translation has done over the last couple of decades is to introduce us not only to new literary traditions but also to link the new literary experience to a modern martyrology, a record of courage and sacrifice which elicits our unstinted admiration. So, subtly, with a kind of hangdog intimation of desertion, poets in English sense the locus of poetic greatness shifting away from their language.

Suddenly, Eliot's separation of the person who suffers and the mind that creates vanishes; suddenly, the old "impertinence" that Heaney had felt whenever he spoke of the "excessively vehement adjectives and nouns" in Wilfred Owen's poetry is ratified ("Nero, Chekhov's Cognac and a Knocker"). By comparison, American poets, submerged in their "permissive, centrally heated, grant-aided pluralism of fashions and schools," have begun to yearn, almost subliminally, for the extreme conditions in which the poetry of the Eastern Bloc writers has survived admirably. The reason for this yearning is not difficult to fathom. Artistic expression within a repressive, totalitarian regime mounts an eloquent argument for what Heaney characterizes as "the continuing efficacy of poetry itself as a necessary and a redemptive mode of being human."

Objections to Heaney's notion of a redemptive poetics pale in comparison to the gravity of his observation. We must be as clear as Heaney is committed. If there are redemptive modes of "being human," then clearly the pursuit of untrammeled artistic expression within a totalitarian regime satisfies the requirements for such redemption. The engagement of literature with the conditions that would extinguish it, the attempt to explore the psychological, emotional, and formal ramifications of such engagements, the ability to turn these issues into subject matters, thereby frustrating the most noxious aspects of censorship and silence—these issues more and more have engaged Heaney, and it is under this rubric that many of the selections for this volume seem to have been made. The volume, then, records Heaney's growing awareness of the nature of art's efficacy, an awareness that finds its first and clearest crystallization in the poems of *North*.

Heaney first encountered the bog people that populate *North* in a book on the subject by P. V. Glob. A genealogical recognition seized him as he viewed the photographs of the Iron Age corpses that had survived centuries in the preserving peat: "The Tollund Man," Heaney has said, "seemed like an ancestor almost, one of my old uncles, one of those moustached archaic faces you used to meet all over the Irish countryside." With its heightened awareness of the redemptive human sacrifices that organized Iron Age culture in northern Europe, *North* addresses many of the issues that would later engage Heaney in his prose. Of the thirteen poems that he has chosen to include, eight of them treat specifically the matter of Ireland's ritualistically violent prehistory, and several of these have become hallmarks of Heaney's accomplishment: "Bone Dreams," "Bog Queen," and "The Grauballe Man," to name three. The essential purpose of these and several other poems like them—a purpose that Heaney has freely acknowledged—concerns the construction of an analogy between the practice of human sacrifice during the Iron Age and the sectarian violence of contemporary Northern Ireland. The poetry of *North* grimly locates the barbarities of life in Northern Ireland within the fertility rituals of Ireland's distant ancestors; political violence becomes genetic in origin. Poetry of this sort, or something like it, successfully transforms the dull malaise of secular martyrdom, a condition hostile to traditional notions of the vigorous imagination, into subject matters for poetry. This, presumably, is a model of the imagination susceptible to the adjective "redemptive." This, certainly, is the model of the imagination that becomes more and more visible in Heaney's selection.

The "inner émigré" that appeared in the last poem of *North*, "the wood-kerne" who had escaped from the "massacre," closed Heaney's *Poems: 1965–1975*, but here in this new volume, we move swiftly into *Field Work* (1979), which begins with the voluptuous ritual of eating oysters and "toasting friendship, / Laying down a perfect memory / In the cool of thatch and crockery." The harsh doctrines of *North* yield to the sudden surprise of hedonistic pleasure, so much so that *Field Work* seems now in its new context to inaugurate the second stage of Heaney's development. But always in this volume Heaney insists on the irreconcilable tug of a loyal guilt that chastens, however slightly, the pleasures arising in a country plagued by violent partitions. Yet Heaney's early loyalties have lost their monolithic stridency, and their loss has given rise to a poetry more oblique in its announced intention, but more straightforward in confronting the essential issues of homeland and nationality. Here are two stanzas from "The Badgers":

> And to read even by carcasses
> the badgers have come back.
> One that grew notorious
> lay untouched in the roadside.
> Last night one had me braking
> but more in fear than in honour...
>
> How perilous is it to choose
> not to love the life we're shown?
> His sturdy dirty body
> and interloping grovel.
> The intelligence in his bone.
> The unquestionable houseboy's shoulders
> that could have been my own.

The anecdotal story line of "Singing School," the poem that ended *North*, is replaced in this poem by the less determined narrative of the parable. Renunciation of "the life we're shown," and the conviction that must attend such a renunciation, are the subject matters of this poem, and they have obvious implications for anyone who has moved from Belfast to Dublin. But just as significant are the two narrative innovations that structure the poem: the nearly Dickinsonian ability to reflect the essential quandary of the poem in a slanted representation of a badger; and the casual efficiency with which Heaney depicts a consciousness inured to violence by the single phrase "to read even by carcasses." Heaney develops here a shorthand of political engagement, but one that with its parablelike command of implication quickly transgresses its own limitations.

But Heaney never forgoes his gift for anecdote and his love of the densely textured line; now, however, one of his standard styles confronts its genealogy. The English resonances of blank verse have not gone unheeded by Heaney: "'I won't relapse / From this strange loneliness I've brought us to. / Dorothy and William—' She interrupts: / 'You're not going to compare us two ... ?'" But the comparison has been made; the 'faint note of duplicity, even of heresy, that attends Heaney's description of his retreat to the Republic finds its representative figures in Dorothy and William Wordsworth. Heaney has included two elegies in *Field Work*—the one for Robert Lowell is omitted—and "Casualty" records a sectarian murder, but the elegiac sensibility of the volume is assuaged by the kind of domesticities that resonate from the intensely personal vision of the sonnets. A burnished familiarity warms Heaney's lines now—the austerities of *North* have vanished—and they serve as the formal consolation framing the dire occasions that more and more engender his verse.

From the beginning of his career, however, Heaney has indulged the note of veneration, holding up for his praises everything from pottery crocks reeking milk to a chip of granite, and finally in *Station Island* Heaney comes to terms with what has been for him a reflexive response to his writing. There are consequences, perhaps even a price, affixed to his obsession, as evidenced in "Sandstone Keepsake"; here are the last two stanzas:

> Anyhow, there I was with the wet red stone
> in my hand, staring across at the watch-towers
> from my free state of image and allusion,
> swooped on, then dropped by trained binoculars:
>
> a silhouette not worth bothering about,
> out for the evening in scarf and waders
> and not about to set times wrong or right,
> stooping along, one of the venerators.

The freedom of the poet, if there is such a thing, lies in veneration, in teaching us how to praise, as Auden had it, but the trained binoculars—they seem almost canine—introduce the neurotic voyeurism of the state, and although Heaney is "stooping along" harmlessly, it is a posture that momentarily seems as crippled by the invasive observation of the guard as it does reflective of the hallowing curiosity of the poet.

The vignette of "Sandstone Keepsake"—the poet going about his seemingly useless business as the state looks on—returns, variously disguised, in many of the poems that Heaney has written during the past decade. Much of his work seems drawn by a subliminal gravitation toward the figure of the citizen and state, and none has so dramatized the protean relation between the two as "Station Island," Heaney's most ambitious poem to date. The twelve sections of the poem glitter with that particular clarity that Joseph Brodsky has found in Auden's "September 1, 1939" and memorably labeled the "lucidity of despair." Based on the penitential vigil of fasting and prayer that still constitutes the pilgrimage to Lough Derg in County Donegal, the poem seizes the occasion to confront the ghosts that have influenced the poet's life—the Dantean parallels are pronounced, acknowledged, and informing. This confrontation often elicits from the figure in question the voice of self-counsel and mediation, a technique that Heaney used in the short lyric "North" and "Making Strange." In "Station Island," this summoning of advice reaches a fever pitch, establishing as one of the dominant notes of the poem a purgative ritual of scrutiny.

The roster of advisors and their collective wisdom effectively locate the poem within a larger catechistic tradition. Here are the principal advisors and a snippet of their counsel: Simon Sweeney: "Stay clear of all processions!" William Carlton: "Remember everything and keep your head." A young priest: "And the god has, as they say, withdrawn." Heaney's second cousin: "You confused evasion and artistic tact." A monk: "Read poems as prayers ... and for your penance / translate me something by Juan de la Cruz." And most dramatically, James Joyce:

> " ... Your obligation
> is not discharged by any common rite.
> What you do you must do on your own.
>
> The main thing is to write
> for the joy of it. Cultivate a work-lust ...
> You've listened long enough. Now strike your note."

The second stanza in this quotation had begun in the original version with the admonitory phrase, "so get back in harness," and Heaney's decision to drop it from this selection does more than simply streamline the narrative; it allows the poem to end on a pronounced note of correction, even rehabilitation. Writing as redemption—as we saw earlier, Heaney's latest criticism has begun to explore the redemptive paradigm that he finds structuring the Eastern Bloc writers, and although he is vulnerable, as are all apologists for poetry, to the sober-minded political theorists who would see the dissident poet as a recalcitrant citizen who happens to write poetry, Heaney's argument for the essential efficacy of the art arrives at a time when

simplistic notions of poetic form too often pass for critical engagements of
intellectual integrity. His dogged insistence on posing the unwieldy question
of efficacy, a question that tolerant and well-conceived theories of poetic
form will certainly help to answer, refocuses much of the purposeless debate
that now constitutes many discussions about traditional poetics.

In Heaney's hands this debate has moved in an unexpected direction.
In *The Haw Lantern* (1987), there is evidence to suggest that, for Heaney,
patterns of social behavior cohere in the broad categorization of nouns and
verbs, and as he has written in "The Impact of Translation," abstractions and
"conceptually aerated adjectives" had long been part of a forbidden word
hoard, one that spoiled the vigorous particularity expected of poets who
matured under authoritative strictures against generality and didacticism. Yet
his admiration of Czeslaw Milosz is based on just this quality: "[Milosz]
seemed ... to know exactly what he wanted to say before he began to say it,
and indeed the poem aspired to deliver what we had once long ago been
assured it was not any poem's business to deliver: a message."

But abstraction for Heaney, particularly in *The Haw Lantern*, extends
beyond the framework of diction, ultimately positing a lyrical form that has,
as I have indicated, much in common with the parable (the last poem of the
original volume significantly does not appear in this selection—it is
accurately titled "The Riddle"). Heaney's anecdotal talents are much in
abundance here, and his sonnet sequence "Clearances" rivals the earlier
sequence in *Field Work*, but nothing prepares us for the encompassing
obliquities of a poem like "The Mud Vision" which, after numerous
readings, creates a generalized and abstract sense of torpor and indolence,
but does so by attending to the old particularities that are Heaney's stock-in-
trade:

> One day it was gone and the east gable
> Where its trembling corolla had balanced
> Was starkly a ruin again, with dandelions
> Blowing high up on the ledges, and moss
> That slumbered on through its increase. As cameras raked
> The site from every angle, experts
> Began their *post factum* jabber and all of us
> Crowded in tight for the big explanations.
> Just like that, we forgot that the vision was ours,
> Our one chance to know the incomparable
> And dive to a future. What might have been origin
> We dissipated in news....

A richly allusive idiom, slightly reminiscent of the memorable fore, bodings of early Auden and much of Muir, the poem maintains a more stolid demeanor than Auden's "The Watershed," for example, or Muir's "The Interrogation." Heaney's willingness to experiment with poetic strategies that might further extend the "efficacy" of his art has obviously brought him a measure of equanimity, and even though selections from *The Haw Lantern* regularly address the kinds of social conflicts that have engaged Heaney for most of his career, their resolutions now rest more in the fictive patterning of narrative than—to use one of Wilde's phrases—in "the violence of opinion." Heaney's new parable is fraught, with advice, however, a sure sign of his continuing engagement with a social poetics, but his new parable is prophetically intoned, an even surer sign that his legislations will go unacknowledged. The last section of "From the Canton of Expectation" italicizes two lines of epigraphic pith: "*What looks the strongest has outlived its term. / The future lies with what's affirmed from under.*" In their iconoclastic model of the imagination, these lines enthrone the autocratic changes that have invigorated and sped Heaney's development; in their quiet insistence on hope as the bellwether of emotions, they situate his work within the perfectly human community where its citizens still speak of redemption and efficacy.

YVONNE OCHILLO

Aspects of Alienation
in the Poetry of Derek Walcott

W hen Arnold proposed that poetry be a substitute for religion, he
conceived of the poetic genre as the artistic medium that is most likely to
produce an intimacy of communion between poet and reader. His premise
was that, in poetry, the writer "comes nearest to being able to utter the truth"
and to incite his reader, through the power of language, to participate
imaginatively in his experience of "the world made flesh".[1] The underlying
assumption is that the poet's work is "genuine". He writes not what is
necessarily pleasing but what he must for, as he engages in the creative act,
he is—as it were—a passive agent, freed from the intrusion of will or
personal desires, reacting to and interpreting a variety of experiences in the
light of their possibilities for human fulfilment. But it is this very sensitivity
to the pulses and impulses of life which induces his alienation.

Leon Gottfried claims that a number of Arnold's poems suggests his
"attempt to fly *from* the modern world *into* poetry rather than fuse the two".[2]
While valid arguments may be raised against Gottfried's idea of flying from,
Arnold himself recognized that coming to terms with ourselves, with what
we feel, does entail a kind of separation or alienation from societal demands
or expectations. In his "Lines Written in Kensington Gardens", he
apostrophizes the spiritual calm and insights that may accrue when one is
removed from the jangling discords of everyday life:

From *Journal of West Indian Literature* 3, no. 2 (September 1989). © 1989 by The University of
the West Indies.

Calm soul of all things! make it mine
To feel, amid the city's jar,
That there abides a peace of thine,
Man did not make, and cannot mar.

By detaching oneself from the world's multitudinousness, one may experience the soul of things—be it the potency of one's being or what Arnold calls "the true condition of humanity". And yet, this attitude of detachment does not necessitate a negation of the affairs of mankind but rather a passive stance, a kind of disinterestedness that affords one "the power to feel with others". This sense of detachment—an aspect of alienation—harks back to Rousseau and the Romantics (whose works Arnold read with eagerness), and includes not so much a conscious separation from or avoidance of the world as a freedom from its conflicts and anxieties. He believed that it is in these rare moments of serenity that the sensitive individual "becomes aware of his life's flow / And hears its winding murmur" (p. 275).[3] Ironically, then, while the poet's sensitivity to the "rush and glare" of life may trigger his alienation, distancing himself from his surroundings affords him new perceptions pertaining to the human condition.

The dividedness which Arnold experienced and which proliferates throughout his works is also characteristic of Derek Walcott, the man and poet. Arnold anticipated the alienation of modern man ravaged by "mental strife" and "divided aims" (pp. 342–3); Walcott describes himself as "the divided child"—a condition that later translates into the passionate plea of "Where shall I turn, divided to the vein?"[4] Both poets have been ever mindful of the sea. For Arnold, "The unplumbed, salt estranging sea" is a poignant symbol of human isolation (p. 125). Walcott also employs the metaphor of the "raging sea between each bed" as he pursues the implications of both insular and individual separateness. However, the intention here is not to compare both writers, but rather to use Arnold's treatment of the subject of alienation in his poetry as a springboard for the exploration of the same theme that marks Walcott's work. The term "alienation" is used here to denote a phenomenon of estrangement, isolation, separation (sometimes treasured), even withdrawal: any condition in which the individual is alienated from some "other", be that "other" himself, his vision of life, or the world in which he lives. Yet, in discussing the various dimensions of alienation in Walcott's poetry, one must move beyond Arnold and consider Walcott's socio-cultural background, which inevitably marked him with a sense of rootlessness or homelessness.

In "In A Green Night",[5] in a volume of that name, Walcott lays before us a mind that "enspheres all circumstance", a mental attitude that prepares us for the variegated moods of his poetry. In "Allegre", a poem in this volume, he celebrates the dawn. We hear:

Some mornings are as full of elation
As these pigeons crossing the hill slopes,
Silver as they veer in sunlight and white
On the warm blue shadows of the range.

(p. 58)

With a Romantic's eye for detail, Walcott depicts scenes that bubble with the vitality of youth, and the freshness and buoyancy of Nature:

... the slopes of the forest this sunrise
Are thick with blue haze, as the colour of
The woodsmoke from the first workman's fire
A morning for wild bees and briersmoke,
For hands cupped to boys' mouths, the holloa
Of their cries in the cup of the valley.

The pastoral scene that is depicted here is reminiscent of Wordsworth's "Tintern Abbey". Just as Wordsworth was prompted to look beyond the external landscape, Walcott, too, falls into a meditative mood which generates more serious thoughts about the whole panorama of West Indian history:

No temples, yet the fruits of intelligence
No roots, yet the flowers of identity.

Implicit reference is made to the rootlessness of West Indians, to their lack of cultural traditions; and so in spite of his previous elation, the poet concludes that "to find the true self is still arduous". Hence his search for self-affirmation contributes to his alienation. By the same token, it is this unusual dimension of his genial spirit that nurtures his susceptibility to impressions and, ironically, allows him to transcend his fragmentation as he engages in the creative act.

It is in a poem with as subtle a title as "Mass Man"[6] that Walcott projects the almost alienated temper of the poet. The setting is a town that rocks with the frenzied merriment of Carnival. Every activity is symptomatic of the playful spirits of the revellers as they assume their various guises. There, a black clerk growls from "a great lion's head clouded with mange". Next, what appears to be a "goldwired peacock" is really a mechanical contraption; then there is Boysie's apparatus, "two golden mangoes bubbling for breastplates, barges / like Cleopatra down her river, making style" (p. 31).

The persona's frantic interjections of "what metaphors! what coruscating, mincing fantasies!" transport us to the scene of the activity. Caught up in the fever of their excitement, the maskers find it odd that the onlooker can remain calm: "Join us", they shout, "O God, child you can't dance?" For the West Indian reader, the poet's use of popular idioms such as "making style" and "child, you can't dance?" evokes the reality of the scene. Yet he remains aloof—and justifiably so for it is his very detachment that gives him insight into the simulacrum of the parade, and enables him to pierce through it to discover the discrepancy between what *seems* and what really *is*:

> But I am dancing, look, from an old gibbet
> my bull-whipped body swings, a metronome!
> Like a fruit-bat dropped in the silk-cotton's shade,
> my mania, my mania is a terrible calm.
>
> (p. 31)

Emphasized here is the contemplative activity of the poet. He cannot scorn society because he is of society, sharing with the revellers a common heritage—"an old gibbet" and a "bull-whipped body". But as poet he must remain detached, the better to record and interpret the panorama of life. He reminds the revellers of the significance of his stance:

> Upon your penitential morning,
> some skull must rub its memory with ashes,
> some mind must squat down bowling in your dust,
> some hand must crawl and recollect your rubbish,
> someone must write your poems.
>
> (p. 31)

In *Another Life*,[7] Walcott intimates that society needs its spots of time captured and enshrined against the ravages of time—a function that is primarily suited to the artist than the historian. Why? Such a one must have the sensitivity, even the elemental creativity, of

> a child without history, without knowledge of its pre-world,
> only the knowledge of water runnelling rocks...
> that child who puts the shell howl to his ear

hears nothing, hears everything
that the historian cannot hear...

(p. 136)

The poet, then, must tolerate his alienation. And yet, that terrible calm that is a necessary prerequisite for the creative act is also the poet's mania, for as he engages in his quest for a better understanding of the world, no human voice reaches him. The inference is that as attractive as isolation may seem, it is jeopardizing, because it creates chasms between its creator and the world beyond that of art. Tennyson had to choose between his palace of art and the imperfect human world. And Walcott, too, realized that the world of art is no substitute for the real world because, in a sense, the poet is equally a stranger in the universe he creates.

The nature of the poet's existence is also implied in "The Castaway". The castaway's separation from society does invite a comparison with the lonely existence of the poet. Refusing to march to the music of society, the castaway becomes an alien. Solitude excites his imagination as he contemplates the varied phenomena of life:

Pleasures of an old man
. . . .
In the sun, the dog faeces
Crusts, whitens like coral.

(p. 16)

Solitude gives him power. Like Alexander Selkirk's exile, he is monarch of all he surveys. He is "godlike". But solitude underscores his mortality, even his kinship with humanity:

We end in earth, from earth began.
In our own entrails, genesis.

(p. 16)

The poet, like the castaway, cannot find fulfilment in isolation. Alienated from humanity, his "creative / powers weaken, rot". They nurture not life-giving images, but a "babel of sea lice, sandfly and maggot". Hence the poet, like the castaway, craves communion with things human:

The starved eye devours the seascape for the morsel
Of a sail.

. . . .
The horizon threads it infinitely.

(p. 16)

If the poet's inherent alienation sustains his poetic sensibility, it also increases his susceptibility to social and cultural alienation. According to Lloyd Brown, "the very modes of perception which he owes to isolation separate the castaway from others. Hence not only does isolation engender perception, but, in turn, perception intensifies one's aloneness".[8] As the poet fabricates his vision, he gives us a broad sweep of life, and provides us with a glimpse of the relationships between truth and reality. He envisions man in time with his potentials and limitations, a vision which promotes our sense of historicity, and enables us to reconcile us to ourselves. The poet is thus likely to reprehend the modern-day values which have degraded man to a cash nexus, and Walcott sometimes writes as though the modern world makes alienation man's destiny.

The theme of the writer in exile, along with the sense of alienation that such a condition engenders, is treated in "Forest of Europe", a poem dedicated to Joseph Brodsky, Russian exile and poet. The poem opens with a scene in winter that is evocative of the loneliness of the things of Nature:

> The last leaves fell like notes from a piano
> and left their ovals echoing in the ear;
> with gawky music stands, the winter forest
> looks like an empty orchestra, its lines
> ruled on these scattered manuscripts of snow
>
> (p. 87)

The scene of desolation that marks the surroundings is also present in man. Brodsky recites lines of poetry as if to forge a link with the poet who gave them birth—"the wintry breath / of lines from Mandelstam" (p. 87). But Brodsky's activity merely serves to underscore the precarious condition of the writer, since Osip Mandelstam was himself forced into exile under the Stalin regime. Walcott warns, however, that nowhere is there really a safe haven for the poet, since the United States, too, contains its

> ... Gulag Archipelago
> under this ice, where the salt, mineral spring
> of the long Trail of Tears runnels these plains.
>
> (p. 88)

Walcott is specifically referring to the elimination of Indians, to the horrors of slavery, to those dark periods of America's history when human beings were sacrificed for causes. The implication is that in any society which debases humanity, the poet will inevitably experience isolation—physical perhaps, but ultimately spiritual—be he in Europe, America or the Caribbean. Concomitantly, his consciousness of his rejection heightens his sense of alienation:

> ... watching the evening river mint
> its sovereigns stamped with power, not with poets
>
> (p. 89)

The juxtaposition of "power" and "poets" stimulates the intellect by way of the ear for, ironically, it is the consonant pattern of both disyllables which serves to establish their contrast—"power" becomes the antinomy of "poet". Yet the poet feels a compulsion to create, confident that his poetry will be alive even "when systems have decayed".

It is in this poem that Walcott unequivocally underscores the painstaking demands of the artistic process—a lonely and agonizing one which involves ardent concentration and a surrender of the self. The skill exacted from the artist is vividly described. In spite of his predicament, the artist seeks to communicate his vision as he

> ... circles, chewing the one phrase
> whose music will last longer than the leaves,
> whose condensation is the marble sweat
> of angels' foreheads, which will never dry
>
> (p. 89)

Paradoxically, however, the poetic craft involves consciousness at its very highest because of the arduous labour the finished product demands:

> ... every
> metaphor shuddered him [Mandelstam] with ague,
> each vowel heavier than a boundary stone
>
> (p. 90)

In an article "Poetry—Enormously Complicated Art",[9] Walcott delineates the seriousness of the craftsmanship that is a prerequisite of great poetry. He visualizes the poet as setting out on a quest, "charting the subconscious, taking the temperature of the senses and any number of undefined feelings, hesitations and memories all disciplined by the logic of the imagination". The poet's engagement with mining words, fashioning and refashioning metaphors, is a necessary activity if his product, the poem, is to be a composite of what Coleridge defines as "the best words in the best order". For while Coleridge adhered to the Romantic theory of the spontaneity of poetic activity, he sought in his poems to unite passion and will, spontaneous impulse and voluntary purpose. T. S. Eliot argues that the poet must abandon himself completely to his task. He affirms the poetic act to be "a concentration, and a new thing resulting from the concentration, of a very great number of experiences which to the practical and active person would not seem to be experiences at all". While he agrees that the poet does induce this meditative act, he concedes that "there is a great deal in the writing of poetry which must be conscious and deliberate".[10]

The poet is thus engaged in a sacrificial act. And yet, he cannot lay claim to bringing about any significant changes. True, his poetry may serve as a beacon for those who follow, even as years after his death Mandelstam's poetry became, for Walcott and for Brodsky, "a fire whose glow / warms our hands". But while Walcott seeks to be reconciled to the idea that his poetry, however unproductive, may have given utterance to a "people's grief", his discontent—even anger—with society's attitudes towards the poet and his work is evident.

It is the sense of loneliness, then, which is a corollary of alienation, that induces in the poet a desire to escape. In "Castiliane", Walcott depicts an environment haunted by

> ... flies, molasses, donkey carts,
> Above the clash of voices from the pier
> Of stevedores gambling over tepid beer
>
> (p. 9)

The sordidness disturbs him. Consequently, he takes flight into the ornate period of the past as is manifested by the remnants of Spanish culture. But his escape is ephemeral, for the substantial nature of the wraith that graces that period is called into question:

> ... Why is that haunted face,
> Dim as an antique faun's, fin de siècle style,
> Imprisoned in the grillwork's leafless green?
>
> (p. 9)

Introspection sets in, and the poet realizes that were his wraith durable, it would not necessarily insulate him from reality. What if she, too, father-like, were conditioned to jeer "at poets with a goldtoothed curse"? The persona concludes that societal values are predisposed towards the material, and although he does not lose faith in the "spirit" of the wraith, his recognition that "the future is in cheap enamel wares" affords cause for neither solace nor hope.

But the persona incriminates neither the hawker nor the bar owners for the sterility of his environment. Led by rulers too confused to rule, the masses lack a proper sense of direction. Walcott affirms that the ordinary people are not the enemy of the artist, not their "crude aesthetic ... refined and orchestrated, but ... those who had elected themselves as protectors of the people ... who cried out that black was beautiful ... without explaining what they meant by beauty."[11]

Art is essentially a mirror of life because it is out of his experiences that the artist speaks. In other words, his art reflects his spiritual, cultural and socio-political milieu, and can legitimately be regarded as a barometer by which the temper of his society may be gauged. In fact, one is likely to sympathize with the view that the artistic creation which is void of human concern is worthless, for how can a thing of beauty run counter to the well-being of man? Indeed, it is his concern for humanity that often constrains the poet to write. And Walcott, at home, finds much that is uncongenial and alienating as he surveys the larger Caribbean scene.

In "Parades, Parades", a poem that is ostensibly political, the focus is on events in Trinidad but the allusions in the poem make the situation applicable to any colonized people. The repetition and intonation of the title "Parades, Parades" evoke a sense of the hullabaloo, the pomp and ceremony that are about to be displayed. But the most cursory reading of the poem reveals the superficiality of the parade: it features a regression, even betrayal, and the shout of excitement that the title seemed initially to convey, manifests a cry of desperation.

Ironically, "Parades, Parades" conjures up images of the past, not with nostalgia but disgust. Nothing new is ventured. New horizons beckon but the politicians travel the same outworn paths without any awareness of their charlatanism,

> without imagination, circling
> the same sombre garden.

(p. 72)

Nothing can accrue from their march, neither milk nor honey nor manna, not even plain water to quench their people's thirst, because they follow beaten paths. In the garden, the fountain is dry, with the "gri-gri palms desiccating / dung pods like goats". Too unimaginative to lead, the politicians ape their models who were themselves buffoons. Thus, what ought to be a celebration of independence is essentially a puppet show of reactionaries.

The poet then follows with a searing attack on Caribbean leaders. If their pageantry contents them, what of its effects on young, unmarked minds, exposed to the impressions of the parade? If their uniforms symbolize independence, then why are the children's eyes

> bewildered and shy,
> why do they widen in terror
> of the pride drummed into their minds?
>
> (p. 72)

The rhetorical nature of the question exacerbates the children's condition. Uniforms can be dictated, but not so people's eyes. The preposterousness of the children's situation is further underscored by a comparison between the "independent" leaders and the colonial masters they mimic. Perhaps distance lent to colonial rule a certain amount of credibility. But here reasons are not important. That conditions in the Caribbean can provoke a Caribbean writer to react negatively to independence induces another question that Aidoo asks of Ghana: "What then does independence mean?"[12] But even the question is redundant, for once the poet—through the use of the conversational tone—transports us to the scene, we too witness the inanity of the puppets' acts:

> Here he comes now, here he comes!
> Papal Papal with his crowd...
>
> (p. 73)

The electorate act out their part; "Papa" likes hosannas, so they let them ring. But the look on their faces, as in the eyes of the children, are the real aspects of the parade.

Walcott seems to suggest that the new consciousness, whether its origins were national or ethnic, did not promote the flowering of humanity. Rather, it alienated people from their very selves by obstructing human freedom and dignity. For an individual can claim true freedom only when he joins in a common purpose that will afford him, like other individuals, spiritual fulfilment. But a common purpose necessitates common values. Where these are wanting, chaos sets in and there can be neither group nor individual fulfilment. "Parades, Parades" is thus a scathing commentary on socio-political situations in countries like those of the Caribbean where politicians have succumbed to large-scale corruption and have thereby estranged themselves from those they represent. It is not surprising that he wrote the poem "The Swamp", a physical feature of the islands but also an adverse symbol of the conditions which prevail there.

Little wonder that Walcott seems at times to be homeless at home. The sense of identity which home should foster he never really found. In "Homecoming: Anse la Raye", expectations are soured when the poet confronts the images similar to those of "The Swamp". One finds none of the hallowed charms that should grace the exile's return, only symbols of worsening times:

> ... sugar-headed children race
> whose starved, pot-bellied children race
> pelting up from the shallows
>
> . . . .
>
> They swarm like flies
> round your heart's sore
>
> (p. 33)

And sore indeed is the heart when cherished dreams are shattered, when "there are homecomings without home". The implication is that home has degenerated into an alien shore, and so homecoming has brought not the ecstasy kindled by memory but emptiness, a sense of nothingness. Disillusioned and dazed, he conjures up images of desolation in the midst of which nods the fisherman "with a politician's / ignorant, sweet smile". The slow, lumbering movements of the lines, with their heavily-accented syllables, underscore their significance, for when the fisherman-politician "nods" arrogantly to the scene, the poet seems to be inviting our reflections on the accountability of West Indian politicians for the disintegrating conditions of the islands.

Social scientists assert that alienation is generic to colonized peoples because they are pursued by what Jan Carew calls "Shadows of the Past". The caste or class system engenders societal divisions and, further, there is cultural alienation, a situation in which the individual is torn between two cultures. While he is intellectually drawn to those values which he acquires from the colonized, he is emotionally drawn to the life of the masses in which run his roots.

The experience of Walcott himself is a classic example of this condition. For in St Lucia, as in other islands, children of the enlightened were not encouraged to associate with the activities of the masses. In "What The Twilight Says", Walcott records a moving account of the alienation one experiences when one's values collide:

> ... two pale children staring from their upstairs window, wanting
> to march with that ragged barefoot crowd, but who could not

because they were not black and poor, until for one of them ...
that *difference* became a sadness, that sadness rage, and that
longing to share their lives ambition.[13]

Many have experienced this divided self, this pull between their
intellectual and emotional selves. But Walcott's alienation is further
compounded by his obsession with his mixed ancestry—his paternal and
maternal grandfathers were both white. In "A Far Cry From Africa", he asks:

I who am poisoned with the blood of both,
Where shall I turn, divided to the vein?

(p. 18)

His mixed ancestry increased his self-consciousness about racial issues
and recurrently we see him standing in the middle as if reluctant to take
sides.

Izevbaye argues that Walcott's psychic division is not just a division
between two cultures, "but mainly a division between an inner and a literary
experience, and an experience of reality".[14] However, he sees this division as
being resolved through the poet's actual experience of "belonging to a
particular place and time". Perhaps it was Walcott's ability to resolve
differences that enabled him to respond soberly to radical movements of
black consciousness: "There are certain values here", he says, "that regardless
of the violence of the revolution we need to preserve if we want the society
to work."[15]

The possibilities which so many West Indians visualized as a hallmark
of independence still remain a dream, for the activities of post-colonial
leaders have largely served to exacerbate those conditions which militate
against the achievement of justice, of liberation in its true sense, of selfhood.
The resultant fragmentation experienced by wakeful minds is typified by
Derek Walcott, whose work reflects the strivings, the anxieties of his people,
and indeed his own, since he is a part of that society. And yet he stands apart
because as artist, he is too sensitive to dance to the discordant music played
by politicians. Ironically, however, it is this detachment which permits him to
contemplate life and to yield, through his art, a vision that may impose order
and beauty on the surrounding chaos.

NOTES

1.   "The Study of Poetry", *Norton Anthology of English Literature II* (New
     York: Norton, 1979), pp. 1444–1466.

2.   *Matthew Arnold and the Romantics* (London, 1963), p. 21. His italics.

3.   References to Arnold's poems are from Kenneth Allott, ed., *The Poems of Matthew Arnold* (London: Longman, 1965).

4.   *In a Green Night* (London: Jonathan Cape, 1962), p. 18.

5.   *In A Green Night*, p. 73.

6.   Wayne Brown, ed., *Selected Poetry* (London: Heinemann, 1981), p. 31. All other poems discussed in this paper, except otherwise indicated, are from this volume.

7.   *Another Life* (New York: Farrar, Straus & Giroux, 1973).

8.   Lloyd Brown, "The Isolated Self in West Indian Literature", *Caribbean Quarterly* 23 (June–September 1977), p. 58.

9.   "Poetry—Enormously Complicated Art", *Trinidad Guardian*, June 19, 1962.

10. "Tradition and The Individual Talent", in *Norton Anthology of American Literature II* (New York: Norton, 1979), p. 1231.

11. "What the Twilight Says" in *Dream on Monkey Mountain and Other Plays* (New York: Farrar, Straus & Giroux, 1970), pp. 34–35.

12. See Aima Aidoo, *No Sweetness Here* (London: Longman, 1970).

13. "What the Twilight Says", p. 2.

14. D. S. Izevbaye, "The Exile and the Prodigal", *Caribbean Quarterly*, 26 (March–June 1980), p. 82.

15. See Raoul Pantin, "Any Revolution Based on Race is Suicidal", *Caribbean Contact*, 1 (August 1973), p. 14.

STEVEN MEYER

Jay Wright: Transfigurations: Collected Poems

J ay Wright is an unsung wonder of contemporary American poetry. To be sure, he has received some choice acknowledgments: he's been a MacArthur Fellow, a Guggenheim Fellow, and a Hodder Fellow, as well as the recipient of awards from the Ingram-Merrill Foundation, the Lannan Foundation, and the American Academy and Institute of Arts and Letters. Still, each of his seven previous volumes has quickly gone out of print or, due to the obscurity of the press, been all but impossible to find. As a result, Wright has barely registered with the broader poetry audience. If this means that most readers will experience *Transfigurations* as a first book, then *what* a first book— displaying both the proverbial promise and the astonishing fulfillment of that promise.

Jay Wright has been writing *Transfigurations* for more than thirty years. Volumes of collected poems often force together earlier collections which cohere only because they were written by the same person, not because of any internal logic. With Wright, things are very different. In 1983—after he had published five of the eight volumes included here—Wright said that he had initially conceived of a series of volumes that would take the dynamic form of "an octave progression." Having completed the first five volumes, however, he realized that what he actually had was "a dominant one" and that he was "working toward the tonic in a new progression." Translated, this

---

From *The Boston Review* (April/May 2002). © 2002 by *The Boston Review*.

means that Wright's first book, *The Homecoming Singer*, set the basic tone for his eight-volume sequence; that the fifth volume, *The Double Invention of Komo*, stands in an especially close relationship to the first; and that the eighth volume, *Transformations*, which collects thirty-three new poems, returns at a higher pitch to the matter initially introduced by the tonic (even as, in conjunction with volumes six and seven of the sequence, *Elaine's Book* and *Boleros*, it resolves tensions introduced by the dominant).

Wright recalls having "discovered the pattern" of *The Homecoming Singer* "almost *a posteriori*. I had, as I looked at it, the record of my developing black African-American life in the United States, but I also saw that I had the beginning of forms to express lives that transcended that particular life." From early to late, Wright has been concerned to express "black people acting in history." As he put it memorably in "The Albuquerque Graveyard," in his second volume, *Soothsayers and Omens*,

> I am going back
> to the Black limbo,
> an unwritten history
> of our own tensions.
> The dead lie here
> in a hierarchy of small defeats.

These defeats ("small") match the triumphs ("small") he celebrated in "Wednesday Night Prayer Meeting," the poem that opened *The Homecoming Singer* and consequently opens *Transfigurations*, articulating

> the uncompromising
> need of old black men and women,
> who know that pain is what
> you carry in the mind,
> in the solemn memory of small triumphs,
> that you get, here,
> as the master of your pain.

So uncompromising are these adepts of "the insoluble / mysteries of being black / and sinned against, black / and sinning in the compliant cities," that Christ himself, who joins them, writhing "as if he would be black," is ignored. "He stands up to sing, / but a young girl, / getting up from the mourner's bench, / tosses her head in a wail." The poem concludes "This is the end of the night," and thus opens the way for the persistent questing of the poems still to come:

and he has not come there yet,
has not made it into the stillness
of himself, or the flagrant uncertainty
of all these other singers.
They have taken his strangeness,
and given it back, the way a lover
will return the rings and letters
of a lover who hurts him.
They have closed their night
with what certainty they could,
unwilling to exchange their freedom for a god.

They are unwilling, that is, to compromise the small triumphs of self-mastery, the freedom that inheres in "the small, / imperceptible act" ("Benjamin Banneker Helps to Build a City"), for the sake of a "god / who chains us to this place"—a master enslaved to himself, "pitiable," "without grace, / without the sense of that small / beginning of movement, / where even the god / becomes another and not himself, / himself and not another." In place of *the* Transfiguration on Mount Tabor, we are presented, as we progress across Wright's octave, with many, many *transfigurations*, as Wright seeks to define in his poetry "a new and capable personality at home in the transformative and transformed world."

This last remark, closing his 1987 manifesto, "Desire's Design, Vision's Resonance: Black Poetry's Ritual and Historical Voice," designates the task that distinguishes "Afro-American poetry" from its African counterpart, even as "black experience in the Americas ... challenges the African world to examine itself." Although Wright meticulously reconstructs the initiation ceremonies of the Komo cult among the Bambara people of West Africa in *The Double Invention of Komo*, he does not do so in the spirit of returning to some putative origin. On the contrary, he aims to contribute to a New World "redefinition of the person" through the "formal juxtaposition" of "African, European, and American ... voices and persons" in the book-length poem.[1] Poetry's "extreme manipulative consciousness" fits this task of redefinition: because it "handles its 'facts'" with a certain "disdain" and "its spiritual domain" with a degree of "critical detachment," poetry is especially well suited to creating the sort of "awareness of differing and seemingly incompatible relationships" demanded by such redefinition, or transfiguration.

As Wright suggests, a pretty fair "record of [his] developing black African-American life in the United States" may be gleaned from the poems he chose to include in *The Homecoming Singer*. Born in Albuquerque, he was raised by guardians—see "The Hunting Trip Cook" as well as "The Faithful

One" in *Soothsayers and Omens*—after his parents separated when he was three years old. At fourteen, he joined his father (who was light-skinned enough to pass for white) in the "naval city" of San Pedro, California. (See "Jason's One Command" and "A Non-Birthday Poem for my Father.") Poems about summer and winter jobs ("The Fisherman's Fiesta," "Two House Painters Take Stock of the Fog," "Track Cleaning") are concerned with a young man's growing awareness of what it means to be black in the United States at mid-century, as, more obviously, are "W.E.B. Du Bois at Harvard" and "Crispus Attucks." So, too, the poems about Mexico, where Wright taught in 1964 ("You come, black and bilingual, / to a passage of feeling, / to a hall of remembered tones, / to the acrylic colors of your own death"), about visiting New Hampshire ("I amble in this New England reticence, / cocksure of my blackness, / unsure of just how white / and afraid my neighbors are"), or about living in New York—where he moved in 1961 after three years in the army and three more as an older undergraduate at Berkeley ("I wait, here near the ocean, for the north wind, / and the waves breaking up on ships. / At this point, the slave ships would dock, / creeping up the shoreline, / with their bloody cargo intact ...").

In his stunningly intransigent "Sketch for an Aesthetic Project," Wright says: "I have made a log for passage, / out there, where some still live, / and pluck my bones. / There are parchments of blood / sunk where I cannot walk. / But when there is silence here, / I hear a mythic shriek." In these lines, Wright sketches the shape of the "aesthetic project" he hears reverberating in that shriek. Call it *Transfigurations:* a work of neither fixed ends nor established beginnings, but of "passage" and "beginning again," as the title of *The Homecoming Singer*'s final poem has it. If the volumes collected in *Transfigurations* proceed rhythmically by means of rigorous renewals, in the end they form an astonishing New World epic—or anti-epic, since this is no tale of founding but of re-founding, of continuing re-creation, of creative juxtaposition. The victor may get the spoils, but the vanquished don't vanish. This multicultural engine—which Wright characterized in the early 1980s as "the fundamental process of human history"—has always been at work, even in the most isolated communities, but its recognition has been broadly resisted. For Wright (and he is surely not alone in this impression) the fact of an ever-widening community of humankind required the peculiar dynamics of the New World in order to be articulated and acknowledged. For this reason, "the African world," for instance, is challenged to self-examination by black experience in the Americas; and for this reason, *Transfigurations* may be viewed as a work of genuinely epic proportions and ambitions, albeit with a very different sort of hero: that "new and capable personality at home in the transformative and transformed world," seeking to understand what Wright refers to in the book-length poem *Dimensions of History* as "our life among ourselves."

Wright's progressive definition of this new personality may be charted in a series of poems that transfigure his basic device of "beginning again" in the terms and imagery of baptism. These include both "The Baptism" and "Baptism in the Lead Avenue Ditch" in his first two volumes, followed by the remarkable "MacIntyre, the Captain and the Saints" in *Explications/ Interpretations*, in which Wright *elects* a Scottish heritage for himself; by "Landscapes: The Physical Dimension," suturing Mexico and the United States with Venezuela, Colombia, and Panama, in *Dimensions of History*; by "The Opening of the Ceremony / the Coming Out of Komo" ("I will be written in water, / measured in my body's curative syntax"); by "The Lake in Central Park" in *Elaine's Book* ("It should have a woman's name"); by "17 / [Melpomene ba]" in *Boleros* ("When, tonight, under a new moon, / the soul's calendar turns another page, / I will go down, ash laden, and walk / the transforming light of Banaras," the great North India pilgrimage destination on the Ganges); and, in *Transformations*, by "The Anti-Fabliau of Saturnino Orestes 'Minnie' Miñoso" ("I had heard reports of a sanctified / woman in the town, one who could provide / hope in a dry season ... / But how could I bring myself to confide / in one who would bathe me in a flood tide / of improprieties ...").

Wright has always been exceptionally attentive to the formal possibilities of poetry, but he usually avoids traditional forms of versification. In *Transformations*, however, he embraces a broad range of rhyme and syllabic schemes. There are seguidillas and zejels, redondillas and sonnets, sextillas, dactylic hexameter, and a villancico to match the earlier "Villancico" in *Dimensions of History*, as well as the unique transformations that he works on a Keats ode ("The Navigation of Absences: An Ode on Method"), on the Spenserian stanza ("Intuition: Figure and Act"), on Donne's "Nocturnal upon St. Lucy's Day" ("Love's Augustine or, What's Done is Donne"), on blues rhythm ("The Healing Improvisation of Hair"), on both the Provençal retroencha ("The Hieroglyph of Irrational Force") and the dansa Provençal ("Lichens and Oranges"), on the busy bees of Oulipo, the late-twentieth-century "workshop of potential literature" ("Coda V"), and on Thelonious Monk ("Coda VI"). These are *all* remarkable works, but no less remarkable is the way that Wright, by placing them at the close of so substantial a volume of intricate formal patterning, enables his readers to experience these formal schemes as *chosen* rather than imposed, emergent rather than imitated.

In 1969 Wright published an article in *Sports Illustrated* on baseball, the "diamond-bright art form." Partly autobiographical—Wright played minor-league ball in the St. Louis Cardinals organization after he graduated from high school—and partly analytic, the article ends with a commentary on a third-strike pitch to a close friend who was then home-run champion of the Mexican league:

> That pitch, more than any other, bothered me. It was such a blatant challenge, such a perverse reward for 15 years.... And at that moment I could think of baseball as the realization, the summit of a masculine esthetic—an esthetic, which, as in the highest art, summarizes a man's life, sets him in a historical context where he measures himself against the highest achievement and where he feels that he is perpetuating the spirit of the best of his chosen work. Aggressive, at times mean, at times petty and foolish, the ballplayer still tries to transcend, by the perfection of his craft, the limitations that are inherent in it, and in himself.... Where we end is in the seemingly absurd realization that, for a good many, the game looks like life.... Our Yankee scout would say that is the American way. I would say it is something more, that baseball offers the ballplayer what any man can learn of art, and of his life as art.

In the thirty-odd years since he wrote these words, Jay Wright has written poetry in a similar spirit. He has composed an extraordinary epic of human transfiguration and transformation, of nothing less than the great work of art that is "our life among ourselves."

NOTES

1. This description comes from the "Afterword" appended to the original edition of *Double Invention*; unfortunately, like explanatory material in several of the volumes, it does not appear in the present edition.

C. K. DORESKI

Decolonizing the Spirits: History and Storytelling in Jay Wright's Soothsayers and Omens

The soothsayers who found out from time what it had in store
certainly did not experience time as either homogeneous or empty.
Anyone who keeps this in mind will perhaps get an idea of how past
times were experienced in remembrance—namely, in just the same way.
—Walter Benjamin, "Theses on the Philosophy of History"

What is happening in the world more and more is that people are
attempting to decolonize their spirits. A crucial act of empowerment,
one that might return reverence to the Earth, thereby saving it, in this
fearful-of-Nature, spiritually colonized age.
—Alice Walker, "Clear Seeing Inherited Religion
and Reclaiming the Pagan Self"

In 1976, during the national enactments of the Bicentennial, Jay Wright published *Dimensions of History* (Corinth) and *Soothsayers and Omens* (Seven Woods Press), two independent sequences of poems dealing with the cultural and aesthetic imperative to construct an enlarged historical path into the cultural geographies of the diaspora. Like Ezra Pound's *Cantos*, these collections are more than poems "containing history"; they are active attempts to reconstruct the very method and modes of the aestheticized historical, the energized field of narrative threads: storytelling and national

From *Reading Race in American Poetry: "An Area of Act,"* edited by Aldon Lynn Nielsen. © 2000 by the Board of Trustees of University of Illinois Press.

(de)construction.[1] For Wright, national*isms* serve as oppositional sponsors of an emerging aesthetic of history. Such efforts require more than the invention or discovery of new historical certainties: they necessitate the deconstruction of received history itself. And what better time than the Bicentennial to investigate the problematic boundaries of nationality, modernity, and reason in this historically suspect construction: the United States of America.

Wright's poetry, seeking "imaginative dissolution and reconstruction of its material" (Rowell 1983:4), responds not simply to the miscarried extensions of Enlightenment dicta, historical revolutionary manifestos, and received national identity; it seeks to escape the oppression of reason and national coherence embedded in even more recent countercultural stirrings such as black nationalism.[2] Recalling Frederick Douglass's determination to authenticate the Centennial celebration through an honest appraisal of the promise and fulfillment of life in America, Wright's aestheticized history moves to supplant the temporal, inherited, and brittle constellation of the founding fathers with a centering pan-African patriarchy[3] curiously akin in impulse to Alice Walker's decentering, womanist rift with mediated history in her Bicentennial novel, *Meridian*. Wright, as if responding to Pound's lament that "*le personnel manqué* ... we have not men for our times" (1995:344), invents a postnational[4] narrative in which his "founding fathers" actually dissolve national corridors, boundaries, and chronology to construct an ephemeral, transactional tale.

Like the Centennial, which followed and apotheosized the Civil War, the Bicentennial was a postwar, mercantile ode to *Pro*gress as well as a subtextual charge to progress through national cohesion and ambitions.[5] Such epochal celebrations are anathema to Wright, who believes that their sole function is the sheer obliteration of the living consciousness of historical and cultural trace memories. The Bicentennial was an enactment of what Homi Bhabha defines in "DissemiNation" as "the construction of a discourse on society that *performs* the problem of totalizing the people and unifying the national will" (1994:160–61). Bhabha further remarks that "this breakdown in the identity of the will is another instance of the supplementary narrative of nationness that 'adds to' without 'adding *up*'" (1994:161). Inadequate constructions of history serve no one, least of all a poet who seeks authentic and vital commemorative linguistic structures.

Although his aesthetic deliberations are born out of Vietnam-era cynicism and Bicentennial tawdriness, Wright owes much of his antihistoricism to the broader historical tide of the twentieth century.[6] No writer has better captured the elegiac note of humanity's loss of history and the leisure of historical time sounded by Walter Benjamin in his 1936 disquisition on narrative, history, community, and solitude, "Der Erzähler" ("The Storyteller"). Written in the late 1920s, it laments an aesthetic and historical concern: "the art of telling stories is coming to an end" (1968:83). And with that simple assertion Benjamin displaces the very meanings of "story," "experience," and "history" as he reinscribes that which began with the First World War: "a process began to become apparent which has not halted since then. Was it not noticeable at the end of the war that men returned from the battlefield grown silent—not richer, but poorer in communicable experience? ... A generation that had gone to school on a horse-drawn streetcar now stood under the open sky in a countryside in which nothing remained unchanged but the clouds, and beneath these clouds, in a field of force of destructive torrents and explosions, was the tiny, fragile human body" (1968:84). Unwilling to fetishize the emblematic ruins of the past and unable to presume attachment to the received history of Pound and Eliot, Wright, adapting and extending the tradition of Emerson, makes a commitment to what Wallace Stevens called, in "Notes toward a Supreme Fiction," "this invention, this invented world" (1954:380). Stevens's "major man," an example of the exemplary figure thought to be essential to historical constructions, will undergo a startling subordination as Wright creates a decentered counterdiscourse to a national epic. Stridently postnational and aggressively transnational, he posits a new (w)hole: a poetic of history that attempts utter effacement of a mediating force, either in the person of the poet or in the presence of the text. History, stripped of its numbing informational qualities, demographic insistence, and subservience to pastness and nationalisms, will thrive in the fluid immediacy of a story being told. "Mean egotism" will vanish, as Emerson's and Whitman's poet-priests are effaced by an experiential elder, the patriarch-storyteller, who fades into the story being told.

Suggestive of what Bhabha identifies as the "postcolonial passage through modernity ... in [which] the past [is] projective" (1994:253), this chronotropic aesthetic underwrites the historiographical intent of *Soothsayers and Omens*. In this collection, Wright will extend Benjamin's insight that stories represent more than the possibility for experience; they are human history. The figure of the storyteller, which assumes constellatory outline in the opening section of Benjamin's essay, will authorize the potential grandeur and spectacular remove of Wright's poetic of history.

Soothsayers and Omens, a poetic sequence that attempts to provide an opening into discontinuous and simultaneous history, rejects received national and linguistic structures in a lyric alternative to the epic. In its sly echo of Wallace Stevens's "The Comedian as the Letter C" (1954:65),[7] *Soothsayers and Omens* circumscribes a field of poetic resonance that is at once canonical—and therefore recognizable—and foreign. A worldly "pleasure of merely circulating" invests the sequence with a simultaneous familiarity and strangeness (Stevens 1954:149–50). Poems self-reflexively call to mind Eliot, Pound, Stevens, Crane, and Hayden even as they thwart such patterned allusions with echoes of anthropologically summoned texts. Wright enacts Stevens's "Tea at the Palaz of Hoon," creating the very "compass" of these new landscapes in which readers find themselves "more truly and more strange" (1954:65).

Unlike Pound, who trod the accepted path of westerners seeking perceptual extensions through the art and religion of the Orient, Wright investigates the transatlantic prophetic realms of the Western Hemisphere and Africa to emphasize the crux of Westernization as well as its expansiveness. Pound's contributions to the aestheticization of history originate in his ability to fracture and assemble the received European historical script. Wright's appropriation of an earlier modernist text yields a decentered inversion of European literatures and inscribes a startling dependence on African and Western Hemispheric literary artifacts. Revoking Pound's summary of the Enlightenment—

> rights
> diffusing knowledge of principles
> maintaining justice, in registering treaty of
> peace
> changed with the times (1995:351)

—Wright advances beyond the formal historical landscape to a local, associative geography that relies on the routine, not the spectacular, for effect. As if to answer Pound's revolutionary capsule of national assemblage and cooperative cohesion—"not a Virginian / but an American Patrick Henry" (1995:363)—Wright asks: "not an American but ...?"[8] In sounding this cultural ambiguity, Wright thwarts the nationalist ends of continuous narrative with the possibilities inherent in the open silences of a discontinuous narrative.

A historically informed poetic, retrieved from the stagnation of chronology and fact associated with history and news, necessitates an enlarged aesthetic, one that embraces the sense of storytelling that Walter Benjamin had associated with "the ability to exchange experiences" in the "realm of living speech" (1968:83, 87). Benjamin's "The Storyteller" asserts that the evolution of the novel and "information" in modern society are the primary means by which the life of experience, culture, and history is nullified in favor of a stable and isolating product. Recalling Thoreau's hostile ambivalence toward the invention of the telegraph, Benjamin deplores the subversion of narrative by news: "Every morning brings us the news of the globe, and yet we are poor in noteworthy stories. This is because no event any longer comes to us without already being shot through with explanation" (1968:89). Such information, anticipating the mediated and isolating depletion of television news, surrenders to its immediate, mediated context and dies into history. The spiritual and aesthetic lapses in such constructions were rooted, Benjamin thought, in the difference between "the writer of history, the historian, and the teller of it, the chronicler" (1968:95). And it is in this conjoined spirit of orality and textuality in the "act of the poem" (Rowell 1983:4) that Wright locates his progressively unmediated, historically charged aesthetic. Explanation, if it is to come at all, comes through the grander, suggestive history of the shared experience of a poetry (curiously reminiscent of Stevens's) "in the service of a new and capable personality at home and in the transformative and transformed world" (Rowell 1983:9).

The four-part, architectonic structure of *Soothsayers and Omens* is at once a reconstruction and a resituation of the Romantic poet in the landscape. Wright frustrates a pattern of mere imitation by shuttling between the Emersonian and the transcendental conjurers of many cultural traces. Three sequences detail a grounding and departure, historically and socially, before fulfilling their aesthetic and cultural promise in a concluding, bold-titled excursion into simultaneous discontinuity, "Second Conversations with Ogotemmêli."

The untitled opening sequence progresses from a declamatory initiation of birth and its attendant installation of an alternative patriarchy through a sequence of mythological potential and shifting chronologies (indebted to Hart Crane) and ends with paired portraits of the exemplary and historical. Poetry inverts history into "a livable assertion" (1976b:II), insisting on what Wright calls "spiritual resonance" (Rowell 1983:4).

"The Charge" initiates Wright's subversion of the chronological in history by means of its ritual-centered, rigidly present-tense installation of patriarch and storyteller. The earlier, foreboding structure of "death as history" yields to its cultural inverse, "history as birth," a dying into a new narrative sequence and coherence:

> This is the morning.
> There is a boy,
> riding the shadow of a cradle,
> clapping from room to room
> as swift as the memory of him. (1976b:II)

The faint disjunction between the present-tense, gestural insistence of these opening lines—"This is," "There is"—establishes the sequence's attitude toward temporal and spatial ideas of order. Like Benjamin's soothsayers, Wright's personae will not "experience time as either homogeneous or empty." Through the confluence of memory, history, preexistence, and death, "The Charge" begins the work of the sequence: the denial of death as history.

Suffused with a Blakean and Emersonian insistence of "infant sight," the five-part sequence displaces English lyrical conventions into a startling and strange reconfiguration. From Vaughan and Milton to Whitman and Thoreau, Wright culls a lexicon that denies the conventional distinctions of life and death. Whitman's "Out of the Cradle" and Vaughan's "They Are All Gone into the World of Light!" shrug off their shrouds and don the unexpected raiment of life:

> Now,
> I hear you whistle through the house,
> pushing wheels, igniting fires,
> leaving no sound untried,
> no room in which a young boy,
> at sea in a phantom cradle,
> could lurch and scream
> and come and settle in the house.
> You are so volubly alone,
> that I turn,
> reaching into the light for the boy
> your father charged you to deliver. (11)

The denial of presence and time, of reference and sequential continuities, persists throughout the poem. Generational superiority fades into a Wordsworthian simultaneity at the transitional moment of the birth of a child who resembles Moses in his circumstance and presence: "where the women will hold the boy, / plucked from the weeds, / a manchild, discovered" (12). Pronouns, in their seemingly logical array, realign into suspect, logic-thwarting reference, until the I's, we's, and you's forge a collective and cross-referential community of ill-determined genealogy. Even what appears to be the familiar punning of "sun" and "son"—"where the sun forever enters this circle. / Fathers and sons sit"—fails to assume its conventional duality, as the poem advances toward a binary-resistant, structural integrity that departs from lyric and semantic convention.[9]

Enlarging the realm of circumspection and locution to include the finite and infinite tasks the poet to "prepare a place" of history-nullifying, timeless continuities "where the sun forever enters this circle" (12). Wright extends Blakean particulars" to create a "whole" where "All things here move / with that global rhythm" (13). What began as a descent into birth ritual has concluded as a startling revision of a death-defying, liberation narrative: "This is the moment when all our unwelcome deaths / charge us to be free" (13).

Such an imperative insinuates itself into Wright's originary "Sources."[10] Evocative of Crane's "Voyages" in *White Buildings*, another six-poem excursion into "time and the elements," "Sources" bridges the immediate and individual world of "The Charge" with the exemplary and historical realms of the concluding Benjamin Banneker poems. Wright embarks on an epical journey of vast interiority as he plumbs the potential depths of historical narrative. The sequence moves beyond that which Crane found "answered in the vortex of our grave" to a moment of communicative display of communion and grace (1966:36). A nourishing rain replaces Crane's tempestuous sea, instilling a certainty and cycle in the consecrated ground.

Orphean strains mix with alien modalities to stress the complexities of cultural weave and historical moment in these poems. The familiar is rendered strange, as allusions drift into tangential relation with barely perceived scripts and recombine into an apparent whole. "Sources" offers an elemental reweaving of the received and intuited histories. Ecclesiastical proffering sustains and restores—"I lift these texts, / wanting the words / to enter my mind like pure wind" (1976b:16)—even as the sequence evokes poems as distant as Stevens's "To the Roaring Wind."

The revolutionary passage from source to moment, from ancestor to poet, necessitates both the "life / and death of all our fathers" if history is to assume what James Baldwin called its "literal presence" (1985:410). The reanimated historical moment for Wright is one in which liberated ancestral moments are praised and carried in the living descendants. Such freedom resides in the ability of the living to fetch history from the dead, the "new and capable imagination" that refuses to fossilize the exemplary dead into memorial history. As Eliot explains in "Little Gidding":

This is the use of memory:
For liberation—not less of love but expanding
Of love beyond desire, and so liberation
From the future as well as the past. (1971:142)

The incipient cosmology of the first section solidifies around the arrested figures of Benjamin Banneker and Thomas Jefferson to form constellations of apparent national coherence and construction—apt characters for deconstructive poetics in the season of Bicentennial celebration.[11] In these paired poems, storytelling becomes the means by which Wright creates poems out of history, not poems of history. Remote, historical substrata establish Baldwin's present tense notion of history. Prefiguration and historical spectacle constitute an enactment, not a reenactment, of encounter and speculation. An extension of the birth ritual of "The Charge," "Benjamin Banneker Helps to Build a City" and "Benjamin Banneker Sends His 'Almanac' to Thomas Jefferson" invoke historical motifs to impose structure on the flux of the present.

Constellatory, like the figure of a poem, the city enlarges beyond its vision; its design escapes the logic of reason to enter into an aesthetic realm with its own spatial order.[12] Just on the secular side of Saint Augustine's City of God, Banneker's realm is at once celestial and earthly, thematizing the Enlightenment projection of attainable, worldly—"heavenly"—cities.[13] The creativity doubles as history, "moving as though it knew its end, against death" (1976b:22). History succumbs to a world of consuming plans and prefigurations. To shed the confines of either inspiration, the poet forces an encounter:

> I call you into this time,
> back to that spot,
> and read these prefigurations
> into your mind,
> and know it could not be strange to you
> to stand in the dark and emptiness
> of a city not your vision alone. (22)

"This time" and "that spot" form the nexus, "that spot where the vibration starts" (22–23). As a descendant of Pound and Eliot, Wright must search "the texts / and forms of cities that burned, / that decayed, or gave their children away" (22). Histories and offspring yielded or were lost.

The juxtaposition of an alternate mode of perception, an aestheticized history that accommodates the irrational in speech and actions, requires the displacement of the ideational constructs and informational models of culture by the astrological force of the metaphysical and mythological. Reason, chronology, and national identity must retire in the face of an enhanced cultural logic. A superimposition of a simultaneous, sanctifying presence serves to redeem and transport the reason-stranded poet and astronomer:

> Over the earth,
> in an open space,

you and I step to the time
of another ceremony.
These people, changed,
but still ours,
shake another myth
from that egg. (23)

Such betweenness epitomizes the hybridity of the black Atlantic cultures in which imposed, culture-severing boundaries stranded lives from their mythic structures and historical context.[14] Alternative theologies sustain competing cosmologies and lead to a potential sanctification upon rebaptism: "A city, like a life, / must be made in purity" (23).

Crane's sonorities and Pound's textualities inspired Wright's reconstruction of the historical path by which personage and place are known. Yet Wright's renewing script cannot make use of Pound's syntactical and historical disruptions. A retraction into the "stillness" before genesis—

Image of shelter, image of man,
pulled back into himself,
into the seed before the movement,
into the silence before the sound
of movement, into stillness (24)

—allows for an inspired new story, for restorative annals. Skirting the allure of myth, that protean antagonist of history, Wright advances into a stylized recapitulation of call-and-response that will allow the documentary presence of Banneker to thrive within an aestheticized frame:

Recall number.
Recall your calculations,
your sight, at night,
into the secrets of stars. (24)

Banneker's epistle to Jefferson, unorchestrated by Wright, serves as the authentic excursion into the rational and purposeful models of history. Unheeded in his time, Banneker slips within the broader compass of prophetic utterance and invocation, challenging the Promethean and Protestant order of this inherited cosmology and spawning the poem's rhetorical challenge to "the movement, / the absence of movement, the Prefiguration of movement" in this place (25). The astronomer becomes the very incarnation of the Enlightenment, a transformative cosmology. The authentication of Enlightenment pledges of liberty resides in a historical inversion:

> So they must call you,
> knowing you are intimate stars;
> so they must call you,
> knowing different resolutions. (25)

Instead of the modernist clock that drives the collating impulse of Stevens's "souvenirs and prophecies," impelling time into anterior and posterior space, Banneker posts "calculations and forecasts" by which to realign "the small, / imperceptible act, which itself becomes free" (25). Attuned to celestial harmonies and earthly disjunctions, the astronomer represents the unease with which the ideological legacy of the Rights of Man was received by African Americans:

> Free. Free. How will the lines fall
> into that configuration?
> How will you clear this uneasiness,
> posting your calculations and forecasts
> into a world you yourself cannot enter? (25)

The proximate "configuration" of lyric space and transtemporality allow this poem to seek a counterdiscourse, one in which "vision" traverses the boundaries of "the city a star, a body" (26) into that still-potential space of aestheticized history, the province of the poem.

When Thomas Jefferson received Benjamin Banneker's *Almanac*, he responded instantly to its synecdochic force: "Sir,—I thank you sincerely for your letter of the 19th instant and for the Almanac it contained. No body wishes more than I do to see such proofs as you exhibit, that nature has given to our black brethren, talents equal to those of the other colors of men" (1984:982). "Benjamin Banneker Sends His 'Almanac' to Thomas Jefferson" countermands Jefferson's presidential approbation with its own lyrical reinvestment of speculative reason and prophetic vision. Though it lacks the intense communion of the earlier poem, it nonetheless collaborates in Wright's evolving historical display.[15] For here, the poet visits the astronomer, not in some interstitial space, but rather "in mind," in historical setting. At once a colloquy and a dialogue, the poem necessitates a larger view of "calculation," "language," and "form"—the things that submit to reason and those that do not. Verifications of celestial truths, those of Banneker's purview—"Solid, these calculations / verify your body on God's earth"—give way to mythological extractions, those of Wright's aesthetic:

I, who know so little of stars,
whose only acquaintance with the moon
is to read a myth, or to listen
to the surge
of the songs the women know. (1976b:27)

The celestial order posited by Banneker's science is one that conducts
a historically sound and metaphysically charged dialogue:

So you look into what we see
yet cannot see,
and shape and take a language
to give form to one or the other,
believing no form will escape,
no movement appear, nor stop,
without explanation,
believing no reason is only reason,
nor without reason. (27)

The prophetic realm of the soothsayer or seer is one that both
formalizes and accepts an utter lack of formality in the perceived order of
things. The aesthetic gaps or "silences" that Wright requires for his
interventions into history are to be found in the "crack of the universe" of
the previous poem or the "flaw" of this one. Beyond the compass of the
perfect number, the numerical whole forwarded by Banneker, beyond the
reach of "the perfect line," the lyrical snare offered by Wright, rest the
"omissions" of the historical and the aesthetic. Within this silenced realm
lurks the quarrel between "the man and the God," the free and the captive.

Banneker becomes the mediating force between the genealogical and
historical imperatives that order the received texts. The challenge of
Banneker's *Almanac* is more than one of cognitive display: it is one of justified
existence. To argue with reason in the person of Jefferson is to quarrel with
the ordering principle of the nation itself. "Your letter turns on what the man
knows, / on what God, you think, would have us know" (28). Wright inverts
the cosmological relationship into one where Banneker scrutinizes the order
of being itself:

All stars will forever move under your gaze,
truthfully, leading you from line to line,
from number to number, from truth to truth,
while the man will read your soul's desire,

searcher, searching yourself,
losing the relations. (28)

"Losing the relations" is an encumbered line, resonant with the promise of calculations as well as the frailty of transactions even as it suggests the ultimate sacrifice of a stabilizing genealogy. Like the one "so volubly alone" in "The Charge," Banneker moves beyond the barely perceptible relations to assume the potential charge of a space of silence and imperfection.

The transient arc from the "livable assertion" to "losing the relations" is one that guides both poet and reader to a cunning instability, a moment and place of irrationality and aesthetic crisis. Within part 1, Wright has succeeded in moving in and through history in such a way that even the most mundane occurrence has become one of speculative poise and abiding uncertainty. Part 2 requires an application of this emerging knowledge, an unseating of domestic ordinariness in the light of this newly found celestial turbulence.

Readers of *Soothsayers and Omens* have expressed relief upon reaching the collection's middle sections, mistaking them for familiar, confessional, anecdotal lyrics "grounded in 'personal' experience" (Rowell 1983:6). The Baedeker surface of familiar detail obscures the restless lines of call-and-response, false seculars and spirituals, Catholic and Protestant rituals—the unsettled logistics of history surging beneath the surface. Ceremonies of possession and rituals of sacrifice fail to quiet the dead of many cultures, lost inhabitants of the once-named and noble New Mexican landscape. What Adrienne Rich has called "contraband memories" suffuse the history emergent in this shifting landscape that is "still untouched by the step and touch / of the sons of slaves, where no slave could ever go" (1976b:32).[16] In "Entering New Mexico," one does not know what might be summoned from the depths of local or national histories.

> Call,
> and some pantalooned grandfather may come,
> with the leisure of Virginia still on his tongue,
> and greet you uneasily.
> Here, he holds uneasy land
> from which he pistols out intrusions (32)

Naming itself assumes unpredictable and prophetic powers; in "The Master of Names," it summons "A history that is none, / that may never be written, / nor conceived again" (34). Within the proper name resides "a power ... almost forgotten" (36).

Extending Walter Benjamin's reflection that "Counsel woven into the fabric of real life is wisdom" (1968:86), Wright surmounts the difficulty of his predetermined landscape—one in which reason and order have been disabled—by weaving his determinations into local historical and genealogical sites in order to discover the matrix of historical wisdom. "The Albuquerque Graveyard" and "Family Reunion" may be seen as application sites for his evolving aesthetic structures of history.

At once an excursion and an incursion into the borderland of grief and remembrance, "The Albuquerque Graveyard" occasions an aesthetic debate on memory, literacy, and history.[17] The incremental advance into the scene of commemoration—

> take three buses,
> walk two blocks,
> search at the rear
> of the cemetery (38)

—echoes grander historical slights, as "buses" and "rear" metonymically realign into "the back of the bus." "The pattern of the place" anticipates a deeper historical disquisition:

> I am going back
> to the Black limbo,
> an unwritten history
> of our own tensions. (38)

This apparent historical act of recovery is balanced by the tugging immediacy of "our." Steeped in the catholicity of the place, the poem toys with its racial and cultural inversions of Dante as well as its hemispheric soundings. History expresses itself in the silence of the ruins; Wright discovers himself in the volatile "tensions" of the buried curse[s] and rage."

If history is to be extracted from this fossilized underlayer of neglect,[18] Wright must turn beyond the evidential to a correspondence between the exemplary and the collective:

> of one who stocked his parlor
> with pictures of Robeson,
> and would boom down the days,
> dreaming of Othello's robes. (38)

Dreaming here has a nearly astrological force as it locates the individual within a commemorative historical sweep of potential realized. In reminiscence, the recognition scenes of "small heroes" resonate locally and nationally, as the poet fades into the persona of Frederick Douglass:

> Here, I stop by the simple mound
> of a woman who taught me
> spelling on the sly,
> parsing my tongue
> to make me fit for her own dreams. (38–39)

The ordered summoning of "unwritten history" produces discontent. The quest yields to an enactment of a modest call-and-response in which the poet "search[es] the names / and simple mounds [he] call[s] [his] own / ... and turn[s] for home" (39). "Home," having acquired an internal and external voice in Wright's canon, recalls the historical cascade of the title poem of *The Homecoming Singer*:

> her voice shifting
> and bringing up the Carolina calls,
> the waterboy, the railroad cutter, the jailed,
> the condemned, all that had been forgotten
> on this night of homecomings. (1971:31)

To "turn for home" is to position oneself in direct relation to the genealogical site of history itself. If history is to be rescripted into a living and inclusive form, it must be superimposed on its recognizable origins: the family. Home is where Wright will reacquaint himself with Benjamin's "source" for storytelling, the place of "the securest among our possessions ... the ability to exchange experiences" (1968:83).

Unlike "the hierarchy of small defeats" populating "The Albuquerque Graveyard," "the elders and saints" of "Family Reunion" confront the traces of that earlier, "unwritten history." Semblance becomes resemblance as "an unfamiliar relative's traces" are confronted (39). Cropped and candid, the snapshots aestheticize lives into glimpsed, historical extensions. Images engender familiar narratives, exchanged experiences, and recognition scenes. Graveyard ruins surrender to the always spontaneous, genealogical accord with the living:

> of hearing a voice, and being able to coax
> the speaker into echoes of himself, his selves,
> his forgotten voices, voices he had never heard:
> of calling your own name, and having it belled

back in tongues, being changed and harmonized
until it is one name and. all names. (40)

Historical recognition depends on individuation, which must then
evolve into a harmonious whole, recognition insisting initially on cognition.
Because authentication of his aesthetic demands the restorative sound of a
vox humana without, as Benjamin Banneker knew, "losing the relations,"
Wright must open his discontinuous narrative to the hemispheric pulse of
historical antecedent.

Readers of *The Homecoming Singer* will recall Wright's initial
fascination with the Mexican fortress Chapultepec: "This is the castle where
they lived, / Maximilian and Carlotta, / and here is where Carlotta slept"
(1971:40). What may be seen as the primary historical grounding of that
earlier collection has slipped into duplicitous aesthetic service in part 3 of
Soothsayers and Omens, as the recurrent sounding of Chapultepec recalls the
euphonious slopping of Stevens's "November off Tehuantepec" in "Sea
Surface Full of Clouds" (1954:98–102). The preparatory path to Wright's
new history lies along abbreviated recapitulations of "The Comedian as the
Letter C," in which tone and circuit shift to include "The Sense of Comedy:
I" (roman numeral or personal pronoun?) in hope of circumventing Crispin's
"faint, memorial gesturings" (1954:29).

Unlike Stevens's "introspective voyager," Wright's persona in "The
Museums of Chapultepec" prefers "Moore's concrete apples, / Giacometti's
daggers" to Crispin's porpoises and apricots (1976b:49). And yet he, like
Crispin, is drawn by "A sunken voice, both of remembering / And of
forgetfulness, in alternate strain" (Stevens 1954:29). So enmeshed is this
section of *Soothsayers and Omens* in the aesthetic web of Stevens that the
poetic sequence seems proximate to its ancestor, steadily moving toward
Crispin's discovery: "*The Idea of a Colony* / Nota: his soil is man's intelligence"
(Stevens 1954:36). Wright, like Crispin, writes "his prolegomena, / And,
being full of caprice, inscribe[s] / Commingled souvenirs and prophecies"
(Stevens 1954:37).

The confluence of history and literature occurs in the announcement
of "The Birthday." Shuttling between the Emersonian and Blakean
contraries of temporal and spatial logic, Wright seeks a fixed and fluid
identity for the historical. The speaker is as focused as Benjamin Banneker:

and my eyes kept focussed
at one point in the light,
as though I would fix
the face and name of a friend
absent even from my memory. (1976b:52)

Caught "between one day and another, / between one age and another," the poet seeks to resolve an apparent conundrum at the center of his debate: "a chosen point to celebrate / the fact of moving still" (52). The definitional instability of "still" has troubled the entire collection, nagging the lines into an uncertain correspondence; but here, it offers the promise of reflection and endurance: the promise of history itself.

The prophetic trajectory of desire and reminiscence coalesces in "Jason Visits His Gypsy." This poem of agitated display attempts to define history linguistically. Even as the gypsy's spectacle draws one simultaneously into and away from the unraveling truth, it becomes the very celebration of "the fact of moving still":

> [she] moves,
> raveling the sand into her sleeve,
> past your still body,
> past your stilled desires. (1976b:54)

Nomadic, nationless, the gypsy seems the ideal simulacrum for Wright's emerging transhistorical and transnational identity:

> The gypsy knows what you have forgotten,
> . . . .
> knows the rhythm of raveling
> the sand into the dark and closeness
> of a space, where only she can live. (54)

The section comes to a rest with another "Homecoming: *Guadalajara*— New York, 1965," a bifurcated tradition and hemispheric ellipsis that reannunciates as well as terminates the earlier sequential debates of reason, history, identity, and narrative. The disembarkation, to use the language of Gwendolyn Brooks, necessitates a conceptual and linguistic pastiche: syntax and diction strain to accommodate competing visions, and allusions collide as architect and poet debate the structural integrity of inheritance. Insistent on its lineage, the poem echoes Stevens's "The Worms at Heaven's Gate," noting that "The strange and customary turns / of living may coincide" (58).

In a different city, at a different time, the poet transgresses; the boundaries of language, nation, history, and time. The Enlightenment constructions so in favor during the Bicentennial have lost even their oppositional, aesthetic value for Wright:

From line to line,
from point to point,
is an architect's end of cities.

But I lie down
to a different turbulence
and a plan of transformation. (58)

The disease between "turbulence" and "plan" intensifies the undetermined path to come. Suspension of the defining boundaries of individual and collective identity will enable Wright to proceed into a history tolerant of "the strange and customary turns / of living" (58).

"Second Conversations with Ogotemmêli," the final section, is doubly estranged from the text proper in that it bears the only subtitle and commits wholeheartedly, and perhaps unexpectedly (to those who neglected the note on the verso of the half-title page), to structures and silences inherent in Marcel Griaule's version of Dogon tribal cosmology. Though previous historical, geographical, and biographical references may have been unfamiliar to the reader, they were inevitably assimilated and accommodated by the overlap of the poems. "Second Conversations," with alienating familiarity, presumes an antecedent, a "first" that signals Wright's dependence on Griaule; "Ogotemmêli" becomes the *named* initiator, the medium through which disclosure (if it is to come at all) will come. Unlike *Dimensions of History*, *Soothsayers and Omens* offers neither "cautionary remarks" nor explanation; except for the prefatory notes, it insists on the aesthetic self-sufficiency of its materials. Wright's cautionary and sly modernist introduction to the notes appended to *Dimensions of History*, on the other hand, shares his expectations for readers of this collection: "The notes are offered as an aid in reading the poem, not as the poem itself, nor a substitution for it. The notes could have been more extensive, and more detailed. I have given only so many because I must, ultimately, rely on the good will and intelligence of the reader. If the reader trusts the poem as much as I trust him or her, he or she should have no difficulty with my exploration of these dimensions of history" (1976a:105).[19] The acute intimacy of these extended poetic explorations in *Soothsayers and Omens* transfers responsibility for coherence and vitality to the reader. In this final, elaborate response to Stevens's Western world of "inconstancy," Wright pilots an excursion into the deepest recesses of transatlantic narrative literatures and histories, allusions and mythologies, in the hope of grasping the weave of the design.

Reading initiates this conversation: Wright's reading of a translation of Griaule's *Conversations with Ogotemmêli: An Introduction to Dogon Religious Ideas* (1962). Poetic invention, the mind creating, closes the silences between poet, who is alienated by successive mediation and remove—stories "heard" through the scrim of translator, text interposed, allusive field (Emerson, Stevens, Pound, Crane, Hayden, Derrida, Bloom)—and experience; it also bridges the gap between the poet and the Dogon storyteller. The anthropological study sponsors the radical subversion of texts inherent in the collection as a whole, extracting poetry in recital. Wright has acceded to Benjamin's situational definition of storytelling—"A man listening to a story is in the company of a storyteller; even a man reading one shares this companionship" (1968:100)—and, in doing so, has relinquished poetic authority to the patriarchal storyteller in the act of disclosure. Emblematic discontinuities abound as conversations, auditorily ephemeral, evade the structures of time and reason and create a momentarily reciprocal aesthetic. Anxious to move beyond the totalizing fields of myth or history, Wright locates coherence and correspondence in that space where poetic and epistemology are one.

Although scholarly attention to the source reveals the imitative array of poems and descriptive language, received diction, and gloss, it does little to disclose the aesthetic of Wright's evolving cosmology. As Hugh Kenner cautions: "It is hard alone to wring song from philology" (195). Immersion in the contextual source leads to an informational gloss that is counterproductive to the revealed revisionary attitude toward aesthetic form and history. This overlapping series reinscribes as it reanimates the lost voice—and the silences—of Ogotemmêli on the accreted, Western canonical context of Wright's experience. Polyphony and polyvocality display the syncretic instability of history and biography under erasure.

"Ogotemmêli" originates the concluding sequence through an intimate dialogue between speaker and storytelling mediator—described by Griaule as one with an "eagle mind and considerable shrewdness" (14)—that is at once instructive and obfuscating. The three-part poem startles with its patterned and excluding repetitions; it is, indeed, a series of "second conversations," exchanges with a history at once textual and informal, European and African, "civilized" and "primitive," historical and simultaneous. The stanzas resemble reliquaries, storing barely contained allusions, artifacts, and utterances as they threaten to sound a tide of discontinuous meanings. Even as the image of Ogotemmêli begins to take visual and linguistic form in parallels and transmutations of its textual origin, it shades into a dimly perceived auditory presence—"But your voice comes clearly / only where I found you" (61)—

insisting on the phenomenological instability of the poetic record. If this "you" grows in familiarity—

> You tilt your head like a bird,
> and wait until my step stops.
> You squint and sniff,
> as though you would brush away
> some offensive smell or movement (61)

—it does so in its tangential and immediate relationship to antecedent visions. Recalling earlier, ambiguously aligned descriptions—"These others stand with you, / squinting the city into place, / yet cannot see what you see" (22)—these actions coalesce to form an enlarged and enlarging series of qualities associated with the historical and eternal in Wright's world.

The second stanza's clustered reduplications of the original force an immediacy and contrariness that spirals into arch parodies of the pastoral—"trace the fat, wet sheep"—and startling inversions of Miltonic atmosphere: "when no light comes, / you will lead me into the darkness" (61). These lines then resolve into aversions and reversals of Cotton Mather's patriarchal speculations on an invisible world: "Father, your eyes have turned / from the tricks of our visible world" (62). The display of correspondences, far from insisting on relation and wholeness, advances the poem into a provisional world of displacement and disjunction. Closure of this final history can be achieved only through a tolerance of what Walter Benjamin has termed *Stillstand* (1968:84), a gap in temporality itself

> So I arrive,
> at the end of this, my small movement,
> moving with you, in the light you control,
> learning to hear the voice in the silence,
> learning to see in the light
> that runs away from me. (62)

That moment of static, enduring immediacy of "reaching into the light for the boy" (11) or "learning to see in the light" is the time of Benjamin's storytelling, the moment of Wright's history.

The figure of the named Dogon elder reinscribes and decenters the collection's originating patriarchal figure, the poet-patriarch of "The Charge," prompting a regenesis and realignment of the phenomenal world. The open yet culminating sequence—from "Beginning" to "The Dead"—articulates the newness of Wright's transcultural diasporic aesthetic.

Semantic and linguistic disjunction denies the verifiable and informational qualities of the history embedded in this discontinuous narrative of postnational consciousness. Emerson's poet-priest and Wright's own poet-patriarch dissolve into Benjamin's storyteller as patriarch, one who (as Benjamin concludes) "has borrowed his authority from death" (1968:94).

"Beginning" appears to dismantle the raiment and facades of received cultural hierarchy and to establish a modernist tableau relative to the "dung and death" of Eliot's "East Coker" or the dust swirling about Pound's cage at the U.S. Army's Detention Training Center north of Pisa:

> Alive again,
> you wait in the broken courtyard.
> Oblivious of its dungheap and ashes,
> you sit once more,
> near the main façade,
> and listen for this unfamiliar footstep. (63)

The historicity of Maximilian and Carlotta, essential to the poems of *The Homecoming Singer*, fractures into the postmodernist shards of this "broken courtyard," an abandoned system of figuration. The discontinuity of "arrive, / at the end of this, my small movement" extends this celebratory, posited continuum: "Alive again." The return signaled is more complex than being to origins; it cycles through a temporality as yet unannounced—or at least unclear. Movement, life's linear creep or history's expected chronological order, meets with immediate status: the weight of "wait." All of this seems to echo Benjamin's "Ur-history of the 19th Century," in which truth was found in the garbage heap" of modernity, the "rags, the trash" of commodity production. And yet readers of the antecedent text will recall more than the atmospheric sponsor of these descriptions: they will recognize clusters of the details themselves. The essential confrontation is not with the prefigured storyteller but with his linguistic trace, fossilized in Griaule's "Conversations." The inspiration of that unmediated, original space will come not from the figure but from the word—"Facing you, / I cannot tell what word, / or form of that word, I shall face" (63)—or soundings of the exchange. The word, the thread that Robert Duncan called "The Torn Cloth" (1984:137–39), initiates the "reaving" of Wright's aesthetic.

If the epistemologically charged aesthetic is to redeem history, it must offer an unmediated space of enactment or realization that is at once provisional and whole. Nathaniel Mackey sees such constructions, in the light of Griaule, as "fabrications": "What this means is not only that our purchase on the world is a weave but also that the word is a rickety witness, the telltale base on which our sense of the weave sits. *Fabric* echoes *fabrication*, as both go back to a root that has to do with making. The creaking of the word calls attention to the constructedness of the hold on the world fabrication affords" (1993:180). Such "purchase" affords little if it fails to secure trust. For Wright, trust responds to dependency and cultural reversals as he relinquishes history to conversation, word to silence. "Lurking near the borders of speech" in "The First Word," Wright succumbs to "the craft of the first word, / weaving speech into spirit" (64).

The evanescence of form thematizes the perceived cosmography of the Dogon tribe, its "world system associated with constellations" (Griaule 1965:32), as well as the canonical tide of poems under erasure. "The Third Word"—

> this seed
> being broken there
> on the smithy's anvil
> will burst to stars,
> design a man (67)

—reduplicates a system of parallels expansive enough to claim Griaule, the Stevens of "The Auroras of Autumn," Ogotemmêli, and Eliot. Decipherings yield analogues that share a global urge for the construction of provisional structures to define and stabilize the existential mysteries of being human.

Ogotemmêli incarnates the problematic of Wright's evolving, historical poetic: the denial of the emblematic, the effacement of the authorial self. Ogotemmêli's ego inheres in the story. From the Poundian personae—"these masks, / with a place at last" (73)—Wright posits an essential emancipation: "Living, we free them; / dying, we learn / how we are freed ourselves" (73). No longer is the Emersonian equation of poet as seer applicable:

> I come here,
> .... attuned to some animal's
> tentative step,
> ... the design
> that escapes my eyes. (74)

The New World extension of this ancient, received covenant will be "to design / your own prefiguration" (76).

The Dogons' supernatural fear of naming, a "marked reluctance, arising from respect and fear, to mention the names or picture the forms of supernatural powers" (Griaule 1965:113), denies the possibility of narrative or lyric coherence in the Western sense. The simultaneous weaving and unweaving of Ogotemmêli's conversations result in the absence of an aesthetic construction; the story exists only in the telling. The "reluctance" to name refuses linguistic access to the Emersonian poet as "namer" but not to the poet as "language-maker" or as "the only teller of news." If, as Benjamin asserts, "a man's knowledge or wisdom, but above all his real life—and this is the stuff that stories are made of—first assumes transmissible form at the moment of his death" (1968:94), then the unresisted lines of "The Dead" initiate the transmission of the sequence's discontinuities and disjunctions. Epistemology and poetic come under erasure in this final telling.

Movement subordinates death in a progressive distancing from Western aesthetics and traditions. Silence (and silences) animate the internal path of allusion to the Banneker poems and their attendant histories and cosmologies, as well as to the forlorn and fetishized dead in "The Albuquerque Graveyard." The indeterminate silence of the animistic and ill-defined displaces the beginnings and endings, the linearity and logic of the articulate, creating a space where contraries embrace "moves still," "living dead." Poundian masks and Yeatsian dances fail to unify perceptions and resolve disjunction; so the poems slip:

> into the rhythm
> of emptiness and return,
> into the self
> moving against itself,
> into the self
> moving into itself,
> the word, and the first design. (78)

"Design," the province of the creator, yields to self-designation as Wright advances into the ultimate, because self-determined, liberation narrative—"Now, / I designate myself your child" (78)—in which covenant and circumstance "will have their place" and the poet, now subservient to the patriarch, will "learn these relations." The transmutation of "design" from nominal to verbal status reduplicates the pattern of this provisional, and often self-negating, collection. The progressive disabling of the textual field intensifies Wright's earlier judgment on Thomas Jefferson, "the man [who] read [Banneker's] soul's desire, losing the relations" (28).

The linguistic trace of "The Dead" restlessly echoes from Governor John Winthrop of the Massachusetts Bay Colony to Ogotemmêli, from religious predestination to aesthetic prefiguration. If Wright's cultural inversions constitute a temporizing, postnational, postmodern aesthetic, they do so with an ironic, solipsistic imperative: Trust the telling, not the tale. The split pairing of death and freedom advances a new "covenant" of admitted contraries: "a sign, / that your world moves still" (78). Wright has invented a simultaneous historical field in which language, culture, and nation are subsumed by the telling of the tale of the tribe.

With his invention of a historical consciousness independent of nation and narration, Jay Wright evolves beyond the chaotic "carnival of gods, customs, and arts ... the alien and disconnected" that Nietzsche had most feared (1980:10, 28) into the uncharted ambivalence of the "cultural space ... [of] the nation with its transgressive boundaries and its 'interruptive' interiority" (Bhabha 1994:5). The discrete representational strategies of race rhetoric that once had underwritten the narrative of black America resolve in Wright's poetry into a simultaneous field of textual orality, a site of critical memory in which the postnational and postmodern continue to write America black.

NOTES

1. Seeking to foreground Wright's aesthetic confrontation with national narratives, I risk invoking "America" as a received (desig)nation for the United States. See Kutzinski (1987:49–50) for a rationale for its de-emphasis: "Wright's territory is the New World, and I am employing this term very self-consciously to de-emphasize as much as possible the nationalistic connotations the term 'America' has acquired as a result of being used as a shorthand expression for the United States. If 'America' in anyway suggests a potentially unified area of study, it does so, as we have already seen, only by subordinating all cultural elements of a non-European origin to the claims of the so-called Anglo-North American cultural establishment."

2. For further discussion of the political field of the Black Arts movement, see the contemporaneous criticism included in the following anthologies: Redmond (1976); Baraka/Neal (1968); Henderson (1972). For contemporary assessment of the aesthetic consequences of these nationalist stirrings, see C. K. Doreski (1992), Gates (1987), Nielsen (1994), and Mackey (1993).

3. See, for example, Hollander (1981:n.p.), a review of Wright's *The Double Invention of Komo*, in which he identifies among the book's "subsidiary quests": "mythologies of the manly." See Mullen (1992:37) for a terse overview of "threatened black masculinity" in African-American letters, specifically Nathaniel Mackey's *Bedouin Hornbook*.

4. For a justification of this problematic term, see Bhabha (1994:4): "If the jargon of our times—postmodernity, postcoloniality, postfeminism— has any meaning at all, it does not lie in the popular use of the 'post' to indicate sequentiality—*after*-feminism; or polarity—*anti*-modernism. These terms that insistently gesture to the beyond, only embody its restless and revisionary energy if they transform the present into an expanded and ex-centric site of experience and empowerment."

5. See Benjamin's "The Storyteller," "The Image of Proust," and "Theses on the Philosophy of History" (1968: 83–110, 201–15, 253–64) for discussions of Enlightenment notions of progress in historical materialism; see Foner (1976) for documentary evidence of alternative declarations of independence; see Bhabha (1994:142) for the ultimate question of nation as narration: "How do we plot the narrative of the nation as narration that must mediate between the teleology of progress tipping over into the 'timeless' discourse of irrationality?"

6. See White (1978:36): "The First World War did much to destroy what remained of history's prestige among both artists and social scientists, for the war seemed to confirm what Nietzsche had maintained two generations earlier. History, which was supposed to provide some sort of training for life ... had done little to prepare men for the coming of the war."

7. Although Wright was obviously responding to Wallace Stevens's "The Comedian as the Letter C," not Holly Stevens's *Souvenirs and Prophecies*, it is interesting to note that her project was also published during the Bicentennial.

8. See Bhabha (1994:246) regarding de Certeau's formulation of the "non-place from which all historiographical operation starts, the lag which all histories must encounter in order to make a beginning."

9. See Wilson Harris (1967:10) for an expanded discussion of the "sun" and its "terrible" reality in the West Indian world and its metaphorical weight "in the American world [where] energy is the sun of life."

10. See Griaule (1965) and Turner (1974) for the cosmological ground of this partially shared system that underwrites the ontology of these earlier poems.

11. See Kutzinski (1987:54–72) for a compelling discussion of the Banneker poems as they serve to foreground her study of myth and history in Wright's *Dimensions of History*. All readers of Wright's poetry should be grateful to this model exercise in philology. Though I often take issue with her insistent readings that facilitate the "history as myth" equation (substituting one fixity for another), I am throughout this chapter indebted to her research.

12. Banneker's urban sophistication continues to inspire. See, for example, Rita Dove (1983:36–37) for her curatorial reading of "Banneker": "At nightfall he took out / his rifle—a white-maned / figure stalking the darkened / breast of the Union—and / shot at the stars, and by chance

one went out. Had he killed? / *I assure thee, my dear Sir!* / Lowering his
eyes to fields sweet with the rot of spring, he could see / a government's
domed city / rising from the morass and spreading / in a spiral of
lights."

13. For consideration of Benjamin's "readings" of cities, see Bahti
    (1992:183–204); Buck-Morss (1989); Benjamin (1986).

14. Gilroy (1993) and Bhabha (1994) provide essential readings of
    postcolonial transatlantic culture.

15. I strongly disagree with Kutzinski's reading of "Benjamin Banneker
    Sends His 'Almanac' to Thomas Jefferson," which subordinates the
    poem to "a shorter version a kind of double which revoices most of the
    important aspects of the former poem" (1987:55). Such an
    interpretation ignores the metaphysical and metaphoric vitality of the
    thing itself: the almanac.

16. See Rich (1993:130): "Africans carried poetry in contraband memory
    across the Middle Passage to create in slavery the 'Sorrow Songs.'"

17. In many ways, Wright's poem extends a genre familiar to readers of
    Allen Tate's "Ode for the Confederate Dead" and Robert Lowell's "For
    the Union Dead" (see William Doreski [1990:24–25, 78–80, 139–45]).
    Wright's elegiac response addresses not the failure to commemorate
    but the inability to do so.

18. See Alice Walker (1975:93–118).

19. See Rowell (1983:4), where Wright defines the collectivity of the poetic
    enterprise: "The *we* is the corporation of human beings who require
    and accept poetry's charter within it."

WORKS CITED

Bahti, Timothy. 1992. *Allegories of History, Literary Historiography after Hegel.*
    Baltimore, Md.: Johns Hopkins University Press.

Baldwin, James. 1985. "White Man's Guilt" (1968). In *The Price of the Ticket:
    Collected Nonfiction, 1948–1985.* New York: St. Martin's Press. 409–14.

Baraka, Amiri, and Larry Neal, eds. 1968. *Black Fire: An Anthology of Afro-
    American Writing.* New York: William Morrow.

Benjamin, Walter. 1968. *Illuminations: Essays and Reflections.* Trans. Harry
    Zohn. New York: Schocken Books.

———. 1986. "Paris, Capital of the Nineteenth Century" (1955). In
    Reflections: Essays, Aphorisms, Autobiographical Writings. Trans. Edmund
    Jephcott. New York: Schocken Books. 146–62.

Bhabha, Homi K. 1994. *The Location of Culture.* New York: Routledge.

Buck-Morss, Susan. 1989. *The Dialectics of Seeing: Walter Benjamin and the
    Arcades Project.* Cambridge, Mass.: MIT Press.

Crane, Hart. 1966. *White Buildings* (1926). In *The Complete Poems and Selected Letters and Prose of Hart Crane*. New York: Liveright Publishing. 3–44.

Doreski, C. K. 1992. "Kinship and History in Sam Cornish's *Generations.*" *Contemporary Literature* 33:663–86.

Doreski, William. 1990. *The Years of Our Friendship: Robert Lowell and Allen Tate*. Jackson: University Press of Mississippi.

Dove, Rita. 1983. *Museum*. Pittsburgh: Carnegie-Mellon University Press.

Duncan, Robert. 1984. *Ground Work: Before the War*. New York: New Directions.

Eliot, T. S. 1971. "Little Gidding" (1942). In *The Complete Poems and Plays, 1909–1950*. San Diego, Calif: Harcourt Brace Jovanovich. 138–48.

Foner, Philip, ed. *We, the Other People: Alternative Declarations of Independence by Labor Groups, Farmers, Women's Rights Advocates, Socialists, and Blacks, 1829–1975*. Urbana: University of Illinois Press, 1976.

Gates, Henry Louis, Jr. 1987. *Figures in Black: Words, Signs, and the "Racial" Self*. New York: Oxford University Press.

Gilroy, Paul. 1993. *The Black Atlantic: Modernity and Double Consciousness*. Cambridge, Mass.: Harvard University Press.

Griaule, Marcel. 1965. *Conversations with Ogotemmêli: An Introduction to Dogon Religious Ideas*. Trans. Ralph Butler, Audrey Richards, and Beatrice Hooke. New York: Oxford University Press.

Harris, Wilson. 1967. *Tradition: The Writer and Society—Critical Essays*. London: New Beacon Publications.

Henderson, Stephen E. 1972. *Understanding the New Black Poetry: Black Speech and Black Music as Poetic References*. New York: William Morrow.

Hollander, John. 1981. "Tremors of Exactitude." Review of *The Double Invention of Komo*, by Jay Wright. *Times Literary Supplement*, 30 January, n.p.

Jefferson, Thomas. 1984. "Letter to Benjamin Banneker" (1791). In *Writings: Autobiography, Notes on the State of Virginia, Public and Private Papers, Addresses, Letters*. New York: Library of America. 982.

Kenner, Hugh. 1971. *The Pound Era*. Berkeley: University of California Press.

Kutzinski, Vera M. 1987. *Against the American Grain: Myth and History in William Carlos Williams, Jay Wright, and Nicholas Guillin*. Baltimore, Md.: Johns Hopkins University Press.

Mackey, Nathaniel. 1993. *Discrepant Engagement: Dissonance, Cross-Culturality, and Experimental Writing*. Cambridge: Cambridge University Press.

Mullen, Harryette. 1992. "'Phantom Pain': Nathaniel Mackey's *Bedouin Hornbook*." *Talisman* 9:37–43.

Nielsen, Aldon Lynn. 1994. *Writing between the Lines: Race and Intertextuality*. Athens: University of Georgia Press.

Nietzsche, Friedrich. 1980. *On the Advantage and Disadvantage of History for Life*. Trans. Peter Preuss. Indianapolis: Hackett.

Pound, Ezra. 1995. *The Cantos of Ezra Pound* (1972). New York: New Directions.

Redmond, Eugene B. 1976. *Drumvoices: The Mission of Afro-American Poetry—A Critical History*. Garden City, N.Y.: Doubleday-Anchor.

Rich, Adrienne. 1993. "History Stops for No One." In *What Is Found There*. New York: W. W. Norton. 128–44.

Rowell, Charles H. 1983. "'The Unravelling of the Egg': An Interview with Jay Wright." *Callaloo* 6.3:3–15.

Stevens, Wallace. 1954. *The Collected Poems of Wallace Stevens*. New York: Alfred A. Knopf.

———. 1966. *Letters of Wallace Stevens*. Ed. Holly Stevens. London: Faber and Faber.

———. 1976. *Souvenirs and Prophecies: The Young Wallace Stevens*. Ed. Holly Stevens. New York: Alfred A. Knopf

Turner, Victor. 1974. *Dramas, Fields, and Metaphors: Symbolic Action in Human Society*. Ithaca, N.Y.: Cornell University Press.

Walker, Alice. 1975. "Looking for Zora." In *Search of Our Mothers' Gardens: Womanist Prose*. San Diego, Calif: Harcourt Brace Jovanovich. 93–118.

———. 1997. "Clear Seeing, Inherited Religion and Reclaiming the Pagan Self" *On the Issues* 6 (Spring): 16–23, 54–55.

White, Hayden. 1978. *Tropics of Discourse: Essays in Cultural Criticism*. Baltimore, Md.: Johns Hopkins University Press.

Wright, Jay. 1967. "Death as History." In *Death as History*. New York: Poets Press. N.p.

1971. *The Homecoming Singer*. New York: Corinth Books.

1976a. *Dimensions of History*. Santa Cruz, Calif: Kayak.

1976b. *Soothsayers and Omens*. New York: Seven Woods Press.

FABIAN CLEMENTS WORSHAM

The Poetics of Matrilineage: Mothers and Daughters in the Poetry of African American Women, 1965-1985

"The image of the mother," according to critic Andrea Benton Rushing, "is the most prevalent image of black women" in African American poetry ("Afro-American," 75). These images have been developed through a long and distinguished literary history, reaching back through the diaspora to ancient African cultures in which "the African woman is associated with core values" and is revered as "guardian of traditions, the strong Earth-Mother who stands for security and stability" (Rushing, "African," 19). These values, passed down through an oral tradition in which women have played a major role, as well as through the medium of print, continue to define the ways black women are represented in African American literature and the ways they perceive themselves and their daughters and act upon these perceptions. Christine Renee Robinson argues that "self-reliance, independence, assertiveness, and strength are inherent characteristics of Black women which are passed on to Black girls at a very early age" (Nice, 68). And it has been widely noted that, contrary to the experience of most white women, black mothers and daughters prosper through relationships that are mutually loving and supportive (Nice, 197; Washington, 148). A recent landmark study by Vivian E. Nice not only points out the relevance of these literary images to sociological and psychological explorations of black motherhood, but also suggests the possibility of using these artistic representations of

From *Women of Color: Mother-Daughter Relationships in 20th Century Literature*, edited by Elizabeth Brown-Guillory. © 1996 by the University of Texas Press.

relationships between black mothers and daughters as models of the kind of supportive, interdependent relationships possible between mothers and daughters of any race once freed from the distorting influences of patriarchal culture.

The writings of African American women hold particular interest for Nice and other feminist theorists who seek to replace the Freudian model of female adolescent development (which emphasizes conflict) with a model based on interdependency and "growth through relationships" (Nice, 66), thus fostering stronger positive bonds between all mothers and daughters and between members of the larger community of women. Nice is aware, however, that ambivalence and conflict will be part of even the most loving relationships, and she applauds contemporary black women writers for revealing ambivalence "in all its glory." In the works of the contemporary poets she cites, there exists "the connection between mothers and daughters and the legacy of strength between them without denying the anger, guilt, and difficulties in communication which can also exist and the fact that connection and anger can in fact co-exist" (187).

In African American poetry, however, there have been at least three forces working to limit the depth of characterization and fullness of description in representations of black mothers and daughters:

1. the symbolic nature of the mother in the African American tradition;
2. the dominant white culture's insistence on what it identifies as universality;
3. the necessity of promoting "positive images" of blacks in order to achieve social change.

With regard to the first of these forces, Rushing notes that "women often symbolize aspects of black life that are valued by the race"; she claims that "that usually unconscious thrust has been something of a straightjacket" ("Afro-American," 74). She calls these symbolic images "epic," "heroic," or "archetypal" ("Afro-American," 82). In another instance, she reflects that poetry may not be a suitable instrument for creating realistic characters ("African," 24). Nan Bauer Maglin agrees that these depictions are often symbolic, but she emphasizes the legitimacy of symbolic representation:

> In the literature of matrilineage often the strength of the women in our past is sentimentalized or is magnified so that our own strength appears to be negligible—especially in terms of the hard physical and social conditions of the past. Sometimes our

genealogical and historical mothers become not persons but symbols (which we need) and lose their multidimensionality. (263)

Maglin cites Lucille Clifton's "My Mama Moved among the Days" as an example of such symbolization, but she argues that Clifton's depiction is "not simplistic" since the poem reveals the mother's fear as well as her strength (263).

Taking a different approach, Arnold Rampersad in his article "The Universal and the Particular in Afro-American Poetry" writes of the dominant white culture's insistence on universality and its equally vehement insistence that the particulars of black experience cannot be construed as universal. Such strictures led to the propagation of "raceless virtues" as black writers attempted to "elevate" their writing while effectively binding it in shackles. Rampersad says of this verse that it "is sometimes executed in glorious fashion, but in many instances it is much like the efforts of a man bound and gagged who is trying to get one's attention" (9). True universality is rooted in the specifics of everyday life; false universality (that prescribed by the dominant culture) "thrives on vagueness; it abhors the specific in any form that stresses concrete experience" (8). Rampersad identifies Amiri Baraka as the poet who, in the 1960s, initiated "a violent assault on the obsessively universal in Afro-American writing" (14).

Finally, the necessity of promoting "positive images" of blacks in general and of black women in particular may have contributed somewhat to the limiting range of characterization of mothers and daughters (for references to the need for positive images, see Ward, 189; Giovanni, 40; Parker, xxx). The projection of positive images, of course, is essential to the development of black pride and self-worth and is a key element in countering stereotypes such as "the Mammy" and "Sapphire." However, this inherently good and useful prescription for change may have produced a somewhat paradoxical side effect: a positive stereotype. As Rushing observes, "in almost all the mother poems, mother is above criticism, the almost perfect symbol of black struggle, suffering, and endurance" ("Afro-American," 76). Ward warns, though, of the problems inherent in judging the adequacy of these representations:

Whether visions of Black women in literature are positive or negative, true or distorted, good or bad, real or surreal, satisfying or inadequate is relative. Evaluation of the vision depends in part on some understanding of the cultural imperatives that governed its creation and in part on whether those imperatives (linguistic, social, psychological, etc.) are constant with our own. (188)

In the intensely autobiographical poems of contemporary African Americans, such as Alice Walker, Lucille Clifton, Carolyn Rodgers, Audre Lorde, and Colleen McElroy, images of black mothers and daughters have achieved a fullness and depth of representation which indicate the individuality of black women and the diversity of their experience. Although the poems are at times more abstract and symbolic, at times more concrete and specific, taken together they provide the model of interdependency which Nice speaks of, with its welter of love, ambivalence, admiration, and anger.

An impressive example of the strong traditional mother appears in Alice Walker's sequence "In These Dissenting Times" (Adoff, 475–480). In carefully crafted, spare verses, Walker employs incremental description to build, piece by piece, an image of a woman of her mother's generation, a mighty gold-toothed woman who dragged her children to church. The third poem in the sequence is entitled "Women," and it is here, primarily, that Walker consciously creates an iconography of traditional black motherhood. As is apparent from the poem's title, Walker has no intention of creating individualized, idiosyncratic portraits of these women. Here she continues the generalized, fragmentary descriptions begun in the prologue. She describes the women's voices as husky, their steps as stout, and their hands as fists. And she shows the women acting not in isolated, separate incidents, but in actions which have become mythologized, embedded in the cultural consciousness of African Americans because of their persuasiveness and the intense emotion—the pain, the humiliation, and the fortitude—which those actions symbolize. The persona notes that these "Headragged Generals" (477) demolished barriers and marched across mined fields to secure an education for their children. Yet when her purpose is individual representation, she does that equally well. In the fourth poem of the sequence, "Three Dollars Cash," she particularizes a representation of her own mother by retelling the story of how her family paid the midwife who brought her into the world. Most of the poem is spoken by the mother, and the diction and cadences of the mother's speech further particularize the poem. The mother's language also creates a casual, informal atmosphere, as does Walker's use of the word "Mom" rather than "Mother."

Whether Walker speaks symbolically or specifically, throughout the sequence she restricts herself to the idealized representation of black motherhood. According to Mary Burgher,

> Values specifically attributed to Black mothers include the belief
> that there is a promised land beyond this life of bondage and
> oppression, that one has within oneself the natural wit and

resourcefulness to find strength in apparent weakness, joy in sorrow, and hope in what seems to be despair, and that the love of a mother cannot always be determined by physical presence or material gifts. (116)

The faith and determination of these women is shown in their insistence that life will be better for their children, even if that involves physical hardship and sacrifice for themselves. Burgher emphasizes these qualities: "It is not she separately who is significant and it is not what she attains personally and immediately that matters; instead it is what the future brings from the ideas she expresses, the consciousness she reflects, the action she takes" (120).

In much of the poetry of these contemporary writers, the mother is a figure of such mythic proportions that her life haunts her daughters through the duration of their own lives. Lucille Clifton, whose mother died in mid-life (at age forty-four), has written extensively upon this theme. In her poem "Breaklight," she speaks of her own intellectual and spiritual growth, which culminates in a new understanding of her mother. She says that when her mother's fears approached her she listened as they explained themselves to her. The persona notes with certainty, "And I understand" (*An Ordinary Woman*, 85). These experiences of mystical enlightenment culminate in a very intense, personal understanding. It is useful, in considering this poem, to look at Clifton's "My Mama Moved among the Days" (Adoff, 308). Part of what Clifton finally "understood" in "Breaklight" may have been what she was unable to understand earlier: her mother was able to get them "almost through the high grass," but seemingly turned around and ran back into the wilderness. The mother here is loved and yearned for, but is not idealized, even though the language is highly symbolic. She has not fully carried out her responsibilities to her daughter. These may be particular responsibilities which remain unnamed and which the mother left undone out of fear or they may simply be her obligation to live and to nurture her daughter, which she was unable to do. Both poems are dreamlike: Mama moves "like a dreamwalker in a field," the disembodied fears knock at the door, trying to "explain themselves." In coming to understand her mother's fears through these dreams, Clifton resolves the bewildering unfinished relationship (at least momentarily, to the extent that poetry can serve that therapeutic function) and assuages her pain.

In a poem commemorating the twenty-first year of her mother's absence ("february 13, 1980"), she speaks again of her grief and pain, naming her mother "the lost color in my eye" (*two-headed woman*, 15). Clifton, whose middle name is Thelma, after her mother, feels that her mother's name has continued to protect her despite her mother's physical absence. She says that she has worn her mother's name like a shield. Her complex feelings are apparent when she notes that the shield has both ripped her up and safeguarded her. And since her mother's absence has come of age, Clifton determines that she must now accept the responsibilities that go along with womanhood. But she assures her absent mother that although she has grown into a self-sufficient woman, she nonetheless remains spiritually close to her. Her mother, though dead, is a continuing presence in her life; lest she disappoint the lingering spirit, the daughter must reassure her that she is still loved and needed.

Approaching the age at which her mother died, Clifton ruminates more darkly upon her mother's death in two poems, "the thirty eighth year" and "poem on my fortieth birthday to my mother who died young." In the first one, the tone is resigned and melancholy, as Clifton reflects upon her life and finds herself merely "an ordinary woman." Implicitly, she compares herself to her mother, finding herself inadequate. She says that she had expected to be more than she was. Instead she views herself as "plain as bread" (*An Ordinary Woman*, 93). In contrast, she remembers her mother as very wise and beautiful. Despite these perceived differences, she identifies strongly with her mother, saying that she has surrounded herself with memories of her mother so that her mother's dreams could be fulfilled through her. The persona clearly sees herself as a continuation or replication of the mother. The implication is that daughters cannot truly find voice until they validate their mother's voice or experiences. Having rescued her mother from death by living for her, she now faces the death which swallowed up her mother. She associates life with images of Africa and death, in contrast, with images of Europe. The prospect of death creates in her an intense loneliness which she had not anticipated; if she is coming to the end of her life, she asks that she be allowed to come to it without fear and loneliness. She says that before she dies, she wants to come "into [her] own" (95). Here she is not seeking to escape from her mother's life (and thus from death), but to emerge from her mother's life equipped with the emotional resources which will allow her to live her own life fully before it ends.

The image of "turning the final turn" derived from the footrace is used again in "poem on my fortieth birthday" (*two-headed woman*, 14). Here the tone is not at all melancholy; rather than growing more abject as the fateful date nears, Clifton (perhaps drawing upon the emotional resources she has inherited and cultivated) seems to rally as she approaches the homestretch. Defiant, strong, goal-oriented, she informs her mother that she intends to keep running. Yet she is not convinced of victory: "if I fall / I fall." The vortex of her mother's death continues to pull her into its spiral.

A truly grueling example of this intense mother/daughter identification is Carolyn Rodgers's "The Children of Their Sin," a double narrative in four parts (21–25). Three of the parts relate the daughter's decision to change seats on a public conveyance; one part tells of the mother's being mugged. As the mother's and daughter's experiences are interwoven, the daughter's changing seats becomes even more intense, violent, and emotionally wrenching than her mother's mugging.

In the first section of the poem, Rodgers explains that she decides to change seats on a bus (or possibly a train) because the man who sat down next to her seems unsavory. Because she has money in her pockets (and because she bears her mother's experience in mind, as is revealed later), she moves to a seat by a stylishly dressed white businessman. Yet as she does so, she "smother[s] faint memories and / shadows and things." The dramatic and passionate narration of the mother's mugging (by a "mean nigger") in section two is followed in section three by the riveting protest of the shadows which she had "smothered" in section one. While she fears that this poor, hungry black brother might mug her, she is reminded by a coliseum of black women ancestors of all the atrocities that white slaveholders heaped upon blacks. These ancestors scream to her to remember the whips, the bodies hanging from trees, the women who were raped and whose children were sold away. The poem moves toward a crescendo of anguish and guilt as Rodgers hears her mother's desperate screams juxtaposed against the agonies of the black race at the hands of white slaveholders. Identifying with her mother, she chooses white over black (she changes seats). Although at first she is only vaguely uncomfortable at this decision, ultimately she understands that her choice is a true act of treason against her race.

Produced at the heart of the Black Arts Movement and promoted by Dudley Randall's Broadside Press, Carolyn Rodgers's work is widely known and often discussed. Her poems "Jesus Was Crucified, or It Must Be Deep" and a companion piece, "It Is Deep," in which Rodgers refers to her mother as "a sturdy Black bridge that I / crossed over, on," are well known (8–12). Rodgers is especially skilled in the depiction of conflict, whether internal or interpersonal. In "Jesus Was Crucified," the points of contention between mother and daughter are apparent: the mother does not approve of her daughter's rejection of religion or her association with revolutionaries (whom she accuses of being Communists); the daughter resents the mother's complacency and lack of political awareness. The daughter's tone throughout is sarcastic and sassy; the mother appears backward and ridiculous, and there is little in this poem to indicate that the daughter has any compassion for her. In the collection *how i got ovah*, however, this poem is followed by "It Is Deep," which serves as a sort of retraction and reconciliation. This poem indicates a complete shift in the daughter's awareness; suddenly she understands that despite their differences they are united by their love and strengthened by the hardships they have come through together.

Discussions of these poems are included in studies by Maglin (265) and Nice (187). Both critics recognize that these poems show the ambivalence characteristic of any intense, enduring relationship, and both recognize the relationship depicted as a model of their ideal mutual support and interdependency. Maglin also notes that "It Is Deep" "articulates some of the themes of the literature of matrilineage: the distance between the mother and daughter; the sudden new sense the daughter has of the mother; the realization that she, her mother, is a strong woman; and that her voice reverberates with her mother's" (265).

Although Maglin and Nice focus on a pair of poems in which conflicts are neatly worked out, in a growing number of mother–daughter poems conflicts are not resolved so neatly, and some are not resolved at all. Despite the tendency for relationships between black mothers and their daughters to be supportive, there are individual exceptions, and some of them are poets. Audre Lorde appears to be one of these, though her struggle to understand her mother is evident in her poems. One of them, "Story Books on a Kitchen Table" (*Coal*, 27), opens, "Out of her womb of pain my mother spat me / into her ill-fitting harness of despair."

Lorde's diction here is sharp and effective; the connotations of *spat*—disgust, disdain, and filthiness—in this context, the act of giving birth, are intended to shock and offend. The child is immediately harnessed—confined—in the mother's despairing world view. The mother undoubtedly fears that her child will shame her by not turning out properly, that she will reject her mother's views and values. Her mother leaves her, for reasons unstated, in the care of "iron maidens." Needing the warmth and tenderness of a "perfect" mother, the child is left with emotionally distant old women. She is (mal)nourished on European witch tales rather than stories of her African-Caribbean heritage. The table is empty, the mother vanished. The poem suggests that there are mothers who seek to control and manipulate; when their daughters resist, the conflict intensifies. The child's loneliness and desperate needs are manifested as heartache—the ache of the ill-fitting harness, a despair like her mother's.

In the poem "Prologue" (*From a Land*, 43–46) Lorde says that in her mother's attempts to teach her survival strategies she tried to beat her whiter every day. She refers to her mother's "bleached ambition" as her motivation for teaching her children about her mother's errors. In her integrity and determination to speak the truth as she understands it, Lorde does not minimize the mother's error; yet the insertion of one word, *survival*, associated as it is with the fabric of oppression, clarifies the complexity of the situation. The mother is not infallibly good or innately evil. And as her mother tried to beat her into whiteness, Lorde recalls her "loving me into her blood's black bone." Here the paradoxical identification of physical punishment with love and Lorde's recognition that she and her mother are bound the more strongly for it are evident. Lorde's attempts to understand her mother are also revealed in "Black Mother Woman," where she imagistically represents the process of this understanding: she has peeled away her mother's anger "down to the core of love" (*From a Land*, 16).

Another contemporary black woman who has written exceptional poems on the theme of mother–daughter conflict is Colleen McElroy. The image she presents of the mother in the poem "Bone Mean" could not in any way be construed as positive. The persona notes that the mother has stacked the world against her daughter. Intentionally mean and vindictive, this mother serves mint-flavored ice cream at the child's birthday party, fully aware that the child dislikes it. As her daughters have matured, she has "Pruned and pinched / them into bonsai symmetry" (*Queen*, 25). A harsh, domineering, cronelike woman, she seeks to control everything around her, until her daughters have no voices and no wins of their own.

Although such a poem is not politically useful in the interests of feminism or race struggle, it is nonetheless a valid and skillfully constructed work of art. If one insists that all art is political, then this poem might be construed as misogynist. If one holds, however, that a poem should be the artist's representation of the truth of her experience as she conceives it, then this poem is a work of integrity, and perhaps also of courage, for the view presented here has not been "politically correct" since the mid-sixties.

Intense, unresolved conflict is the theme again in McElroy's poem "Ruth" (Stetson, 287–288). The daughter has been haunted for twenty-seven years by her memory of her mother falling down a flight of stairs during one of their arguments. She remembers the terror she felt as she was unable to prevent her mother from falling. Immobilized, she felt like the famous statue of Venus (the Aphrodite of Melos) without arms to catch her mother. Here imagery reveals her complex feelings: on the one hand, the mother is "larger than life," "a great vulture"; on the other, she is "fragile ... plunging in wingless flight." McElroy has been unable to write about this incident for twenty-seven years, all attempts thwarted by the memory of her mother's angry words. Nonetheless, her relationship with her mother has been an obsession, as is evident in the countless unfinished verses about her mother which she has stuffed away in closets. Writing the poem, she has finally recognized the cycle of pain and blood in which she and her mother (and all women) are trapped. She has been unable to see herself in her mother, to recognize the forces that unify them, including perhaps their shared oppression. And she understands that she will someday continue the cycle in her relationship with her own daughter. However, the ending of the poem does not indicate a complete reversal—anger and bitterness have not completely been replaced by love and understanding. Modifying the words of the biblical Ruth, McElroy says, "Wherever I go you have gone." Not only does she see her mother as having prepared the way for her, but she cannot find a path that is uniquely hers—a path her mother has not taken before her—and she finds this frustrating. The persona is in search of a space to call her very own, perhaps, one in which she will be able to break the cycle of pain and begin a new legacy which includes joy.

As is apparent in quite a few of these poems, including this one, feelings are complex. They result from a lifetime of experience and, like thunder-heads, are continuously roiling. The poems about mothers and daughters reflect the shifting configurations of feelings.

McElroy's poems do not exclusively present conflicts, though she does that with great skill. Perhaps the most beautiful poem she has written is "Mother," a birth poem rich with the imagery of the African jungle (*Music*, 34–35). The poet imagines her mother, sedated while giving birth to her, dreaming of "emerald green forests," "queleas and touracos." The mother's dream of Africa symbolizes her role in the generational continuity of the black race. Her daughter, the poet, sits in an easy chair, happy and comfortable, trying to remember what it was like to be in her mother's womb. Continuity of lineage is emphasized as the daughter hums her mother's song while her own children watch her.

Two other notable birth poems are Audre Lorde's "Now That I Am Forever with Child" and Lucille Clifton's "light." Lorde's poem deals with the birth of her daughter, including the experience of pregnancy, her thoughts about the baby's prenatal development, the birth itself, and (in a brief conclusion) the child's individuation. Clifton's poem is about her own birth, particularly her mother's choice of the name Lucille for her, and includes the story of her ancestor whose name she is given. All of these birth poems are romantic, magical representations.

According to Nice, "there is much less written by mothers than by daughters on the mother–daughter relationship" (70). Indeed, this is true with regard to poetry. Outstanding poems by mothers on daughters are rare, the strongest having been written by Audre Lorde. Several have also been produced by Alice Walker. These poems focus on misgivings and insecurities which the mother experiences as she attempts to raise her daughter.

In "What My Child Learns of the Sea," Lorde ponders the intellectual growth of her daughter, who, despite what Lorde has passed on to her, will one day be a "strange girl ... cutting my ropes" (*Coal*, 22). Yet Lorde herself will feel responsible for her daughter's view of the world, her optimism or pessimism. In "Progress Report" Lorde deals with her daughter's adolescence and, despite the apparent love between the two, the growing distance between them. When her daughter asks her about love, Lorde doesn't know whether to recommend "a dictionary / or myself" (*From a Land*, 13). She feels unsure whether she has taught her daughter enough about blackness and she knows that behind the closed door of her room her daughter is reading secret books. Lorde's respect for her maturing daughter, her acceptance of her as an individual, is obvious throughout the poem. She appreciates the child's strength of spirit, tenderness, and fearlessness, qualities she admires; and she remembers to knock before entering her daughter's room.

Alice Walker's poems about her daughter are very different from Lorde's—more direct and less evocative. Nonetheless, they reveal similar insecurities. Only a few lines of the poem "Mississippi Winter III" focus on her daughter, but what emerges clearly is Walker's anticipation of her daughter's adolescence, even though the child is only four. Walker is "alarmed" that her little daughter already "smells / of Love-Is-True perfume" (*Horses*, 38). This experience leads Walker to muse upon her own preference to avoid romance. "My Daughter Is Coming!" (*Horses*, 38–39) shows Walker frantic as she prepares a room for her daughter, who has been living far away in the custody of her father. Joyous, excited, and insecure, she worries that her daughter will only notice the torn curtains. Poems of this kind, in which mothers reveal their feelings about their daughters and illustrate the difficulties of motherhood, prove to be a valuable resource in understanding the mother's role.

Poems in which the poet deals with her role as both a mother and a daughter are especially rare. However, it is in these poems that the continuity of generations can be seen most clearly. Colleen McElroy's "In My Mother's Room" not only reveals the linkage of women from generation to generation within her own family, but also points to the connection of all women within a larger women's culture (*Queen*, 5–6). McElroy's images of her mother are not idealized, yet they achieve symbolic power. Her unflattering description of her mother's vulnerable naked body, with its childbearing scars, her mouth sagging open, suggests that this is a woman of flesh and blood and that McElroy is able to see beyond her role as mother to her physical existence as a woman. Though they are torn by conflict, she and her mother are "shadows of black into black," and she expects to follow her mother in "age-old patterns." Her connection with her mother and with all women is apparent in her assertion that she will follow the path of her foremothers in childbirth. Thus, here again as in "Ruth" is the "cycle of blood and pain" with its connection to fertility, childbirth, the continuation of one's genetic line, and the propagation of one's race. Though McElroy's daughter is innocent about what lies ahead for her, the poet understands that her continuation of this female role is inevitable.

Lucille Clifton also links three generations of women in her family in her poem "i was born with twelve fingers" (*two-headed woman*, 4). Using the extra fingers which she, her mother, and her daughter were born with as a symbol of magical power and generational continuity, she says that members of their community were afraid that they would learn to cast spells. Here Clifton alludes to the mythological woman of power, the African conjurer. Although the fingers were surgically removed, the power is not so easily excised. She speaks of the missing fingers as ghosts with powerful memories. This line of women remains powerful: "we take what we want / with invisible fingers." And she closes the poem with a beautiful image of the three women—one dead, two living, linking those amazing hands across the boundaries of death.

Contemporary African American women poets, whose cultural traditions have primed them for this task, are speaking of these connections between women and in doing so are creating a poetics of matrilineage. The simple direct verses of Alice Walker, the terse, mystical writings of Lucille Clifton, the passionate lines of Carolyn Rodgers, the evocative encodings of Audre Lorde, and the richly imagistic poems of Colleen McElroy are diverse representations of black women as mothers and as daughters. These writers are "beginning to piece together the story of a viable female culture" (Washington, 147). A part of that culture will be a full understanding of what it means to be the mother of a daughter or the daughter of a mother. Additionally, these poets are finding ways to see beyond those relationships, to see their mothers and their daughters as unique, individual women within a larger community of women. The mother–daughter poems produced by these talented and wise black women suggest that both mothers and daughters grow spiritually when they recognize and valorize each other's experiences as women.

Works Cited

Adoff, Arnold, ed. *The Poetry of Black America: Anthology of the Twentieth Century*. New York: Harper and Row, 1973.

Bell, Roseann P., Bettye J. Parker, and Beverly Guy-Sheftall, eds. *Sturdy Black Bridges: Visions of Black Women in Literature*. Garden City, N.Y.: Anchor Doubleday, 1979.

Burgher, Mary. "Images of Self and Race in the Autobiographies of Black Women." In Bell et al., 107–122.

Clifton, Lucille. *An Ordinary Woman*. New York: Random House, 1974.

———. *two-headed woman*. Amherst: University of Massachusetts Press, 1980.

Giovanni, Nikki. *Re:Creation*. Detroit: Broadside Press, 1970.

Lorde, Audre. *Coal*. New York: W. W. Norton, 1976.

———. *From a Land Where Other People Live*. Detroit: Broadside Press, 1973, rpt. 1983.

Maglin, Nan Bauer. "Don't never forget the bridge that you crossed over on: The Literature of Matrilineage." In *The Lost Tradition: Mothers and Daughters in Literature*, ed. Cathy N. Davidson and E. M. Broner, 257–267. New York: Frederick Ungar, 1980.

McElroy, Colleen J. *Music from Home: Selected Poems*. Carbondale: Southern Illinois University Press, 1976.

———. *Queen of the Ebony Isles*. Middletown, Conn.: Wesleyan University Press, 1984.

Nice, Vivian E. *Mothers and Daughters: The Distortion of a Relationship*. New York: St. Martin's, 1992.

Parker, Bettye J. "Introduction." In Bell et al., xxv–xxxi.

Rampersad, Arnold. "The Universal and the Particular in Afro-American Poetry." *CLA Journal* 25, no. 1 (1981): 1–17.

Rodgers, Carolyn. *how i got ovah: New and Selected Poems*. Garden City, N.Y.: Anchor Press / Doubleday, 1975.

Rushing, Andrea Benton. "Images of Black Women in Afro-American Poetry." In *The Afro-American Woman: Struggles and Images*, ed. Sharon Hartley and Rosalyn Teborg-Penn, 74–84. Port Washington, N.Y.: National University Publications–Kennikat Press, 1978.

———. "Images of Black Women in Modern African Poetry: An Overview." In Bell et al., 18–24.

Stetson, Erlene, ed. *Black Sister: Poetry by Black American Women 1746–1980*. Bloomington: Indiana University Press, 1981.

Walker, Alice. *Horses Make a Landscape Look More Beautiful*. New York: Harcourt, 1984.

Ward, Jerry D. "Bridges and Deep Water." In Bell et al., 184–190.

Washington, Mary Helen. "I Sign My Mother's Name: Alice Walker, Dorothy West, Paule Marshall." In *Mothering the Mind: Twelve Studies of Writers and Their Silent Partners*, ed. Ruth Perry and Martine Watson Brownley, 142–163. New York: Holmes and Meier, 1984.

JOHN F. CALLAHAN

"Close Roads": The Friendship Songs of Michael S. Harper

"Jesus Christ," I used to say when the phone bills came ten, fifteen, or twenty years ago, "Did I talk to goddamn Michael that long?" (And that's only half of what I really meant!) But as I paid those bills over the years, I came to realize how precious those minutes, seconds, and sometimes those hours were, how much the spirit flowed during those calls. Now when the bills come, almost but not quite as finely calculated as the final minute of the fourth quarter in the NBA, I'm glad of every second and every penny of every last bill:

> our voices rising over gray Portland skies.

Not because I love the phone company—there's Michael's clarifying cadence slipping into the breaks of my prose as it does from time to time in my conversation. ("I can always tell when you've seen Michael," my eldest daughter, Eve, tells me in her direct, loving, slightly headstrong way, "because you talk like him." And then she must notice a new line in the creases around my eyes. "You're still you," she'll add to soften the blow, "but I hear Uncle Michael in your voice.") No, I don't love the phone company, but the older I get, the more I love having a record of those calls "amidst the circuits / of brain waves" in the computer bank of the universe.

From *Callaloo* 13, no. 4. © 1991 by John F. Callahan.

I won't tell much about my first meeting with Michael Harper; the space was too sealed off, too much a place of hibernation, the occasion too dependent on the orchestration of others; the time too unpropitious except for feelings of rage or grief:

> say nightmare, say it loud
> panebreaking heartmadness:
> nightmare begins responsibility.

I met Michael the Sunday after Martin Luther King was murdered and the day before the funeral. I had marched, never more conscious of the whiteness of my skin, through Albina, the black section of Portland, yes, Albina. Everyone marching, black and white, had been excruciatingly nice. Together we walked on eggshells amidst slivers of broken glass so invisibly cruel I almost wished there'd been a riot in Portland. Afterwards, I went to the house of new friends who were old friends of Michael's from Iowa City days:

> Now I live in the bear's house
> marking the spare implements
> he's used, with intense impunity.

Few eggshells there at first when Michael, Shirley, and Roland (almost two) arrived. Soon enough familiar slivers of glass sprouted like weeds through the old hardwood floors in the person of a know-it-all graduate student, someone's relative. I was the designated wedding guest to this young ancient mariner without a story to tell. Against my better judgment I stayed for dinner but left soon after when the talk turned to politics and pragmatism, never passion, because I had committed all the artillery of body and soul I possessed to the Oregon campaign of Eugene McCarthy:

> As for the president, Gene McCarthy, the poet who only
> got into the White House to read his poems, the body-politic
> and sang the clearest song to Sterling Brown and Robert Hayden.

So in the literal sense I met Michael Harper in April 1968 but knew him hardly at all then, or him me. For all the extenuating circumstances, I don't think there was yet the charge or connection that sometimes marks a lifelong friendship from the start. When he returned to Oregon a month later to read his poems in a show-and-tell performance for a one-year job at Lewis and Clark, I was so far off the deep end making my rounds of the fifteen McCarthy storefronts in my charge that I missed the reading. No, my friendship with Michael Harper began differently, unexpectedly, some lucky combination of affinity and curiosity overcoming the measured guard each of us probably thought he should have up against the other:

> out of nowhere
> *confirmation, confirmation, confirmation.*

"'Young mahn, what have you thar?'" Sterling Brown, in his mimicking best *basso profoundo*, used to swear the good Doctor Du Bois had asked him and Ralph Bunche early, early one morning after rising from a cot in a tent on the Spingarn estate in an effort to swipe Bunche's applejack (read moonshine). Somehow that line strikes me as apropos of my chance encounter with Michael after an English Department meeting which he was told not to bother attending and for that reason attended:

> The conservatives, the lower division,
> always against war, negotiate
> our flints, feathered gowns, tenure,
> genteel wines, and this song.

Now, in the strictest sense those lines characterized Reed College, not Lewis and Clark; I know that, and I know they were written for a man named Robert Michael. In this connection one of my few gripes with Michael (or is his publisher the culprit?) is that *Images of Kin* excises the names of people to and for whom many of the poems were written, but maybe that's Michael's way of making readers and critics who would understand his poems do their homework:

> "———T. S. Eliot!———his———."

Who knows, to paraphrase Ralph Ellison—and each individual's variation on Invisible Man's riddle of identity—but that "The Faculty Club, Portland, Oregon" speaks to Lewis and Clark in 1968 as well as Reed, though in more inchoate ways:

> These are liberals in starched
> dungarees the color of sharkskin,

A lingering at any rate, after that English Department meeting: two guys on the stone steps of a decrepit building smelling of the chemistry experiments carried on and often misfiring in the basement. Lingering and in the lingering a beginning:

From man to man, *contact high*, to man.

So it goes, Ralph Ellison likes to say, and so it went. The truth is that only rarely do more than a few seconds tick off on memory's dock of my life these past twenty-two years when I don't have some vivid image of Michael Harper and his poems where, as he wrote apropos of my elder daughter's then newly pulsing life, his "heart-center funnels its loam."

Yes, as I struggled to write my dissertation on F. Scott Fitzgerald and American history but, equally, as Michael knew better than I, about F. Scott Fitzgerald, American history, and one John F. Callahan, he finished *Dear John, Dear Coltrane*. Though he'd written the poem in 1966, once I'd crossed over—"Where are my pages?" or "you're breaking discipline / baby"—he showed me "American History," my name below it and told me: "That's for you, mf, you earned it!":

> Can't find what you can't see
> can you?

Yes, and when I'd finished my dissertation, "Dear John, Dear Callahan" was the salutation on Michael's letter of response to the pages of my last chapter. Earlier, with patient, painstaking refrains of long-distance advice from Michael in my head, I had maneuvered my oral defense for September 1969—"heart mysteries there"—but then I stopped short realizing Michael as my invisible, unofficial dissertation advisor had to be present, had to be seen and heard. Fortunately, I was able to wire a poetry reading to provide him cover and cash enough to come. Years later, I discovered some folks in Urbana still talked about the magical coincidence that had put Michael in town on the very afternoon of my defense. Magic, yes: black Irish magic it was. That oral defense yielded more fruit than my Ph.D.; it occasioned a Harper poem—cryptic, playful, complex—on a reverse ritual in which tutored and untutored changed places:

> Beacons: the cat teeth
> refracting boycotted angles
> of personality, here,

Yes, and there is a companion poem to "Oral Light" written in response to an interview Michael arranged for me at Hayward a couple of months later. Indeed, who and for what reason and in what guise interviews whom in the academy?

Murder is the academic game
opting in a soporific name;
vision, vision, personality,
make redemptive, manly polity.

The rest of the poem is full of puns drawing distinctions between the black church and the academy, between "the chant of saints" and the whining songs of isolatoes.

Yes, and although Michael, in this one respect like Fitzgerald's Dick Diver about whom I was too harsh in my dissertation and book, "like[s] his friends without reservations," his poems send us messages, too. He worked the Morse recount in December 1968 as a favor to me and in remembrance of Wayne Morse's service to that true republic of Robert Lowell's "For the Union Dead" and Ralph Ellison's "Brave Words for a Startling Occasion." In his Black Panther beret, toothpick sliding from side to side in fair warning of the pick-and-roll moves he was soon to put on the Junior League Republican poll watchers, Michael increased Morse's Portland vote total as much as the other twelve watchers combined. Still, I am only talking about thirty votes, and so later on as a poet Harper gave the metaphorical count of this and other elections in that time, that place:

      nothing at stake
but our buttons, callousing
over high-tension feet, the game
lost, the urge to piss
on our cards on the auction table.

That lesson was a hard one for me. When I ran for Congress, declaring on St. Patrick's Day, 1970, in what six weeks later became a campaign of Cambodia, Kent State, Jackson State—not trigger-happy, those latter forgotten Mississippi murders but cold-blooded, colder-hearted fusillades into a dormitory by National Guardsmen reviving the lynching posses of their ancestors—Michael sent me a hundred dollars and urged me to spend it on a good dinner, preferably French, he said, for my fiancée to be, Susan, and me. He knew I hadn't and wouldn't take his advice, but he called anyway from a motel room in upstate New York—his father's and grandfather's country—where, marooned after a poetry reading, he'd written a new poem. The words, the lines, the passion, the fury crackled through the wires of a bad connection:

Blow Bird! Inside out Charlie's
guts, *Blow Bird*! get yourself killed.

In the first wave, the musicians,
out there, alone, in the first wave.

There are tangential memories evoked by those lines and that poem—its first
public reading at a benefit in San Francisco's Glide Memorial Church for the
Native Americans occupying Alcatraz that summer of 1970, not to mention
the uncoincidental importance of the last seating at a French restaurant the
four of us had planned to go to weeks before the organizers of the benefit
asked Michael to read, and would not take no for an answer because not a
single black poet was on the program. There's more to say about "Bird Lives"
and about Harper's reading that evening in a voice so full of fury and power
that he electrified an audience antagonistic with booze and drugs; there's
always more to say, but the years run on.

"Michael, will you be my best man?" I asked—over the phone,
naturally.

"Well, man, ... (silence: pleasure tempered perhaps by a sense of the
journey involved; the ambiguity, ambivalence, and intricacy of the scene; the
knowledge that readings would have to be sought, chits incurred to pay the
freight). Sure, I'll be best man, if that's what you want." Here too, Michael
had a poem to thank (or curse) for his dilemma, if there was a dilemma which
I doubt. How could the man who had written these lines refuse the office of
best man?

membranous hands, paired,
loving membranes touching
contact-high: as you touch you.

At the wedding, at Susan's parents' house in Seattle, Michael proposed
a toast so brief some were disappointed, for they did not know and I, who
liked the toast just fine, did not know that like an evening in Berkeley the
previous summer, his afternoon silence was germination for a subsequent
poetic toast that is both charge and counsel for us and for the generations to
come:

If in the old crystal
ball there are no images,
make them, pure and round,
and close to the heart.

Elsewhere, in a poem for my then fiancée, now my wife, Susan
Kirschner, Michael wrote that "Culture tells us most about its animals." Yes,

and children are the keepers of a culture's animals and children are often the vital mediating term in Michael's friendship songs. That's a truth, too, about the man as well as the poet, about Uncle Michael as my daughters, Eve and Sasha call him. When Eve was a little over a year-old, and Michael who had not met her but had written a poem, "Eve (Rachel)," for her and for his own daughter, Rachel, after whom Eve is named, was coming to Portland, Susan, anxious in a motherly way for Eve to take to Michael, explained to the wide-eyed, all ears little girl that Michael, though quite a bit bigger than most people, was a gentle man. As it happened, Michael arrived when Eve was alone with her babysitter. He relieved the young woman, and spent an hour with Eve. Once we had returned and Michael left for a little while, Eve looked up at us. After a pause, with great seriousness, almost solemnity, she spoke her child's fine of poetry:

"Michael Harper beeg mahn, nice mahn."

Now Eve was too young to have remembered much of that poem Michael had written for her from a photograph or two and no doubt our descriptions, but maybe she caught some of the feel; I'm not sure, but I am sure of her love now, for the man and his poetry:

I have been waiting to speak to you
for many years.

In that same poem Harper performed the poet's lonely, austere, lovely, continuing office of best man by speaking things too true of my dead father for me to speak them; how he knew so much of my father's sensibility—the thistles of bitterness choking off the few remaining tender shoots in his soul—when the man had passed away before I met Michael, is a mystery of poetry and personality:

I was there among the family faces
strung on violin and cello,
your Irish grandmother's song of the bogs,
your hidden grandfather's raging at your loveliness,
at his own daughters swimming amidst swans.

From the wedding of her parents—our wedding, my wedding—Harper comes to the living child:

the lush green of your eyes
shuttered in springtime,

In "Eve (Rachel)" Harper calls the child—the children really, for he includes his own sung-and-unsung daughter—and himself back to an incessant troubling and intriguing riddle:

To be here in America?

That's a question surely and one, who would argue, all of our children will struggle to answer for their time and in their place.

These little known poems of Michael's that I write of here are love poems, really, along the trajectory of my life and my family's life. There are poems for my daughters—to be fair I better quote from "Little Song of the Sun," for Sasha, later changed to "Night Letter, I":

I hear you curse your big sister, Eve,
her real name, and only a little biblical,
but what you kiss is her cheek
of an apple on the sly.

And for my wife, Susan, a poem that is dance and song of a European past all mixed up with hope and illusion, eloquence and euphemism, myth and history, and, beyond the old world, the subsequent mysteries of change in America. "The Dance of the Elephants" enacts Michael's view, a variation of Yeats's, that memory transfigures the present moment and opens up experience to a new scale of possibilities, painful, yes, but richer, too, than the old unexamined or painlessly examined past:

a small girl cuddles her elephant,
the song in the streets
leaping the train windows
and what love as the elephant chimes.

Michael Harper speaks to his friends in other ways, too, ways simultaneously familiar and unfamiliar, cryptic and unspeakably, *utterly* intimate. I know, for he has "wait[ed] to speak to me" about certain things until utterance has been made flesh in poems. Matters professional:

I'm not blaming anyone either,
but authorial control is a reality,
does lie within the nexus of race,
and elsewhere also,

And matters so personal they tremble with the terrible, dangerous beauty of intimacy:

> You can cut the hair so short
> on a mother's head and not fool a child,
> but the man who listens is fooled
> over and over by the quaint images of women.

Later in that poem, "The Fiddle," there is a passage of pizzicato taut enough to cut the very bone of any fingers careless in the plucking:

> He is a father because he learned to listen;
> he does not do this without receivers.

Lately, as he has done from time to time, Michael wrote and sent a poem to Susan and me on our wedding anniversary, a poem harking back to memory's old identities even in its focus on the unbearable, bearable immediate present of the changing self. "Extremes are what we need" begins "Motel Room" (for John and Susan), dated by hand "20 Mar 90." Here and elsewhere Michael Harper's friendship songs begin to make something happen between the lines in the lives of his friends:

> Right now it is this bed,
> kingsized, a crack
> in the middle,
> no space necessary
> to hold your own
> so you can hold each other—
> permission is given,
> and it is taken.

In these poems of love and friendship, metaphor becomes a key to what Harper calls "the room number of change" in the different ways of language and life. As always, to receive and absorb Michael's work is to acknowledge truly that "there is no substitute for pain"—and not the world's pain either but our own.

So Michael Harper keeps coming on with his songs. For instance, I thought I had finished with this piece; it had been literally signed, sealed, delivered, and received at the other end when Michael came to Portland in July. There, in response to a hot blue summer day's excursion to the coast—

and I'm sure other times, other places, other things and other people, too—
he wrote a poem called "The Kite" for Sasha, my daughter. For a day or so
before he wrote it in a nest of secretaries outside my office, he was silent
except for the camouflage of an occasional bravado riff to keep the household
at bay. In the poem the twelve-year-old girl and her kite are Michael's
emblems for the embodied soul, that elusive bird of personality soaring and
dipping by turns in the constant struggle to create "one's own sonata."
Fathom the kite, the girl, the poet straining to ascend:

> on a spool
> and when reined in
> blisters with exhilaration,
> torment, struggle,
> freedom near the Columbia River Gorge.

And "The Kite" wasn't all. On Sasha's birthday a card arrived
postmarked Providence. Typed on the inside, dated 11 Sept 90, was "Kite
Coda." In the poem Michael speaks of another stringed object, kin to the kite
in the girl's struggle to ascend in her life and her art.

> The violin had strings
> and had defeated her
> in practice, in recital;
>
> but at thirteen
> new hope in the numb
> wrists, resutured, nuanced
> fingers on the planes of the bow.

Reading Sasha her poem on her birthday, without warning I cried. Only
Michael's cadence of struggle enabled me to keep alive some vestige of
concentration. As Sasha stood before me wondering and in wonder on the
cusp of her emerging self, I felt the rush of many losses and defeats from
adolescence to boyhood and back to the present moment through succeeding
decades of manhood. The girl, my daughter, looked back at me with warm
and steady eyes, and Michael's words became the very breath and balm of
possibility—more needfully, I realized, for me than for her.

> as if from breath in the woman to be
> as she was before, after, right now.

Ah, I thought, hearing the theme of my coda: There's nothing off limits and little beyond the reach of Michael Harper's imagination as he calls the roll, in poems, of his expansive, ever-expanding congregation of friends:

> those who travel
> those who ride
> close roads of images
> and make their own.

SHAMOON ZAMIR

The Artist as Prophet, Priest and Gunslinger: Ishmael Reed's Cowboy in the Boat of Ra

I

In 1963 Reed published "Time and the Eagle," a somber poetic meditation on the burden of history upon the Afro-American people. Its studied and effected sense of tragedy and pathos make the poem unique in Reed's published oeuvre, a body of work almost entirely satiric in nature. While Reed's exclusion of this poem from his collected poetry rightly acknowledges its status as apprentice work, "Time and the Eagle" provides an invaluable point of departure for understanding Reed's poetic development. This development can be charted as a radical shift in the relationship of self to history and as a struggle between passivity and agency. These are the first two out of eight verses from Reed's poem:

I
The shackled Black, being torn in innocence;
Molded his advent through cyclical time.
Surging, flowing, rising, falling time.
Begatting contraries which fuse and breakaway
like fire, water, wood and metal.

From *Callaloo*, 17, no. 4. © 1994 by Shamoon Zamir.

In the ashes of the bird, a new egg and the moon
Bring a second coming.
Golgotha and the knocking at the tomb
Comes with the blood of the moon.

II
The dog of the moon bays with the tide,
And cacophony of each age of madness.
Each gloomy age has its dying Gods and is
Marked by the scaly sea creatures.
Each rope dancing age made the demon
Pact and is marked by the heavy winged
Bird, who soars and dives like the
Rhythm of the blood tide.
Each age, an interminable ceremony,
As time flows in heroes, Gods, scaly
Heavy winged creatures.[1]

The poem was published just a year after Reed's arrival in New York
from Buffalo. In 1963 Reed was only just starting out on his writing career,
and "Time and the Eagle" is one of his earliest published works. Looking
back on his years in New York, Reed later claimed that he went there
thinking he "was going to be a W. B. Yeats"[2] and that he was "writing
visionary poetry" during his early years in the East Village.[3] "Time and the
Eagle" is a confused adaptation of "The Second Coming" and "Leda and the
Swan" that reads almost like a parody.[4] As yet there is little in the poem that
is not immediately derivative of Yeats, but the groundwork for *Conjure:
Selected Poems, 1963–1970* (1971), Reed's first major collection of poetry, and
related works from the same period, is laid here. Reed is attracted to Yeats's
deterministic poetics of history and borrows the Irishman's symbols of
cyclicality, contrariety, and violent annunciation as a framework of prophecy.
The "interminable ceremony" recasts the "ceremony of innocence ...
drowned" from "The Second Coming," as the "cacophony of each age of
madness" refigures Yeats's "Mere anarchy ... loosed upon the world."[5] The
eagle and the egg as signifiers of the violent birth of a new age are taken from
Yeats's interpretation of the myth of Leda's rape by Zeus. Yeats's swan
incarnates the immutable force of history; the violation engenders further
history and myth. Reed's adaptation of Yeats's bird symbolism is as yet vague.
It is clear that Reed has studied *A Vision* together with the poetry. "I
imagine," writes Yeats in *A Vision*, "the annunciation that founded Greece as
made to Leda, remembering that they showed in a Spartan temple, strung up

to the roof as a holy relic, an unhatched egg of hers; and that from one of her eggs came Love and from the other War. But," he adds, "all things are from antithesis...."[6] The Virgin and the dove are replaced by Leda and the swan: "The new birth is to be ... a welter of blood and pain, full of the screams of the new birds of prey...."[7] In Reed, "The heavy winged bird swoops down / Upon a yard of innocence and kills."[8]

"I am a cowboy in the boat of Ra" (1968), Reed's most frequently anthologized poem, is a comic reworking of "Time and the Eagle." It moves towards the transformation of passivity into agency. The heroization of the poetic persona is dramatized within the struggle for mastery between satire and prophecy within the poem. In the "Foreword" to *Conjure* Reed offers himself as America's "son, her prophet" and proceeds to quote from Madame Blavatsky's *Isis Unveiled*: "Philo Judaeus makes Saul say, that if he banishes from the land every diviner and necromancer his name will survive him." Reed adds, "if the government ever created a Bureau of Prophecy, Saul and his cronies would certainly stack it."[9] If the combination of satire and prophecy seems at first incongruous, it should be familiar from Blake. As Northrop Frye notes, "condemnation is only part of the satirist's work.... the great satirist is an apocalyptic visionary like every other great artist, if only by implication, for his caricature leads irresistibly away from the passive assumption that the unorganized data of sense experience are reliable and consistent, and afford the only means of contact with reality." But "satire is not necessarily revolutionary in itself, though its hostility to the world of its time may be pressed into revolutionary service.... a poet cannot depend on satire alone if he wants to show his revolutionary sympathies and point out what such revolutions signify."[10]

The Blakean analogy is invited self-consciously by Reed. When he synthesizes the multiple personas of his poem prior to the final showdown into the figure of the poet-priest, or the artist as necromancer, the poet-priest's call for his ritual paraphernalia refers the reader to Blake's *Milton*:

> bring me my Buffalo horn of black powder
> bring me my headdress of black feathers
> bring me my bones of Ju-Ju snake
> go get my eyelids of red paint.
> Hand me my shadow. (*C* 18)

Here are the corresponding lines from Blake's preface to *Milton*:

> Bring me my Bow of burning gold:
> Bring me my Arrows of desire:

Bring me my Spear: O clouds unfold!
Bring me my Chariot of fire![11]

Reed's invocation of Blake at a climactic point in the poem—when the
cowboy Horus announces his return from exile—establishes Romantic
literary structures as necessary interpretive frames for Reed's poem: *Milton* is
a paradigmatic text of Romanticism's exploration of the imagination's
struggle against duality and its quest for resolution through the higher
synthesis of culture—in Blake's case through the restoration of prophetic
vision. This process of consciousness is commonly dramatized by the
Romantics in terms of the Homeric journeys away from and back to home,
the *Iliad* and the *Odyssey* serving as the respective halves of the dialectic.[12]
Reed simply substitutes the Nile voyage for the Mediterranean one. But
while Reed organizes his poem by referring to the Romantic plot, the
sequence of his poem is as a partial inversion of this plot, concluding in a
New World configuration that is not easily assimilable into Romantic
synthesis.

Reed's poem offers variations on the theme of culture clash organized
within an overarching plot of exile, return, and renewed war. Two other
frames overlap with this larger structure. The return of the exiled hero is also
the resurfacing of the repressed and the suppressed. The urge towards the
psychologizing of history borders on the Spenglerian and remains true to the
politics of the 1960s counterculture in the context of which the poem takes
shape. And the drama of departure and journey home narrativizes the
dialectic of dualism, of unity lost and regained, that is the central plot of
Romanticism and undergirds its obsession with immanent teleology and a
metaphysics of integration, laying the foundations for the modern divided
self[13]—a fragmentation described most notably in the Afro-American
context by W.E.B. DuBois. The processes of duality and synthesis are staged
both as the irresolvable confrontation of satire and prophecy and as a
dialogue amongst poets. Reed engages the poetics of Blake and Yeats,
resisting the conflation of the two and finding in this differentiation both a
range of possibilities and a set of closures for the black poet. The Nile
journey of "I am a cowboy" is also an Afro-American recasting of Whitman's
"Passage to India" (1871).

In the midst of the Second World War, the Afro-American poet Robert
Hayden had questioned the possibility of the transcendental vision even in
Whitman's own time. "Middle Passage," a long section of an uncompleted
book on slavery and the Civil War, imagined the "Voyage of death, / voyage
whose chartings are unlove" that was part of Whitman's reality.[14]
Continuing an Afro-American dialogue with Whitman, "I am a cowboy" was

one among many revisions of Whitman's prophecy of America, undertaken by American writers in the 1950s and 1960s. Like Reed, many poets' attempted to retrieve the idealism of the frontier myth in the age of the New Frontier when that idealism had been significantly tarnished. Inevitably, the attempted recuperation simultaneously acknowledged the strength of the contemporary barriers to the Romantic dream of spiritual and cultural synthesis and the recovery of unity in "Passage to India."[15] In 1956 Allen Ginsberg had used the verse-line of Whitman to voice the end of the dreamed-of garden of the New World. In the apocalyptic parody of *Howl*, "Visions! omens! hallucinations! miracles! ecstasies!" are all "gone down the American river!"[16]

II

Reed's poem retells an ancient Egyptian myth of divine conflict as a wild west showdown. The outlaw gunman, once "vamoosed from / the temple" and now fighting for "the come back of / Osiris" (*C* 17, 18) is the exiled Horus who returns to avenge the murder of Osiris, his father, at the hands of Set, the brother of Osiris. Osiris, the black fertility god and culture hero who, according to Plutarch, civilized Egypt through the power of his songs, introducing agriculture, the observation of laws and the honouring of gods, is sacrificed in a manichean drama to the forces of chaos. Horus's aim is to restore cultural and political order.[17] Although never named as such in the poem, the cowboy is clearly identifiable as Horus. According to the myth, even while Horus was under the protection of Isis, Set managed to have him "bitten by savage beasts and stung by scorpions."[18] Reed alludes to this in the poem's first strophe ("sidewinders in the saloons of fools / bit my forehead"). Having obtained magical powers of transformation from Thoth, Horus fought the battle against Set from the boat of Ra.[19]

But the poem's persona is multiple in its identities. As one who "bedded / down with Isis" (*C* 17), the cowboy is also Osiris; as the "dog-faced man" (*C* 17) he is Anubis; later he appears as "Loup Garou" (*C* 18), a Vodoun loa of the fierce Petro cult of Haiti; he is also an African priest and necromancer demanding his "bones of Ju-Ju snake"(*C* 18); and a gangster calling his "moll" ("C / mere a minute willya doll?" [*C* 18]). The quotation that provides the epigraph to "I am a cowboy," taken from the *Rituale Romanum* and endorsed by Cardinal Spellman, insists that "the devil must be forced to reveal any such physical evil (potions, charms, fetishes, etc.) still outside the body and these must be burned" (*C* 17). But the devil, the poem demonstrates, is more slippery. The liturgical book of the Roman rite and the cardinal are over-confident in their belief in the mimetic abilities of the Word as a guarantee of that alliance of logos and law that has been an alibi for conquest. In *Yellow-Back Radio Broke Down* (1969), Reed's second novel and a work closely tied to "I am a cowboy" in its preoccupations, John Wesley Harding explains to the cattle baron Drag Gibson: "I got so strung out behind the Bible, that I went on to study law. Got my degree in jail. I've always been on the side of the Word, killing only those who were the devil incarnate—you know—black fellows."[20] Spellman, among America's most prominent Catholics and a favorite target of Reed's, combined his social work with energetic support for McCarthy and the Vietnam war.[21] Taking up the challenge of the *Rituale Romanum*, "I am a cowboy" appears to trace the imminent return of all that would be exorcised or repressed. The poem follows the pattern of *The Marriage of Heaven and Hell*; this is Reed's Bible of Hell. Like Blake's "Mental Traveller," it threatens the revival of pagan forms and the decline of Christianity. And like Blake, the poet-prophet becomes the satiric advocate of the "Devil's Party" against the priestly order and its books of law. Used for the administration of sacraments and blessings as well as for conducting processions and *exorcisms*, the *Rituale Romanum*'s authority depends to a large extent on its formulas being followed with minimal variation.[22] The history of this liturgical text from the 16th to the 20th century represents precisely the attempt at codification that Reed and Blake resist and which Reed parodies in his poem "Neo-HooDoo Aesthetic."[23]

The rapid, seemingly gratuitous proliferation of personae in "I am a cowboy" does more than resist the confessional or lyric voice in Afro-American poetry and the politics of identity and interiority these modes represent. Reed's illusive shape-changers recognize with Emerson that reality is "the endless passing of one element into new forms, [an] incessant metamorphosis." It is upon this ground that Emerson concludes that "all thinking is analogizing, and it is the use of life to learn metonymy," or, as Lawrence Buell explicates, "the inter-substitution of images for the same principle."[24] This principle of identity is not a stable self in Reed, any more than it is in Emerson. Rather it is that Manichean duality that is a universal description of the world in the occult and which allows all heresies to crowd at one pole as a community of identity. Here Transcendentalist Neo-Platonism and Reed's counter-cultural melange of Vodoun and Yeatsian theosophy find alignments.[25]

In a move characteristic of the 1960s, Reed conflates Vodoun and gnostic traditions into a subculture of heresy as a reservoir for his poetic mythology. In *Yellow Back Radio* Reed identifies his Vodoun hero with a gnostic idea of the devil and his uprising with that of the Albigenses and Waldenses (*YBR* 164–65, 151). Black Diane from the novel re-appears in the poem as "Pope Joan" (*C* 18), a woman who, disguised as a man (it is fabled), became pope sometime between the 9th and 11th centuries.[26] Reed associates Joan with the composite figure of Ptah, the creator god of Memphis, and Ra, the great sun god,[27] but moves her quickly into the personae of a gangster's moll and a ritual assistant to an African priest. The same year that Reed's novel was published, Gary Snyder wrote of a "great subculture of illuminati ... a powerful undercurrent in all higher civilizations ... which runs ... without break from Paleo-Siberian Shamanism and Magdalenian cave-painting; through megaliths and Mysteries, astronomers, ritualists, alchemists and Albegensians; gnostics and vagantes, right down to Golden Gate Park."[28] Reed's continued identification of the appearance of ancient gods in a Chinese American novel as "Cantonese Hoodoo"[29] and of Kabbalistic traditions in his own work as "Jewish Vodoun"[30] suggests that "Hoodoo" is for him a term of general inclusivity. "Old country writing, backwoods writing, medicine shows, nineteenth century speeches," like genres of popular fiction and Afro-American folklore, are part of "a subculture in American literature that never makes the institutions" (*S* 133). This subculture is a repository of all those cultural histories excluded from that version of cultural history installed by "Egyptologists who do not know their trips" and "School marms with halitosis" (*C* 17). (Pope Joan is also a card game in which one of the cards, the nine of diamonds, is removed from play.)[31]

Such conflations are congenial to the mythology of the devil within Afro-American folk traditions. In this folklore "Satan or the Devil is not a personification of evil or of the demon in man; he is almost a comic figure, a scapegoat for human failings and errors." The reimagining of Satan is in part a resistance to the missionaries' forced identification of trickster gods of African descent (such as Legba or Labas) with their own devil.[32] At the same time that these gods had their complexities partially distorted within Christian manicheanism, the Christian devil emerged as a personification of a process of cultural hybridization that stands against the Church's extension of imperial control through religious indoctrination. Following Blake's' heretical model, Reed takes the New World devil hero as the upholder of the poet-prophet's vision.

III

The second stanza of Reed's poem dramatizes a struggle between contending representations of history. It is cultural, not political history that is at stake here, and the site of contention is the artist's consciousness and his work.

School marms with halitosis cannot see
the Nefertiti fake chipped on the run by slick
germans, the hawk behind Sonny Rollins' head or
the ritual beard of his axe; a longhorn winding
its bells thru the Field of Reeds. (*C* 17)

Reed's "school marms" are descendants of Yeats's "kind old nun in a white hood" in "Among School Children" who teaches her students a stale, uninspiring curriculum:

The children learn to cipher and to sing,
To study reading-books and history,
To cut and sew, be neat in everything
In the best modern way ... (Yeats 215)

The "momentary wonder" of the children is only aroused by the appearance of the sixty-year-old smiling public man" (Yeats 216). The "school marms" in Reed's poem represent a perpetuation of that ignorance about other cultures personified by the untrustworthy "Egyptologists" in the previous stanza (*C* 17). Specifically, they are oblivious to three things: "the Nefertiti fake," "the hawk behind Sonny Rollins' head" and "the ritual beard of his axe."

The famous bust of Nefertiti in Berlin is dismissed as a fake here because its features are so conspicuously "high yellow." While the bust remains one of the best known pieces of Ancient Egyptian sculpture, the features of the Queen, Reed seems to suggest, are acceptable precisely because they hide any trace of the ancient history of cultural exchange between Egypt and West Africa. As Reed points out in the foreword to *Conjure*, "Egypt is located in Africa, you know, even though certain Western Civ. fanatics pretend that it lay in the suburbs of Berlin" (*C* vii). It is due to, the invisibility of this history that the school marms cannot "see" the Nefertiti bust as a fake. This elliptical relativization of Western European aesthetics reconfirms the deathly image of the "Ledean" woman (Maud Gonne) in "Among School Children." The "present image" of the once beautiful woman floats into the poet's mind as a "Quattrocento" painting, "Hollow of cheek as though it drank the wind / And took a mess of shadows for its meat" (Yeats 216).

The "hawk" behind Sonny Rollins' head is a more complex pun at the center of the staged dialogue between Yeats and Blake in this poem. It is Reed's counterpoint to Yeats's falcon, swan and golden bird. The figure of the bird is a multiple symbol of order, art and history in Yeats. The familiar

Yeatsian vacillation between history as necessity and the terror of change, evident in "Leda and the Swan," is more succinctly captured in "A Second Coming" where the divorce of the falcon and the falconer, whose union is a symbol of equilibrium, results in the famous collapse of the center and the nightmare of "things fall[ing] apart" (Yeats 187). The bird as symbol of order reappears at the close of "Sailing to Byzantium" as a supreme work of art ("such a form as Grecian goldsmiths make") that will gather up the aging poet out of historical time ("what is past, or passing, or to come" becomes the song of the golden bird) "Into the artifice of eternity" (Yeats 193–94).[33]

Having lived through two revivals of spiritualism in Europe, Yeats had found many confirmations of myths and stories learned at any early age. He knew *The Book of the Dead* and "the great falcon that hovers over the God Horus."[34] Reed's hawk, however, is more than the recollection of this falcon (or hawk), the animal form of both Horus and his protector Ra. The witty move from Egyptian iconography to the famous profile of Sonny Rollins extends the cultural continuity between Egypt and West Africa, suggested earlier in the poem, to Afro-America. And as the unraveling of the pun on hawk will show, it is significant that the personification of this continuity is a jazz musician. The startling coincidence of familiar Egyptian relief paintings and the musicians' portrait constructs Rollins as an image come to life, stepping off the wall, in a subtle revision of the "sages standing in God's holy fire / As in the gold mosaic of a wall" in "Sailing to Byzantium" (Yeats 193). It is to these sages that the aging poet, sensing his divorce from the sensual life, calls to come "And be the singing-masters of my soul" and "Consume my heart away" (Yeats 193). Yeats seeks an escape from history. "The poet," Harold Bloom concludes, "is asking for transfiguration." But the flight "is not so much from nature as from a new dispensation of the young."[35] But Reed seeks no such transcendent "tangible analogue" of eternity[36] and the conflation of Horus and Rollins announces just such a new dispensation.

The shore from which Yeats sets sail "is no country for old men" (Yeats 193). The image of the "tattered coat upon a stick" (Yeats 193) reappears with dismissive levity in "Among School Children":

> Plato thought nature but a spume that plays
> Upon a ghostly paradigm of things;
> Soldier Aristotle played the taws
> Upon the bottom of a king of kings;
> World-famous golden-thighed Pythagoras
> Fingered upon a fiddle-stick or strings
> What a star sang and careless Muses heard:
> Old clothes upon old sticks to scare a bird. (Yeats 217)

But Reed is interested neither in a conflict of young and old, nor in the
hackneyed universalism of the dialectic of bodily decrepitude and art's
eternity (though he would most likely twist Yeats's sense and take the old
clothes upon a stick as the flag that marks the end of a cultural race for the
famed Greeks). Against Yeats's elegaic turn to an idealized vision of
Byzantium in the age of Justinian (c. A.D. 550) as a response to generational
discontinuity, Reed offers a vital, living tradition. For Reed, Yeats's feared
anarchy becomes a new order. In its association with Rollins, a leading
exponent of hard bop, "hawk" resonates with the names of other jazz
musicians: Coleman *Hawkins*, "the first noted 'traditional' jazz musician to
play with the young bebop revolutionaries"[37] Charlie *'Bird'* (or 'Yardbird')
Parker, the most celebrated of these revolutionaries, and most obviously *Sun
Ra* and his *Ark*estra, major exponents of the free jazz movement in the 1960s.
(The name of saxophonist Sonny Rollins, of course, echoes that of Ra [*Sun*-
ny *Ra*-llins, American pronunciation]). Rollins and the figures that cluster
around him in "I am a cowboy" encapsulate an entire musical history (indeed
a musical genealogy if not an ornithology) from pre-bebop jazz to free jazz.
No fingering upon a fiddle-stick here.

In the end Reed's own idea of jazz is perhaps no less utopian than
Yeats's idea of Byzantium. It becomes in the poem a container for community
imagined as the dialogue of living tradition within the visionary
consciousness of the artist. During performances Sun Ra and the Arkestra
dress in robes and ceremonial head-dress, and the lyrics of their songs
evangelize Sun Ra's particular blend of mysticism and space-age
consciousness. In 1967 Sun Ra gave a concert in New York's Central Park
with about a hundred players, singers and dancers and a large crew of light
and sound technicians; the concert was a tribute to "Nature and Nature's
Gods."[38] In 1970 the Arkestra toured Europe and, at the Berlin
Kongresshalle the concert included a light show, bizarre costumes, dancing
girls, a fire-eater, "songs extolling the 'joys of space travel,' a march through
the audience (a la Living Theater), and Sun Ra's pretended star gazing with
a telescope through the solid" roof of the hall.[39] Critics and audience, for the
most part, were either perplexed or furious at both concerts. As Ekkehard
Jost argues, the critics' reaction "revealed an ignorance of the cultural
background in which this kind of 'musical theater' is rooted, a background
that has as little to do with the stupid flashiness of Broadway shows as it does
with the intellectually calculated surrealism of Mauricio Kagel's
'instrumental theater'": "The roots of this show lie rather in the origins of
Afro-American music: in the rites of the Voodoo cult, a blend of magic,
music and dance; and in the vaudeville shows of itinerant troupes of actors
and musicians, where there was room for gaudily tinseled costumes and the

stunts of supple acrobats, as well as for the emotional depths of blues sung by a Ma Rainey or a Bessie Smith."[40] And Berendt, enlarging this catalogue, brings home the point that the label of "avant garde" is finally inappropriate for an artist like Sun Ra:

> Sun Ra's music is more than just avant-garde, free big-band jazz. It certainly is that, but behind it stands the whole black tradition: Count Basie's Swing riffs and Duke Ellington's saxophone sounds; Fletcher Henderson's "voicings"; old blues and black songs; African highlife dances and Egyptian marches; black percussion music from South, Central and North America, and from Africa; Negro show and voodoo ritual; trance and black liturgy—celebrated by a band leader who strikes one as *an African medicine-man skyrocketed into the space era.*[41]

The blend of traditional and avant-garde elements in this music calls into doubt the usual definitions and usages of both terms—as Jost's comments on the initial response to Sun Ra indicate, the perception of his music as a destruction of jazz, or as "anti-jazz," often depended upon the listener's own ignorance rather than on the music's alleged discontinuities. Both Reed and Sun Ra are uncomfortable with the label "avant garde" when it is applied to their work, and here the coinage of "inter-galactic" and "myth" terminology by the latter, and of "neo hoodoo" by the former, are attempts to "change the joke and slip the yoke." Concerning the music of Archie Shepp and Cecil Taylor, and the differences of his own music from theirs as *he* conceived it, Sun Ra said in 1970 that "they were doing their thing, but they were not talking about Space or Intergalactic things ... They were talking about the Avant Garde and the New Thing."[42] In "if my enemy is a clown, a natural born clown," one of the poems in *Conjure,* Reed writes:

> i called it pin the tail on the devil
> they called it avant garde
> they just can't be serious
> these big turkeys. (*C* 53)

In his *The Theory of the Avant-Garde,* Renato Poggioli argues that the modern artist's alienation from society is also an "*alienation from tradition*": "In contrast to the classical artist, who had recourse to tradition as a stable and recurrent series of public epiphanies, the modern artist works in chaos and shadow, and is overcome by feeling that language and style are in continual apocalypse."[43] But, as Gerhard Putschogl's discussion of tradition and innovation in jazz suggests, Poggioli's equation of the avant-garde with historical discontinuity does not seem to apply to Afro-American art. "The stereotyped equation of tradition with reaction," he writes, "is generally not applicable to Afro-American culture. [Archie] Shepp defines the term avantgarde in a 'strictly historical sense'.... This is a major reason why the tradition is a point of reference for the black musicians of the sixties."[44]

The interdependence of tradition and innovation has been referred to above in Blakean terms as an idealized image of community embodied paradoxically in the figure of the individual prophetic artist. In Milton the later Blake moves from the earlier idea of "Poetic Genius" to an idea of the artist as representative of a brotherhood that is also a body of poetry, what Leonard Deen has called "identity-as-community" and what elsewhere in Blake is personified by the creative genius Los:

> Blake's prophecies show a community of "Eternals" falling asunder, but surviving and recreating itself through the love and labors of the figure he calls "Los".... For Blake the community may not only act or recreate itself in the individual person: it may *be* that person, as Jesus is for Blake the community of mankind. Identity is community. For Blake, community achieved as a conversing in paradise is Jesus; struggling to create itself, it is Los.
> ... Los not only signifies but also embodies and enacts "divine humanity" and the ideals and salient characteristics of Blake's own poetry; and identity-as-community describes the form of a body of poetry as well as an ideal of brotherhood.[45]

It is this dual sense of community as a body of work and a brotherhood of individuals or artists that is also captured in the pun on the hawk behind Sonny Rollins' head. And out of all the jazz musicians Reed conjures up, it is Sun Ra who best embodies the full resonances of Blake's meaning. The mythological affiliations of his name with the Egyptian sun god make him kin to Blake's Los whose name is most likely the sun's name in reverse.[46]

IV

Reed's version of identity-as-community is generated in the context of historically specific social collapse. In 1973, after his move to the West Coast, Reed recalls that "walking down St. Mark's Place in New York's East Village [he] was often able to observe key members of several generations of the American 'avant-garde,' before breakfast, or chat with Archie Shepp,

Ornette Coleman, Sun Ra, Bill Dixon, Albert Ayler, Cecil Taylor, and members of a splendid generation of young painters" (*S* 111). All the men named were musicians of free jazz or the new music. But all, except Ayler, were also members of the Jazz Composers' Guild, a mutual aid organization initiated by Bill Dixon. Umbra, a group of Afro-American poets to which Reed belonged in the early 1960s and with which Dixon had some contact, saw the "new musicians as representing a kind of strength and poetry of the black experience" with which they "strongly identified."[47] But while the "new music" became a major resource for Afro-American writers at this time, the history of the Jazz Composers' Guild also provided a pointed social parallel to the fragmentation and collapse of many art groups in the 1960s.

Dixon, one of the musicians Reed mentioned in his 1968 interview, was one of the first to set up a mutual support organization along more traditional lines than Sun Ra's Arkestra. He organized the now famous 'October Revolution in Jazz' of 1964 which brought together most of the leading free musicians of that time for a series of concerts at the Cellar Cafe on New York's West Ninety-Sixth Street. The idea for the Jazz Composers' Guild grew directly out of the experience of the concerts. Dixon wanted to create an organization that would protect jazz musicians and composers from economic exploitation, and he opened the door to white musicians as well as to blacks.[48] The members agreed to turn down work unless it was considered advantageous to the Guild as a whole, and contracts for concerts and recordings were to be negotiated with the Guild rather than with the individual musicians. Due to internal differences, the Guild collapsed, but it was to set a model for organizations that followed after it. According to Taylor, the Guild did not survive because its members "lacked a social consciousness.... If certain members had shown themselves strong, more loyal to their promises, if their actions matched their ideas, the Guild would exist today."[49]

The idealism implicit in Reed's turn towards a Romantic model for artistic practice cannot be read as a disavowal of history; it was in fact a recognition of the political limits of experiments such as the Jazz Composers' Guild that sought to explore democratic models within severely embattled cultural spaces. In the conclusion of his chapter on Sun Ra and his book on free jazz, Jost writes that "the politically accentuated reminiscences in the music of the Art Ensemble, Don Cherry's efforts toward 'musical world peace' and Sun Ra's mysticism dressed in the costumes of *a utopian minstrel show*, all represent levels of consciousness that can by no means be reduced to the equation 'free jazz = Black Power.' Nevertheless, there is in the style changes manifest in the music ... a tendency that is probably tied up with the change of consciousness that took place in the Sixties among the black population."[50] While Jost is overly cautious about the political nature of free jazz and could easily have added the names of Cecil Taylor, Ornette Coleman and John Coltrane to his list, he is right to resist the *potentially* reductive readings of Frank Kofsky's *Black Nationalism and the Revolution in Music* (1970) and Philippe Carles and Jean-Louis Comolli's *Black Power/Free Jazz* (1971). This is not to discredit either of these excellent studies but to suggest that free jazz may reveal a path not coterminous with or identical to that of the Civil Rights movement or Black Power.

At the same time, resistance to this easy equation has led some cultural theoreticians into extreme fantasy as the only means by which to retrieve the radical potential of this art. Jacques Attali for instance believes that "Free jazz was the first attempt to express in economic terms the refusal of the cultural alienation inherent in repetition to use music to build a new culture. What institutional politics, trapped within representation, could not do, what violence, crushed by counterviolence, could not achieve, free jazz tried to bring about in a gradual way through the production of new music outside of the industry."[51] This escapism testifies to its own impotency. Attali burdens an exemplary cultural moment with a political weight it cannot sustain; there is no confrontation of society's organized power, control and violence here. Nathaniel Mackey's comments on the political nature of collective improvisation (note that Attali takes improvisation as the formal counterpart of the economics) state the matter more realistically: "black music—especially that of the sixties, with its heavy emphasis on individual freedom within a collectively improvised context—proposed a model social order, an ideal, even utopic balance between personal impulse and group boundaries."[52]

The attraction to collective improvisation as a utopian model was indeed strong among Afro-American writers in the 1960s.[53] For one who both listens to jazz and reads Blake, there are obvious cross-overs between the two. For in Blake (and other Romantics) there is a complex balance of individuation and unity; community arises not through common denomination but through the aggregate of difference: "The poet as man aims at a society of independent thinkers, a democratic 'republic,' but on the smaller and more intensive scale of community. The poet as prophet seeks to create a community of prophets, a New Jerusalem."[54] Blake seeks not the regaining of Eden in the present but the full potential of creative imagination in the fallen world. The poet-prophets form an apostolic succession, and through them history is turned back to its sources in myth, divided humanity is transformed into community.[55] This is the third cultural blind-spot of Reed's school marms.

The "ritual beard" of Sonny Rollins' "axe" holds Reed's ambivalent transitions between sacrifice and performance in the poem; in the terms of the Blakean scheme, poetry and art, and not the priests, are the sources of culture. But Reed does not clearly sustain that distinction (just as he does not explicitly distinguish between priest and prophet). The musician and his instrument and the priest and his ritual tool are, intertwined. "Ritual beard" again refers not only to Rollins' physiognomy but also to the pictorial analogy between the curved shape of beards in Egyptian (Assyrian?) iconography and the form of the saxophone ("axe" is jazz slang for the saxophone). In the second stanza of the poem the cut of the axe initiates the reader into the community of tradition and the "longhorn winding / its bells thru the Field of Reeds" completes the synthesis. The dance of the Sidhe, the ancient gods of Ireland, in the wind, and the poetic refiguration of the "philosophic gyres" as the "winding stair" of the tower of Thoor Ballylee in Yeats now resurface as a different motion of history and myth.[56] For one, the meandering movement of the cattle looks ahead to the mythic west of the Chisholm Trail in the fourth stanza. Rollins' saxophone (the "long horn" with the open "bell" of its mouth) threads its own voice with the music of other players of the reed instrument configured as a vibrant synchronic "field": "Tradition, in a word, is the sense of the total past as *now*."[57] The sounding of the bell may well reach to the boxing ring in which the Afro-American boxer. Ezzard Charles is defeated later in the poem, but the competition in this stanza is something altogether different; the "cutting sessions" among the improvising soloists in jazz clubs perform a finer marriage between the group and self. The "Field of Reeds" is also the Egyptian Elysium and the Nile bank where the Horus child, like Moses, was hidden from Set, and Rollins is finally identified with Osiris, the god crowned with horns who weighs the hearts of the dead in Fields of Satisfaction that are the after-world.[58] These dizzying metamorphoses are gathered up as the domain of the artist's active imagination in the pun on the author's name.

   That these transformations should occur within Ra's boat or Sun Ra's jazz Ark continues the Blake analogy. In *Milton* the "Tabernacles" (Blake's "holy place for an ideal")[59] of Osiris, Isis and Horus (Orus in Blake) float on the Nile during the night, "till morning break & Osiris appear in the sky" (Blake 138). But it is at the climax of the poem that Ololon, the spiritual form of Milton's Emanation from which the poet has been divorced, descends in "the Moony Ark" heralding the restoration of the poet and her mystical union with Jesus, the wedding of love and wisdom that will bear man, like Noah's Ark, across the Sea of Time and Space, across the expanse of history:

Then as a Moony Ark Ololon descended to Felphams Vale
In clouds of blood, in streams of gore, with dreadful thunderings

> Into the Fires of Intellect that rejoic'd in Felphams Vale
> Around the Starry Eight: with one accord the Starry Eight became
> One Man Jesus the Saviour. wonderful! around his limbs
> The Clouds of Ololon folded as a Garment dipped in blood
> Written within & without in woven letters: & the Writing
> Is the Divine Revelation in the Literal expression:
> A Garment of War, I heard it named the Woof of Six Thousand
> Years. (Blake 143)

The marriage of the Starry Eight (Milton's Humanity and his seven guardian angels)[60] and Jesus restores Milton's divided self and his imaginative powers. The successor Blake faints on his garden path at the sight of this vision, and as he recovers, the Lark, Los's messenger and Blake's bird-symbol for "the new idea which inspires the entire poem,"[61] heralds the new dawn (Blake 143).

By contrast to Blake, Reed's hawk descends towards the start of his poem, just as Blake's prefatorial invocation is echoed in the final movement of "I am a cowboy." The reversal of the narrative movement of *Milton* is significant; Reed's poem is structured as an inverted epic. The three stanzas that follow the second one consider the failure of synthesis. Isis, like Leda, gives birth to war, and the ringmanship of Ezzard Charles is defeated. The fifth stanza then acknowledges the exile of art. This pattern is in fact closer to Blake's satiric meditation on the impossibility of art and the failure of Los in a fallen world in *The Book of Urizen* (1794). In reversing the transcendent sequence of *Milton*, Reed dramatizes the pressures of history and the social upon the ideal of the synthetic imagination. In Blake the aquatic Polypus symbolizes human society because some forms of this animal are "colonial" organisms of individuals.[62] Ololon, descending to find Milton, must first enter "the Polypus within the Mundane Shell ... [the] Vegetable Worlds" (Blake 136). "Human society," S. Foster Damon explains, "must be taken into account before the creation of art is possible; or as Blake puts it, 'Golgonooza cannot be seen till having passed the Polypus / It is viewed on all sides round by a Four-fold Vision / Or till you become Mortal & Vegetable in Sexuality'" (Blake 135).[63] This full humanity is never imagined in Reed. The Afro-American poet attracted to an idealist aesthetic finds himself caught between American Transcendentalism's rejection of the relevancy of society and Romanticism's dialectic of self and society, and this dilemma becomes the central political drama of his work.[64]

V

Following Yeats's occult model for a poetics of history, Reed's poem figures history as the incessant alternation of conflict and *coniunctio*. This pattern is already present, in the larger narrative of the poem where war is a prelude to the restoration of order. But each stanza repeats the drama as an almost independent unit. While the Horus-Cowboy narrative of exile and return shapes the poem, an over-emphasis on the overarching structure of the poem can undermine the experience of local transitions and image by image progression.[65] The links between (and within) stanzas follow no principle of logical or historical connection. The violent juxtaposition of diverse materials which disrupts the linear flow of narrative is held together by formal principles derived from Yeats's poetics.

> I am a cowboy in the boat of Ra.
> I bedded down with Isis, Lady of the Boogaloo, dove
> down deep into her horny, stuck up her Wells-Far-ago
> in daring midday getaway. 'Start grabbing the
> blue', I said from top of my double crown. (*C* 17)

The rapid transitions in this third stanza are representative of the procedures of the whole poem and extend the flamboyant punning of the poem into a collagist aesthetic. A pun reminiscent of the sexual innuendos of blues lyrics allows Reed to leap from Egyptian mythology to nineteenth-century America and from an image of sexual union to a history of political and economic conflict, a parody of the rape of Leda by the Swan, used here to engender North American history. Isis's "Wells-Far-ago" is a distortion of the name of the Wells Fargo company, established in 1852 by Henry Wells, William G. Fargo and associates, founders of the American Express. The company carried mail, silver and gold bullion and provided banking services. "In less than ten years," Alvin F. Harlow explains, the company had "either bought out or eliminated nearly all competitors and become the most powerful company in the Far West." Wells Fargo later extended its operations to Canada, Alaska, Mexico, the West Indies, Central America, and Hawaii, as well as the Atlantic coast.[66] The economic monopoly of Wells Fargo parallels the monotheism of Judaism and Christianity, which not only banished other gods (Osiris and the Voodoo loa) but also suppressed its own heretical traditions. The outlaw cowboy's cry, "start grabbing the / blue," is slang for "put your hands up" but also refers to "blueback," an archaic term for a bank note of Confederate money, so called for the contrast of blue ink on its back with the green ink used on the Northern "greenback." With

Horus speaking from the "top of [his] double crown" in the next line, the
blueback carried by the Wells Fargo Company can be taken as a symbol of
the division between North and South in the "United" States. This is
confirmed by the double crown as symbol of a unified Egypt in Egyptian
iconography, and one of the manifestations of Horus was "Har-mau," or
"Horus the uniter," upholder of the unity of northern and southern Egypt.[67]
The aggressive lover of Isis is of course Osiris (the "longhorn" in the
previous stanza refers, among other things, to the horned crown of Osiris,
and the rather obvious sexual pun on "longhorn" and "horny" completes the
link). The product of this intercourse is Horus, whereas in Yeats the rape
leads to the birth of Helen and Clytemnestra, Love and War. The outlaw
Horus initiates the fall of the Confederacy and the rise of the Union, while
Leda hatches the fall of Troy and the ascendancy of Greece. The same
pattern is repeated in the next stanza.

> I am a cowboy in the boat of Ra. Ezzard Charles
> of the Chisholm Trail. Took up the bass but they
> blew off my thumb. Alchemist in ringmanship but a
> sucker for the right cross. (C 17)

Here each sentence is a yoking together that, like the rest of the poem,
brazenly defies the facts of history. The conjunction of Ancient Egypt and
the American West is, by this point in the poem, familiar. The cowboy then
appears as the Afro-American heavyweight boxing champion from the early
1950s riding the famous 19th-century cattle trail that stretched from south
Texas to Kansas City.[68] His transformation into a musician, linking back to
Sonny Rollins in the second stanza and to the "Lady of the Boogaloo" in the
third, is aborted by gun law. The last sentence is a characteristically
condensed pun, welding together boxing and alchemy—again, confrontation
and synthesis. Not only is the allusive hero's boxing prowess weak, but his
"talismanic rings [are] no match for the symbols of Christianity."[69] The
alchemist's dream of *coniunctio*, of the philosopher's stone, is defeated. The
ring, occult symbol for such unity and wholeness but also representative here
of the boxing ring, encapsulates the balance of conflict and *coniunctio*
throughout the poem.[70] But this very balance is shattered by a blow from the
cross, a re-match between the gnostic traditions and Christianity in which
the later once again emerges as victor. After being knocked out by "Jersey"
Joe Walcott in seven rounds in Pittsburgh in 1951, Charles was never able to
make a successful comeback in boxing. He was defeated again by Walcott in
1952 and by Rocky Marciano in 1954.[71] In the next stanza the artist-hero
accepts that an "outlaw alias copped my stance" but the exile is only a

temporary set-back: "Vamoosed from / the temple," he explains, "i bide my time" (*C* 17).

Yeats had adopted the idea of war and conflict as agents of renewal largely from his occult studies.[72] But unlike in Blake, there is in Yeats no progression through the interplay of contraries, no transcendence of that image of history. War becomes the only possible form of the world, "a dramatic universe where conflict is the dance-form of life."[73] Dance is, of course, like the bird, Yeats's multivalent symbol of order and chaos. In the dream of the beggar Billy Byrne in "Under the Round Tower," dance and conflict imagery is related to sexual imagery (Yeats 137–38).[74] And Reed's Isis, in the midst of sexual union and physical conflict, appears as "Lady of the Boogaloo."[75] Referring to Yeats's characteristic techniques as they are evident in Billy Byrne's dream, Hazard Adams writes that, "with the building up of a mass of metaphorical suggestion, Yeats's multiverse, like Blake's, becomes a single macrocosmic metaphor; a universe. All things finally relate themselves to all other things in a unified vision."[76] This is also an accurate description of the procedures of "I am a cowboy." But Adams continues: "The difference from Blake lies in the fact that conflict becomes the form of the only world Yeats knows, not simply, as in Blake, the delusion to be transcended."[77] This too is ultimately true of Reed. The danger for a satirist like Reed, who is also attracted to the possibilities of the poet-prophet, is one of entrapment within a closed system that psychologizes history as the unchanging clash of antinomial forces. The static nature of this model makes it fundamentally ahistorical as a poetics of history. The prophecies of a new age simply become predictions of repetition, so that the poet aspiring to vision can too easily become a mere magician. And the satirist, requiring perpetual conflict as a necessary condition for his art, is hard pressed to sustain a vision of identity-as-community or to fulfill the prophetic quest for *polis*.

In *Milton* Blake distinguishes between "Mental War" and "Corporeal Strife," immediately after those lines from Blake's preface which Reed parodies and invokes, the poet declares:

> I will not cease from Mental Fight,
> Nor shall my Sword sleep in my hand:
> Till we have built Jerusalem,
> In England's green & pleasant Land. (Blake 95–96)

Later in the poem Blake distinguishes Mental Fight from actual war. The "Four Elements" that are "Gods of the Kingdoms of the Earth" are caught "in contrarious / And cruel opposition: Element against Element, opposed in War / Not Mental, as the Wars of Eternity, but a Corporeal Strife" (Blake 130).

The intellectual war and hunting that goes on in heaven, which is of course a mental state in Blake, not a place beyond the sky, is the proper contrary form of those dreadful "negations" known as war and hunting in nature. Yeats thinks of that symbolized by the sphere as things-in-themselves, which fall into antinomies in experience. Blake's heaven is the life of intellect itself, which proceeds by dialogue and contrariety.

... this difference leads Yeats to an ironic welcoming of violence, while Blake was always horrified by war, which he regarded as the result of the repression of true contrariety.[78]

As in Blake's preface to *Milton*, the poet-priest of "I am a cowboy," after calling for his "Buffalo horn of black powder," his "bones of Ju-Ju snake" and other ritual instruments, launches his *mental* war against the cultural domination of Set, an archetype for all forms of religious, ideological and cultural monisms in Reed's mythology:

I'm going into town after Set

I am a cowboy in the boat of Ra

look out Set   here i come Set
to get Set   to sunset Set
to unseat Set   to Set down Set

                usurper of the Royal couch
                imposter RAdio of Moses' bush
                part pooper O hater of dance
                vampire outlaw of the milky way
                                    (*C* 18)

The return of the outlaw cowboy is in fact the return of art to the arena of effective cultural struggle since earlier in the poem the exile of the outlaw hero is defined as the exile of art:

                Vamoosed from
the temple i bide my time. The price on the wanted
poster was a-going down, outlaw alias copped my stance
and moody greenhorns were making me dance;
    while my mouth's
shooting iron got its chambers jammed. (*C* 17)

It is the poet's voice, the *"mouth's* / shooting iron," that is silenced. Despite his obvious parodic and comic intent, Reed's obsessive use of the rhetoric of aggression can sometimes be misleading.[79] But Reed takes care in many of his works to forestall such readings. The exchange between the slave 40s and Raven Quickskill, the artist-hero, in *Flight to Canada* (1976) offers just one example. When the militant 40s tells Raven Quickskill, "you take the words, give me the rifle," Quickskill replies that "words built the world and words can destroy the world." Quickskill eventually learns that a flight to Canada is a false promise of freedom; for him "freedom was his writing. His writing was his HooDoo."[80] The unjamming of the "mouth's / shooting iron" narrativizes the release of the creative and playful potential of language and simultaneously stages this release as a moment of self-genesis for the poetic persona. But what does genesis mean for Reed and his personae?

VI

The action of "I am a cowboy" begins to turn in the seventh stanza. Though still in exile, the poet no longer has his mouth's shooting iron jammed. He is now writing "the mowtown long plays for the comeback of / Osiris" (*C* 18). just as the climax of *Milton* is moved to the opening verses of Reed's poem, so Blake's prefatory invocation to his truncated epic is echoed towards the end of "I am a cowboy" (in the eighth stanza). By ending his narrative where Blake begins his, the point at which the poet calls for inspiration to arm him for the task of Mental War, Reed deliberately ends in limbo. The battle is yet to come or it is perpetual; in any case, the Afro-American poet is uncomfortable about projecting resolution.

The return of the exiled hero is no longer imagined as Horus's revenge. Instead of the more familiar and culturally more distant mythology of Egypt, Reed now turns to a New World transformation of African folklore and works his own syncretic changes upon it. In the eighth stanza the sexual union of Osiris and Isis is re-formulated in more traditional occult and astrological terms as the *coniunctio* of Pisces and Aries. But the product is "the Loup Garou Kid," "Lord of the Lash," not Horus, a "half breed son," a reincarnation of the Afro-American divided self, not an incarnation of national unity (*C* 18). In occult and astrological lore, Osiris and Isis are taken to be representatives of the Sun and Moon respectively, and so as the father and mother of "sublunary nature" who, "by their conjunctions renew all life in its generations, and at their oppositions bring forth that which is generated."[81] The Loup Garou Kid is, of course, literally generated out of dramas of union and opposition in the course of the poem. The union of

Pisces and Aquarius appears to be the first successful *coniunctio* in the poem, an alchemical wedding of "the prototypical male and female opposites—identified in alchemical symbolism as sulfur and mercury, or Sol and Luna, or king and queen."[82] But this is clearly not the case since the "half breed son" is not the reunited, complete man. Loup Garou in fact represents only the masculine half of the conjunction: where, in Blake, the *female* Ololon descends in the "*Moony ark*," Reed's cowboy rides in the solar barge. In an 1896 letter Yeats wrote that "we belong to the coming cycle. The sun passes from Pisces into Aquarius in a few years. Pisces is phallic in its influence. The waterman is spiritual so the inward turning soul will catch the first rays of the new Aeon."[83] The counter-culture, too, was obsessed with the Aquarian Age and its promise of the transformation of human consciousness.[84] In parts of his aesthetic formulations Reed is clearly sympathetic to the Yeatsian prediction of an inward turn, the metaphysical country behind the eyes, but with Loup Garou he makes the representative hero of the age a figure of aggression and outward confrontation.

Loup Garou, derived from the French, is the name given to werewolves and vampires in Haiti. Though the werewolves can be male, loups garous are more commonly known to be female vampires who suck the blood of children, as they are generally in West African societies.[85] Most significantly for Reed, loup garous are associated with the Petro, not the Rada cult of Vodoun.[86] Petro is, in Maya Deren's words, "a New World answer to New World Needs."[87] Where the loa of Rada, a cult of Dahomean origin, are generally protective, guardian powers, the Petro loa represent aggressive action, a response to the history of enslavement and violence: "For it was the Petro cult, born in the hills, nurtured in secret, which gave both the moral force and the actual organization to the escaped slaves who plotted and trained, swooped down upon the plantations and led the rest of the slaves in the revolt that, by 1804, had made of Haiti the second free colony in the western hemisphere, following the United States."[88] Loup Garou is, then, an appropriate choice of protagonist in a poem that satirically masks its own complex cultural kinships behind a polarized drama of cultural slavery and revolt. (The parentage of Reed's hero is, once again, telling here since Pisces is the "symbol of confinement and restraint, the fishes being tethered together," and Aquarius one of the aerial signs, a symbol of freedom.)[89]

"The crack of the slave-whip," Deren reminds the reader, sounds constantly in Petro rites like "a never-to-be-forgotten ghost."[90] Reed's hero is also "Lord of the Lash" but Reed, with his characteristic penchant for the humour of the incongruous, reincarnates a now-forgotten hero from B-movie westerns in the grim shadow of the Petro cult. According to *The Film Encyclopedia*, Al La Rue, a.k.a. "Lash" La Rue, was

Born on June 15, 1917, in Michigan. Cowboy hero of miniscule-budget Hollywood Westerns of the late 40s, known as "Lash" for his principle weapon, a 15-foot bullwhip, which he used on his enemies with great skill. His film career was brief and unmemorable. He later performed in carnivals and toured the South as a Bible-thumping evangelist, preaching the gospel and contemplating astrology and reincarnation. He had several brushes with the law, answering charges of vagrancy, public drunkenness, and possession of marijuana. He claims to have been married and divorced 10 times.[91]

At the start of *Yellow Back Radio*, run out of too many towns, Loop Garoo has joined "a small circus" (*YBR* 10).

Following the syncretic principles of New World religions, Reed takes the transformation of African vampire folklore one step further than it has already been taken in Vodoun. The Petro Loup Garou is reborn as a North American cowboy (and in recent years a new cowboy loa has in fact appeared in Brazil), though this is not quite accurate; rather, he is reborn as a popular culture *idea* of a cowboy and much more. La Rue stands at the other end of American mythology from Will Rogers. The bundle of paradoxical collisions represented by La Rue's career, like the heterogeneity of Vodoun, rather than the deceptively sanitized Christian imperialism of his more famous colleague, stands as the true groundwork for a usable indigenous mythology. It is in his vertigenous blend of New World religion and an Emersonian mythology of Americana that Reed discovers weapons for his Mental War against cultural exclusionism.

VII

In Blake the female Ololon returns to Milton and is gathered up around Jesus. Reed does not follow this occult sexual law, the merging of male and female, the return of the Shekinah to God.[92] The Afro-American offspring of Pisces and Aries is instead a divided self, a "half breed son." Reed significantly erases all elements of the female from the mythology of loup garous and transfers the figure into a classical American male mythology of self-regeneration through violence.[93]

Those 1960s poets who adopted the gunslinger as hero in their re-engagement with Whitman dramatized the ambivalent potential of the Transcendentalist self.[94] While the conflictual poetic narratives made explicit the blurred boundaries between Whitman's trans-continental visionary journey and the violent history of Manifest Destiny, the hero wrapped in the aura of the six gun mystique was at the same time himself a reincarnation of what Quentin Anderson has called the "imperial self." In the 1950s and 1960s writers adopted the figure of the outlaw as representative for the creative artist. The outlaw was an ideal actor in the dramatization of the antagonistic relationship between self and society, but the myth of the Western outlaw contained within it an ambivalent resolution of this conflict through acts of violence.[95] Emerson had accepted war as a function of self-reliance and a permanent condition of nature, suggesting that self-reliance was in fact initially a stance against society.[96] While the emergence of the outlaw as artist-hero in the 1960s was also part of an oppositional stance, the literary anarchism could not escape a degree of association with the logic of the then prevalent consensus ideology that offered itself as the end of ideology.[97] The interest here is in Reed's turn to the gunslinger as hero as an acceptance of the unavailability of the prophetic model of resolution in the late 1960s. The alternative of satiric narratives, based on occult rather than dialectical models, maintains double consciousness as an arena of perpetual conflict. Reed's persona takes the moment of conflict as the bridge to the triumph of satire in the vacuum left by the failed Blakean brotherhood of artists. While the final showdown between the Cowboy and Set, initiated as a new beginning at the end of Reed's poem, must still be seen as a continuation of Mental War, the poetic rhetoric there leaves little room for a possible mutuality through art. This turn in the second half of Reed's poem is part of a much broader problematic in Reed's work that is not easily absorbed by sympathetic understanding.

The "I" of "I am a cowboy" is a descendent of the expansive and incorporative selves of Whitman and Emerson. Reed's cowboy hero, confronted with the double-consciousness of a divided self, adopts a strategy of inflation, an "unrealistic aggrandizement" of the ego.[98] This process is part of the "shifts from communal modes of self-validation to a psychic self-reliance [that] have always been part of magic and religion, and perhaps of action itself," and have characterized classic texts of American literature.[99] The transition from the Blakean notions of artist and community to the model of the gunslinger reverses the transition from sacrifice to performance in the second stanza and reincarnates the artist as sacrificial priest. This section examines this shift as the site of the imperial self's fullest manifestation and Reed's use of the possibilities of immanence in magic as the vehicle of this appearance.

In the sixth and seventh stanzas Reed repeats the wedding of Afro-American music, Ancient Egyptian religion and another classic scene of western mythology, but the movement now, unlike that of the second stanza, is from performance back to sacrifice:

I am a cowboy in the boat of Ra. Boning-up in
the ol West i bide my time. You should see
me pick off these tin can wippersnappers. I
write the mowtown long plays for the comeback of
Osiris. Make them up when stars stare at sleeping
steer out here near the campfire. Women arrive
on the backs of goats and throw themselves on
my Bowie.

I am a cowboy in the boat of Ra. Lord of the lash,
the Loup Garou Kid. Half breed son of Pisces and
Aquarius. I hold the souls of men in my pot. I do
the dirty boogie with the scorpions. I make the bulls
keep still and was the first swinger to grape the taste.

(*C* 18)

Compare this to the take-over of Video Junction by Loop Garoo and the
children in *Yellow Back Radio* reported by "the shotgun messenger from the
Black Swan Stagecoach":

Everybody dead except for the kids up in the mountains dancing
and smoking tobaccy and some women arriving on a shindig on
the backs of obscene goats. Without no floogers on. Nekkid. Was
bettern a topless. One of them hookers had knockers on her that
was biggern a helliummed grapefruit. Three black cowboys were
seated on tree stumps drinking from some wooden bowl and
grinning. One of 'em was playing the slide trombone.

Then everybody got on the ground. They was gnashing their
teeth and rolling over each other and the air got all hot and funky.
Finally they took some woman and put her on a platform on a
log, then this one black cowboy took a Bowie and jugged the
woman in the chest. She didn't even yell but said some furriner
jaw-breaking word, exquisite exquisite, said it over and over
again. (*YBR* 55)

A little later in the chapter Loop chants a black mass, conjuring up the devil,
Vodoun loa and "his personal Loa, Judas Iscariot, the hero who put the finger
on the devil" (*YBR* 61–64).

Dionysus descends too easily here. The parody works within the terms
of a discourse it seeks to subvert. The obvious sexism (as with the "school

marms" and Isis) and show of phallocentrism are facile alternatives to Yeats's
anxieties about sex and age. Reed's emotions of excess come as easy as Yeats's
losses. The implied construction of this Yeats as representative of the sterility
of Western culture (Blake notwithstanding) offers the instant gratification of
cliché. To be sure the heathen rites are Cardinal Spellman's worst nightmares
made flesh, the Afro-American adopting his stereotypical association with
the devil not as a mark of condemnation but as a sign of his status as *fellahin*,
but the satiric resurfacing of the repressed uncritically maintains the counter-
cultural psychoanalytic model as political arena. The 1960s were witness to
the fact that, without adequate social forms to hold it, the erotic release of
the Bacchae was likely to result in disaster not revolution.[100] This is where
malign priests like Charles Manson stepped in. Reed is forced to revert from
the controls of art to the repetitive regeneration of violent sparagmos. The
eroticism of the famous "mowtown long plays" heralds the return of the
Bacchus prototype, the Egyptian god of viticulture. The trombone playing
artist stands on the periphery, providing accompaniment for the
hallucinogenic orgy; this is Reed himself, a one-time player of that
instrument.[101] In "I am a cowboy" and *Yellow Back Radio* this is Eros's reply
to Logos. While the ecstatic ceremony of "I am a cowboy" may restore the
"limb scattered" Osiris of "Time and the Eagle," transforming the poetic
hero from passive to active agent, and may be compatible with the patterns
of artistic regeneration in Blake, perpetual sacrificial renewal is finally
antithetical to the visionary sense. Blake's "The Mental Traveller" rejects the
delusions of determinism for the potential of spiritual progress. As Hazard
Adams has detailed, when Yeats wrote of Blake's poem in the first version of
A Vision, he isolated the single pattern of the poem as the myth of "the
perpetual return of the same thing": "Yet the myth must include the Traveller
himself, the visionary who comprehends delusion. The Mental Traveller
finds his way out of the circle and affirms that man may discover something
more than the 'perpetual return of the same thing.'"[102] Unlike the
Spenglerian Yeats, Blake asserts "that the cycle whirls to a vortex instead of
rolling endlessly in space. That is, one proceeds toward vision if one rejects
the idea of history as a simple straight line for the idea of history as cycle. But
one *attains* to vision only when one sees time as a point."[103] In his vacillation
between vision and satire the anarchist poet finds himself attracted to the
magical powers of the priest as model.[104] But Sun Ra's captaincy of his Ark
is finally incompatible with the fully democratic experiment of the Jazz
Composers' Guild, and it is telling that, unlike Melville's Pequod, it is the
Arkestra, not the Guild, that has survived. While it is true that Sun Ra
embodies the spirit of Los, he also steps into a stance ultimately antithetical
to Blake and to Whitman by confusing the roles of prophet and priest. Not

only does Sun Ra gather up the multiplicity of tradition and innovation in his music into his performance persona of ritual priest and utopian prophet, he presides as priestly leader over the famous, strangely monastic community of his Arkestra. A unique phenomenon in the history of jazz, the members of the Arkestra have often lived together as a commune, following not only Sun Ra's musical leadership, but also his esoteric mystical teachings and his self-help (even dietary) doctrines.

Also in the 1960s, the Jewish American poet Jerome Rothenberg takes the shaman as a figure for the poet. Extending the sense of shamanism as a "technique of ecstasy" and of the shaman as a "technician of the sacred" in Mircea Eliade's cross-cultural study of the phenomenon,[105] he argues in 1968 that "the shaman can be seen as a protopoet, for almost always his technique hinges on the creation of special linguistic circumstances, i.e., of song and invocation."[106] Himself moving between various "primitive" cultures and contemporary poetic forms, Rothenberg is interested in "a common (shamanic / not priestly) pattern."[107] In a 1984 interview, pushed to define this delicate politics more fully against the developments of the preceding decades, Rothenberg acknowledges the susceptibilities of the archaic poetic model inside contemporary culture. Discussing the increased preoccupation with Dionysian release in American society, the growth of the Daemonic in popular culture, and figures like Jim Jones, he senses the dangers of a malign spill-over into poetic and social explorations seeking release from established frameworks into the unknown: "These are powers of the mind and they still remain—and some of the worst of it is probably a result of their release in what has been an extremely repressed, repressive culture"; "If shamanism depends somehow on a one-to-one relationship—the presence of the shaman and the other—then I don't think you can deal with it in mass-communication terms. I think it is ultimately irresponsible to try and do so and that was the tremendous failure of such as Timothy Leary ..."[108] Such strategies become, in fact, a disastrous over-compensation for the lack of social integration that distinguishes the modern poet from the shaman.[109]

At the end of "I am a cowboy," the returning hero seeks to chase out Set, the "imposter RAdio of Moses' bush" (*C* 18). In *Yellow Back Radio* Loop's magic is directed as invasive noise within existing mass media and communication systems. In both instances the artist-magician aims simultaneously for his own immanence within the circuits. While there is no nostalgic dismantling of technology here, the media extensions of the human offer an effective diffusion of magical control. The "Old Woman" who runs the talk show in the town of Yellow Back Radio leaves town after "the Loop Garoo Kid came in there and put some bad waves into her transmitter." She explains that "the 'demons of the old religion are becoming the Gods of the new,' cause he put something on her that had her squawking like a chicken" (*YBR* 83). Chief Showcase, referring to this and other incidents, explains the power of "nigger words— ... how they move up and down the line like hard magic beads out riffing all the language in the syntax" (*YBR* 129). Within Reed's dramatization of cultural wars in terms of information theory paradigms, the "nigger words" are forces of anti-chance, not entropy; they create new meanings as they dissolve existing ones.[110] Examining literature in the light of theories of negentropy in information theory, physics and biology, William Paulson acknowledges that the supposition of self-organization from noise in literature depends to some degree on romantic notions of literary autonomy but suggests that "romantic autonomy itself can now be reread in the context of contemporary, non-vitalistic and non-teleological approaches to the autonomy of organisms."[111] Reed's easy moves between romantic models of the artist and contemporary technological frameworks is similarly suggestive. Along with the destruction of Video Junction, Loop Garoo is concerned "with the serious business of closing every conceivable repair shop available to Yellow Back Radio, whose signals were needless to say becoming very very faint" (*YBR* 118). But the Pope realizes that Loop wants to broadcast his own "strange fixes" (*YBR* 119) without interference. Not surprisingly, Loop's hideout is a cave under "the Peak of No Mo Snow" (*YBR* 155), snow, of course, being the term for the effect of deteriorated image quality or), television or video tape.

Reed is an admirer of Marshall McLuhan. In the late-1960s he reiterates the vision, of a heterogenous global village:

> With a televised technology tribalism and separatism are impossible. Given what McLuhan and Buckminster Fuller have shown us, you *can't* be a separatist.... Once You become an international mind-miner it's all over. That's where the Afro-American artist is today: John Coltrane going to Ali Akbar Khan, Afro-American ragas, Bill Dixon doing science-fiction music, Sun Ra into Gustav Holst.[112]

And commenting on the title of his second novel, Reed explains that he "based the book on old radio scripts in which the listener constructed the sets from his imagination—that's why radio, also because it's an oral book, a talking book; people say they read it aloud, that is, it speaks through them, which makes it a loa" (*S* 134).[113] "Given only the *sound* of a play," McLuhan writes, "we have to fill in all of the senses, not just the sight of the action."[114] For the Catholic McLuhan, the transformation of human consciousness promised by the technologies of the global village will be the modern day second coming. It is in this sense that George Steiner is correct in stressing that "McLuhan is [Blake's] successor over and over again."[115] Reed's singling out of musicians whose work is marked by a cross-cultural imagination acknowledges as much. But in his explanation of his novel's sources in orality and radio he uncritically extends his meaning into the processes of possession. McLuhan, however (and despite his own religiosity), knows that within the magic of "the tribal drum" of radio "the old web of kinship" can begin "to resonate once more with the note of fascism."[116]

As Richard Poirier has argued, there is in a great deal of American literature a crisis of failure at that point in the work when the author attempts to externalize the ideal consciousness (the "visionary eye" / I) of his hero, "tries to insert it, to borrow William James's metaphor, into social and verbal environments that won't sustain it. And the crisis is confronted not only by the heroes but also by their creators when it comes to conceiving of some possible resolution to the conflict of inner consciousness or some suitable external reward for it."[117] The point at which Loup Garou emerges and takes on the mantle of the priest-magician is such a moment of crisis for both protagonist and author in "I am a cowboy." It is also the point at which we can most fully grasp those principal forms of the self in Reed that permit Yeats, Transcendentalism and Vodoun to perversely cohabit in the same body.

Terence Diggory has recorded the very significant impact of American poetry on the work of Yeats and of the subsequent engagement with Yeats in the work of several American poets. Yeats was initially attracted to Whitman as a poet who spoke to shared concerns of nationhood. But after his failure to establish the national theatre and a communal tradition through the recuperation of ancient Irish legend and folk beliefs, Yeats found in Emerson and Whitman poets who "had discovered in the self an alternative to tradition that was at the same time a new source of tradition."[118] This is what Diggory calls "the tradition of the self," a tradition fundamentally different to the Romantic tradition of self-expression:

> For Wordsworth, the self was given or, at most, discovered; for Yeats, the self was created. In the process of being created, the self becomes distanced or externalized. It is literally *ex-pressed*, but not as in romantic expression, because Yeats's externalized self differs from the internal self where it originated. Once externalized, the self is viewed not as the poet's content but rather as a form to be entered into; it is the mask or antiself that must be pursued throughout life.

Though it has roots in Blake's *Four Zoas* and Shelley's *Alastor*, Yeats's postulation of a dual or even multiple self marks another

signal divergence from romantic self-expression, since that
theory demands an identity between what is expressed and what
is contained in the poet's true self. The romantic desires harmony
between subjective and objective experience, a harmony that
Yeats could preserve only by expanding the definition of the self
to include what appeared to him as quite disparate modes of
experience. Subjectively, Yeats felt himself to be the creator of the
world, but, objectively, he felt himself the helpless victim of the
world's intransigence. By granting a measure of truth to both
selves, Yeats could adopt a heroic stance in his poetry without
diminishing the obstacles he faced.[119]

From its inception in 1917 onwards, the philosophy of *A Vision* was
formulated in the context of World War I and its aftermath, the Russian
Revolution and unending insurrection, guerrilla warfare, civil disobedience
and civil war in Ireland that destroyed that class of landed gentry which was
Yeats's symbol for civilization and tradition.[120] Yeats's response to the times
was the assertion that "a civilization is a struggle to keep self-control," an act
of "an almost superhuman will" that is doomed to failure within his own
deterministic system: "The loss of control over thought comes towards the
end; first the sinking in upon the moral being, then the last surrender, the
irrational cry, revelation...."[121] This paradox of "superhuman will" and
determinism is what Diggory is referring to in his contrasting of the duality
of "creator" and "helpless victim." As Diggory goes on to argue, it is through
the tradition of the self and its use of the mask that the poet attempts to
overcome his sense of passivity and victimization before the forces of history.

> ... Yeats was able to retain a sense of inspiration as coming from
> outside—a sense demanded by the feeling of helplessness before
> the world—and yet to know also that his inspiration came from
> himself, since there was also a self that was outside. To enjoy the
> sanction of external authority and yet to recognize that authority
> as the self is the definitive experience of the tradition of the
> self.[122]

Reed's personae are his masks. Through them he too enacts the drama
of dual or multiple selves caught between the constraints of history and the
promise of heroic action and self-genesis. The imperial self retrieves its own
projected self as its sanction and inspiration. It is through this poetic device
that Reed overcomes the experience of history as absolute fate in "Time and
the Eagle." What Diggory refers to as subjective and objective experiences

in Yeats, Anderson, in connection with American poetry, calls "the two imaginative modes" of the "imperial self," "incorporation" and "agency."[123] "But," as far as Yeats's work is concerned, "English romanticism checked [his] American Adamic impulse, freeing him to conceive a poetry distinct from either of its sources. The tradition of the self grows less distinctively American as Yeats shapes it to accommodate the communal concerns that he shared with the English romantics."[124] These concerns may be among the principal reason why an Afro-American writer may be attracted to the romantic tradition. And Yeats, as the poet who mediates between this tradition and the Transcendentalist tradition of the self in the context of colonialist politics, understandably engages the attention of Afro-American poets. While Reed turns, at the start of his poem, to Blake for a model of communitas, he cannot sustain this collectivity and increasingly incorporates Yeats into the more traditionally American and anarchist patterns of the "imperial self."[125]

NOTES

1. Ishmael Reed, "Time and the Eagle," *Umbra* 1.2 (December 1963): 5.

2. John O'Brien, *Interviews with Black Writers* (New York: Liveright, 1973), 170.

3. Ishmael Reed, *Shrovetide in Old New Orleans* (Garden City: Doubleday, 1978), 5. Hereafter cited parenthetically as *S*.

4. Before coming to New York Reed had written a short story that was a parody of the second coming. The story was called "Something Pure." It was never published and is now lost. See Henry Louis Gates, "Ishmael Reed," in Thadious M. Davis and Trudier Harris, eds., *Afro-American Fiction Writers Since 1955, Dictionary of Literary Biography* (Detroit: Gale Research Co., 1983), 33:219–32.

5. *The Collected Works of W. B. Yeats*, Vol. 1, *The Poems*, rev. ed., ed. Richard J. Finneran (New York: Macmillan, 1989), 187. All subsequent quotations from Yeats's poetry are from this edition and page numbers will be cited in the text.

6. W. B. Yeats, *A Vision* (1937; New York: Collier Books, 1966), 268. Compare also page 214: "The bird signifies truth when it eats, evacuates, builds its nest, engenders, feeds its young; do not all intelligible truths lie in its passage from egg to dust?" The poem "Leda and the Swan" does not mention eggs of Leda, hence my argument for the likelihood of Reed's having read *A Vision*. The bloody tide and the bloodied moon are also common Yeatsian images.

7 Northrop Frye, "Yeats and the Language of Symbolism" (1954), *Fables of Identity: Studies in Poetic Mythology* (New York: Harcourt, Brace & World Inc., 1963), 225.

8   Reed, "Time and the Eagle," 6.

9   Ishmael Reed, *Conjure: Selected Poems, 1963–1970* (Amherst: University of Massachusetts Press, 1971), viii. Hereafter cited parenthetically as *C*.

10.   Northrop Frye, *Fearful Symmetry: A Study of William Blake* (1947; Princeton: Princeton University Press, 1978), 200, 202.

11.   William Blake, *The Complete Poetry and Prose of William Blake*, ed. David E. Erdman, rev. ed. (New York: Doubleday, 1988), 95. Hereafter cited parenthetically as Blake.

12.   M.H. Abrams, *Natural Supernaturalism: Tradition and Revolution in Romantic Literature* (1971; New York: W.W. Norton & Co., 1973), 191, 223–24.

13.   Abrams, *Natural Supernaturalism*, 177–83.

14.   Hayden, *Collected Poems*, 51. On the composition of the poem and its place in the uncompleted project, see John O'Brien, *Interviews with Black Writers* (New York: Liveright, 1973), 118.

15.   For a reading of "Passage to India" in the context of the Romantic plot of dualism, see Martin Bickman, *American Romantic Psychology: Emerson, Poe, Whitman, Dickinson, Melville*, 2nd ed. (Dallas: Spring Publications, 1988), 32–37.

16.   Allen Ginsberg, *Howl and Other Poems* (San Francisco: City Lights, 1956), 18.

17.   See George Hart, *A Dictionary of Egyptian Gods and Goddesses* (London: Routledge & Kegan Paul, 1986), 151–67.

18.   *New Larousse Encyclopaedia of Mythology* (1955), cited in J.M. Linebarger and Monte Atkinson, "Getting to Whitey: Ishmael Reed's 'I am a cowboy ...'," *Contemporary Poetry* 2.1 (1975): 10. Linebarger and Atkinson identified the Horus myth in the poem.

19.   See M. A. Murray, *Ancient Egyptian Legends* (New York: E.P. Dutton, 1913), chapter viii, "The Battles of Horus."

20.   Ishmael Reed, *Yellow Back Radio Broke Down* (Garden City: Doubleday, 1969), 115. Hereafter cited parenthetically as *YBR*.

21.   John J. Delany, *Dictionary of American Catholic Biography* (New York: Doubleday, 1984), 546. See also Reed's poem in *Conjure*, "for cardinal spellman who hated voodoo" (58).

22.   "Besides the rites, it also contains *rubrics that must be followed*, hymns that may be used, and formulas employed in parish records." G. J. Sigler, "Roman Ritual," *New Catholic Encyclopaedia*, Vol. 12 (New York: McGraw Hill, 1967), 523–24.

23.   Sigler, "Roman Ritual," traces the various attempts to codify the rituals of the church from the *Liber Sacerdotalis* compiled by Albert Castellani in 1523 through various revisions in the 16th and 17th centuries to the most recent and definitive revision in 1952. Only minor changes have been made since (524).

24. Lawrence Buell, *Literary Transcendentalism: Style and Vision in the American Renaissance* (Ithaca, NY: Cornell University Press, 1973), 175. The first two quotations are from Emerson.

25. The metamorphosis of personae in Reed's poetry also serves self-creation, and insofar as this entails an externalization of the self in a "mask," it is very much part of the drama of duality and of Reed's attraction to Yeats. But more of that later.

26. C. M. Aherne, "Fable of Popess Joan," *New Catholic Encyclopaedia*, 7:991–92. See also Lawrence Durrell, *Pope Joan*, translated and adapted from the Greek of Emmanuel Royidis (Woodstock, NY: Overlook Press, 1960) for further information and bibliography. Pope Joan was discovered only when she gave birth during a procession between the Colosseum and St. Clements in Rome.

27. For Ptah, see Hart, *A Dictionary*, 172–77.

28. Gary Snyder, *Earth House Hold* (New York: New Directions, 1969), 105, 115.

29. Joseph Henry, "A MELUS Interview: Ishmael Reed," *MELUS* 11.1 (Spring 1984): 85.

30. See interview with Reed in the present issue of *Callaloo*.

31. See Robert H. Abel, "Reed's 'I am a cowboy in the boat of Ra,'" *Explicator* 30.9 (May 1981): item 81, n.p.

32. James Haskins, *Witchcraft, Mysticism and Magic in the Black World* (Garden City, NY: Doubleday, 1974), 9, 50.

33. Geoffrey Thurley, *The Turbulent Dream: Passion and Politics in the Poetry of W. B. Yeats* (St. Lucia: University of Queensland Press, 1983), 174–79, summarizes the debate about Yeats's use of "artifice."

34. T. R. Henn, *The Lonely Tower: Studies in the Poetry of W. B. Yeats*, rev. ed. (London: Methuen, 1965), 215.

35. Harold Bloom, "from *Yeats*," ed. William H. Pritchard, *W. B. Yeats: A Critical Anthology* (Harmondsworth: Penguin, 1972), 335, 337. Bloom notes that one cancelled line in an early draft of the poem reads "I fly from nature to Byzantium" and another applauds the city as the place "where nothing changes" (335).

36. The phrase is from Arra M. Garab, *Beyond Byzantium: The Last Phase of Yeats's Career* (DeKalb: Northern Illinois University Press, 1969), 20.

37. Joachim Berendt, *The Jazz Book*, trans. D. Morgenstern and H. and B. Bredigkeit (1953; Westport: Lawrence Hill, 1975), 77.

38. Tam Fiofiori, "Space Age Music: The Music of Sun Ra," *Negro Digest* 19.3 (1970): 25.

39. Ekkehard Jost, *Free Jazz* (1974; New York: DeCapo Press, 1981), 191.

40. Jost, *Free Jazz*, 191.

41. Berendt, *Jazz Book*, 359, my emphasis.

42. In Jost, *Free Jazz*, 181.

43. Renato Poggioli, *The Theory of the Avant-Garde* (1962; Cambridge: Harvard University Press, 1968), 127.

44. Gerhard Putschogl, "Black Music-Key Force in Afro-American Culture: Archie Shepp on Oral Tradition and Black Culture," *History and Tradition in Afro-American Culture*, ed. Gunter Lenz (Frankfurt: Campus Verlag, 1984), 268. However, the emphasis on historical research and the exploration of cross-cultural materials in the work of many "white modernists" clearly challenges both Poggioli and Putschogl. We can no longer conceive of the avant-garde in terms of a perpetual historical discontinuity as Poggioli's emphasis on futurism, early surrealism and dada perhaps allows him to do. Nor can we accept the idea that an attachment to tradition is an exclusive preserve of "ethnic" modernists.

45. Leonard Deen, *Conversing in Paradise: Poetic Genius and Identity-as-Community in Blake's Los* (Columbia: University of Missouri Press, 1983), 1.

46. The sun is also "the axis upon which the entire Voodoo cult turns." See Milo Rigaud, *Secrets of Voodoo*, 8–9.

47. Tom Dent, "Umbra Days," *Black American Literature Forum* 14.3 (1980): 108.

48. "Rosewald Rudd, John Winter, Mike Mantler, Burton Greene and Paul and Carla Bley ... were the charter members of the Guild, together with Sun Ra, Archie Shepp, John Tchicai, Cecil Taylor and Dixon himself." Valerie Wilmer, *As Serious as Your Life: The Story of the New Jazz* (London: Allison & Busby, 1974), 214. Most of my information on the Guild and Dixon is taken from Wilmer, 213–15. See also Robert Levin, "The Jazz Composers' Guild: An Assertion of Dignity," *Downbeat* 32.10 (May 6, 1965): 17–18, and Dan Morgenstern and Martin Williams, "The October Revolution: Two Views of the Avant Garde in Action," *Downbeat* 31–30 (November 19, 1964): 15, 33.

49. Jean-Louis Noames, "Le System Taylor" (interview), *Jazz Magazine* No. 125 (December 1965): 33. My translation. The history of the Jazz Composers' Guild must have been an all too familiar story to Reed since it closely paralleled the history of Umbra, the poetry group to which he belonged. There is no space here to examine the history of Umbra. For further information, see Michel Oren, "A '60s Saga: The Life and Death of Umbra," Part 1, *Freedomways* 24.3 (1984): 167–81. Part II of this study appeared in *Freedomways* 24.4 (1984): 237–54. Together the two parts comprise the most sustained social and literary history of Umbra to date. See also Dent, "Umbra Days," 105–08 and Lorenzo Thomas, "The Shadow World: New York's Umbra Workshop & Origins of the Black Arts Movement," *Callaloo* 4.1 (October 1978): 53–72. Thomas' article, like Dent's piece, is a useful source because

written by a former member of Umbra. Reed gives his own brief account of Umbra in the introduction to 19 *Necromancers from Now*, xx–xxi.

50. Jost, *Free Jazz*, 199, my emphasis.

51. Jacques Attali, *Noise: The Political Economy of Music* (1977; Minneapolis: University of Minnesota Press, 1985), trans. Brian Massumi, 138. Attali is discussing the Jazz Composers' Guild, the Association for the Advancement of Creative Musicians, the Jazz Composers' Orchestra Association and other similar mutual-aid organizations that developed around the free jazz scene.

52. Nathaniel Mackey, "The Changing Same: Black Music in the Poetry of Amiri Baraka," *Boundary* 2, 6.2 (1978): 368, my emphasis. For Attali's comments on improvisation, see *Noise*, 142.

53. See LeRoi Jones, *Black Music* (New York: Quill, 1967), 194–95.

54. Deen, *Conversing in Paradise*, 12.

55. Deen, *Conversing in Paradise*, 9.

56. For the Yeats references, see *The Wind Among the Reeds* (1899) and *The Winding Stair and Other Poems* (1933). For Yeats's own glosses on the key images in these books, see Yeats 592, 599.

57. Marshall McLuhan, *Understanding Media: The Extensions of Man* (1964; New York: Signet, 1966), 263.

58. For Osiris, see E. A. Wallis Budge, *Osiris: The Egyptian Religion of Resurrection* (1911; New York: University Books, 1961, two vols. bound as one), 50; for the afterworld's nomenclature, see Rudolf Anthes, "The Mythology of Ancient Egypt," *Mythologies of the Ancient World*, ed. Samuel Kramer (Garden City: Doubleday's Anchor Books, 1961), 19. Shadle, "Mumbo Jumbo Gumbo Works," has remarked on some of these references previously (129–30).

59. S. Foster Damon, *A Blake Dictionary: The Ideas and Symbols of William Blake* (1965; rev. ed., Hanover: University Press of New England, 1988), 395.

60. Damon, *A Blake Dictionary*, 307.

61. Damon, *A Blake Dictionary*, 234.

62. Damon, *A Blake Dictionary*, 332–33.

63. Damon, *A Blake Dictionary*, 333.

64. For this contrast between Transcendentalism and Romanticism, see Quentin Anderson, *The Imperial Self: An Essay in American Literature and Culture* (New York: A. Knopf, 1971), 5.

65. Buell, *Literary Transcendentalism*, 173–74, makes the same point about Whitman's poetry.

66. Alvin F. Harlow, "Wells, Fargo and Company," *Dictionary of American History*, rev. ed. (New York: Charles Scribner and Sons, 1976), 7:267.

67. Hart, *A Dictionary of Egyptian Gods and Godesses*, 89.

68. For Ezzard Charles, see "Ezzard (Mack) Charles," *The New Encyclopaedia Britannica*, Vol. II (15th ed., 1974), 763. For a brief note on the Chisholm Trail, see *The Encyclopaedia of Americana*, vol. 6 (New York: Americana Corp., 1973), 608–09.

69. Abel, "I am a cowboy," n.p.

70. The imminent return of the outlaw in this stanza is laden with the same desire that awaits the day when Osiris will "be scattered over 100 ghettoes" (*C* 4). But in his recurrent satire of Christian atonism, Reed never acknowledges that the Osirian sparagmos is identical to Christian mythologies of regeneration through sacrifice. In the dreamed of restoration of the alchemist's ring, Osiris and Christ are interchangeable. "In Christian alchemy," M. H. Abrams reminds us, "the Philosopher's Stone was held to correspond to Christ, the Messiah of Nature, who has the apocalyptic function of restoring both fallen and divided man and the fallen and fragmented universe to the perfection of their original unity" (*Natural Supernaturalism*, 160).

71. *Encyclopaedia Britannica* Vol. II, 763.

72. Fahmy Farag, *The Opposing Virtues* (Dublin: The Dolmen Press, 1978), 6.

73. Hazard Adams, *Blake and Yeats: The Contrary Vision* (Ithaca: Cornell University Press, 1955), 199.

74. For the dance as order and equilibrium, see "The Double Vision of Michael Robartes" (170–72) or "The Song of the Happy Shepherd" (7–8).

75. Compare also the other dance references in the poem: the "winding" motion of the saxophone in the second stanza; the forced "dance" in the fifth; and the dance music of the "mowtown long plays" in the sixth.

76. Adams, *The Contrary Vision*, 178.

77. Adams, *The Contrary Vision*, 178.

78. Hazard Adams, "The Seven Eyes of Yeats," in *William Blake and the Moderns*, ed. Robert J. Bertholf and Annette S. Levitt (Albany: State University of New York Press, 1982), 6.

79. See for example Madge Ambler's "black power" reading of the poem. Ambler, "Ishmael Reed: Who's Radio Broke Down," *Negro American Literature Forum* 6.4 (Winter 1972): 125–31.

80. Ishmael Reed, *Flight to Canada* (New York: Doubleday, 1976), 82, 89.

81. Sepharial, *New Dictionary of Astrology* (New York: Galahad Books, 1963), 82.

82. Abrams, *Natural Supernaturalism*, 160.

83. Richard Ellmann, *Yeats: The Man and the Masks* (1948; New York: E.P. Dutton, n.d.), 121.

84. Theodore Roszak, *Unfinished Animal: The Aquarian Frontier and the Evolution of Consciousness* (1975; London: Faber & Faber, 1976), 3.

85. Alfred Metraux, *Voodoo in Haiti*, trans. Hugo Charteris (1959; New York: Schocken Books, 1972), 300.

86. Metraux, *Voodoo in Haiti*, 89; Hurston, *Tell My Horse*, 180.

87. Maya Deren, *The Voodoo Gods* (London: Paladin, 1975), 65. Originally published as *The Divine Horsemen* (1953).

88. Deren, *Voodoo Gods*, 66–67. Deren also notes that "it is still true, and extremely significant, that wherever Vodoun has been especially suppressed (at the insistence of the Catholic Church) it is the Petro rites that become dominant (66). Petro combines African and Indian elements (6870) and we remember that in *Yellow Back Radio* Chief Showcase is the ally of Loop Garoo.

89. Sepharial, *Dictionary of Astrology*, 84, 7.

90. Deren, *Voodoo Gods*, 66.

91. The quote and the information on La Rue are from Mark Shadle, "Mumbo Jumbo Gumbo Works: The Kalaedoscopic Fiction of Ishmael Reed," Ph.D., University of Iowa, 1984, 151. La Rue also made a pornographic film called *Hard on the Trail*.

92. See the section on "The Sexual Law," in Denis Saurat's *Literature and Occult Tradition: Studies in Philosophical Poetry*, trans. Dorothy Bolton (London: G. Bell and Sons, 1930), 94–121.

93. See Richard Slotkin, *Regeneration Through Violence: The Mythology of the American Frontier, 1600–1860* (Middletown, CT: Wesleyan University Press, 1973).

94. The exploration of the outlaw in the works of writers as diverse as Gore Vidal, Samuel R. Delany, Charles Olson, Michael McClure, Michael Ondaatje, and Jack Spicer, as well as other relevant materials from the post-war period are examined in Chapter 6 of Stephen Tatum's *Inventing Billy the Kid: Visions of the Outlaw in America, 1881–1981* (Albuquerque: University of New Mexico Press, 1982). Two works not mentioned by Tatum are particularly revealing companion pieces for both "I am a cowboy" and *Yellow Back Radio*: Ed Dorn's long poem *Stinger* (1975), the first two books of which appeared in 1968 and 1969, and Jerome Rothenberg's "Cokboy," part one of which appeared in 1972 and part two in 1973. There is, unfortunately, no space here to pursue a dialogue among these works.

95. Tatum, *Inventing Billy the Kid*, 117, 123, 146.

96. Frederick Ives Carpenter, *Emerson Handbook* (New York: Hendricks House, 1953), 149–50.

97. Cf. the comments on the ideological biases of historians at this time in Tatum, *Inventing Billy the Kid*, 140–41. On the relationship of the American concept of representative selfhood and consensus ideology to

the mythology of the expansive frontier, see Sacvan Bercovitch, "The Rites of Assent: Rhetoric, Ritual, and the Ideology of American Consensus," in Sam B. Girgus, ed., *The American Self: Myth, Ideology, and Popular Culture* (Albuquerque: University of New Mexico Press, 1981), 9, 13.

98. Bickman, *American Romantic Psychology*, 83: "The double consciousness can be collapsed into a condition that has been called 'inflation,' where the ego confounds its own aims and powers with those of the entire psyche. The process can result in an unrealistic aggrandizement of the ego and in a sense of power not fully apprehended or controlled. Perhaps one of the reasons that Emerson's transparent eyeball passage in Nature is such an easy target of satiric and critical deflation is that it suggests this hazardous identification of the ego with the self...."

99. Anderson, *The Imperial Self*, 237.

100. For an investigation of the 1960s' obsession with the Dionysian, see Eric Mottram, "Dionysus in America," *Other Times* 1 (1975): 38–48.

101. Shadle, "Mumbo Jumbo Gumbo Works," makes the identification (138). See also the interview with Reed in this issue of *Callaloo*, where Reed talks about his early playing.

102. Adams, *The Contrary Vision*, 243.

103. Adams, *The Contrary Vision*, 244. Abrams notes that the return of the divided man to wholeness in Blake is dependent upon his breaking out of "what Blake calls 'the circle of Destiny'—the cyclical recurrences of pagan history—into a 'Resurrection to Unity' which is the full and final closure of the Christian design of history" (*Natural Supernaturalism*, 260).

104. Although Yeats dissociates the artist and magician, and, like his mentor Blavatsky, rejects the priests as model, his sense of the relationship of art and magic is not always clear. See George Mills Harper, *Yeats's Golden Dawn* (New York: Harper and Row, 1974), Chapter 8; and Ellman, *Yeats*, 56–57, 90–91.

105. Mircea Eliade, *Shamanism: Archaic Techniques of Ecstasy* (Princeton, NJ: Princeton University Press, 1964).

106 Jerome Rothenberg, "Pre-Face," *Technicians of the Sacred: A Range of Poetries from Africa, America and Oceania*, ed. Rothenberg (1968; Garden City: Anchor Books, 1969), 424.

107. Rothenberg, "Pre-Face," 440.

108. Gavin Selerie and Eric Mottram, *The Riverside Interviews* 4: *Jerome Rothenberg* (London: Binnacle Press, 1984), 31, 32.

109. For a consideration of this social distinction between modern poet and shaman, see Kevin Powers, "A Conversation with Jerome Rothenberg," *Vort* 7, 3.1 (1975): 146–47; Fedora Giordano, "Translating the Sacred: The Poet and the Shaman," in *North American*

Indian Studies: European Contributions, ed. Pieter Hoverns (Gottingen: Edition Herodot, 1981), 109–22; Michael Castro, *Interpreting the Indian: Twentieth Century Poets and the Native American* (Albuquerque: University of New Mexico Press, 1983), 122.

110. On the principles of information theory, see Jeremy Campbell, *Grammatical Man: Information, Entropy, Language and Life* (1982; Harmondsworth: Penguin, 1984), especially 11–12. William R. Paulson explains that noise, the collective term for all causes of interrupted and altered transmission, "may be the interruption of a signal, the pure and simple suppression of elements of a message, or it may be the introduction of elements of an extraneous message ... or it may be the introduction of elements that are purely random" (*The Noise of Culture: Literary Texts in a World of Information* [Ithaca: Cornell University Press, 19881, 67.)

111. Paulson, *The Noise of Culture*, 121.

112. Walt Sheppard, "When State Magicians Fail: An Interview with Ishmael Reed," *The Journal of Black Poetry* 1.2 (1969): 73. And in the late-1980s he continued to hold a positive, McLuhanite sense of the possibilities of technology. See also the interview with Reed in this issue of *Callaloo*.

113. Regarding the other elements in the title, Reed explains that "Yellow Back" was the name given to old, popular Western novels after their yellow covering. "Broke Down" is a "takeoff" on Lorenzo Thomas' poem "Modern Plumbing Illustrated" (1966). "When people say 'Break it down' they mean to strip something down to its basic components. So *Yellow Back Radio* is the dismantling of a genre done in an oral way like radio" (*S* 134).

114. McLuhan, *Understanding Media*, 264.

115. In Gerald Emanuel Stearn, ed., *McLuhan: Hot & Cool* (New York: Dial Press, 1967), 242.

116. McLuhan, *Understanding Media*, 259.

117. Poirier, *A World Elsewhere*, 29.

118. Terrence Diggory, *Yeats and American Poetry: The Tradition of the Self* (Princeton: Princeton University Press, 1983), 5.

119. Diggory, *Yeats and American Poetry*, 5–6. The externalized or dual self, of course, refers to Yeats's ideas of the antithetical and primary selves. See *A Vision*, 71–72.

120. A. G. Stock, *W. B. Yeats: His Poetry and Thought* (1961; Cambridge: Cambridge University Press, 1964), 176–78.

121. Yeats, *A Vision*, 268. The urge behind *A Vision* is the conservative's anxiety to stabilize history through the construction of a system in which poetics is finally sacrificed to metaphysics. Yvor Winters hits the mark when he writes that Yeats's was a "medieval method"

masquerading as "Mallarmean method." Winters, "from *Forms of Discovery*" (1967), *W. B. Yeats: A Critical Anthology*, ed. William H. Pritchard (Harmondsworth: Penguin, 1972), 272.

122. Diggory, *Yeats and American Poetry*, 6.

123. Anderson, *Imperial Self*, 241.

124. Diggory, *Yeats and American Poetry*, 7.

125. This same development can be traced over a longer period in the novels. Although the first two novels subscribe to an anarchist individualism, in *Mumbo Jumbo*, *The Last Days of Louisiana Red*, and *Flight to Canada*, Reed returns to narratives of community in the form of mutual aid organizations. But the later novels abandon this attempt and return to a less optative version of the masculine heroism of the earlier novels.

PETER ERICKSON

Rita Dove's Shakespeares

every song he sings
is by Shakespeare
and his mother-in-law.
                    —"Shakespeare Say"

Fig newtons
and *King Lear*, bitter lemon as well
for Othello, that desolate
conspicuous soul.
But Macbeth demanded dry bread,
crumbs brushed from a lap
as I staggered off the cushions
contrite, having read far past
my mother's calling.
                    —"In the Old Neighborhood"

Black writers' approaches to Shakespeare have never been monolithic. Two of the most memorable passages on Shakespeare in twentieth-century African-American letters define the opposite ends of a very broad spectrum. In the paragraph that concludes chapter VI of *The Souls of Black Folk* (1903),

---

From *Transforming Shakespeare: Contemporary Women's Re-Visions in Literature and Performance*, edited by Marianne Novy. © 1999 by St. Martin's Press.

W.E.B. Du Bois declares: "I sit with Shakespeare and he winces not."[1] Fifty years later Du Bois's mood of serene mutuality is sharply undercut by the angry sense of exclusion articulated in James Baldwin's 1953 essay "Stranger in the Village": "The most illiterate among them [white Europeans] is related, in a way that I am not, to Dante, Shakespeare, Michelangelo, Aeschylus, Da Vinci, Rembrandt, and Racine; the cathedral at Chartres says something to them which it cannot say to me."[2]

Du Bois's triumphant placement of "not" as the positive final word in the sentence—"he winces not"—is reversed by the insistent negative force of Baldwin's stress on "not"—"in a way that I am not," "which it cannot say to me." Baldwin thus explicitly questions and denies Du Bois's central image of harmonious communication—"Across the color line I move arm in arm"—in an idealized cultural realm where "wed with Truth, I dwell above the veil."

"Shakespeare Say" in *Museum* (1983) and "In the Old Neighborhood" in *Selected Poems* (1993),[3] two poems in which Rita Dove presents different images of Shakespeare, need to be read in this larger context of the history of African-American responses to Shakespeare. The purpose of the plural Shakespeares in my title is to suggest not only that Dove inherits a tradition with multiple versions of Shakespeare but also that she actively intervenes in this tradition by ranging across its spectrum, playing with her own combinations and freely creating new variations.

The present essay is organized in two parts. The first consists of the full transcript of Rita Dove's comments in response to a set of questions concerning Shakespeare, while the second part presents my commentary on her two poems involving Shakespeare. I am extremely grateful to Rita Dove for her participation in this project and for her permission both to print the interview and to quote from her poetry.

I. SHAKESPEARE QUESTIONS

PE: As background, I am working with two of the greatest Shakespearean touchstones in African-American letters: W.E.B. Du Bois's "I sit with Shakespeare and he winces not" in *The Souls of Black Folk* and James Baldwin's "The most illiterate of them is related, in a way that I am not, to Dante, Shakespeare" in "Stranger in the Village," the final essay in *Notes of a Native Son*. I am interested in any observations you may have about these two passages.

I am also wondering whether you encountered either of these when you were growing up. If so, what do you recall about the specific moment and the specific meaning of the encounter?

RD: The difference between W.E.B. Du Bois's comment in *The Souls of Black Folk*—"I sit with Shakespeare and he winces not"—and my first encounter with Shakespeare is rather radical. I encountered Shakespeare as an innocent—that is, I was not "introduced" to Shakespeare but rather stumbled upon him, much as one would bump into a stranger at a party and discover that one had a lot in common to talk about. Shakespeare was on the bookshelves in my parents' home, and though I knew he was a Famous Writer, at the age of 10 or 11 I did not truly comprehend just what that meant. I began reading Shakespeare as a challenge to myself, not a challenge set up by an Authority Figure, and I believe that has made all the difference in the world regarding my entry into literature, for I found Shakespeare a kindred soul. My discovery of James Baldwin, on the other hand, is a different story. My first contact with him was the startling encounter with his portrait on the back of his essay collection *Notes of a Native Son*. My parents had bought the book, and I remember my mother taking it along to read while I had my private cello lessons at the Akron Conservatory of Music. In a way, Baldwin might have been amused by the irony of such a situation, since the essay you mention, "Stranger in the Village," discusses this very question of legacy.

PE: I assume that "Shakespeare Say" may have originated in your seeing an actual live performance by Champion Jack Dupree. If so, could you comment on the circumstances and on your reactions at the time? How would you characterize the relation between the event and the poem? Do you see the poem at all as a reflection or reconsideration (though not necessarily as an emotion recollected in tranquillity!)?

Also, do you have any feelings about the European context of the poem? Does it make a difference that the setting is Munich rather than somewhere in the U.S.?

RD: I did experience a live performance by Champion Jack Dupree. It occurred not in Munich, as the poem claims, but in the city of Bielefeld, where I spent ten weeks as part of a group of international writers and critics in the fall of 1980. How I relate the event, however, is pretty much true to the way it happened. Champion Jack Dupree did use "Shakespeare Say" as a running joke throughout his banter; the audience was enamoured by his "exoticism —and completely unaware of their own ignorance. Of course, I imagined the thoughts that Champion Jack entertains while playing his sets. I think it does make a difference that the setting is Germany rather than somewhere in the United States, for the very same reasons that James Baldwin's Reflections on the White Man's Privilege [were] sparked by his experiences in Europe. Sometimes one needs to get away to see clearly the conflicting circumstances from which one has arisen.

PE: Concerning "In the Old Neighborhood," I continue to be struck by your use of the 1970 epigraph from Adrienne Rich's emotionally explosive

The Will to Change. Could you comment on how you discovered and responded to Rich's work?

RD: It's difficult for me to comment on Adrienne Rich, except to say that she has always been an example to me—not only for the quality of her work, which I admire, but also for the paradigm of her life. Here is a poet who was willing to jettison all of the easy trappings of fame—after all, her first book was chosen by Auden for the Yale Younger Poets Prize—in order to discover what kind of language would be capable of bearing witness to the life she was experiencing.

PE: How did the two "wine-red" "bouillon cubes" enter your family library? Were the Shakespeare volumes associated with a particular family member? Did you discuss your reading?

With regard to Othello, that desolate / conspicuous soul," can you recall your experience on first looking into this play and where, in the overall sequence of reading Shakespeare's works, did you read *Othello*? Did you see it as an equal part of the great tragic sweep of *Hamlet, Othello, Lear, Macbeth*, or did you experience it as set apart, different? Finally, have you witnessed any performances of *Othello* that had a powerful impact?

RD: I never discussed my early reading of Shakespeare with anyone. And I do not know exactly how the Shakespeare volumes appeared in my family library. My father has always read voraciously; when my older brother and I were not quite in our teens, my father ordered the entire Great Books of the Western World, as much for his own pleasure as for our education. I can only imagine that the two "wine-red" volumes of Shakespeare were part of his hunger to understand as much about the umbrella culture under which he was born as possible. I cannot recall exactly when I read *Othello*, except to say that I know I read it before I turned thirteen. The very first Shakespeare play I read was *Macbeth*, mainly because I heard my mother reciting from it at length; it was rapidly followed by *Romeo and Juliet, Julius Caesar*, and *A Midsummer Night's Dream*. I started *Lear* but didn't finish it (nor did I read *Hamlet*) until years later, in school. *Othello* must have happened sometime around *Romeo and Juliet* (I read all of these in one summer!), and I did read *Othello* because I was intrigued by the fact that this British Elizabethan had such a large mind that he was able to imagine a black man as a prince in Italy! It was certainly not the kind of imagination that I saw bearing any fruit in the more contemporary literature I had come across up to then. Interestingly enough, I have never seen a live performance of *Othello*.

PE: I need to ask you about the way stanzas 10 to 12 in "In the Old Neighborhood" are bracketed in parentheses because these seem to mark a separate zone that disrupts the temporal counterpoint between 1993, the present moment when the poet returns home for a family reunion occasioned by her younger sister's wedding, and 1973, "twenty years before," the moment when the poet at 21 with a new B.A. perhaps first left the home within which she had lived so completely up to that point. But when I reach the section in parentheses, I don't know where I am! The verbs don't allow me easily to identify the timeframe. The tone and mood of "I'll ask" make me imagine the final Lear–Cordelia encounter—no doubt the result of my excessively Shakespeare-steeped intellect! In any event, the transition from "*All weeds*" to "*Chink. Chink.*" is so excitingly abrupt that I hardly know how to talk about it. I would welcome your comments here.

RD: Actually, the present in the poem is closer to 1982, when the poet is 30, and the "twenty years before" refers to about 1962, an "innocent" age of 10 when the child was taught to read the newspaper "correctly"—maybe so she would begin to understand what was going on in our country at that time of social and racial upheaval. But back to the gist of your question: These parenthetical stanzas in the poem "In the Old Neighborhood" are a dream sequence interrupting the collage of memory and present activity in the poem at large. In a way, these stanzas are like an invocation to memory— an attempt, through incantatory language, to summon up a kind of psychic landscape through which the speaker can travel and discover the subconscious significance of familial relationships. The speaker asks to go back to "the white rock on the black lawn." There is actually a huge white rock in the front yard of my parents' house; and on this rock they have painted the house number in black paint. I did not expect the casual reader to figure this out through the poem; instead, I think that in these stanzas the house looms as the "white rock" "moored in moonlight." The speaker, therefore, is in this dream landscape, one in which the house appears as an impenetrable brightness and the speaker is walking along the dark grass, in effect almost sinking into the darkness. Everything around her is quieted and sealed away from her understanding—even the pansies have been placed behind bars of the picket fence. When the speaker dares to address the father directly, ostensibly to ask him a gardener's question, all the father can offer is another image of failure. We discover, however, that the father is not out in this psychic landscape with the speaker; rather, he "intuits" her presence outside the house—the house she dare not / cannot enter—he mutters from his pillow that all of these plants that he has tried to nourish are not presentable but are "*All weeds.*"

The first words after these parenthetical stanzas represent a sound, because sounds are often what will snatch us out of a deep reverie. *Chink* could be the sound of a hoe hitting rock; it also suggests, rather disconcertingly, an unsavory racial epithet. But just as the reader is confused, fascinated and a little bit repulsed by the sound, the speaker of the poem struggles to make sense of it—and finds in the true reason an even more horrifying event.

PE: Could you please comment on whether you ever met the novelist Leon Forrest? I realize this may seem an odd, off-the-wall question but as I am rereading *Divine Days*, I'm struck by two connections between his work and yours. You both explicitly address the limitations of the Black Aesthetic and you both engage Shakespeare. If you did meet Forrest, was there any discussion of these themes?

RD: I met Leon Forrest only once—and very briefly—in the spring of 1995. I was in Chicago for the American Booksellers Association's annual fair, and after my reading he approached me and gave me a copy of *Divine Days*. Unfortunately, I never had the opportunity to meet him again. We had no time to discuss our affinities, but I have always felt him to be a kindred spirit.

II. POETIC TRANSFORMATIONS

My approach in this section is twofold. First, I aim to establish the multiplicity of Rita Dove's invocation of Shakespeare's name by suggesting that as an initial step we think of "Shakespeare Say" as her Baldwin poem and "In the Old Neighborhood" as her Du Bois poem. Though I shall subsequently explore connections between the two poems, I want first to bring out their differences in order to emphasize the extraordinary range that Dove encompasses, and, in particular, her capacity to embrace both sides of the Baldwin–Du Bois opposition. Second, I hope to demonstrate that Dove does not merely reproduce two received images of Shakespeare but also plays with them to create new effects and novel outcomes. My strategy for this part of the argument will be to show how convergences between Baldwin and Du Bois may be seen as providing a flexible basis on which Dove can conduct her mobile experiments in poetic transformation.

The contrasting tones of "Shakespeare Say" and "In the Old Neighborhood" stem from the divergent status of their speaking voices: in the former, Dove speaks through, and is partly hidden behind, the black blues singer Champion Jack Dupree, whereas in the latter she speaks directly in her own voice. The ease with which Dove herself claims access and connection to Shakespeare in "In the Old Neighborhood" follows from his location within the family home: "I've read every book in this house," and the second line of the poem indicates that the family has reunited for her sister's wedding, an event that signifies family renewal and continuity. The poem builds the family constellation by introducing each member in turn—sister, mother, father, self, brother—and celebrates their unity in a summary italicized line: "*whole again whole again now.*" In keeping with this spirit, Shakespeare is so congenial as to be almost part of the family. The affirmation of familial harmony is matched by her harmonious initiation as a reader of Shakespeare, an activity portrayed as natural as the specific images of eating associated with each play. Like Du Bois, the Dove of this poem can positively imply that Shakespeare "winces not."

As we might expect, Champion Jack Dupree in "Shakespeare Say" seeks oral satisfaction of a rawer sort. The image of Champion Jack wielding "the bourbon in his hand" as he readies himself for the third set is both raucous and strangely subdued. Alcohol signals release—the license to transcend codes of politeness and to speak without constraint. Yet, at the same time, the singer's mirroring of the audience's "stinking on beer" testifies to his need for emotional numbness in the face of underlying sadness and pain. As early as lines 10 and 11, the expansive, genial, affectionate portrayal of Champion Jack is cross-cut with a disturbingly harsh note that pulls us up short: "with sand / in a mouthful of mush." Like the Baldwin of "Stranger in the Village," Champion Jack is an artist in European exile and a figure of alienation.

His alienation is double-edged. As an outsider, he mocks and rejects the Western tradition epitomized by Shakespeare's dominant canonical position. Shakespeare is the most quotable of authors: Champion Jack parodies this cultural reflex by violating the sacred status of Shakespeare's actual words and using Shakespeare's name as an ironic all-purpose endorsement for whatever the Champion improvises on the spot. This is an effective way of making Baldwin's point that Shakespeare does not speak to or for everyone. But the other side of this subversive public performance is the unredeemable loss he expresses in his private voice—"so no one hears"—at the poem's culmination: "*my home's in Louisiana, / my voice is wrong.*"

The "near-tragic" depth of this final self-negation may be understood in terms of Ralph Ellison's definition of the blues: "The blues is an impulse to keep the painful details and episodes of a brutal experience alive in one's aching consciousness, to finger its jagged grain, and to transcend it, not by the consolation of philosophy but by squeezing from it a near-tragic, near-comic lyricism."[4] Yet despite the aptness of Ellison's eloquent statement to Champion Jack's situation, the enormity of the pain this poem evokes can perhaps be fully measured only by reference to June Jordan's ringing counterassertion in "Poem about My Rights": "*I am not wrong. Wrong is not my name.*"[5] This is a response of which we feel Champion Jack's entrapment makes him incapable. Of course Dove herself cannot be identified with the poem's main character in this regard. Although she allows him to retain a basic dignity and even an endearing flair, she is also unsentimentally clear-eyed about his self-pity, his limited view of women, and his musical deficiencies—the word "mistakes" in "even the mistakes / sound like jazz" has a sting that is not entirely forgiving.

Having established the counterpoint between Champion Jack cut off from home in "Shakespeare Say" and Rita Dove ensconced in family environment in "In the Old Neighborhood," I now want to explore the possibility of a more comprehensive perspective from which, without canceling the contrast, we might begin to see points of overlap that could lead to a larger synthesis.[6] My starting point is a reconsideration of the Baldwin–Du Bois tension. While the perception of tension remains valid, we can also discern elements of convergence that qualify the idea of absolute diametrical opposition.

On Baldwin's side, the total rejection of Shakespeare registered in "Stranger in the Village" is substantially modified when he reverts to Shakespeare and Chartres twenty years later in *No Name in the Street*. Baldwin now envisions a two-step process in which "throwing out" Shakespeare is followed by a second "Move: "Later, of course, one may welcome them back, but on one's own terms."[7] On Du Bois's side, the "I sit with Shakespeare" declaration is frequently distorted because it is excerpted in a decontextualized manner.[8] Du Bois's homage to Shakespeare is in fact counterbalanced in the immediately preceding paragraph by an equally strong assertion of the power of American blacks to make an innovative cultural contribution: "Herein the longing of black men must have respect: the rich and bitter depth of their experience, the unknown treasures of their inner life, the strange rendings of nature they have seen, may give the world new points of view and make their loving, living, and doing precious to all human hearts." Although the contrasting emphases are indeed present in their key passages on Shakespeare, Baldwin's subsequent shift to "on one's own terms" and Du Bois's commitment to "new points of view" nonetheless bring the two authors closer together in a shared conceptual arena. Similarly, while the contrast between "Shakespeare Say" and "In the Old Neighborhood" still stands, at another level points of connection emerge when we take a second look at the latter poem.

"In the Old Neighborhood" is easy to underestimate because of the way its amiable surface tone is carried by a flood of genuine family affection. Yet there is an underlying complexity that pulls back away from this emotional tide and moves the poem in another direction: a meditation on reading and, by extension, on the writing career into which the poet has been led by this childhood habit.

After portraying her parents' respective styles of imaginative profusion and extravagance, Dove turns to herself in the poem's fourth stanza, where she intimates a slight tension between two versions of reading:

I am indoors, pretending
to read today's paper
as I had been taught
twenty years before:
headlines first,
lead story (continued on A–14),
followed by editorials and
local coverage. Even then
I never finished, snared
between datelines—*Santiago,*
Paris, Dakar—names as
unreal as the future
even now.

The first version, defined by the phrase "as I had been taught," portrays the act of reading as an orderly process of gleaning factual information. The resistance to this mode is quietly pursued through the ongoing motif of the newspaper: "I skip to the daily horoscope," "I fold the crossword away." The horoscope and the crossword puzzle are not, one is made to feel, part of the authorized agenda. The poem's concluding lines involving the newspaper's obliteration in recycling pick up and linger over the telltale phrase— "properly, / as I had been taught to do"—as though definitively to set it aside by repeating it with an ironic twist.

The alternative version of reading is harder to define since its pleasure is portrayed in part as the evasion of regulation: "as I staggered off the cushions / contrite, having read far past / my mother's calling." A hint is given in the way the child is drawn by the single words of the cities in the datelines into a global expanse that entices the imagination far beyond the domestic household. The goal, however, is not merely escape or adventure but also a worldview in a deeper sense. It is no coincidence that Dakar appears as the decisive final term in the list, for it points to Africa and to the history of race. This motif is subtle but recurrent: we hear it again in the reference to Othello as "that desolate / conspicuous soul." Compressed as this notation is, it introduces a moment of troubled questioning that counteracts the easygoing appreciation of Shakespeare. Othello is the only character who is accorded adjectives, and the two adjectives attract attention because their apposition lacks a comma and is split over two lines. Othello is not only conspicuous because he is desolate; his desolation has its mainspring in his conspicuousness, his visibility as a black man in a white culture. The child reader is tacitly shown stumbling on discoveries, though these are presented with a restraint that avoids intruding on the overall upbeat atmosphere.

The poem's characteristic deftness is displayed in the understated quality of the epigraph citing Adrienne Rich: "*To pull yourself up by your own roots, / to eat the last meal in your own neighborhood.*" Without counterpoising Rich and Shakespeare in direct confrontation, Dove nevertheless implicitly indicates alternatives to Shakespeare for authoritative reading experiences.[9] In contrast to the generally pleasurable mix of eating and reading associated with Shakespeare, Rich presents a sterner image of food involving renunciation of comfort and security in favor of change and the development of new identity. The positioning of Rich's lines as the epigraph casts the entire poem in a retrospective frame: the Dove who is writing the poem is no longer the Dove described within the poem. She has already grown up and moved on. If she returns now, it is only to confirm her departure by symbolically "eating the last meal." The Rich quotation also subtly provides "In the Old Neighborhood" with a literary genealogy of far more explosive intensity than we might at first glance realize. Dove's identification with Rich's lines has larger ramifications because they are the very last two lines in *The Will to Change: Poems, 1968–1970* and hence poised on the cusp of the dramatic transition to *Diving into the Wreck: Poems, 1971–1972.*[10]

In order to test the thesis that "In the Old Neighborhood" is structured by means of a strategy of deceptive understatement, I turn to the question of the poem's pattern of color imagery. "Color" in relation to Dove's father's roses is an announced theme. But there is a distinct strand that has specifically racial significance whose impact depends on the cumulative power of slight effects to convey a larger metaphorical resonance.

The first instance, the raccoons' "black-gloved paws" with which the opening stanza ends, is so slight that it passes by unnoticed. Like "Shakespeare Say" ("He drums the piano wood, / crowing"), "In the Old Neighborhood" begins with an energetic, colloquial tone turned up full volume. But the heightened mood concentrates our attention on the single arresting word "faggy." Our uncertainty thus engaged elsewhere, the detail of the "black-gloved paws" strikes us as vivid but innocent. Surely, we conclude, no subliminal allusion to "coon" as a racial slur can be intended here.

The references to Dakar and Othello put us sufficiently on alert to hear the potential for something more than a race-neutral night scene: "(Let me go back to the white rock / on the black lawn, the number / stenciled in negative light. / Let me return to the shadow / of a house moored in moonlight." The eeriness of Dove's chiaroscuro has its playful, teasing aspect even as it seems haunted, driven. To apply Dove's word for Othello, the color scheme is "conspicuous": it stands out, calls out, suggestively. We are forced to consider the possibility that racial reverberations are metaphorically present in this overdetermined language of white and black. Her father's spectacular success with mutant roses—"this sudden teacup / blazing empty, its rim / a drunken red smear"—is now unaccountably turned to failure.[11] The "negative light" makes his flowers seem worthless: "Weeds, my father mutters / from his pillow. *All weeds*." Only the fragile wedding corsage at the end pulls back from this image of despair-a precarious recovery.

The final drama of the destruction of the starling by the attic fan's blades reads like such an outlandish parody of the caged bird in Paul Laurence Dunbar's "Sympathy" that it at first appears more like comedy than "the first tragedy of the season." Yet how do we interpret the seemingly offhand dismissal in the rhetorically loaded question: "Who could guess it would be / a bird with no song, / no plumage worth stopping for?" If we are willing to see an analogy between the weeping girl trapped in the tent and the bird, then the latter's destruction expresses in hyperbolic form a danger faced by the former. The fear of a black poet's failure is registered in the bird's triple negative: the starling has "no plumage worth stopping for" because it is black; the "bird with no song" signifies poetic inability; the bird's annihilation, concluded by the unceremonious disposal with the fan's reverse switch, condemns it to anonymity. Dove's own poetic splendors are proof against this fate, but her cruelly macabre farce of the starling's demise ruefully acknowledges the lingering force of the stereotype that she has had to overcome.

Closer examination reveals that, contrary to the initial impression of pure congeniality, "In the Old Neighborhood" has an attitude as questioning as that of "Shakespeare Say." In both poems the allusion to Shakespeare prompts not an occasion for simple celebration but rather an exploration of a problematic inheritance.

III. Coda

I began by placing Rita Dove's poems in relation to an African-American literary tradition; I conclude by situating them in a wider American context. Far from being mutually exclusive, the terms African-American and American are mutually constitutive. Perhaps the single most important feature of Dove's work as a whole is the remarkable sense of freedom conveyed by her verbal exuberance, dexterity, and audacity. A central challenge is how to describe the culturally specific American implications of this freedom.

Helen Vendler, the dominant shaper of Dove studies to date, is right to emphasize Dove's freedom from separatist formulas of racial identity and hence from rigidly circumscribed expectations of what it means "to make a poet black, and bid him sing."[12] However, valuable as Vendler's critical perspective is, it is ultimately limited and one-sided because she does not devote equal attention and sophistication to the critique of universalism, even though she is aware of the problem of "false 'universality.'"[13] In order to perceive the full scope of the freedom Dove asserts with regard to race, it is necessary to present a balanced analysis of the simplifications of universalism as well as of separatism. For the freedom Dove enacts in her poetry is not just freedom from race but also freedom to address racial issues by rejecting both separatist and universalist constructions of them.

With a view to reopening and expanding the racial significance of Dove's work, I turn to the nineteenth-century American phenomenon of minstrelsy, of which Champion Jack Dupree can be seen as a distant descendant. Two of the most potent signifiers for exploring a distinctive American identity are Shakespeare and race; this potency is intensified by their conjunction in instances of Shakespeare burlesque involving blackface.[14] In one paradigm the intersection of representations of Shakespeare and representations of blackness leads to a double satire in which one stone kills two birds by licensing the display of both anti-Shakespeare and anti-black feeling.[15] Mockery of Shakespeare that signals American cultural independence is thus fundamentally compromised at the outset because such self-definition is simultaneously tied to a racist outlook.

This particular formation is tantalizingly suggested as a central motif in Mark Twain's *Adventures of Huckleberry Finn*. Jim's characterization draws in part on blackface minstrelsy,[16] while the King and the Duke perform Shakespeare burlesque. But although the two elements are placed in proximity, they are not joined, with the result that the problem of race is incompletely probed and therefore left unresolved.[17]

This is the sensitive cultural zone in which Dove's poems intervene to perform their liberating work. Dove does not sidestep but rather works with the given materials of Shakespeare and of blackness so as innovatively to recast them. Using her own vigorous poetic presence to reconstitute these basic categories, Dove develops new possibilities for American self-fashioning. The consequence is a transformative poetic space that frees us from the endlessly problematic monopoly that Othello and *Huckleberry Finn* seemed to hold over our literary discourse on race. As black poet, Dove empowers us to think in new ways about the significance of blackness and hence to reenter the central crux of American national identity.

NOTES

1. W. E. B. Dubois, *The Souls of Black Folk* (New York: Bantam, 1989), 76.

2. James Baldwin, "Stranger in the Village," *Notes of a Native Son* (New York: Dial Press, 1955), 148.

3. Rita Dove, *Museum* (Pittsburgh, PA: Carnegie-Mellon University Press, 1983); *Selected Poems* (New York: Pantheon, 1993).

4. Ralph Ellison, "Richard Wright's Blues" (1945), in *Shadow and Act* (New York: Random House, 1964), 90.

5. June Jordan, "Poem about My Rights," *Passion: New Poems, 1977–1980* (Boston: Beacon Press, 1980), 89.

6. In "On Voice," in *Dwelling in Possibility: Women Poets and Critics on Poetry*, ed. Yopie Prins and Maeera Shreiber (Ithaca, NY. Cornell University Press, 1997), 111–15, Dove describes Europe and home as two points in her own overall trajectory: "In *Museum* (1983) I was very concerned with presenting a type of antimuseum, a collection of totems that would not be considered 'essential' to the canon of Western culture—and to that end I adopted a voice that was distanced, cool, ironic; of all my books, this is the most 'European.' After *Museum* I felt I had gone away from home and was now able to return, like a prodigal daughter" (111).

7. James Baldwin, *No Name in the Street* (New York: Dial Press, 1972), 47–48. In a short piece chronologically midway between "Stranger in the Village" and *No Name in the Street*—"'This Nettle, Danger'" (1964), in *James Baldwin: Collected Essays* (New York: Library of America, 1998), 687–91—Baldwin defined the terms that enabled his return to Shakespeare: "Every man writes about his own Shakespeare—and his Shakespeare changes as he himself changes, grows as he grows—and the Shakespeare that I am reading at this stage of my life testifies, for me, to this effort" (688). However, Baldwin's new acceptance goes so far as to remove Shylock and Othello from critical scrutiny; in my view, this reaction goes too far in the other direction.

8. For further discussion of this decontextualization, see the section on Du Bois in Peter Erickson, "The Two Renaissances and Shakespeare's Canonical Position," *Kenyon Review*, n.s., 14, no. 2 (Spring 1992): 58–60.

9. An extended account of Rich's work is given in my essays: "Adrienne Rich's Re-Vision of Shakespeare," in *Rewriting Shakespeare, Rewriting Ourselves* (Berkeley: University of California Press, 1991), 146–66; "Singing America: From Walt Whitman to Adrienne Rich," *Kenyon Review*, n.s., 17, no. 1 (Winter 1995): 103–19; and "Start Misquoting Him Now: The Difference a Word Makes in Adrienne Rich's 'Inscriptions,'" *Shakespeare and the Classroom* 5, no. 1 (Spring 1997): 55–56.

10. The Rich quotation that Dove chooses belongs to the same moment as Rich's critical shift in "When We Dead Awaken: Writing as Re-Vision" (1971) in *On Lies, Secrets, and Silence* (New York: Norton, 1979), 33–49. Rich's concept of "re-vision" inspired the three-volume project edited by Marianne Novy: *Women's Re-Visions of Shakespeare* (Urbana: University of Illinois Press, 1990), *Cross-Cultural Performances: Differences in Women Re-Visions of Shakespeare* (Urbana: University of Illinois Press, 1993), and the present collection. A full picture of black writers' responses to Shakespeare can be completed only when male authors are taken into account; in addition to Du Bois and Baldwin discussed here, examples can be found in my essays: "Contextualizing *Othello* in Reed and Phillips," *The Upstart Crow: A Shakespeare Journal* 17 (1997): 101–107, and a work in progress on Leon Forrest's Shakespeare-saturated texts.

11. In the final "Autobiography" section of *The Poet's World* (Washington, D.C.: Library of Congress, 1995), Dove locates a source for the father's despair in the racial discrimination that thwarted his career, despite his university degree (75–76), while, in poignant contrast, the recording of her own career landmarks demonstrates the expanded possibilities for black Americans in the very next generation. The encounter with her father at the poem's center negotiates the emotional terrain of this generational shift.

12. Vendler's work on Dove consists of six items: "Louise Glück, Stephen Dunn, Brad Leithauser, Rita Dove," in *The Music of What Happens* (Cambridge, MA: Harvard University Press, 1988), 437–54; "An Interview with Rita Dove," in *Reading Black, Reading Feminist*, ed. Henry Louis Gates, Jr. (New York: Meridian, 1990), 481–91; "A Dissonant Triad: Henri Cole, Rita Dove, and August Kleinzahler" and "The Black Dove: Rita Dove, Poet Laureate," in *Soul Says* (Cambridge, MA: Harvard University Press, 1995), 141–55 and 156–66; "Rita Dove: Identity Markers," in *The Given and the Made: Strategies of Poetic Redefinition* (Cambridge, MA: Harvard University Press, 1995), 59–88; and "Twentieth-Century Demeter," *The New Yorker*, May 15, 1995, 90–92.

Dove herself provides ample testimony to her rejection of a purist Black Aesthetic mode in favor of a stance open to multiple, hybrid influences. See especially her extraordinary comprehensive historical survey of black poetry co-authored with Marilyn Nelson Waniek: "A Black Rainbow: Modern Afro-American Poetry," in *Poetry After Modernism*, ed. Robert McDowell (Brownsville, OR: Story Line Press, 1991), 217–75, as well as her revealing commentaries on two individual poets in "Telling It Like It I-S *IS*: Narrative Techniques in Melvin Tolson's Harlem Gallery," *New England Review* 8 (1985): 109–17, and "'Either I'm Nobody, or I'm a Nation,'" *Parnassus* 14, no. 1 (1987):

49–76. On the other hand, we must also note Dove's equally strong dismissal of the traditionalist posturing represented by Harold Bloom in "Screaming Fire," *Boston Review* 23, nos. 3–4 (Summer 1998): 31.

13.   Vendler, *The Given and the Made*, 80.

14.   The brilliant recent work on blackface—the chapter on "Blackface Minstrelsy" in Alexander Saxton's *The Rise and Fall of the White Republic* (London: Verso, 1990), the chapter on "Black Skins, White Masks: Minstrelsy and White Working Class Formations before the Civil War" in David Roediger's *The Wages of Whiteness* (London: Verso, 1991), and Eric Lott's *Love and Theft: Blackface Minstrelsy and the American Working Class* (New York: Oxford University Press, 1993)—pays virtually no attention to Shakespeare. The extremely important exception is Joyce Green MacDonald's "Acting Black: Othello, Othello Burlesques, and the Performance of Blackness," *Theatre Journal* 46 (1994): 231–49.

15.   In "William Shakespeare in America," in *Highbrow/Lowbrow: The Emergence of Cultural Hierarchy in America* (Cambridge, MA: Harvard University Press, 1988), Lawrence W. Levine emphasizes the continuity between Shakespeare's plays and Shakespeare burlesques: "It is difficult to take familiarities with that which is not already familiar; one cannot parody that which is not well known" (15–16). However, burlesque transformations frequently have a parodic bite that pays no respect to the original; hence Levine underestimates the extent to which familiarity with Shakespeare is employed to register a characteristically American form of contempt.

16.   Jim's partial derivation from blackface roles is noted both by Ralph Ellison, *The Collected Essays of Ralph Ellison*, ed. John F. Callahan (New York: Modern Library, 1995), 731, "Jim is flawed by his relationship to the minstrel tradition," and by Toni Morrison, *Introduction to Adventures of Huckleberry Finn* (New York: Oxford University Press, 1996), xxxv ("the over-the-top minstrelization of Jim").

17.   Anthony J. Berret is unconvincing when he argues in *Mark Twain and Shakespeare* (Lanham, MD: University Press of America, 1993) that "it is probable that Twain thought of Othello while composing" *Huckleberry Finn* (176). The link to Othello represents a critical fantasy of what we would like to have happened in Twain's novel but does not in fact occur. The connection between Shakespeare burlesque and blackface minstrelsy that could have been illuminating is never actually made. The novel's lack of resolution has produced an ongoing debate exemplified by Jane Smiley's "Say It Ain't So, Huck," *Harper's Magazine*, January 1996, 61–67.

Works by the Poets

ROBERT HAYDEN (1913–1980)

Angle of Ascent: New and Selected Poems, 1975.
The Night-Blooming Cereus, 1972.
Words in the Mourning Time, 1970.
Selected Poems, 1966.
A Ballad of Remembrance, 1962.
Figure of Time: Poems, 1955.
The Lion and the Archer (co-authored by Mryon O'Higgins), 1948.

GWENDOLYN BROOKS (1917–2000)

In Birmingham, 2001.
Selected Poems, 1995.
Children Coming Home, 1991.
Winnie, 1988.
Gottschalk and the Grand Tarantelle, 1988.
Blacks, 1987.
The Near Johannesburg Boy and Other Poems, 1986.
Mayor Harold Washington and Chicago, the I Will City, 1983.
To Disembark, 1981.
Black Love, 1981.

Beckonings, 1975.
The Tiger Who Wore White Gloves: Or What You Are, You Are, 1974.
Black Position, No. 2, 1972.
Aurora, 1972.
Jump Bad: A New Chicago Anthology, 1971.
A Broadside Treasury, 1971.
The World of Gwendolyn Brooks, 1971.
Black Position, No. 1, 1971.
Black Steel: Joe Frazier and Muhammad Ali, 1971.
Aloneness, 1971.
Family Pictures, 1970.
Riot, 1969.
In the Mecca, 1968.
The Wall, 1967.
We Real Cool, 1966.
Selected Poems, 1963.
The Bean Eaters, 1961.
Bronzeville Boys and Girls, 1956.
Annie Allen, 1949.
A Street in Bronzeville, 1945.

AMIRI BARAKA (LEROI JONES) (1934–)

Funk Lore: New Poems (1984-1995), 1996.
Transbluesency: The Selected Poetry of Amiri Baraka/Leroi Jones (1961–1995),
       1995.
WiseWhy's Y's: The Griots's Tale, 1995.
The Leroi Jones/Amiri Baraka Reader, ed. William J. Harris, 1991.
Selected Poetry of Amiri Baraka/LeRoi Jones, 1979.
Hard Facts, 1975.
Spiritual Reach, 1972.
It's Nation Time, 1970.
Black Magic: Collected Poetry 1961-1967, 1969.
Black Art, 1966.
The Dead Lecturer, 1964.
Preface To A Twenty Volume Suicide Note, 1961.

MAYA ANGELOU (1928–)

A Brave and Startling Truth, 1995.
The Complete Collected Poems of Maya Angelou, 1994.
Wouldn't Take Nothing for My Journey Now, 1993.
I Shall Not Be Moved, 1990.
Now Sheba Sings the Song, 1987.
Shaker, Why Don't You Sing?, 1983.
And Still I Rise, 1978.
Oh Pray My Wings Are Gonna Fit Me Well, 1975.
Just Given Me a Cool Drink of Water 'fore I Diiie, 1971.

DEREK WALCOTT (1930–)

Tiepolo's Hound, 2000.
Bounty, 1997.
Collected Poems (1965-1980).
Midsummer, 1984.
The Fortunate Traveler, 1981.
Selected Poetry, 1981.
The Star-Apple Kingdom, 1980.
Sea Grapes, 1976.
Another Life, 1973.
The Gulf and Other Poems, 1969.
The Castaway and Other Poems, 1965.
Selected Poems, 1964.
In A Green Night: Poems 1948-60, 1962.
Epitaph For The Young, 1949.
Twenty Five Poems (privately printed in 1948).

JAY WRIGHT (1935–)

Transfigurations: Collected Poems, 2000.
Boleros, 1991.
Selected Poems of Jay Wright, 1987.
Elaine's Book, 1986.
Explications/Interpretations, 1984.
The Double Invention of Komo, 1980.

Dimensions of History, 1976.
Soothsayers and Omens, 1976.
The Homecoming Singer, 1971.
Death as History, 1967.

LUCILLE CLIFTON (1936–)

Blessing the Boats: New and Selected Poems 1988–2000, 2000.
The Terrible Stories, 1995.
The Book of Light, 1993.
Quilting: Poems 1987–1990, 1991.
Next: New Poems, 1987.
Good Woman: Poems and a Memoir, 1969–1980.
Two-Headed Woman, 1980.
An Ordinary Woman, 1974.
Good News About the Earth, 1972.
Good Times, 1969.

MICHAEL S. HARPER (1938–)

Songlines in Michaeltree: New and Collected Poems, 2000.
Honorable Amendments, 1995.
Healing Song for the Inner Ear, 1985.
Images of Kin, 1977.
Nightmare Begins Possibility, 1975.
Debridement, 1973.
Photographs: History as Apple Tree, 1972.
Song: I Want a Witness, 1972.
History Is Your Own Heartbeat, 1971.
Dear John, Dear Coltrane, 1970.

ISHMAEL REED (1938–)

New and Collected Poetry, 1988.
A Secretary to the Spirits, 1978.
Chattanooga: Poems, 1973.
Conjure: Selected Poems, 1963-1970, 1972.
Catechism of D Neoamerican HooDoo Church, 1970.

Rita Dove (1952–)

On the Bus with Rosa Parks, 1999.
Mother Love, 1995.
Selected Poems, 1993.
Grace Notes, 1989.
The Other Side of the House, 1988.
Thomas and Beulah, 1986.
Fifth Sunday, 1985.
Museum,1983.
Mandolin, 1982.
The Yellow House on the Corner, 1980.
The Only Dark Spot in the Sky, 1980.
Ten Poems, 1977.

Works about the Poets

Allen, Donald M., ed. *The New American Poetry: 1945–1960*. New York: Grove, 1960.

Anaporte-Easton, Jean. "Healing Our Wounds: The Direction of Difference in the Poetry of Lucille Clifton and Judith Johnson." *Mid-American Review* 14, no. 2 (1994).

———. "She Made Herself Again': The Maternal Impulse as Poetry." *13th Moon: A Feminist Literary Magazine* 9, no. 1–2 (1991).

Antonucci, Michael A. *Cryptic Cartography: The Poetry of Michael S. Harper and the Geopoetic Impulse*. Doctoral Dissertation: Emory University, October 2000.

Brown, Fahamisha Patricia. *Performing the Word: African American Poetry as Vernacular Culture*. New Brunswick, N.J.: Rutgers University Press (1999).

Brown, Joseph A. "Their Long Scars Touch Ours: A Reflection on the Poetry of Michael Harper." *Callaloo* 9, no. 1 (Winter 1986).

Buschendorf, Christa. "White Masks: Greek Mythology in Contemporary Black Poetry." *Crossing Borders: Inter- and Intra- Cultural Exchanges in Multicultural Society*. Edited by Heinz Ickstadt. Frankfurt am Main, Germany and New York: Peter Lang, 1997.

Chrisman, Robert. *Robert Hayden: Modernism and the Afro-American Epic Mission*. *DAI* 60, no. 7 (Jan 2000).

Clarke, Cheryl. "The Loss of Lyric Space and the Critique of Traditions in Gwendolyn Brooks's 'In the Mecca.'" *The Kenyon Review* 17, no. 1 (Winter 1995).

Dawson, Emma Waters. "Vanishing Point: The Rejected Black Woman in the Poetry of Gwendolyn Brooks." *Obsidian II* 4, no. 1 (Spring 1989).

Dean, Michael P. "Magnolias, Mayhem, and Malice: Two 'Mississippi Poems' by Robert Hayden." *Publications of the Mississippi Philological Association* (1986).

De Silva, Lilamani. "The Poetry of African-American Women: Making Cultural Difference Meaningful." *Sri Lanka Journal of the Humanities* 21, no. 1–2 (1995).

Edmundson, Mark. "Rita Dove's Mother Love: A Discussion." *Callaloo* 19, no. 1 (Winter 1996).

Ellison, Mary. "Jazz in the Poetry of Amiri Baraka and Roy Fisher." *Yearbook of English Studies* 24 (1994).

Fisher, Dexter and Robert Stepto. *Afro-American Literature: The Reconstruction of Instruction.* New York: MLA (1979).

Frankovich, Nicholas and David Larzelere, eds. *The Columbia Granger's Index to African-American Poetry.* New York: Columbia University Press, 1999.

Gayle, Addison, Jr. "Gwendolyn Brooks: Poet of the Whirlwind." *Black Women Writers (1950–1980): A Critical Evaluation.* Edited by Mari Evans and Stephen E. Henderson. Garden City, New York: Anchor-Doubleday (1984).

Georgoudaki, Ekaterini. "Rita Dove: Crossing Boudaries." *Callaloo* 14, no. 2 (Spring 1991).

Gibson, Donald B., ed. *Modern Black Poets: A Collection of Critical Essays.* Englewood Cliffs, N.J.: Prentice-Hall, 1973.

Goldstein, Laurence. "The Greatest Poem in the World." *The Southern Review* 35, no. 4 (1999).

Hamner, Robert D. *Critical Perspectives on Derek Walcott.* Washington, D.C.: Three Continents, 1993.

Harney, Steve. "Ethnos and the Beat Poets." *Journal of American Studies* 25, no. 3 (December 1991).

Harper, Michael S., Robert B. Stepto and John Hope Franklin, editors. *Chant of Saints: A Gathering of Afro-American Literature, Art, and Scholarship.* Urbana: University of Illinois Press, 1979.

Hayes, Ned Dykstra. "Whole 'Altarity': Toward a Feminist A/Theology." *Divine Aporia: Postmodern Conversations about the Other.* Hawley, John C., ed. Lewisburg, PA: Bucknell University Press; London: Associated University Press, 2000..

Henderson, Theodore. *Understanding the New Black Poetry: Black Speech and Black Music as Poetic References.* New York: Morrow, 1973.

Holladay, Hilary. "'I Am Not Grown Away from You': Lucille Clifton's Elegies for Her Mother." *College Language Association Journal* 42, no. 4 (June 1999).

Hudson, Theodore. *From LeRoi Jones to Amiri Baraka: The Literary Works.* Durham, N.C.: Duke University Press, 1973.

Huggan, Graham. "Blue Myth Brooding in Orchid: A Third-World Reappraisal of Island Poetics." *Journal of West Indian Literature* 1, no. 2 (1987).

Hughes, Gertrude Reif. "Making It Really New: Hilda Doolittle, Gwendolyn Brooks, and the Feminist Potential of Modern Poetry." *American Quarterly* 42, no. 3 (September 1990).

Hull, Akasha Gloria. "In Her Own Images: Lucille Clifton and the Bible." *Dwelling in Possibility: Women Poets and Critics on Poetry.* Prins, Yopie and Maeera Shreiber, eds. Ithaca, N.Y.: Cornell University Press, 1997.

———. "Channeling the Ancestral Muse: Lucille Clifton and Dolores Kendrick." *Feminist Measures: Soundings in Poetry and Theory.* Edited by Lynn Keller and Cristanne Miller, Ann Arbor: University of Michigan Press, 1994.

Johnson, Joyce. "The Theme of Celebration in Lucille Clifton's Poetry." *Pacific Coast Philology* 18, nos. 1–2 (November 1983).

Jones, Kirkland C. "Folk Idiom in the Literary Expression of Two African American Authors: Rita Dove and Yusef Komunyakaa." *Language and Literature in the African American Imagination.* Edited by Carol Aisha Blackshire-Belay, Westport, C.T.: Greenwood, 1992.

Jong, Erica. "Three Sisters." *Parnassus: Poetry in Review* 1, no. 1 (1972).

Kellman, Anthony. "Projective Verse as a Mode of Socio-Linguist Protest." *ARIEL* 21, no. 2 (April 1990).

Kent, George E. *A Life of Gwendolyn Brooks.* Lexington: University Press of Kentucky, 1990.

———. "Gwendolyn Brooks' Poetic Realism: A Development Survey Source." *Black Women Writers (1950–1980): A Critical Evaluation.* Edited by Mari Evans and Stephen E. Henderson, Garden City, New York: Anchor-Doubleday (1984).

Keyes, Carol. *Language's 'Bliss of Unfolding' in and through History, Autobiography, and Myth: The Poetry of Rita Dove.* Doctoral Dissertation: University of New Hampshire, 1999.

Kutzins, Vera M. *Against the American Grain: Myth and History in William Carlos Williams, Jay Wright, and Nicolás Guillén.* Baltimore: Johns Hopkins University Press, 1987.

Lacey, Henry C. "Baraka's 'AM/TRAK': Everybody's Coltrane Poem." *Obsidian II* 1, nos. 1–2 (Spring-Summer 1986).

Lazer, Hank. "Blackness Blessed: The Writings of Lucille Clifton." *The Southern Review* 25, no. 3 (Summer, 1989).

Leffler, Merrill. "Eight Contemporary Maryland Poets." *Maryland English Journal* 14, no. 2 (1976).

Lenz, Gunter H. "Black Poetry and Black Music: History and Tradition: Michael Harper and John Coltrane." From *History and Tradition in Afro-American.* Edited by Gunter H. Lenz. *Culture.* Frankfurt: Campus (1984).

Madhubuti, Haki. "Lucille Clifton: Warm Water, Greased Legs, and Dangerous Poetry." From *Black Women Writers (1950–1980: A Critical Evaluation.* Edited by Mari Evans and Stephen E. Henderson. Garden City, N.Y.: Anchor-Doubleday (1984).

Manson, Michael Tomasek. "The Clarity of Being Strange: Jay Wrights's The Double Invention of Komo." *Black American Literature Forum* 24, no. 3 (Fall 1990).

McCluskey, Audrey T. "Tell the Good News: A View of the Works of Lucille Clifton." *Black Women Writers (1950–1980): A Critical Evaluation.* Edited by Mari Evans and Stephen E. Henderson. Garden City, N.Y.: Anchor-Doubleday (1984).

McDowell, Robert. "The Assembling Vision of Rita Dove." *Callaloo* 9, no. 1 (Winter 1986).

Melhem, D. H. "Cultural Challenge, Heroic Response: Gwendolyn Brooks and the New Black Poetry." *Perspectives of Black Popular Culture.* Edited by Harry B. Shaw. Bowling Green, Ohio: Popular, 1990.

Moallem, Minoo and Iain A. Boal. "Multicultural Nationalism and the Poetics of Inauguration." From *Between Woman and Nation: Nationalisms, Transnational Feminisms and the State.* Edited by Caren Kaplan, Norma Alarcon, and Minoo Moallem. Durham, N.C: Duke University Press, 1999.

Nicholas, Xavier, ed. "Robert Hayden & Michael S. Harper: A Literary Friendship." *Callaloo* 17, no. 4 (Fall 1994).

Nielsen, Aldopn Lynn. *Black Chant: Languages of African-American Postmodernism.* Cambridge: Cambridge University Press, 1997.

Okpewho, Isidore. "From a Goat Path in Africa: An Approach to the Poetry of Jay Wright." *Callaloo* 14, no. 3 (Summer 1991).

Ostriker, Alicia. "Kin and Kin: The Poetry of Lucille Clifton." *The American Poetry Review* 22, no. 6 (1993 Nov–Dec).

Ojaide, Tanure. "Branches of the Same Tree: African and African-American Poetry." *Of Dreams Deferred, Dead or Alive: African Perspectives on African-American Writers.* Edited by Femi Ojo-Ade. Westport, Connecticut: Greenwood, 1996.

Perry, Carolyn and Mary Louise Weaks, eds. *The History of Southern Women's Literature*. Baton Rouge: Louisiana State University Press, 2002.

Rampersad, Arnold. "The Poems of Rita Dove." *Callaloo* 9, no. 1 (Winter 1986).

Reece, Erik. "Detour to the 'Alltombing Womb': Amiri Baraka's Assault on Yeats' Muse." In *Learning the Trade: Essays on W. B. Yeats and Contemporary Poetry*. Edited by Deborah Fleming. West Cornwall, Connecticut: Locust Hill, 1993.

Richards, Phillip M. "Robert Hayden (1913–1980): An Appreciation." *Massachusetts Review* 40, no. 4 (Winter 1999–2000).

Rubeo, Ugo. "'In the Inner Ear': Genealogy and Intertextuality in the Poetry of Etheridge Knight and Michael Harper." *GRAAT*, 18 (1998).

Rushing, Andrea Benton. "Lucille Clifton: A Changing Voice for Changing Times." From *Coming to Light: American Women Poets in the Twentieth Century*. Edited by Diane Wood Middlebrook and Marilyn Yalom. Ann Arbor: University of Michigan Press, 1985.

Smith, David Lionel. "Amiri Baraka and the Politics of Popular Culture." From *Politics and the Muse: Studies in the Politics of Recent American Literature*. Edited by Adam J. Sorkin. Bowling Green, Ohio: Bowling Green State University Press (1989).

Smith, Gary. "Gwendolyn Brooks's 'A Street in Bronzeville,' the Harlem Renaissance and the Mythologies of Black Women." *MELUS* 10, no. 3 (Fall 1983).

Spillers, Hortense J. "'An Order of Constancy': Notes on Brooks and the Feminine." *The Centennial Review* 29, no. 2 (1985 Spring).

Stanford, Ann Folwell. "Dialectics of Desire: War and Resistive Voice in Gwendolyn Brooks's 'Negro Hero' and 'Gay Chaps at the Bar.'" *African American Review* 26, no. 2 (Summer 1992).

———. "'Like Narrow Banners for Some Gathering War': Readers, Aesthetics, and Gwendolyn Brooks's 'The Sundays of Satin-Legs Smith.'" *College Literature* 17, no. 2–3 (1990).

———. "An Epic with a Difference: Sexual Politics in Gwendolyn Brooks's 'The Anniad.'" *American Literature* 67, no. 2 (June 1995).

Steffen, Therese. "Movements of a Marriage or, Looking Awry at U.S. History: Rita Dove's

"Thomas and Beulah." In *Families*. Edited by Werner Senn. Tubingen, Germany: Narr (1996).

———. "Beyond Ethnic Margin and Cultural Center: Rita Dove's 'Empire' of Mother Love." From *Empire: American Studies*. Edited by John G. Blair and Reinhold Wagenleitner. Tubingen, Germany: Narr, 1997.

———. "The Darker Face of the Earth: A Conversation with Rita Dove." *Transition* 7, no. 2 (1998).

Stepto, Robert B. "'The Aching Prodigal': Jay Wright's Dutiful Poet." *Callaloo* 6, no. 3 (Fall 1983).

Taylor, Henry. "Gwendolyn Brooks: An Essential Sanity." *The Kenyon Review* 13, no. 4 (Fall 1991).

Vendler, Helen. "Rita Dove: Identity Markers." *Callaloo* 17, no. 2 (Summer 1994).

Wallace, Patricia. "Divided Loyalties: Literal and Literary in the Poetry of Lorna Dee Cervantes, Cathy Song and Rita Dove." *MELUS* 18, no. 3 (Fall 1993).

Waller, Gary. "I and Ideology: Demystifying the Self of Contemporary Poetry." *Denver Quarterly* 18, no. 3 (Autumn 1983).

Ward, Scott. "No Vers is Libre." *Shenandoah* 45, no. 3 (Fall 1995).

Weaver, Afaa Michael. *These Hands I Know: African-American Writers on Family*. Louisville, K.Y.: Sarabande Books, 2002.

Welburn, Ron. "Jay Wright's Poetics: An Appreciation." *MELUS* 18, no. 3 (Fall 1993).

Wheeler, Lesley. *The Poetics of Enclosure: Emily Dickinson, Marianne Moore, H.D., and Gwendolyn Brooks*. Doctoral Dissertation: Princeton University, 1995.

Wright, Stephen Caldwell, ed. *On Gwendolyn Brooks: Reliant Contemplation*. Ann Arbor: University of Michigan Press, 1996.

Wyke, Clement H. "'Divided to the Vein': Patterns of Tormented Ambivalence in Walcott's 'The Fortunate Traveller.'" *ARIEL* 20, no. 3 (1989).

Biographical Notes

ROBERT EARL HAYDEN (1913–1980)

Michael Harper has referred to Robert Hayden as "by far the best chronicler and rememberer of the African-American heritage." As an African-American academic and poet, Hayden balanced the academic demands as a professor at Fisk University from 1946 to 1968 with his vocation as a poet. Hayden was born in Detroit, Michigan on August 4, 1913 to Asa and Ruth Sheffey, who separated during his infancy. He became the foster son of William Hayden and Sue Ellen Westerfield Hayden, with whom he lived in the St. Antoine slum of Detroit. Hayden grew up in a poor neighborhood ironically referred to as "Paradise Valley." Later in his teenage years, Hayden became acquainted with his biological mother who had moved next door—an acquaintance which produced an emotional struggle between his two families. As a child, Robert Hayden was severely myopic although this condition never prevented him from becoming an avid reader of the books Ruth Sheffey sent him. While growing up with his foster parents, Hayden received as many advantages as was possible—he attended school in the summer, was active in the Baptist church, and played violin in the Sunday school orchestra. Upon graduating from Detroit Northern High School in 1932, he entered Detroit College (now Wayne State University) on a scholarship where he majored in Spanish and minored in English. From 1936 to 1938, Hayden worked with the Federal Writers' Project in Detroit where he researched local black folklore and history. Following that, he worked part-time for the *Michigan Chronicle*, a black weekly, where he served as theatre, movie and music critic. In fact, the editor of the *Michigan*

Chronicle, Louie Martin, later founded the Falcon Press to publish Hayden's first poetry collection, *Hart-Shape in the Dust*, in 1940. That same year, Hayden became engaged to and married Erma Morris, a promising concert pianist from a middle-class family who disapproved of the poet's impoverished background. While living in New York City during the summer of 1941, Hayden pursued his historical research but remained jobless as the Federal Writers' Project was dismantled. As a result, he became determined to earn a master's degree and entered the University of Michigan graduate school in 1942, the year that his only child, Maia, was born. There, he studied with W.H. Auden, who was then a visiting professor and who gave Hayden valuable advice for developing his own style. Upon earning his master's degree in 1944, Hayden remained at Michigan for another two years as a teaching fellow and the first black member of the English department's faculty. In 1946, he became an Assistant Professor of English at Fisk University, a black college in Nashville, Tennessee. Robert Hayden received the distinction of becoming the first African American to receive an appointment as poetry consultant to the Library of Congress. From 1968 until his death, Hayden served as Professor of English at the University of Michigan at Ann Arbor. His life's work was dedicated to social protest and pride in celebrating the memory of his Afro-American heritage. In *Elegies for Paradise Alley* (1978), he brings back to life the forgotten residents of his old neighborhood where memory of his individual past is blended with others of the past and present.

GWENDOLYN BROOKS (1917–2000)

One of the most distinguished American poets of the twentieth century, Gwendolyn Brooks was born in Topeka, Kansas on June 7, 1917. Her father, David Anderson Brooks, was the only family member to graduate from high school and attend a year of college at Fisk University. When her father died in November, 1959, Gwendolyn wrote a poem, "In Honor of David Anderson Brooks, My Father," in which she celebrated his zest for life. Her mother, Keziah Corinne Wims, was a schoolteacher. Gwendolyn grew up in Chicago and from her earliest schooldays, she became aware of racial prejudice. From the start, writing became a catharsis for her feelings of rejection. Brooks attended the racially integrated Englewood High School, graduating in 1934, and she graduated from Wilson Junior College in 1936. By 1935 she was mastering traditional poetic forms and experimenting with syntax, sharp comparisons, and color symbolism. One important influence at the time was the poetry of Sara Teasdale, of whom she spoke lovingly. Brooks also corresponded with the Harlem Renaissance poet, James Weldon Johnson, in addition to reading Countee Cullen and Langston Hughes.

Under the guidance of a rich Chicago socialite, Inez Cunningham Stark, who taught a poetry class at the Southside Community Art Center, Brooks was introduced to the groundbreaking modernist poets Ezra Pound and T.S. Eliot. Her first collection of poems, *A Street in Bronzeville* (1945), written during her participation in Stark's workshop, celebrates the unsung heroes of the ghetto. In 1938, Brooks joined the NAACP Youth Council where she met Henry Lowington Blakely II, whom she married on September 17, 1939. Her first child, Henry Lowington Blakely, III was born in October, 1940, and her daughter, Nora, was born in September, 1951. With her second poetry collection, *Annie Allen* (1950), which concerns the maturation of a young black woman, Brooks became the first African American to receive the Pulitzer Prize for poetry. Brooks was now a poet of national reputation. In 1956, she published *Bronzeville Boys and Girls*, a collection of poems for children, and in 1960, she published *The Bean Eaters*, a title which is meant to suggest Vincent van Gogh's poignant depiction of peasant life, *The Potato Eaters*. During the 1960's, Brooks's popularity increased, and in 1962, President John F. Kennedy invited her to read at a Library of Congress poetry festival, where she met Robert Frost. In 1963, she began her teaching career at Chicago's Columbia College and wrote new material for *Selected Poems*. In 1967, Brooks attended the Second Fisk Writers Conference, which was based on the paradigm of America as a broken community. Subsequently, she became involved with young black arts in Chicago. Her poetry collection, *In the Mecca* (1968), reflects this newer consciousness of the black community. Brooks was named Poet Laureate for the state of Illinois in 1968, and served as poetry consultant to the Library of Congress from 1985-1986. In 1994, the National Endowment for the Arts awarded her the Jefferson lecturer, which is the government's highest honor in the humanities. She also was inducted into the National Women's Hall of Fame. Brooks continued to write prolifically and publish her poetry until her death on December 3, 2000 at the age of 83.

AMIRI BARAKA (LEROI JONES) (1934–)

Amiri Baraka (known as LeRoi Jones until 1968) is a brilliant and seminal force in the evolution of contemporary Afro-American literature, and a protean personality, having shifted personas and identities with remarkable alacrity. Born Everett LeRoi Jones on October 7, 1968, he is the son of Coyette Leory Jones, a postal worker, and Anna Lois Russ Jones, a social worker. Jones was raised with his younger sister, Sandra Etaine, in Newark, New Jersey, in a family which was middle class in perspective, if not by economic definition. He attended the Central Avenue School in Newark and became one of the few black students to attend Barringer High School.

Upon graduating from Barringer High School in 1951, Jones attended Rutgers University on a science scholarship in the fall of that year. In 1952, Jones transferred to Howard University, where his interests shifted to philosophy, religion, German and English literature. There he studied with such prominent Afro-American scholars as E. Franklin Frazier, Nathan A. Scott, Jr. (who taught a course on Dante) and Sterling A. Brown (a well-respected patriarch of Afro-American literary critics who also held informal classes on black music). In October 1954, Jones enlisted in the U.S. Air Force and was assigned as weatherman and gunner on a B-36 in Puerto Rico. Jones's return to civilian life in January 1957 coincided with a critical period of intellectual ferment and social conflict in the arts. He moved to New York's Greenwich Village in 1957, where he took a job as clerk at the *Record Changer* magazine and met Hettie Robert Cohen, a young Jewish woman who shared many of his interests in music and literature. On October 13, 1958, they were married, by which time Hettie had become advertising and business manager of the *Partisan Review*. Jones would have two children with Hettie—Kellie and Lisa. By this time, Jones attempted to locate himself within the aesthetic tradition of the new poets of the 1950's, many of whom claimed such poets as Ezra Pound and William Carlos Williams as their forbearers. During the late 1950s, Jones became increasingly absorbed in the civil rights movement and he formed the Organization of Young Men consisting of a group of black intellectuals and artists, including Alvin Simon, A.B. Spellman, Bob Thomason, and Bill White. During the mid-1960s, Jones would adopt a militant, anti-white stance and, consistent with his anti-mainstream, anti-bourgeois perspective, he celebrated the values in Afro-American music with its roots in jazz and bebop, a music he believed resistant to Western ideals and musical styles. In 1963, he began teaching contemporary American poetry and creative writing at the New School for Social Research in New York City and, through his relationship with Charles Olson, in 1964 he secured a teaching position at the State University of New York at Buffalo, the same year he taught at Columbia University. By late 1965, Jones ended his marriage to Hettie Cohen, broke most of his ties with the white literary community and moved uptown to Harlem. In August 1966, Jones married his present wife, Sylvia Robinson (Amina) with whom he would have five children—Obalaji, Ras Jua, Shani, Amiri and Ahi. During this time, in his hometown in Newark, Jones organized a multifunctional black cultural center named Spirit House, and a publishing house named Jihad (Arabic for "Holy War"), a cooperative book and record store, and an African free school. In 1968, Jones adopted the name Imamu Amiri Baraka ("the blessed one"), given him by Heshaam Jaaber, an orthodox Muslim. Baraka played an important role in the organization of the Congress of

African Peoples in 1970 and, in the same year, campaigned for Kenneth Gibson, the man elected as the first black mayor of Newark. In 1974, Baraka proclaimed himself a Third World Marxist-Lenninist and dropped the Muslim title Imamu from his name. Throughout the 1980s and 1990s, Baraka continued to write prolifically and teach in the Department of Africa Studies at SUNY, StonyBrook. He has been the recipient of numerous awards and honors, including the Pen/Faulkner Award and fellowships from the National Endowment for the Arts and the Guggenheim Foundation. In 1999, Baraka retired from teaching at SUNY, StonyBrook, and in 2002 he was appointed Poet Laureate of New Jersey.

MAYA ANGELOU (1928–)
Born Marguerite Johnson in St. Louis on April 4, 1928 to Bailey and Vivian Baxter Johnson, she did not become Maya Angelou until her debut as a dancer in the Purple Onion cabaret in her early twenties. An account of her life is, by necessity, primarily informed by her autobiographies, four of which were published between 1928 and the mid-1960s. When she was three and her brother Bailey was four, the two children were sent by her divorced parents to live in Stamps, Arkansas, to be raised by her maternal grandmother, Annie ("Momma") Henderson, a woman who would be an enormous influence throughout her life and work. However, when she was eight years old, the confidence she had acquired with Momma was overturned during a brief stay with her mother in St. Louis. During this visit, Angelou was raped by her mother's boyfriend, who was later found dead. As a consequence of these events, Angelou returned to Stamps having lost both her bourgeoning pride and her speech, which would take several years to regain. Nevertheless, five years of reading and reciting the world's great literature with Mrs. Flowers, the educated "aristocrat of Black Stamps," would restore her speech and sense of well-being, along with the importance of self-expression and communication. In 1940, after Angelou graduated at the top of the eighth grade class, her mother, now a professional gambler, moved the children to San Francisco. Her formal education now consisted of attending George Washington High School in San Francisco throughout World War II, while taking up dance and drama lessons at the California Labor School. While in high school, Angelou obtained a job as the first black woman streetcar conductor in San Francisco. She also became pregnant at sixteen, giving birth to her son, Guy, one month after her graduation from Mission High School's summer school in 1945. Determined to leave her mother's household, she had a brief stint as a $75 a week cook at the Creole Café before moving to San Diego where she began with a job as a nightclub waitress and was initiated into the world of prostitution. By eighteen years of

age, she had become a "manager" of other prostitutes and developed a feeling of moral superiority as well as an appreciation of her freedom from marriage. Nevertheless, her "reign" was short-lived and she returned to Stamps seeking solace. Angelou tried a few more legitimate jobs, including a nightclub dancing act, but none of them worked out. Eventually, at about the age of twenty-two, Angelou married Tosh Angelos, an ex-sailor, a man she describes as "intelligent, kind and reliable" and white. Nevertheless, the atmosphere of bourgeois respectability became a prison sentence, denying her independent spirit and, thus, she was divorced within three years; She returned to a career as the first black dancer at a local bar. She would later have two more long-term relationships with men: living with Vusumzi Make in Egypt and Ghana in the mid 1960s, and marrying Paul Du Feu in 1973. This second marriage would last until 1980. By her own account, Angelou came of age between 1957 to 1963 along with the development civil rights movement and the women's movement. By the time she was thirty, inspired by her friendship with the distinguished social activist, John Killens, Angelou moved to Brooklyn to be near him, determined to become a writer. In Brooklyn, she attended weekly meetings of the Harlem Writers Guild, accepted by such practicing members as John Henrik Clarke, Paule Marshall and James Baldwin. At the same time, Angelou made a commitment to the black civil rights movement, increasing her circle of friends to include Martin Luther King, Godfrey Cambridge with whom she organized a benefit, "Cabaret of Freedom," for King's Southern Christian Leadership Conference, and Bayard Rustin, who appointed Angelou to succeed him as the SCLC's northern coordinator. In 1981, Angelou was appointed to a lifetime position as the first Reynolds Professor of American Studies at Wake Forest. She composed and recited an original poem for former President Clinton's inauguration in 1993. Angelou is the author of 12 books, including *I Know Why the Caged Bird Sings*, and she is the recipient of several honorary degrees by Smith College, Mills College and Lawrence University, among others. Her poetry expresses strong, jazzy rhythms, themes common to the experiences of many black Americans—such as discrimination, exploitation, and welfare, and the virtue of pride.

DEREK WALCOTT (1930–)

For many years, Derek Walcott has been the preeminent poet and playwright of the West Indies. Indeed, his African and European heritage embodies the cultural matrix of the New World. His questioning of origins, identity and search for meaningful order in a chaotic world lead to an exploration of themes that transcend time, place and racial considerations. Derek Alton Walcott was born on January 23, 1930 in Castries, Saint Lucia, the son of Warwick and Alix Walcott. His father, Warwick, was a civil servant, poet and visual artist who died when Walcott and his twin brother, Roderick, were only one year old. His mother was a schoolteacher and encouraged her sons' early education and love for reading. She was also involved in a community cultural group and was able to expose her sons to the theater. Roderick, along with his brother, was to become a well-known playwright. Walcott earned his B.A. in English, French and Latin in 1953 while on a British government scholarship at the University College of the West Indies in Kingston, Jamaica. Thereafter, he studied for one more year in the Department of Education. In 1954, Walcott married Fay Moyston. He founded the St. Lucia Arts Guild in 1950, and from 1954 until 1957, Walcott taught in various West Indian schools where he also began to devote more and more time to writing and the theater. He then started his career as a journalist, writing features for *Public Opinion* in Kingston and features and drama critics for the Trinidad *Guardian*. He worked as a professor of poetry at the University of Boston, and divided his time between Trinidad and the USA. From 1959 to 1971, Walcott was the founding director of the Little Carib Theatre (later the Trinidad Theatre Workshop). He has written a large number of plays for stage and radio. Of these *Dream on Monkey Mountain* was commissioned originally by the Royal Shakespeare Company in the late 1960s, but produced finally in the USA. Walcott has also collaborated on several musicals with Galt McDermott, best-known from the hippie musical *Hair*. In 1992, Walcott was awarded the Nobel Prize for literature. Walcott studies the conflict between the heritage of European and West Indian culture, the long way from slavery to independence, and his own role as a nomad between cultures. His poems are characterized by allusions to the English poetic tradition and a symbolic imagination that is at once personal and Caribbean. "Poetry, which is perfection's sweat but which must seem as fresh as the raindrops on a statue's brow, combines the natural and the marmoreal; it conjugates both tenses simultaneously: the past and the present, if the past is the sculpture and the present the beads of dew or rain on the forehead of the past. There is the buried language and there is the individual vocabulary, and the process of poetry is one of excavation and of self-discovery." Walcott has referred to himself as "a mulatto of style." His epic poem, *Omeros* (1990) takes its title from the Greek word for 'Homer', and recalls the dramas of Homer's *Iliad* and *Odyssey* in a Caribbean setting. The task of the bard is to sing of lost lives and a new hope.

JAY WRIGHT (1935–)

Praised by some literary critics as the most imaginative and scholarly contemporary black American poet, Jay Wright's books are complex, centered around themes of personal development through spiritual and intellectual quest. These autobiographical elements are assimilated into a mythology borne of his extensive study in Afro-American historical experience and the history of religions, and his vast knowledge of the philosophy of science, anthropology and European literature of the Renaissance and Middle Ages. Wright asserts what he believes to be the African sense of unity the spirit and the physical world. Nevertheless, Wright is working within the American tradition of such writers as T.S. Eliot, Ezra Pound and Charles Olson. Borne on May 25, 1935 to Leona Dailey and Mercer Murphy Wright, Jay Wright grew up Albuquerque, New Mexico. His father, a mechanic and jitney driver, was born in Santa Rosa, New Mexico and his mother in Virginia. After completing high school in San Pedro, California, Wright played semi-professional baseball and served in the Army. In 1961, he earned a bachelor's degree after three years of study at the University of California at Berkeley. For a brief period thereafter, Wright attended Union Theological Seminary in New York and, in 1961, enrolled in graduate school at Rutgers University from which he earned an M.A. (although he had completed all requirements for his doctorate except a dissertation). His other academic appointments include being a Hodder Fellow at Princeton University and a Fellow in Creative Writing at Dundee University in Scotland, a teaching position at Tougaloo and Talladega colleges between 1968 and 1970 and a teaching position at Yale University from 1975 to 1979.

His honors include the Guggenheim and MacArthur Fellowships, the American Academy and Institute of Arts and Letters Literary Award, and the Oscar Williams and Gene Derwood Award. Wright was named a Fellow of The Academy of American Poets in 1995.

LUCILLE CLIFTON (1936–)

Thelma Lucille Sayles Clifton was born on June 27, 1963 in Depew, New York, a suburb of Buffalo, the daughter of Samuel and Thelma Moore Sayle. Lucille Clifton began composing poems at a very early age, and has drawn encouragement from an increasing audience and fine critical reception. In many ways, Clifton's subject matter is conventional, her themes shaped by her concern with family history and relationships, with racial history, and with the possibility of reconciliation with and transcendence of the ghetto experience. Her poems proclaim that her community has its heroes, exemplified by those who manage to lead worthy lives despite their hardship of the black urban experience. Included within the group of heroes is her father, who remained affirmative about life, despite the fact that he had a leg amputated. One of the most influential family members is her great-great-grandmother, Caroline Donald, a remarkable woman of faith, intelligence and integrity, kidnapped, along with mother, sister and brother from her home in Dahomey, West Africa and brought to America as a slave. Caroline would become an enduring symbol of the power of the black female. Lucille attended Howard University from 1953 to 1955 and graduated from the State University of New York Teachers College at Fredonia (near Buffalo) in 1955. In 1958, Lucille married Fred James Clifton, with whom she had four daughters and two sons. From 1958-1960, she worked as a claims clerk in the New York State Division of Employment in Buffalo. From 1960-1971, Clifton worked as a literature assistant in the Office of Education in Washington, D.C. and published *Good Times* in 1969. From 1971 to 1974, while Clifton was poet-in-residence at the historically black school, Coppin State College in Baltimore, she published two books of poetry, *Good News About the Earth* in 1972 and *An Ordinary Woman* in 1974. In 1979, Clifton was named Poet Laureate for the state of Maryland. Her next volume, *Two-Headed Woman* was published in 1980 and was both a Pulitzer Prize nominee and winner of the University of Massachusetts Press Juniper Prize. From 1982 to 1983, Clifton was a visiting writer at Columbia University School of the Arts and at George Washington University. In 1985, she taught literature and creative writing at the University of Santa Cruz and then at St. Mary's College of Maryland. In 1999, Clifton was elected a Chancellor of The Academy of American Poets and served again as Poet Laureate for the State of Maryland. Her honors include an Emmy Award from the American Academy of Television Arts and Sciences, the Charity Randall prize, the Shestack Prize from the American Poetry Review, the Lannan Literary Award, two fellowships from the National Endowment for the Arts, the Shelley Memorial Award, and the YM-YWHA Poetry Center Discovery Award. Lucille Clifton is currently Distinguished Professor of Humanities at St. Mary's College in Maryland.

MICHAEL S. HARPER (1938–)

With the publication of his seventh book of poetry, *Images of Kin* (1977), Michael Harper established himself as a major black poet with a wide appeal amongst white Americans. Harper was born in his parents' home in Brooklyn, New York, 1938. His father, Walter Warren Harper, was employed as a postal worker and supervisor. His mother, Katherine Johnson Harper, worked as a medical stenographer. Although the family was not wealthy, they owned a very good music collection which served as a source for Michael Harper's poetic imagination during his childhood. At the age of thirteen, Harper's family moved to a predominantly white neighborhood in West Los Angeles. When he was enrolled at the Susan Miller Dorsey High School, he was placed in an industrial arts program, rather than an academic one, until his father convinced the school of his son's abilities. As a result of asthma, which he inherited from his mother, Harper failed gym and, consequently, was kept off the honor roll. He worked as a newspaper boy, familiarizing himself with the streets and neighborhood, all the while trying to figure out how to become a doctor. Later on, he would be discouraged from pursuing a career in medicine by a zoology professor who did not believe that blacks could make it to medical school. Such demonstrations of racism and rejection would lead to his concept of a schizophrenic American society. Meanwhile, his enthusiasm for poetry and history remained essentially dormant during his high school years. Following graduation from high school in 1955, Harper attended Los Angeles State College from 1956 to 1961, where he was especially influenced by a course entitled "The Epic of Search," in which the classics were presented with the context of a historical overview of man's quest for self-assertion. At the same time, Harper worked as a full-time postal worker. In the winter of 1961, Harper participated in the Iowa Writers Workshop, and encountered the writer Ralph Albert Dicky and the painter Oliver Lee Jackson. He also became more keenly aware of racial differences as blacks were made to live in segregated sections. Harper returned to Iowa to take his comprehensives in English and was awarded a masters degree in 1963. Following his graduation, Harper's teaching career began at Contra Costa in San Pablo, California from 1964 to 1968, followed by an Associate Professorship of English at California State College from 1968 to 1969 and Hayward from 1969 to 1970. In 1970, Harper received a National Book Award Nomination for his book, *Dear John, Dear Coltrane*. From 1970 to 1971, Harper pursued a post-doctoral fellowship at the University of Illinois and, since 1971, has taught at Brown University. Additionally, he has been a visiting professor at Harvard, Yale, Carleton College in Minnesota and the University of Cincinnati. In 1988, Harper became the first Poet Laureate of the state of Rhode Island, serving until 1993. His poetry has focused on the dual consciousness of being a black American poet and an American poet, and the key to his understanding of the black experience in America is related to musical traditions, most especially blues, spiritual and jazz forms.

ISHMAEL REED (1938–)
Born in 1938 to Henry Lenoir and Thelma Coleman in Chattanooga, Tennessee, Ishmael Reed grew up in the working class neighborhoods in

Buffalo, New York. Reed took his surname from his stepfather, Bennie Stephen Reed, an autoworker. At the age of four, his family moved to Buffalo, where he attended the public schools and the University of Buffalo (now a part of the State University of New York) from 1956 to 1960. Uncomfortable with the academic literary scene, Reed left the University of Buffalo in the middle of his junior year, though he remained in the city for some time, working as a correspondent for the *Empire Star Weekly*, a black community newspaper, along with co-hosting a local radio program. Reed moved to New York City in 1962, working as editor of a Newark, New Jersey weekly, and co-founded the *East Village Other* in 1965, an underground newspaper that achieved a national reputation. He also became a member of the Umbra Writers Workshop, one of organizations instrumental in creating the Black Arts movement. In 1967, Reed published his first novel, *The Freelance Pallbearers*, which set the tone and aesthetic for all his subsequent writings. During that same year, Reed moved to Berkeley, California, and then relocated to Oakland, where he lives today with his wife, Carla Blank, a dancer and choreographer, and daughter, Tennessee. He has taught at the University of California at Berkeley since the late 1960s. He has also held visiting appointments at many other academic institutions, including Yale, Harvard, Dartmouth, Washington University in St. Louis and the State University of New York at Buffalo. Reed was nominated for the Pulitzer Prize and was a finalist for the National Book Award, once in poetry and once in fiction. In 1976, Reed co-founded the Before Columbus Foundation, a multiethnic organization dedicated to promoting a pan-cultural view of America. Though he is a rigorous promoter of African modes of being and performance, and has assumed his own unique aesthetic sensibilities, "neoamerican hoodooism," he is nevertheless a postmodernist, a perspective enabling him to debate conventional ideas of form and genre, as well as canonical issues. Unlike those who argue for a black essentialism, Reed sees his eclecticism as a virtue rather than a betrayal. His placement within contemporary literary studies stems in part from his ability to channel his encyclopedic historical, political and cultural knowledge into poetry and prose that is at once individual and collective.

RITA DOVE (1952–)

Born in Akron, Ohio, Rita Dove is the daughter of well-educated parents. Her father, Ray A. Dove, was the first African-American chemist to break the racial barrier in the tire and rubber industry. Later on, in *Thomas and Beulah* (1986), Dove presents the saga of her family, portraying the generations descended from her maternal grandparents, Thomas Hord and his wife Beulah. Their relationship is a union of body and spirit, a passion which they bestowed upon their children and grandchildren. In 1987, Dove would be awarded the Pulitzer Prize in poetry for *Thomas and Beulah*. In 1970, just before her eighteenth birthday, Dove received was invited to the White House as a "Presidential Scholar," an honor signaling the fact that she was among the top one hundred high school students in the nation for that year. In 1973, she earned a bachelor's degree from Miami University in Oxford, Ohio, where she graduated summa cum laude. It was also at Miami University where Rita Dove met Marian Musgrave, her teacher, mentor and friend, a Renaissance scholar, Germanist and international pioneer in black studies. Her poems, which demonstrate a rhetorical affinity with such other American poets as Robert Frost, Langston Hughes and Gwendolyn Brooks, began to appear in major periodicals in 1974. Following graduation, Dove studied modern European literature as a Fulbright/Hays fellow at the University of Tübingen in Germany. When she returned from Europe, she took an M.F.A. at the University of Iowa in 1977. In 1979, Dove married Fred Viebahn, a German-born novelist, and they became the parents of a daughter, Avivia Chantal Tamu Dove-Viebahn. Later, she taught creative writing at Arizona State University before joining the faculty of the University of Virginia where she is currently Commonwealth Professor of English. During the past two decades, Dove has made frequent trips to Ireland, Israel, France and Germany, indicative of a poetic desire to cross the boundary lines of time and space. From 1993 to 1995, Dove served as Poet Laureate of the United States, and her many honors include The Academy of American Poets Lavan Younger Poets Award, an NAACP Great American Artist Award, and Fulbright and Guggenheim scholarships, to name a few. Dove's aesthetic sensibility is informed by a very diverse poetic spectrum ranging from William Shakespeare to such other major African American poetry of Tolson, Walcott, Clifton, Hughes and Baraka.

Contributors

HAROLD BLOOM is Sterling Professor of the Humanities at Yale University and Henry W. and Albert A. Berg Professor of English at the New York University Graduate School. He is the author of over 20 books, including *Shelley's Mythmaking* (1959), *The Visionary Company* (1961), *Blake's Apocalypse* (1963), *Yeats* (1970), *A Map of Misreading* (1975), *Kabbalah and Criticism* (1975), *Agon: Toward a Theory of Revisionism* (1982), *The American Religion* (1992), *The Western Canon* (1994), and *Omens of Millennium: The Gnosis of Angels, Dreams, and Resurrection* (1996). *The Anxiety of Influence* (1973) sets forth Professor Bloom's provocative theory of the literary relationships between the great writers and their predecessors. His most recent books include *Shakespeare: The Invention of the Human* (1998), a 1998 National Book Award finalist, *How to Read and Why* (2000), and *Genius: A Mosaic of One Hundred Exemplary Creative Minds* (2002). In 1999, Professor Bloom received the prestigious American Academy of Arts and Letters Gold Medal for Criticism, and in 2002 he received the Catalonia International Prize.

BRIAN CONNIFF is an Associate Professor of English at the University of Dayton. He is the author of "Faith and Crisis in the Writing of T. S. Eliot" (1994) and *The Lyric and Modern Poetry: Olson, Creeley, Bunting* (1988).

RONALD E. WALCOTT is a Professor of English at Kingsborough Community College (CUNY). He is the author of "The Novels of Hal Bennett" (1974) and "Some Notes on the Blues, Style & Space: Ellison, Gordone and Tolson" (1972).

BROOKE KENTON HORVATH is a Professor of English at Kent State University. Horvath is the author of *Dropping Out: Spiritual Crisis and Countercultural Attitudes in Four American Novelists of the 1960s* (doctoral dissertation, 1960).

W.D.E. ANDREWS is the author of "'All is Permitted': The Poetry of LeRoi Jones/Amiri Baraka."

CAROLE E. NEUBAUER has been a member of the Department of English and Foreign Languages at Bradley University. She is the author of "Developing Ties to the Past: Photography and Other Sources of Information in Maxine Hong Kingston's China Men" (1983) and "One Voice Speaking for Many: The Mau Mau Movement and Kenyan Autobiography" (1983).

SIDNEY BURRIS is Associate Professor of English and Director of the Fulbright College Honors Program at the University of Arkansas. He is the author of "The Noble Mr. Heaney, Poet" (2000) and "Stephen Dedalus and the New Formalism" (1999).

YVONNE OCHILLO has been a Professor of English at Southern University in Baton Rouge, Louisiana. She is the author of "The Power of the Past in Walcott's Another Life" (1988) and "Black Boy: Structure as Meaning" (1987).

STEVEN MEYER teaches at Washington University. His study, *Irresistable Dictation: Gertrude Stein and the Correlations of Writing and Science*, was published in 2001.

C. K. DORESKI has taught at Daniel Webster College, the University of Massachusetts, Emmanuel College and Boston University. She is the author of *Elizabeth Bishop: The Restraints of Language* (1993) and "Reading Tolson, Reading Pound: National Authority, National Narrative" (2000).

In addition to work on the female image in African American poetry, **FABIAN CLEMENTS WORSHAM** has written for *Pudding Magazine: The International Journal of Applied Poetry*.

JOHN F. CALLAHAN is Professor of English and Morgan S. Odell Professor of Humanities at Lewis and Clark College. Among his works are *In the African-American Grain: The Pursuit of Voice in 20th Century Black Fiction*

(1988); and *The Illusions of a Nation: Myth and History in the Novels of F. Scott Fitzgerald* (1972). He also edited Ralph Ellison's *Juneteenth* (1999).

SHAMOO N. ZAMIR has taught at University of Chicago, York University, and currently at Kings College, London. He is author of *Dark Voices: W.E.B. Du Bois and American Thought* (1995).

PETER ERICKSON is an editor of *Early Modern Visual Culture: Representation, Race, and Empire in Renaissance England* (2000) and "On the Origins of American Feminist Shakespeare Criticism" (1997).

Acknowledgments

"Answering "The Waste Land": Robert Hayden and the Rise of the African American Poetic Sequence" by Brian Conniff. From *African American Review* 33, no. 3. © 1999 by Brian Conniff. Reprinted by permission.

"Calling the Names and Centering the Call in Robert Hayden's *American Journal*" by Ronald Walcott. From *CLA Journal*, vol. XLIII, no. 3 (March 2000). Reprinted by permission.

"The Satisfactions of What's Difficult in Gwendolyn Brooks's Poetry" by Brooke Kenton Horvath. From *American Literature* 62, no. 4 (1990). © 1990 by Duke University Press. All rights reserved. Reprinted by permission of the publisher.

"'All Is Permitted': The Poetry of LeRoi Jones/Amiri Baraka" by W. D. E. Andrews. From *Southwest Review* 67, no. 2 (1982 Spring). © 1982 by Southern Methodist University Press. Reprinted by permission.

"Maya Angelou: Self and a Song of Freedom in the Southern Tradition" by Carol E. Neubauer. From *Southern Women Writers: The New Generation*, edited by Tonette Bond Inge. © 1990 by The University of Alabama Press. Reprinted by permission.

"An Empire of Poetry" by Sidney Burris. From *The Southern Review* 27, no. 3. © 1991 by Sidney Burris Reprinted by permission.

"Aspects of Alienation in the Poetry of Derek Walcott" by Yvonne Ochillo. From *Journal of West Indian Literature* 3, no. 2 (September 1989). © 1989 by The University of the West Indies. Reprinted by permission.

Index

AA (African Americans)
  on being black
    Angelou, 102–105, 111
    Brooks, 49, 58, 174
    Clifton, 280–281
    Dove, 256
    DuBois, 30, 76, 252
    Harper, 30
    Hayden, 6–7, 24, 30, 40–41, 274
    Hughes, 30
    Jones/Amiri Baraka, 64–65, 69–70,
      79–83, 276
    Lorde, 186–187
    McElroy, 188
    Reed, 283
    Rodgers, 185
    Wright, 146–149, 163
  black Africans compared to, 99–101,
    147
  folklore traditions, 211, 225–227
  matrilineage of, 179–190
  poetic sequence, 7–8, 26–29
  responses to Shakespeare, 246–256
Abel, Robert A., 211, 222, 237
Abrahms, M. H., 208, 222, 226, 230,
  236, 240, 242
Achille *(Omeros)*, 117, 119–120
"Acting Black: Othello, Othello
  Burlesques, and the Performance of
  Blackness" (MacDonald), 256, 259
Adams, Hazard, 223–224, 230, 240, 242
Adams, John Quincy, 20–21, 24–25
Adoff, Arnold, 182–183, 190

"Adrienne Rich's Re-Vision of
  Shakespeare" (Erickson), 257
Adventures of an African Slaver (Canot),
  23, 32
Adventures of Huckleberry Finn (Twain),
  256, 259
"The AFL-Aspen Conference"
  interview of Angelou, 112
"After" (Angelou), 102
"After Modernism, After Hibernation:
  Michael Harper, Robert Hayden,
  and Jay Wright" (Stepto), 31, 34
"Afterword" to Wright's *Selected Poems*
  (Bloom), 31–32
*Against the American Grain: Myth and
  History in William Carlos Williams,
  Jay Wright, and Nicholas Guillin*
  (Kutzinski), 176
Aherne, C. M., 210–211, 237
Aidoo, Aima, 140, 143
Alastor (Shelley), 233–234
"The Albuquerque Graveyard"
  (Wright), 146, 163–165, 172
Alexander, Elizabeth, 28
All God's Children Need Traveling Shoes"
  (Angelou), 87–88, 99–101, 111
*Allegories of History, Literary
  Historiography after Hegel* (Bahti),
  175
"Allegre" (Walcott), 133
Allen, Donald, 63
Allott, Kenneth, 132, 143
"Alone" (Angelou), 104–105

Ambler, Margaret, 225, 240
"America" (Angelou), 105
American Academy of Poets, 35
The American Evasion of Philosophy: A Genealogy of Pragmatism (West), 32, 34
"American History" (Harper), 196
American Indian poetry, 9–10
"American Journal" (Hayden), 36–37, 40, 44–46
American Journal (Hayden), 35–46
American Romantic Psychology: Emerson, Poe, Whitman, Dickinson, Melville (Bickman), 209, 228, 236, 242
Amiri Baraka, Imamu. *see* Jones/Amiri Baraka, LeRoi
Amistad mutiny, 17–21, 24–25
"Among School Children" (Yeats), 212–214
"An Appreciation from the White Suburbs" (Jaffe), 50, 58
"An Explanation of the Work" (Jones/Amiri Baraka), 81
"An Interview with Maya Angelou" (Neubauer), 100, 112
An Ordinary Woman (Clifton), 183–184, 191, 281
"Anahorish" (Heaney), 121
Ancient Egyptian Legends (Murray), 209, 236
"And Still I Rise" (Angelou), 106, 108
And Still I Rise (Angelou), 87–88, 106–108, 112
Anderson, Quentin, 220, 228, 234–235, 239, 242, 244
Andrews, W. D. E.
    biographical info, 286
    on Jones/Amiri Baraka, 61–84
Angelou, Maya
    awards
        Commission of International Women's Year, 86
        in general, 278
        Matrix Award, 87
        Woman of the Year (*Ladies Home Journal*), 86
    on being black, 102–105, 111
    biographical info, 85–101, 277–278
    The Blacks, 86
    Cabaret for Freedom, 86
    Clark, Lloyd, 94
    employment
        Arab Observer, 98
        Garden of Allah, 93–94
        Melrose Record Shop, 93
        Organization of Afro-American Unity, 101
        Porgy and Bess role, 86, 94–96
        prostitution, 91–92
        Purple Onion, 86, 94
        Southern Christian Leadership Conference, 86, 97
    family
        Angelos, Tosh, 94–95, 278
        Baxter, Vivian, 85, 88, 90
        Feu, Paul du, 87, 105–106
        Henderson, Annie, 85, 88–92
        Johnson, Bailey, 85, 88, 90, 97, 107–108
        Johnson, Colin Ashanti Murphy, 108
        Johnson, Guy Bailey, 86, 90–91, 96–99
        Make, Vusumzi, 98
        Uncle Willie, 107
    Feelings, Tom, 111
    Ghana (Africa), 99–101
    Harlem Writers Guild, 86, 277
    home is where her son is, 99–101
    hopeful outlook, 91, 99, 107–109
    King, Martin Luther, Jr., 97–98
    marijuana use, 92
    marital bliss scenario, 91, 95, 98
    music as her "refuge," 93
    racism experiences, 88–92, 95–96
    rape of, 277
    Southern roots, 87
    Stamps, AR, 85, 87, 91–92
    on white people, 95–96
Angelou, Maya, style of
    lively, invincible beat, 103–104
    lyrical cadences, 110

rejection of American myths, 102–103
strong metric control, 102, 104
themes
    alienation, 104–105
    displacement, 88, 90, 96, 99
    family, 107–108
    human suffering, 102–103,
        105–106
    love, 102, 105–106, 108–110
    oppression, 110–111
    survival, 108–109
    woman's nature, 106–108, 111
Angelou, Maya, works of
"After," 102
*All God's Children Need Traveling
    Shoes,"* 87–88, 99–101, 111
"Alone," 104–105
"America," 105
"And Still I Rise," 106, 108
"Caged Bird," 110
"The Gamut," 102
Gather Together in My Name, 87–88,
    90–93, 111
"A Georgia Song," 110
"Greyday," 106
"Harlem Hopscotch," 101, 103–104
The Heart of a Woman, 87–88, 96–99,
    111
I Know Why the Caged Bird Sings,
    87–90, 110–111
*Just Give Me a Cool Drink of Water
    'fore I Diiie,* 87–88, 112
"Kin," 107–108
"The Lie," 109
"Miss Scarlett, Mr. Rhett and Other
    Latter Day Saints," 101
"No No No No," 102–103
Now Sheba Sings the Song, 87–88,
    111–112
*Oh Pray My Wings Are Gonna Fit Me
    Well,* 87–88, 104–106, 112
"Passing Time," 105–106
"Phenomenal Woman," 106–107
The Poetry of Maya Angelou, 101–104
"Prelude to a Parting," 109
Shaker, Why Don't You Sing?," 87–88,
    108–112

*Singin' and Swingin' and Gettin' Merry
    Like Christmas,* 87–88, 93–96, 111
"Southeast Arkansia," 105
And Still I Rise, 87–88, 106–108, 112
"Times-Square-Shoeshine
    Composition," 103
"To a Husband," 102
"Touch Me, Life, Not Softly,"
    106–108
"Traveling," 106–108
"Willie," 107
"Woman Work," 107
Angle of Ascent (Hayden), 35
Annie Allen (Brooks), 50–58, 275
Another Life (Walcott), 134–135
Anthes, Rudolf, 219, 239
*Anthology of New American Poetry 1945-
    1960* (Allen, ed.), 63
"Any Revolution Based on Race is
    Suicidal" (Pantin), 142–143
Arkestra, Sun Ra and, 214–215,
    217–218, 230–231
Armageddon school of the Sixties, 50
Arnold, Matthew, 131–132, 142
"As My Blood Was Drawn" (Hayden),
    45–46
*As Serious as Your Life: The Story of the
    New Jazz* (Wilmer), 217, 238
Ash Wednesday (Eliot), 71
"Astronauts" (Hayden), 37, 40
"At a Potato Digging" (Heaney), 121
Atkinson, Monte, 209, 236
Attali, Jacques, 218, 239
Auden: An American Friendship (Miller),
    15, 33
Auden, W. H.
    Hayden influenced by, 1–2, 11,
        14–15, 274
    Niebuhr and, 15–16
    teaching style, 15
    Walcott influenced by, 2
Auden, W. H., works of
    Collected Poems, 32
    For the Time Being, 15
    "New Year Letter," 15
    "September 1, 1939," 127

"The Watershed," 129
"The Auroras of Autumn" (Stevens),
    171
"Author Maya Angelou Raps" (Elliot),
    112
The Autobiography (Williams, W. C.), 64
Avant-garde, 215–217

Baca, Jimmy Santiago, 9–10
Bacchus, 230
"The Badgers" (Heaney), 125
Bahti, Timothy, 175
Baker, Houston, 14, 32, 49–50, 58
Baldwin, James, 157–158, 175, 246–247,
    257
"The Ballad of Nat Turner" (Hayden),
    10
"A Ballad of Remembrance" (Hayden),
    5–6, 10, 39
Banneker, Benjamin, 157–158, 165
Baraka, Amiri. see Jones/Amiri Baraka,
    LeRoi
Barber, John Warner, 19, 32
The Bean Eaters (Brooks), 275
Beat East Coast (magazine), 62–63
Beat Movement, 61–62
"Beginning" (Wright), 170
"Beginnings" (Hayden), 47
Bell, Roseann P., 190
"Belsen, Day of Liberation" (Hayden),
    10
Benjamin, Walter, 153–155, 163,
    169–170, 172, 174–175
"Benjamin Banneker Helps to Build a
    City" (Wright), 147, 158
"Benjamin Banneker Sends His
    'Almanac' to Thomas Jefferson"
    (Wright), 157–162, 172, 176
Benson, C., 112
Bercovitch, Sacvan, 228, 242
Berendt, Joachim, 214–215, 237
Berret, Anthony J., 256, 259
Beyond Byzantium: The Last Phase of Yeats'
    Career (Garab), 213, 237
Beyond the Culture Wars (Graff), 30, 33

Bhabha, Homi K., 152–153, 173, 175
Bicentennial of U.S.A., 151–152
Bickman, Martin, 209, 228, 236, 242
"Big Bessie Throws Her Son into the
    Street" (Brooks), 50–51
"Biographical Sketch" (Williams, P.), 30
"Bird Lives" (Harper), 197–198
"The Birthday" (Wright), 165–166
Black, French, and African: A Life of
    Léopold Sédar Senghor (Vaillant), 5,
    31, 34
Black Aesthetic, 250, 258
"Black Art" (Jones/Amiri Baraka), 81–82
Black Art (Jones/Amiri Baraka), 78–83
Black Arts Movement, 26, 173, 185
The Black Atlantic: Modernity and Double
    Consciousness (Gilroy), 176
Black Cultural Nationalism, 6, 24, 26
"Black Cultural Nationalism" (Karenga),
    6, 33
"Black Dada Nihilismus" (Jones/Amiri
    Baraka), 77–78, 83
"The Black Dove: Rita Dove, Poet
    Laureate" (Vendler), 255–256, 258
Black Fire: An Anthology of Afro-American
    Writing (Jones/Amiri Baraka and
    Neal), 175
Black Magic: Collected Poetry 1961-1967
    (Jones/Amiri Baraka), 78–83
"The Black Man is Making New Gods"
    (Jones/Amiri Baraka), 78–79
"Black Mother Woman" (Lorde),
    186–187
Black Mountain Review, 62
Black Music (Jones/Amiri Baraka), 218,
    239
"Black Music-Key Force in Afro-
    American Culture: Archie Shepp
    on Oral Tradition and Black
    Culture" (Putschogl), 215–215, 238
Black Nationalism and the Revolution in
    Music (Kofsky), 218
Black on White: A Critical Survey of
    Writing by American Negroes
    (Littlejohn), 49, 58
"Black People" (Jones/Amiri Baraka),
    79–80

Black Poetry in America (Jackson and
    Rubin), 58
Black Power/Free Jazz (Comolli), 218
"A Black Rainbow: Modern Afro-
    American Poetry" (Dove and
    Waniek), 258
"The Black Scholar Interviews: Maya
    Angelou" *(Black Scholar)*, 112
*Black Sister: Poetry by Black American
    Women* (Stetson), 191
"Black Skins, White Masks: Minstrelsy
    and White Working Class
    Formations before the Civil War"
    (Roediger), 256, 259
The Black Spear (Hayden, unfinished),
    13–14
Black Writers Conference at Fisk, 6, 8,
    30
*Black Writers in French: A Literary
    History of Négritude* (Kesteloot), 31,
    33
"Blackberry Picking" (Heaney), 122
"Blackface Minstrelsy" (Saxton), 256,
    259
The Blacks (Genet), 86
Blake, William
    artist as representative of
        brotherhood, 216
    conflict as delusion, 223
    cycles have an end, 230
    individuation and unity in, 218–220
    Mental War, 223, 225
    Reed influenced by, 207–208, 211,
        219–220, 225
    Ritual Romanum and, 210
Blake and Yeats: The Contrary Vision
    (Adams), 223, 230, 240, 242
*A Blake Dictionary: The Ideas and Symbols
    of William Blake* (Damon), 219–220,
    239
Blavatsky, HP "Madame," 207
Bloom, Harold
    "Afterword" to Wright's *Selected
        Poems*, 31–32
    biographical info, 285
    introduction, 1–4

on Yeats, 213, 237
Bluebacks vs. greenbacks, 221–222
"Blues Chant Hoodoo Revival"
    (Komunyakaa), 28
Blues People (Jones/Amiri Baraka), 67–68
"Bog Queen" (Heaney), 124
"Bogland" (Heaney), 122
Boleros (Wright), 146
Bollingen Prize, 9
"Bone Dreams" (Heaney), 124
"Bone-Flower Elegy" (Hayden), 2,
    36–37
"Bone Mean" (McElroy), 187
Bontemps, Arna, 7
The Book of Urizen (Blake), 220
"The Bounty" (Walcott), 3
"Brave Words for a Startling Occasion"
    (Ellison), 197
Breadloaf Writers Conference, 35
"Breaklight" (Clifton), 183
Brecht, Bertolt, 80
"Bridge" (Jones/Amiri Baraka), 73
"Bridges and Deep Water" (Ward), 181,
    191
Brodsky, Joseph, 127, 136, 138
Bronzeville Boys and Girls (Brooks), 275
Brooks, Gwendolyn
    Annie Allen, 50–58, 275
    awards and honors, 50, 275
    The Bean Eaters, 275
    on being black, 49, 58, 174
    "Big Bessie Throws Her Son into the
        Street," 50–51
    biographical info, 274–275
    Bronzeville Boys and Girls, 275
    Columbia College (Chicago), 275
    "Do Not Be Afraid of No," 50–58
    emergence of, 8
    "Gang Girls," 50
    "In Honor of David Anderson
        Brooks, My Father," 274–275
    "In the Mecca," 56, 59, 275
    Kennedy, John F., 275
    "Notes from the Childhood and
        Girlhood," 50
    passionate caring of, 11–12

"Pygmies Are Pygmies Still, Though
    Percht on Alps," 58
Selected Poems, 275
A Street in Bronzeville, 275
"We Real Cool," 56, 59
Brooks, Gwendolyn, style of
    artistic control, 49
    broad experiences in, 51
    complex, rhythmic verse, 49–50
    identifying white racism, 52
    images of lapping and fur, 53
    logical conundrum, 57
    multiple meanings, 57
    racism or feminism, 52–53
    rhyming couplets with consonance,
        56
    symbolism and imagery, 54–55
    white style, black content, 50
    "yes" as a denial of life, 54–55
Brown, Lloyd, 136, 143
Brown, Martha H., 50, 58
Brown, Sterling A., 195, 276
Buck-Morss, Susan, 175
Budge, E. A. Wallis, 219, 239
Buell, Lawrence, 210, 220, 237, 239
Burgher, Mary, 182–183, 190
Burris, Sidney
    biographical info, 286
    on Heaney, 121–129
    on Walcott, 113–121

"Caged Bird" (Angelou), 110
Callahan, John F.
    biographical info, 286–287
    on Harper, 193–203
Callaloo, 211, 237, 242–243
Cameron, Dee Birch, 112
Campbell, Jeremy, 232, 243
Canot, Theodore, 23, 32
The Cantos of Ezra Pound (Pound), 177
Cantos (Pound), 151–152
Carew, Jan, 141
Carpenter, Frederick Ives, 228, 241
"The Castaway" (Walcott), 135
"Castiliane" (Walcott), 138

"Casualty" (Heaney), 126
"Ceremony for Minneconjoux" (Osbey),
    27, 34
"Changing Permanences: Historical and
    Literary Revisionism in Robert
    Hayden's 'Middle Passage'"
    (Kutzinski), 33
"The Changing Same: Black Music in
    the Poetry of Amiri Baraka"
    (Mackey), 218, 239
Chapultepec, 165
"The Charge" (Wright), 155–156, 158,
    162
Charles, Ezzard "Mack," 222, 240
"The Children of Their Sin" (Rodgers),
    184–185
"Churning Day" (Heaney), 121
Cinquez (*Amistad* mutiny), 18–21, 25
Clark, Norris B., 50, 58
Clausen, Christopher, 50
"Clear Seeing, Inherited Religion and
    Reclaiming the Pagan Self"
    (Walker), 177
"Clearances" (Heaney), 128
"The Clearing" (Jones/Amiri Baraka),
    67
Clifton, Lucille, 181, 183, 190–191,
    280–281
Clifton, Lucille, works of
    An Ordinary Woman, 183–184, 191,
        281
    "Breaklight," 183
    "february 13, 1980," 183–184
    Good News About the Earth, 281
    Good Times, 281
    "i was born with twelve fingers," 190
    "light," 188
    "My Mama Moved among the Days,"
        181, 183
    "poem on my fortieth birthday to my
        mother who died young," 184
    "the thirty eighth year," 184
    two-headed woman, 183–184, 190–191,
        281
Coal (Lorde), 186, 188–189, 191
"Coda V" (Wright), 149

"Coda VI" (Wright), 149
Coleridge, Samuel Taylor, 137–138
The Collected Essays of Ralph Ellison
    (Callahan, ed.), 256, 259
Collected Poems (Auden), 32
Collected Poems (Hayden), 33, 46,
    208–209, 236
The Collected Poems of Wallace Stevens
    (Stevens, W.), 165–166, 177
Collected Prose (Hayden), 11–14, 27–28,
    30–31
The Collected Works of W.B. Yeats
    (Finneran, ed.), 206, 210, 212–214,
    219, 235
Columbus, Christopher, 113–114
Combustion (magazine), 62–63
"The Comedian as the Letter C"
    (Stevens, W.), 153–154, 165
Commission of International Women's
    Year, 86
Commolli, Jean-Louis, 218
*The Complete Poetry and Prose of William
    Blake* (Erdman, ed.), 207–208, 210,
    219–220, 236
Congress of African Peoples, 276–277
Conjure: Selected Poems, 1963-1970
    (Reed), 206–207, 209, 211–212,
    215–216, 230, 236, 240
Conniff, Brian
    on AA poetic sequence, 26–29
    on the *Amistad* mutiny, 17–21, 24–25
    biographical info, 285
    on Hayden, 5–34
    on post-traditional poetry, 28–29
    on "Schizophrenia," 17
"Contextualizing *Othello* in Reed and
    Phillips" (Erickson), 258
Contingency, Irony, Solidarity (Rorty), 34
"A Conversation with Jerome
    Rothenberg" (Powers), 231, 242
*Conversation with Ogotemmêli: An
    Introduction to Dogon Religious Ideas*
    (Griaule), 167–168, 171–172, 176
*Conversing in Paradise: Poetic Genius and
    Identity-as-Community in Blake's Los*
    (Deen), 215–216, 218, 238–239

Crane, Hart, 2, 154–155, 157, 159, 176
"Crazy Jane" (Yeats), 75
Creeley, Robert, 62
"Crispus Attucks" (Wright), 148
*Cross-Cultural Performances: Differences in
    Women Re-Visions of Shakespeare*
    (Novy), 258
"Crow Jane in High Society"
    (Jones/Amiri Baraka), 75
"Crow Jane" (Jones/Amiri Baraka), 75
"The Crucial Years" (Hatcher), 30
Cry for a Leader (Walcott), 117–118
"Cuchulain Comforted" (Yeats), 9
Cullen, Countee, 274
Culture and Imperialism (Said), 13, 34

Damon, S. Foster, 219–220, 239
"The Dance of the Elephants" (Harper),
    200
Davis, Charles T., 31, 33
The Dead Lecturer (Jones/Amiri Baraka),
    63, 69–70, 74–78
"The Dead" (Wright), 172–173
"Dear John, Dear Callahan" (Harper),
    196
Dear John, Dear Coltrane, 196
Death and dying
    Clifton on, 184, 190
    Hayden on, 41–43, 45–46, 208–209
    Jones/Amiri Baraka on, 71
    Wright on, 146
"Death as History" (Wright), 167, 177
"Death of a Naturalist" (Heaney), 121
"The Death of Nick Charles"
    (Jones/Amiri Baraka), 67
"Debridement" (Harper), 27
"The Decline of Anglo-American
    Poetry" (Clausen), 50, 58
Deen, Leonard, 215–216, 218, 238–239
Delany, John J., 210, 236
Dent, Tom, 217, 238
Deren, Maya, 226, 241
"Desire's Design, Vision's Resonance:
    Black Poetry's Ritual and Historical
    Voice" (Wright), 14, 34, 147

Desperate Circumstances, Dangerous Women (Osbey), 27

Dhomhnaill, Nuala ni, 9

The Dialectics of Seeing: Walter Benjamin and the Arcades Project (Buck-Morss), 175

Dictionary of American Catholic Biography (Delany), 210, 236

A Dictionary of Egyptian Gods and Goddesses (Hart), 209, 211, 222, 236

Diggory, Terrence, 233–234, 243–244

Dimensions of History (Wright), 28, 149, 151–152, 167

"Dionysus in America" (Mottram), 230, 242

Discrepant Engagement: Dissonance, Cross-Culturality, and Experimental Writing (Mackey), 176

"DissemiNation" (Bhabha), 152–153

"A Dissonant Triad: Henri Cole, Rita Dove, and August Kleinzahler" (Vendler), 255–256, 258

Divine Days (Forrest), 250

Dixon, Bill, 217

Dixon, Melvin, 28

"Do Not Be Afraid of No" (Brooks), 50–58

Donald, Caroline, 281

Donne, John, 149

"Don't never forget the bridge that you crossed over on: The Literature of Matrilineage" (Maglin), 180–181, 186, 191

Doolittle, Hilda. *see* HD

Door into the Dark (Heaney), 121

Doreski, C. K.
  biographical info, 286
  on Wright, 151–177

Doreski, William, 176

The Double Invention of Komo (Wright), 28, 146–147

"The Double Vision of Michael Robartes" (Yeats), 223, 240

Douglass, Frederick, 152, 164

Dove, Rita
  awards and honors, 284
  on being black, 256
  biographical info, 283–284
  on Rich, 248, 254, 258
  self-portrait, 253
  Shakespeare and, 247–257

Dove, Rita, style of
  alienation as a theme, 251
  color, use of, 254–255
  parenthetical stanzas, 249
  racial significance in, 254
  ranges from Baldwin-DuBois, 250, 252

Dove, Rita, works of
  "Either I'm Nobody, or I'm a Nation," 258
  "In the Old Neighborhood," 245–246, 248–252, 254–255
  Museum, 176, 246, 257
  "Screaming Fire," 259
  "Shakespeare Say," 245–246, 250–252, 255
  "Telling it Like it I-S *IS*: Narrative Techniques in Melvin Tolson's Harlem Gallery," 258
  Thomas and Beulah, 283–284

Dramas, Fields and Metaphors: Symbolic Action in Human Society (Turner), 177

Dream on Monkey Mountain and Other Plays (Walcott), 114–115, 119, 139–143, 279

Drumvoices: The Mission of Afro-American Poetry—A Critical History (Redmond), 177

DuBois, W. E. B., 30, 76, 208, 245–247, 252, 257

Duncan, Robert, 170, 176

Dupree, Champion Jack, 247, 250–252

Dwelling in Possibility: Women Poets and Critics on Poetry (Prins and Shreiber, eds.), 252, 257

"The Early Purges" (Heaney), 121

Earth House Hold (Snyder), 211, 237

"East Coker" (Eliot), 73, 170

East Village Other, 283
"Either I'm Nobody, or I'm a Nation" (Dove), 258
"El-Hajj Malix El-Shabazz" (Hayden), 10
Elaine's Book (Wright), 146
Elegies for Paradise Alley (Hayden), 274
"Elegies for Paradise Valley" (Hayden), 36–37, 40–42, 45–46
Eliade, Mircea, 231, 242
Eliot, T. S.
  Brooks influenced by, 49
  on challenges of writing poetry, 138, 143
  contribution to poetry, 71
  as Faber and Gwyer poetry editor, 9
  Hayden influenced by, 10–17, 31
  impending social disruption, 27
  Jones/Amiri Baraka and, 63–64, 71, 78–79
  line modulation of, 73
  radical philosophical uncertainty of, 22
  use of language, 14
  Wright influenced by, 153–154, 158
Eliot, T. S., works of. *see also* "The Waste Land"
  Ash-Wednesday, 71
  "East Coker," 73, 170
  Family Reunion, 15
  Four Quartets, 73
  "Little Giddin," 10, 73, 157, 176
  "The Love Song of J. Alfred Prufrock," 11, 31–32, 71
  "Tradition and the Individual Talent," 138, 143
  The Waste Land and Other Poems, 33
Eliotic despair, 17
Elliot, Jeffrey M., 112
Ellison, Ralph, 31, 251, 256, 259
Ellmann, Richard, 33, 226, 240
Emerson, Ralph Waldo, 155–156, 165, 210, 228, 233
Emerson Handbook (Carpenter), 228, 241–242
Empire Star Weekly, 283

"Entering New Mexico" (Wright), 162
Erdman, David E., 207–208, 236
Erickson, Peter
  biographical info, 287
  on Dove, 245–259
Erickson, Peter, works of
  "Adrienne Rich's Re-Vision of Shakespeare," 257
  "Contextualizing *Othello* in Reed and Phillips," 258
  "Singing America: From Walt Whitman to Adrienne Rich," 257
  "Start Misquoting Him Now: The Difference a Word Makes in Adrienne Rich's 'Inscriptions'," 257
  The Upstart Crow: A Shakespeare Journal, 258
"Essay on Colonies" (Smith, A.), 113–114
Evans, Mari, 58
"Eve (Rachel)" (Harper), 199–200
Evergreen Review, 62–63
Every Shut Eye Ain't Asleep: An Anthology of Poetry by African Americans Since 1945 (Harper and Walton, eds.), 30, 32–33
"The Exile and the Prodigal" (Izevbaye), 142–143
"Exposure" (Heaney), 122
"Ezzard (Mack) Charles" (*The New Encyclopædia Britannica*), 222, 240

"Fable of Popess Joan" (Aherne), 210–211, 237
"The Faithful One" (Wright), 147–148
Falling Pieces of the Broken Sky (Lester), 37, 46
Family Reunion (Eliot), 15
"Family Reunion" (Wright), 163–164
"A Far Cry From Africa" (Walcott), 142
Farag, Fahmy, 223, 240
Fargo, William G., 221
Fearful Symmetry: A Study of William Blake (Frye), 207, 236
"February 13, 1980" (Clifton), 183–184

Federal Writers' Project, 273–274
Feldman, Gene, 84
Fetrow, Fred M., 30, 33, 47
"The Fiddle" (Harper), 201
Fiedler, Leslie, 54
Field Work (Heaney), 125–126, 128
*Figures in Black: Words, Signs, and the
    "Racial"* (Gates), 176
Finneran, Richard J., 235
Fiofiori, Tam, 214, 237
First Black Writers' Conference (Fisk
    University), 6, 8
"First Fight, Then Fiddle" (Park), 50,
    52, 56, 58
"The First Word" (Wright), 171
"The Fisherman's Fiesta" (Wright), 148
Fisk University, 6, 8, 30, 274
Flicks, Christopher, 31
Flight to Canada (Reed), 225, 235, 244
The Floating Bear newsletter, 62
Foner, Philip, 176
For the Time Being (Auden), 15
"For the Union Dead" (Lowell), 175,
    197
"Forest of Europe" (Walcott), 136–137
"Foreword" to Hayden's *Collected Prose*
    (Meredith), 33
Forrest, Leon, 250
"Fortunate Fall: W. H. Auden at
    Michigan" (Pearce), 15, 34
Four Quartets (Eliot), 73
Four Zoas (Blake), 233–234
Frazier, E. Franklin, 276
"Frederick Douglass" (Hayden), 10, 39
Free Jazz (Jost), 214–215, 217–218, 237
Freud, Sigmund, 180
From a Land Where Other People Live
    (Lorde), 186–189, 191
"From an Almanac" (Jones/Amiri
    Baraka), 67, 69, 72–74
*From the Auroral Darkness: The Life and
    Poetry of Robert Hayden* (Hatcher), 33
"From the Canton of Expectation"
    (Heaney), 129
"From the Life: Some Remembrances"
    (Hayden), 47

Frost, Robert, 11
Frye, Northrup, 207, 235–236

"The Gamut" (Angelou), 102
"Gang Girls" (Brooks), 50
Garab, Arra M., 213, 237
"The Garauballe Man" (Heaney), 124
Gartenberg, Max, 84
Gates, Henry Louis, Jr., 176, 255–256,
    258
Gather Together in My Name (Angelou),
    87–88, 90–93, 111
Genet, Jean, 86
"A Georgia Song" (Angelou), 110
"Getting to Whitney: Ishmael Reed's 'I
    am a cowboy...'" (Linebarger and
    Atkinson), 209, 236
Gide, André, 80
Gilroy, Paul, 176
Ginsberg, Allen, 67–68, 209, 236
Giordano, Fedora, 231, 242–243
Giovanni, Nikki, 191
The Given and the Made" (Vendler), 256,
    259
"GLR Interview: Gwendolyn Brooks"
    (Brown and Zorn), 50, 58
Good News About the Earth (Clifton), 281
Good Times (Clifton), 281
Gottfried, Leon, 131
The Government of the Tongue (Heaney),
    123
Graff, Gerald, 30, 33
*Grammatical Man: Information, Entropy,
    Language and Life* (Campbell), 232,
    243
Grand Prix award, 5–6, 26, 29
"The Great Hunger" (Kavanagh), 121
Greek myth of Osiris and Horus,
    209–213, 222–225
"Green Lantern's Solo" (Jones/Amiri
    Baraka), 74
Greenbacks vs. bluebacks, 221–222
Greenwich Village, 61
"Greyday" (Angelou), 106
Griaule, Marcel, 167–168, 171–172, 176

Ground Work: Before the War (Duncan), 176
Grundy, Felix, 20
Guy-Sheftall, Beverly, 190
Gwendolyn Brooks; Poetry and the Heroic Voice (Melhem), 8, 33, 50, 58
"Gwendolyn Brooks' *A Street in Bronzeville*, the Harlem Renaissance and the Mythologies of Black Women" (MELUS), 59
"Gwendolyn Brooks and a Black Aesthetic" (Clark), 50, 58
"Gwendolyn Brooks" (Israel), 58
"Gwendolyn Brooks' Poetic Realism: A Developmental Survey" in *Black Women Writers* (Evans, ed.), 51, 58
Gwendolyn Brooks (Shaw), 50, 58
Gypsy Ballads (Lorca), 71

"Harlem Hopscotch" (Angelou), 101, 103–104
Harlem Renaissance, 11
Harlem Writers Guild, 86, 277
Harlow, Alvin F., 221, 239
Harper, George Mills, 230, 242
Harper, Michael S.
    awards and honors, 282
    on being black, 30
    biographical info, 281–282
    Hayden and, 8, 13–14, 27, 32, 37
    racism experiences, 282
    style of, 197, 201
Harper, Michael S., works of
    "American History," 196
    "Bird Lives," 197–198
    "The Dance of the Elephants," 200
    "Dear John, Dear Callahan," 196
    "Debridement," 27
    "Eve (Rachel)," 199–200
    "The Fiddle," 201
    Images of Kin: New and Selected Poems, 27, 33, 195, 281
    "The Kite," 202
    "Kite Coda," 202
    "Little Song of the Sun," 200

"Motel Room," 201
"Night Letter, I," 200
"Oral Light," 196
"Remembering Robert Hayden," 33
Yeats Golden Dawn, 230, 242
Yeats influence on, 200
"Harriet Tubman" (Hayden), 39
Harris, Wilson, 176
Hart, George, 209, 211, 222, 236
Hart-Shape in the Dust (Hayden), 274
Haskins, James, 211, 237
Hatcher, John, 6, 8, 30–31, 33
The Haw Lantern (Heaney), 123, 128–129
Hayden, Robert
    Auden's influence on, 1–2, 11, 14–15
    awards and honors, 5–6, 13, 26, 29, 35, 274
    Baha'i faith, 8
    on being black, 6–7, 24, 30, 40–41, 274
    biographical info, 5–6, 11, 14–15, 35, 273–274
    critical writing of, 10–11
    Federal Writers' Project, 273–274
    on humanity, 39
    Library of Congress speech, 11, 30
    Michigan Chronicle, 273–274
    obscurity of, 26
    on passionate caring, 11–12
    possibility of transcendental vision, 208
    "signpost of sensibility," 32
    University of Michigan, 274
    Wright influenced by, 8, 28, 31, 154
Hayden, Robert, style of
    anonymity of, 6–9
    baroque figures, 39–40
    Eliotic intonations, 10–17, 31
    indirection and disguises in, 37–38
    as medium for change, 11
    paradox on paradox, 43
    portraits, 39–44
    storytelling, 37
    symmetry in, 36–37, 44

themes
    death and dying, 41–43, 45–46,
      208–209
    elegies, 2, 36–37, 40–42, 45–46
    historical consciousness, 13–14, 27
    human dignity, 29
Hayden, Robert, works of. *see also*
    "Middle Passage"
American Journal, 35–46
"American Journal," 36–37, 40, 44–46
Angle of Ascent, 35
"As My Blood Was Drawn," 45–46
"Astronauts," 37, 40
"The Ballad of Nat Turner," 10
"A Ballad of Remembrance," 5–6, 10,
    39
"Beginnings," 47
"Belsen, Day of Liberation," 10
"Bone-Flower Elegy," 2, 36–37
Collected Poems, 33, 46, 208–209, 236
Collected Prose, 11–14, 27–28, 30–31
"El-Hajj Malix El-Shabazz," 10
Elegies for Paradise Alley, 274
"Elegies for Paradise Valley," 36–37,
    40–42, 45–46
"Frederick Douglass," 10, 39
"From the Life: Some
    Remembrances," 47
"Harriet Tubman," 39
Hart-Shape in the Dust, 274
"Homage to Paul Robeson," 36
"The Islands," 1–2, 42–43
"John Brown," 43, 45–46
"Killing the Calves," 45
"Letter," 45
"A Letter from Phillis Wheatley,"
    44–45
"Locus," 46
"manifesto" for the Counterpoise
    Series, 31
"Names," 42
"Nat Turner," 39
"Night, Death, Mississippi," 10, 32
The Night-Blooming Cereus, 35
"O Daedalus, Fly Away Home,"
    27–28

"The Point," 40
"The Prisoners," 39, 43
"The Rag Man," 39
"Runagate Runagate," 2, 10
"Schizophrenia," 16–17, 33
"The Snow Lamp," 36
"The Tattooed Man," 37–39, 46
"Theme and Variation," 42, 46
"Twentieth Century American
    Poetry," 10–11
"Witch Doctor," 39
"Words in the Mourning Time," 10,
    30–31, 38–40
"The Year of the Child," 42, 45
H.D., 12
"The Healing Improvisation of Hair"
    (Wright), 149
Heaney, Seamus
    anecdotes and parables, 122, 126, 128
    densely textured lines, 126
    on Eastern block poets, 123–124,
      127–128
    elegies, 126
    hedonistic pleasure as theme, 125
    intoned implications, 121
    political themes, 123–125
    post-traditional stance of, 9
    self-counsel via ghosts, 127
Heaney, Seamus, works of
    "Anahorish," 121
    "At a Potato Digging," 121
    "The Badgers," 125
    "Blackberry Picking," 122
    "Bog Queen," 124
    "Bogland," 122
    "Bone Dreams," 124
    "Casualty," 126
    "Churning Day," 121
    "Clearances," 128
    "Death of a Naturalist," 121
    Door into the Dark, 121
    "The Early Purges," 121
    "Exposure," 122
    Field Work, 125–126, 128
    "From the Canton of Expectation,"
      129

"The Garauballe Man," 124
The Government of the Tongue, 123
The Haw Lantern, 123, 128–129
"The Impact of Translation," 123, 128
"Making Strange," 127
"The Mud Vision," 121, 128
North, 122, 124–125
"Relic of Memory," 122
"The Riddle," 128
"Sandstone Keepsake," 126–127
Selected Poems: 1966-1987, 121
"Shore Woman," 122–123
"Singing School," 125
Station Island, 9, 126–127
"Station Island," 121, 127
"The Tollund Man," 122, 124
"Trout," 121
Wintering Out, 121–122
"Wintering Out," 121
The Heart of a Woman (Angelou), 87–88, 96–99, 111
Helen *(Omeros)*, 116–117
Henderson, Stephen E., 176
Henn, T.R., 213, 237
Henry, Joseph, 211, 237
Hensen, Matthew, 36
"The Hieroglyph of Irrrational Force" (Wright), 149
Highbrow/Lowbrow: The Emergence of Cultural Hierarchy in America (Levine), 256, 259
A History of the Amistad Captives (Barber), 19, 32
"History Stops for No One" (Rich), 162, 177
Hollander, John, 152, 173–174, 176
"Homage to Paul Robeson" (Hayden), 36
"Homecoming: Anse la Raye" (Walcott), 141
"Homecoming: Guadalajara—New York, 1965" (Wright), 166–167
"The Homecoming Singer" (Wright), 164
The Homecoming Singer (Wright), 146–148, 164–165, 170

Homer, 115–116
Horses Make a Landscape Look More Beautiful (Walker), 189, 191
Horus ("I am a cowboy in the boat of Ra"), 209, 219–220, 222
Horvath, Brooke Kenton
biographical info, 286
on Brooks, 49–59
Hoverns, Pieter, 231, 243
How i got ovah: New and Selected Poems (Rodgers), 184–185, 191
"How You Sound?" (Jones/Amiri Baraka), 69
Howl and Other Poems (Ginsberg), 209, 236
Hughes, Langston, 30, 49, 67–68, 274
"The Hunting Trip Cook" (Wright), 147–148
"Hymn for Lanie Poo" (Jones/Amiri Baraka), 67

"I am a cowboy in the boat of Ra" (Reed), 207–210, 219–222, 224–225, 230–231, 233
I Know Why the Caged Bird Sings (Angelou), 87–90, 110–111
"I Sign My Mother's Name: Alice Walker, Dorothy West, Paule Marshall" (Washington), 179, 190–191
"I was born with twelve fingers" (Clifton), 190
"If my enemy is a clown, a natural born clown" (Reed), 215–216
"If We Must Die" (McKay), 11
Illuminations: Essays and Reflections (Benjamin), 163, 169, 175
"The Image of Proust" (Benjamin), 174
"Images of Black Women in Afro-American Poetry" (Rushing), 179–180, 191
"Images of Black Women in Modern African Poetry: An Overview" (Rushing), 179–181, 191
Images of Kin: New and Selected Poems (Harper), 27, 33, 195, 281

"Images of Self and Race in the Autobiographies of Black Women" (Burgher), 182–183, 190

"The Impact of Translation" (Heaney), 123, 128

The Imperial Self: An Essay in American Literature and Culture (Anderson), 220, 228, 234–235, 239, 242, 244

"In A Green Night" (Walcott), 5, 132–133

"In Honor of David Anderson Brooks, My Father" (Brooks), 274–275

"In Interview with Rita Dove" (Vendler), 255–256, 258

"In Memory of Radio" (Jones/Amiri Baraka), 67

"In My Mother's Room" (McElroy), 189–190

"In the Mecca" (Brooks), 56, 59, 275

"In the Old Neighborhood" (Dove), 245–246, 248–252, 254–255

"In These Dissenting Times" (Walker), 182

In These Houses (Osbey), 27–28, 34

Interpreting the Indian: Twentieth Century Poets and the Native American (Castro), 231, 243

"The Interrogation" (Muir), 129

"Interview: Maya Angelou" (Paterson), 112

Interviews with Black Writers (O'Brien), 47, 206, 235

Introduction to Adventures of Huckleberry Finn (Morrison), 256, 259

"Introduction" to Wright's *Selected Poems* (Stepto), 31, 34

"Intuition: Figure and Act" (Wright), 149

Inventing Billy the Kid: Vissions of the Outlaw in America, 1881-1981 (Tatum), 227–228, 241

Inventions of the March Hare (Flicks, ed.), 31

Invisible Man (Ellison), 31

Irish poetry, 115–116

"Ishmael Reed: Who's Radio Broke Down" (Ambler), 225, 240

Isis Unveiled (Blavatsky), 207

"The Islands" (Hayden), 1–2, 42–43

"The Isolated Self in West Indian Literature" (Brown), 136, 143

Israel, Charles, 50, 58

"It Is Deep" (Rodgers), 185–186

Izevbaye, D. S., 142–143

Jackson, Blyden, 58

Jackson State murders, 197

Jaffe, Dan, 50, 58

James Baldwin: Collected Essays (Baldwin), 257

"Jason Visits His Gypsy" (Wright), 166

"Jason's One Command" (Wright), 148

The Jazz Book (Berendt), 214–215, 237

Jazz Composers' Guild, 217, 230, 238

"The Jazz Composers' Guilde: An Assertion of Dignity" (Levin), 217, 238

Jefferson, Thomas, 157–158, 172, 176

"Jesus Was Crucified, or It Must Be Deep" (Rodgers), 185–186

"John Brown" (Hayden), 43, 45–46

Johnson, James Weldon, 274

Johnson, Marguerite Annie. *see* Angelou, Maya

Jones/Amiri Baraka, LeRoi
 awards and honors, 277
 on being black, 64–65, 69–70, 79–83, 276
 biographical info, 61–64, 275–277
 comic strip heroes' influence, 74–75, 79
 indignation as psychic aid, 80
 poetry venues, 62–63
 prison sentence, 79
 as racial anarchist, 78–83
 revolutionary nationalism, 81
 statement of freedom, 68–69
 Williams' influence on, 63–64
 Yeats' influence on, 75

Jones/Amiri Baraka, LeRoi, style of
 anti-modernism of, 64

Christian/Judeo God, rejection of, 77–79
drama, 82
enchantment and bitterness, 66
hortatory, oratorical style, 82
juxtaposed scenes and images, 67
language and, 64
morality and inhumanity combined, 77–78
multiple images, 73
polyrhythmic music, 67–69
syntax, 68
themes
    disorder, coldness, 73–74
    frustration, loss, death, 71
    images from the unconscious, 65
    mysticism, 83
    personal experience, 65–69, 75–76
    politics, 75
    racial, 77
    rejection of whites, 76, 78–83
Jones/Amiri Baraka, LeRoi, works of
"An Explanation of the Work," 81
Black Art, 78–83
"Black Art," 81–82
"Black Dada Nihilismus," 77–78, 83
Black Fire: An Anthology of Afro-American Writing, 175
Black Magic: Collected Poetry 1961-1967, 78–83
"The Black Man is Making New Gods," 78–79
Black Music, 218, 239
"Black People," 79–80
Blues People, 67–68
"Bridge," 73
"The Clearing," 67
"Crow Jane," 75
"Crow Jane in High Society," 75
The Dead Lecturer, 63, 69–70, 74–78
"The Death of Nick Charles," 67
"From an Almanac," 67, 69, 72–74
"Green Lantern's Solo," 74
"How You Sound?," 69
"Hymn for Lanie Poo," 67
"In Memory of Radio," 67

"Lines to Garcia Lorca," 70
"Look for You Yesterday, Here you Come Today," 67, 74
"The New Sheriff," 74
"A Poem for Black Hearts," 82
"A Poem for Democrats," 74–75
"A Poem for Willie Best," 74
"A Poem Some People Will Have to Understand," 79
"Political Poem," 75
"The politics of rich painters," 75
Preface to a Twenty Thousand Volume Suicide Note, 63–65, 70, 80
"Roi's New Blues," 67, 73–74
Sabotage, 78–83
"The Shadow is Dead," 79
"Short Speech to My Friends," 75
"Statement on Poetics," 63, 68–69
Target Study, 78–83
"There Must Be a Lone Ranger," 74
"The Turncoat," 66, 73
"Vice," 73
"Way Out West," 73
Jordan, June, 251, 257
Jost, Ekkehard, 214–215, 217–218, 237
Joyce, James, 116, 118, 127
Just Give Me a Cool Drink of Water 'fore I Diiie (Angelou), 87–88, 112

Karenga, Ron, 6, 33
Kavanagh, Patrick, 121
Keats, John, 149
Kenner, Hugh, 168, 176
Kent, George, 51, 58
Kesteloot, Lilyan, 31, 33
Kierkegaard, 15–16
"Killing the Calves" (Hayden), 45
"Kin" (Angelou), 107–108
"Kinship and History in Sam Cornish's *Generations* (Doreski), 176
"Kite Coda" (Harper), 202
"The Kite" (Harper), 202
Kofsky, Frank, 218
Komunyakaa, Yusef, 28
Kora in Hell (Williams, W. C.), 64

Kulchur magazine, 62
Kutzinski, Vera M., 33, 176

Language, 14, 64, 118, 128
Language, Contingency, Solidarity (Rorty),
      32
Lash La Rue ("I am a cowboy in the
      boat of Ra"), 226–227
"Leda and the Swan" (Yeats), 206
"LeRoi Jones or, Poetics & Policemen
      or, Trying Heart, Bleeding Heart"
      (Schneck), 84
"LeRoi Jones" (Ossman), 84
Lester, Julius, 30–31, 33, 37
"A Letter from Phillis Wheatley"
      (Hayden), 44–45
"Letter" (Hayden), 45
"Letter to Benjamin Banneker"
      (Jefferson), 176
"Letter to Nathaniel Hawthorne"
      (Melville), 59
Letters of Wallace Stevens (Stevens, H.,
      ed.), 177
Levin, Robert, 217, 238
Levine, Lawrence W., 256, 259
Leyda, Jay, 54, 59
Library of Congress, Hayden's address
      to, 11, 30
"Lichens and Oranges" (Wright)
"The Lie" (Angelou), 109
*A Life Distilled: Gwendolyn Brooks,
      Her Poetry and Fiction* (Mootry
      and Smith, G., eds.), 50, 52, 58
"Light" (Clifton), 188
Limits (Okigbo), 5
Linebarger, J. M., 209, 236
"Lines to Garcia Lorca" (Jones/Amiri
      Baraka), 70
"Lines Written in Kensington Gardens"
      (Arnold), 131–132
Literary criticism, 12–13
Literary Transcendentalism (Buell), 220,
      239
"Little Gidding" (Eliot), 10, 73, 157, 176
"Little Song of the Sun" (Harper), 200

Littlejohn, David, 49, 58
Llorens, David, 6–7, 33
The Location of Culture (Bhabha),
      152–153, 173, 175
"Locus" (Hayden), 46
*The Lonely Tower: Studies in the Poetry of
      W. B. Yeats* (Henn), 213, 237
"Look for You Yesterday, Here you
      Come Today" (Jones/Amiri
      Baraka), 67, 74
"Looking for Zora" (Walker), 177
Loop Garoo *(Yellow-Back Radio Broke
      Down)*, 229, 231–232
Lorca, Frederico Garcia, 63, 70–71
Lorde, Audre, 186–191
Lott, Eric, 256, 259
"Louise Glück, Stephen Dunn, Brad
      Leithauser, Rita Dove" (Vendler),
      255–256, 258
Loup Garou (I am a cowboy in the boat
      of Ra), 209, 225–227, 233
*Love and Theft: Blackface Minstrelsy and
      the American Working Class* (Lott),
      256, 259
"The Love Song of J. Alfred Prufrock"
      (Eliot), 11, 31–32, 71
Lowell, Robert, 175
Lowenthal, David, 118

Macbeth (Shakespeare), 248
MacDonald, Joyce Green, 256, 259
Mackey, Nathaniel, 170–171, 176, 218,
      239
Madam Artelia ("Elegies for Paradise
      Valley"), 40–42
Maglin, Nan Bauer, 180–181, 186, 191
Mailer, Norman, 61–62, 84
Major Dennis Plunkett *(Omeros)*,
      117–120
"Making Strange" (Heaney), 127
Mandelstam, Osip, 136
"Manifesto" for the Counterpoise Series
      (Hayden), 31
Mark Twain and Shakespeare (Berret),
      259

"Market," 39
The Marriage of Heaven and Hell (Blake), 210
"Mass Man" (Walcott), 133–134
Massachusetts Review (periodical), 63
"The Master of Names" (Wright), 162
Masters, Edgar Lee, 11
Mather, Cotton, 169
Matrilineage, 179–190
Matrix Award, 87
Matthew Arnold and the Romantics (Gottfried), 131, 143
Maud Plunkett (*Omeros*), 117
The Maximum Poems (Olson), 12
"Maya Angelou: In Search of Self" (Elliot), 112
"Maya Angelou: The Heart of a Woman" (Oliver), 112
"A Maya Angelou Bibliography" (Cameron), 112
"Maya Angelou Interview" (*Harper's Bazaar*), 112
"Maya Angelou" (Tate), 112
McCluskey, Paul, 47
McDermott, Galt, 279
McDowell, Robert, 258
McElroy, Colleen J., 187–188, 190–191
McKay, Claude, 11
McLuhan: Hot & Cool (Stearn), 233, 243
McLuhan, Marshall, 219, 232, 239, 243
Melhem, D. H., 8, 33, 50, 58
"A MELUS Interview: Ishmael Reed" (MELUS), 211, 237
Melville, Herman, 54, 59
"The Mental Traveller" (Blake), 210, 230
Meredian (Walker), 152
Meredith, William, 10, 33
Metraux, Alfred, 226, 241
Meyer, Stephen
 biographical info, 286
 on Wright, 145–150
"Middle Passage" (Hayden)
 Amistad mutiny and, 17–21
 Cinquez, visions of, 25–26
 cultural schizophrenia as theme, 17, 19

 death in, 46, 208–209
 language in, 14
 moral contradictions in, 20, 24
 opening octave, 2
 racism examined in, 10
 reply to Tiresias' vision, 23–24
 revisionist history and, 13
 schizoid past's brutalities in, 14
 "Schizophrenia" compared to, 22
 tangle of black traditions, 31
 transforms "The Waste Land" theme of transformation, 25
Miller, Charles, 15, 33
Milosz, Czeslaw, 128
Milton (Blake), compared to "I am a cowboy on the boat of Ra" (Reed), 207–208, 216, 219–220, 223–224
"Minority Reporting and Psychic Distancing in the Poetry of Robert Hayden" (Fetrow), 47
"Miss Scarlett, Mr. Rhett and Other Latter Day Saints" (Angelou), 101
"Mississippi Winter III" (Walker), 189
"Modern Plumbing Illustrated" (Thomas), 233, 243
Modernism and the Harlem Renaissance (Baker), 14, 32
Montez (*Amistad* mutiny), 18–21, 24
Mootry, Maria K., 50, 58
Morgenstern, Dan, 217, 238
Morrison, Toni, 256, 259
Morse, Wayne, 197
Moss, Thylias, 4
"Motel Room" (Harper), 201
"Mother" (McElroy), 187–188
Mothers and Daughters: The Distortion of a Relationship (Nice), 179–180, 191
Mottram, Eric, 230–231, 242
"The Mud Vision" (Heaney), 121, 128
Muir, Edwin, 129
Mullen, Harryette, 176
Mumbo Jumbo, The Last Days of Louisiana Red (Reed), 235, 244
"Mumbo Jumbo Gumbo Works: The Kaleidoscopic Fiction of Ishmael Reed" (Shadle), 219, 226–227, 230, 239, 241–242

Murray, M. A., 209, 236
Museum (Dove), 176, 246, 257
"The Museums of Chapultepec"
　　(Wright), 165
Music from Home: Selected Poems
　　(McElroy), 188, 191
"My Daughter Is Coming!" (Walker),
　　189
"My Mama Moved among the Days"
　　(Clifton), 181, 183
"The Mythology of Ancient Egypt"
　　(Anthes), 219, 239
Myths
　　Bacchus, 230
　　dance of the Sidhe, 219
　　"Fable of Popess Joan" (Aherne),
　　　210–211, 237
　　Greek, Osiris and Horus, 209–213,
　　　222–225
　　Parsifal, 24–25
　　of the perpetual return of the same
　　　thing, 230

Naked Ear (magazine), 62–63
"Names" (Hayden), 42
"Nat Turner" (Hayden), 39
Nation (periodical), 63
National Book Award, 35
*Natural Supernaturalism: Tradition and
　　Revolution in Romantic Literature*
　　(Abrams), 208, 222, 226, 230, 236,
　　240, 242
"The Navigation of Absences: An Ode
　　on Method" (Wright), 149
Neals, Larry, 175
Nefertiti, bust of (Berlin), 212
Négritude movement
　　about, 8
　　affinity with AA poetry, 26
　　dimensions of negritude, 31
　　Hayden and the, 29–30
　　militant, 79–81
　　mysteries of, 83
　　Third World Festival of Negro Arts
　　　and, 7–8

"The Negro Artist and the Racial
　　Mountain" (Hughes), 30
"Neo-HooDoo Aesthetic" (Reed), 210
Neruda, Pablo, 11–12
Neubauer, Carole E.
　　on Angelou, 85–112
　　biographical info, 286
New American Poetry, 64
New Black consciousness, 8
New Criticism, 26
New Dictionary of Astrology (Sepharial),
　　225–226, 240
The New Encyclopædia Britannica, 222,
　　240
New Larousse Encyclopædia of Mythology,
　　209, 236
"The New Sheriff" (Jones/Amiri
　　Baraka), 74
"New Year Letter" (Auden), 15
Niagara Frontier Review, 62–63
Nice, Vivian E., 179, 186, 188, 191
Nicholas, Xavier, 13, 33
Niebuhr, Reinhold, 15–16
Nielsen, Aldon Lynn, 177
Nietzsche, Fredrich, 177
"Nigger words," 232
"Night, Death, Mississippi" (Hayden),
　　10, 32
The Night-Blooming Cereus (Hayden), 35
"Night Letter, I" (Harper), 200
"No, In Thunder" (Fiedler), 59
No Name in the Street (Baldwin), 252
"No No No No" (Angelou), 102–103
No Sweetness Here (Aidoo), 140, 143
Nobel Prize for Literature, 279
"Nocturnal upon St. Lucy's Day"
　　(Wright), 149
Noise: The Political Economy of Music
　　(Attali), 218, 239
*The Noise of Culture: Literary Texts in a
　　World of Information* (Paulson), 232,
　　243
Nomad (magazine), 62–63
"A Non-Birthday Poem for my Father"
　　(Wright), 148
North (Heaney), 122, 124–125

Norton Anthology of Modern Poetry (Ellmann and O'Clair, eds.), 7, 33
"Notes from the Childhood and Girlhood" (Brooks), 50
Notes of a Native Son (Baldwin), 246–247
"Notes toward a Supreme Fiction" (Stevens, W.), 153
"November off Tehuantepec" (Stevens, W.), 165
Novy, Marianne, 258
Now Sheba Sings the Song (Angelou), 87–88, 111–112
"Now That I Am Forever with Child" (Lorde), 188

"O Daedalus, Fly Away Home" (Hayden), 27–28
O'Brien, John, 47, 236
Ochillo, Yvonne
  on Arnold, 131–132
  biographical info, 286
  on Walcott, 132–143
O'Clair, Robert, 33
O'Connor, Flannery, 38, 47
"The October Revolution: Two Views of the Avant Garde in Action" (Morgenstern and Williams), 217, 238
October Revolution in Jazz, 217
"Ode for the Confederate Dead" (Tate), 175
Odyssey (Homer), 116, 208
Oh Pray My Wings Are Gonna Fit Me Well (Angelou), 87–88, 104–106, 112
Okigbo, Christopher, 5
Oliver, Stephanie Stokes, 112
Olson, Charles, 12, 63, 68–69
Omeros (Walcott), 9, 114–121, 279
On Lies, Secrets and Silence (Rich), 258
On the Advantage and Disadvantage of History for Life (Nietzsche), 177
"One Big Interview" *(Picked-Up Pieces)*, 59
The Opposing Virtues (Farag), 223, 240

"Oral Light" (Harper), 196
Organization of Young Men, 276
Osbey, Brenda Marie, 8, 27–28
Osiris: The Egyptian Religion of Resurrection (Budge), 219, 239
Osiris ("I am a cowboy in the boat of Ra"), 209–213, 222–225
Ossman, David, 84
O'Sullivan, Maurice J., 47
Othello (Shakespeare), 119, 248, 253, 259
"Out of the Cage and Still Singing: Interview with Maya Angelou" (Benson), 112
"Out of the Cradle" (Whitman), 156

Pantin, Raoul, 142–143
"Parades, Parades" (Walcott), 139–140
Paradise Valley (Detroit, MI), 11, 273
Park, Clara Claiborne, 50, 52, 58
Parker, Bettye J., 190–191
"Parker's Back" (O'Connor), 38, 47
"Passage to India" (Whitman), 208–209
"Passing Time" (Angelou), 105–106
Paterson, Judith, 112
Paterson (Williams, W. C.), 12
Paulson, William R., 232, 243
Pearce, Donald, 15, 34
Penny Poems (magazine), 62–63
Petro cult (Vodoun), 226–227
" 'Phantom Pain': Nathaniel Mackey's *Bedouin Hornbook*" (Mullen), 176
"Phenomenal Woman" (Angelou), 106–107
Phillis Wheatley (A Letter from Phillis Wheatley), 44
Philoctete *(Omeros)*, 114
"Poem about My Rights" (Jordan), 251, 257
"A Poem for Black Hearts" (Jones/Amiri Baraka), 82
"A Poem for Democrats" (Jones/Amiri Baraka), 74–75
"A Poem for Willie Best" (Jones/Amiri Baraka), 74

"Poem on my fortieth birthday to my
    mother who died young" (Clifton),
    184
"A Poem Some People Will Have to
    Understand" (Jones/Amiri Baraka),
    79
The Poems of Matthew Arnold (Allott,
    ed.), 132, 143
"The Poet and His Art: A
    Conversation" (McCluskey), 47
Poet in New York (Lorca), 71
Poetry
    AA limits to fullness of description,
        180–181
    difficulty of writing, 137–138
    of the Eastern block, 123–124,
        127–128
    Eliot's contribution to, 71
    Hayden on, 11
    Irish, contemporary, 115–116
    poet as man/prophet, 218, 223
    post-traditional, 8–10, 25, 28–29, 39
    redemptive, 124
    shamans in, 231
    as substitute for religion, 131
    symbolic representation in, 180–181,
        183
    Walcott on, 279
Poetry After Modernism (McDowell, ed.),
    258
*The Poetry of Black America: Anthology of
    the Twentieth Century* (Adoff, ed.),
    182–183, 190
The Poetry of Maya Angelou (Angelou),
    101–104
Poetry (periodical), 63
"Poetry—Enormously Complicated
    Art" (Walcott), 137–138, 143
The Poet's World (Library of Congress),
    258
Poggioli, Renato, 215–215, 238
"The Point" (Hayden), 40
Poirier, Richard, 233, 243
"Political Poem" (Jones/Amiri Baraka),
    75

"The politics of rich painters"
    (Jones/Amiri Baraka), 75
Pool, Rosey, 5, 29–30, 34
The Portable Melville (Leyda, ed.), 54, 59
A Portrait of the Artist as a Young Man
    (Joyce), 118
Post-traditional poetry, 8–10, 25, 28–29,
    39
Pottawatomie Creek, 43
Pound, Ezra
    activist temperament, 80
    Cantos, 151–152
    (de)construction of history, 151–152
    impending social disruption, 27
    Jones/Amiri Baraka influenced by, 63
    paradisal visions, 9
    revising Eliot's typescript, 23
    Wright influenced by, 153–154,
        158–159
The Pound Era (Kenner), 168, 176
Powers, Kevin, 231, 242
*Preface to a Twenty Thousand Volume
    Suicide Note* (Jones/Amiri Baraka),
    63–65, 70, 80
"Prelude to a Parting" (Angelou), 109
Prima, Diane di, 62
Prins, Yopie, 252, 257
"The Prisoners" (Hayden), 39, 43
Pritchard, William H., 234, 243–244
"The Problem of a 'Black Aesthetic'"
    (Hatcher), 30
"Progress Report" (Lorde), 188–189
"Prologue" (Lorde), 186–187
*Protest: The Beat Generation and the
    Angry Young Men* (Feldman and
    Gartenberg, eds.), 84
Provincetown Review, 62–63
Pulitzer Prize, 50, 275, 284
Putschogl, Gerhard, 215–215, 238
"Pygmies Are Pygmies Still, Though
    Percht on Alps" (Brooks), 58

Queen of the Ebony Isles (McElroy),
    187–191

"The Rabbi," 39
Racism
  Angelou's experience of, 88–92, 95
  Brooks and, 52–53
  Harper's experiences, 282
  Hayden's description of, 10, 32
"The Rag Man" (Hayden), 39
Rampersad, Arnold, 181, 191
Reading Black, Reading Feminist (Gates,
    ed.), 255–256, 258
Re:Creation (Giovanni), 191
Redding, Saunders, 30
Redmond, Eugene B., 177
Reed, Ishmael
  as avant-garde, 215–215
  awards and honors, 283
  on being black, 283
  biographical info, 206, 282–283
  Blake's *Milton* compared to, 207–208,
    211, 219–220, 225, 227–228
  collective improvisation as utopian
    model, 218
  Emerson's influence on, 210
  folklore traditions, use of, 211,
    225–227
  "Hoodoo," 211
  identity-as-community, 216–220
  "Mental War against cultural
    exclusionism," 227
  parodies, use of, 206, 235
  Spengler's influence on, 208
  Sun Ra compared to, 214–215
  Thomas and, 243
  transcendentalism vs. romanticism,
    220, 227
  Yeats, Transcendentalism and Vodoun
    mixed, 233
  Yeats' compared to, 210, 212–214,
    219, 221, 230
Reed, Ishmael, style of
  cultural clash, 208
  dual or multiple selves, 234–235
  jazz, 213–220
  metamorphosis of personae, 210, 237
  obsessive use of aggression, 225
  Romantic literary structures, 208

satire and prophecy, mix of, 207–208,
    218, 223
symbolism, 212–213, 220, 225–226,
    232
transitions between sacrifice and
    performance, 218–219, 228–229
violent juxtaposition of diverse
    materials, 221
Reed, Ishmael, works of
  Conjure: Selected Poems, 1963-1970,
    206–207, 209, 211–212, 215–216,
    230, 236, 240
  Flight to Canada, 225, 235, 244
  "I am a cowboy in the boat of Ra,"
    207–210, 219–222, 224–225,
    230–231, 233
  "if my enemy is a clown, a natural
    born clown," 215–216
  Milton (Blake), compared to "I am a
    cowboy on the boat of Ra,"
    207–208, 216, 219–220, 223–224
  *Mumbo Jumbo, The Last Days of
    Louisiana Red*, 235, 244
  "Neo-HooDoo Aesthetic," 210
  Shrovetide in Old New Orleans, 206,
    211, 235, 237
  "Time and the Eagle," 205–207, 230,
    235
  Yellow-Back Radio Broke Down,
    210–211, 227, 229–230, 236
"Reed's 'I am a cowboy in the boat of
    Ra'" (Abel), 211, 222, 237
"Reflections on the White Man's
    Privilege" (Baldwin), 247
*Regeneration Through Violence: The
    Mythology of the American Frontier,
    1600-1860* (Slotkin), 227, 241
"Relic of Memory" (Heaney), 122
"Remembering Robert Hayden"
    (Harper), 33
Rich, Adrienne, 9, 162, 177, 247–248,
    254
"Richard Wright's Blues" (Ellison), 251,
    257
"The Riddle" (Heaney), 128
Rigaud, Milo, 215, 238

The Rise and Fall of the White Republic
  (Saxton), 256, 259
"Rita Dove: Identity Markers"
  (Vendler), 255–256, 258
"The Rites of Assent: Rhetoric, Ritual
  and the Ideology of American
  Consensus" (Bercovitch), 228, 242
Ritsos, Yannis, 11
Rituale Romanum, 209–210
*The Riverside Interviews 4: Jerome
  Rothenberg* (Selerie and Mottram),
  231, 242
*Robert Hayden: A Critical Analysis of His
  Poetry* (Williams, P.), 6, 30–31, 34,
  47
"Robert Hayden: Poet Laureate" (Pool),
  5, 29–30, 34
"Robert Hayden & MIchael S. Harper:
  A Literary Friendship" (Nicholas),
  27, 33
Robert Hayden (Fetrow), 30, 33
"Robert Hayden's Use of History"
  (Davis), 31, 33
Robinson, Christine Renee, 179
Robinson, Edward Arlington, 11
Rodgers, Carolyn, 184–185, 190–191
Roediger, David, 256, 259
"Roi's New Blues" (Jones/Amiri Baraka),
  67, 73–74
Rollins, Sonny, 213–214, 216, 218–219,
  222
"Roman Ritual" (Sigler), 210, 236
Rorty, Richard, 32, 34
Roszak, Theodore, 226, 241
Rothenberg, Jerome, 231, 242
Rowell, Charles H., 152, 155, 162, 177
Rubin, Louis D., Jr., 58
Ruiz (*Amistad* mutiny), 18–21, 24
Rukeyser, Muriel, 11–12, 14, 17–21
"Runagate Runagate" (Hayden), 2, 10
Rushing, Andrea Benton, 179–181, 191
"Ruth" (McElroy), 187–188

Sabotage (Jones/Amiri Baraka), 78–83
Sachs, Emily, 11–12

Said, Edward, 13, 34
"Sailing to Byzantium" (Yeats), 213
Sandburg, Carl, 11
"Sandstone Keepsake" (Heaney),
  126–127
Saurat, Denis, 227, 241
Saxton, Alexander, 256, 259
"Say It Ain't So, Huck" (Smiley), 256,
  259
Sayles, Thelma Lucille. *see* Clifton,
  Lucille
"Schizophrenia" (Hayden), 16–17, 33
Schneck, Stephen, 84
Scott, Nathan A., Jr., 276
"Screaming Fire" (Dove), 259
"Sea Surface Full of Clouds" (Stevens,
  W.), 165
The Seasons (magazine), 62–63
Second Black Writers' Conference (Fisk
  University), 8, 275
"A Second Coming" (Yeats), 213
"The Second Coming" (Yeats), 206
"Second Conversations with
  Ogotemmêli" (Wright), 155,
  167–169, 171–172
Secrets of Voodoo (Rigaud), 215, 238
Seebohm, Caroline, 112
Selected Poems: 1966-1987 (Heaney), 121
Selected Poems (Brooks), 275
Selected Poems of Jay Wright (Stepto, ed.),
  28, 31, 34
Selerie, Gavin, 231, 242
Senghor, Léopold Sédar, 5
"The Sense of Comedy: I," 165
Sepharial, 225–226, 240
"September 1, 1939" (Auden), 127
Set (magazine), 62–63
"The Seven Eyes of Yeats" (Adams), 224
"The Sexual Law" (Saurat), 227, 241
Shadle, Mark, 219, 226–227, 230, 239,
  241–242
"The Shadow is Dead" (Jones/Amiri
  Baraka), 79
Shaker, Why Don't You Sing? (Angelou),
  87–88, 108–112
Shakespeare, William, 21–22, 119,
  245–256

"Shakespeare Say" (Dove), 245–246, 250–252, 255
Shamanism: Archaic Techniques of Ecstasy (Eliade), 231, 242
Shamans, 231
Shaw, Harry B., 50, 58
Shelley, Percy Bysshe, 233–234
Sheppard, Walt, 232, 243
"Shore Woman" (Heaney), 122–123
"Short Speech to My Friends" (Jones/Amiri Baraka), 75
Shreiber, Maeera, 252, 257
Shrovetide in Old New Orleans (Reed), 206, 211, 235, 237
Sigler, G. J., 210, 236
Signal (magazine), 62–63
Singers of Daybreak: Studies in Black American Literature (Baker), 49–50, 58
Singin' and Swingin' and Gettin' Merry Like Christmas (Angelou), 87–88, 93–96, 111
"Singing America: From Walt Whitman to Adrienne Rich" (Erickson), 257
"Singing School" (Heaney), 125
"Sketch for an Aesthetic Project" (Wright), 148
Slotkin, Richard, 227, 241
Smiley, Jane, 256, 259
Smith, Adam, 113–114
Smith, Gary, 50, 52, 58
"The Snow Lamp" (Hayden), 36
Snyder, Gary, 211, 237
Social and Cultural Pluralism in the Caribbean (Lowenthal), 118
Société Africaine de Culture, 5
"The Song of the Happy Shepherd" (Yeats), 223, 240
Soothsayers and Omens (Wright)
  aesthetic self-sufficiency of, 167
  aesthetic web of Stevens in, 165
  black people acting in history, 146
  Chapultepec, recurrent sounding of, 165
  (de)construction of history, 151–152
  four-part, architectonic structure, 155

personal portraits in, 147–148
restless lines of call-and-response, 162
simultaneous familiarity and strangeness, 154, 157
Souls of Black Folk (DuBois), 30
The Souls of Black Folks (DuBois), 76, 245–247, 257
"Sources" (Wright), 157
"Southeast Arkansia" (Angelou), 105
Souvenirs and Prophecies: The Young Wallace Stevens (Stevens, W.), 177
"Space Age Music: The Music of Sun Ra" (Fiofiori), 214, 237
Spellman, Cardinal, 209–210, 230
Spengler, Oswald, 208, 230
Stark, Inez Cunningham, 275
"Stars," 46
"Start Misquoting Him Now: The Difference a Word Makes in Adrienne Rich's 'Inscriptions' " (Erickson), 257
"Statement on Poetics" (Jones/Amiri Baraka), 63, 68–69
"Station Island" (Heaney), 121, 127
Station Island (Heaney), 9, 126–127
Statue of Liberty, 75, 103
Stearn, Gerald Emanuel, 233, 243
Steiner, George, 233
Stepto, Robert B., 28, 31, 34
Stetson, Erlene, 191
Stevens, Holly, 177
Stevens, Wallace, 2–3, 153–154, 157, 171, 177
Stock, A. G., 234, 243
"Story Books on a Kitchen Table" (Lorde), 186
"The Storyteller" (Benjamin), 153–155, 174
"Stranger in the Village" (Baldwin), 246, 252, 257
A Street in Bronzeville (Brooks), 275
"The Study of Poetry" (Arnold), 131, 142
Sturdy Black Bridges: Visions of Black Women in Literature (Bell, Parker and Guy-Sheftall, eds.), 190

The Sullen Art: Interviews with Modern American Poets (Ossman), 84
Sun Ra, 214–215, 217–218, 230–231
"The Swamp" (Walcott), 140

"Talks with Two Singular Women" (Weston and Seebohm), 112
Target Study (Jones/Amiri Baraka), 78–83
Tate, Claudia, 112, 175
"The Tattooed Man" (Hayden), 37–39, 46
Tatum, Stephen, 227–228, 241
Taylor, Cecil, 217
"Tea at the Palaz of Hoon" (Stevens), 154
Teasdale, Sara, 274
Technicians of the Sacred: A Range of Poetries from Africa, America and Oceania (Rothenberg), 231, 242
"Telling it Like it I-S *IS*: Narrative Techniques in Melvin Tolson's Harlem Gallery" (Dove), 258
The Circus Animal's Desertion" (Yeats), 9
"The thirty eighth year" (Clifton), 184
"Theme and Variation" (Hayden), 42, 46
The Theory of the Avant-Garde (Poggioli), 215–215, 238
"There Must Be a Lone Ranger" (Jones/Amiri Baraka), 74
"Theses on the Philosophy of History" (Benjamin), 174
"They Are All Gone into the World of Light!" (Vaughn), 156
Third World Festival of Negro Arts (Dakar, Senegal), 5–8, 29–30
"This Nettle, Danger" (Baldwin), 257
Thomas, Lorenzo, 243
Thomas and Beulah (Dove), 283–284
"Three Dollars Cash" (Walker), 182
Thurley, Geoffrey, 213, 237
"Time and the Eagle" (Reed), 205–207, 230, 235

"Times-Square-Shoeshine Composition" (Angelou), 103
"Tintern Abbey" (Wordsworth), 133
Tiresias ("The Waste Land"), 22–23
"To a Husband" (Angelou), 102
"To the Roaring Wind" (Stevens, W.), 157
"The Tollund Man" (Heaney), 122, 124
Tolson, Melvin, 6, 50
Topics of Discourse: Essays in Cultural Criticism (White), 177
"The Torn Cloth" (Duncan), 170
Totem Press, 62–63, 69
"Touch Me, Life, Not Softly" (Angelou), 106–108
"Tour Guide: *Le Maison des Esclaves*" (Dixon), 28
Tradition, 28–29
Tradition: The Writer and Society— Critical Essays (Harris), 176
"Tradition and the Individual Talent" (Eliot), 138, 143
Transcendentalism: Style and Vision in the American Renaissance (Buell), 210, 237
Transfigurations: Collected Poems (Wright), 4, 145–150
Transformations (Wright), 146
"Translating the Sacred: The Poet and the Shaman" (Giordano), 231, 242–243
"Traveling" (Angelou), 106–108
"Tremors of Exactitude" Review of *The Double Invention of Komo* (Hollander), 152, 173–174, 176
Trilogy (HD), 12
Trinidad Theatre Workshop, 116–117
"Trout" (Heaney), 121
The Turbulent Dream: Passion and Politics in the Poetry of W. B. Yeats (Thurley), 213, 237
"The Turncoat" (Jones/Amiri Baraka), 66, 73
Turner, Victor, 177
Twain, Mark, 256, 259
"Twentieth Century American Poetry" (Hayden), 10–11

"Twentieth-Century Dementer"
(Vendler), 255–256, 258
Two-headed woman (Clifton), 183–184,
190–191, 281
"Two House Painters Take Stock of the
Fog" (Wright), 148

Ulysses (Joyce), 116
Umbra, 217
"Umbra Days" (Dent), 217, 238
Uncle Crip ("Elegies for Paradise
Valley"), 40–41
"Under the Round Tower" (Yeats), 223
*Understanding Media: The Extensions of
Man* (McLuhan), 219, 232, 239,
243
*Understanding the New Black Poetry: Black
Speech and Black Music as Poetic
References* (Henderson), 176
"The Undertaker's Daughter Feels
Neglect" (Moss)
hallucinatory force, 4
UNESCO, 5
*Unfinished Animal: The Aquarian Frontier
and the Evolution of Consciousness*
(Roszak), 226, 241
"The Universal and the Particular in
Afro-American Poetry"
(Rampersad), 181, 191
"'The Unraveling of the Egg': An
Interview with Jay Wright"
(Rowell), 152, 155, 162, 177
Updike, John, 53
The Upstart Crow: A Shakespeare Journal
(Erickson), 258
"Ur-history of the 19th Century"
(Benjamin), 170

Vaillant, Janet G., 5, 31, 34
Van Buren, Martin, 20
Vaughn, Henry, 156
Vendler, Helen, 255–256, 258
"The Venus Hottentot" (Alexander), 28
"Vice" (Jones/Amiri Baraka), 73

Village Voice (periodical), 63
"Villancico" (Wright), 149
A Vision (Yeats), 206–207, 230, 234
The Voodoo Gods (Deren), 226, 241
Voodoo in Haiti (Metraux), 226, 241
"Voyages" (Crane), 157

W. B. Yeats: A Critical Anthology
(Pritchard, ed.), 234, 243–244
W. B. Yeats: His Poetry and Thought
(Stock), 234, 243
"W. E. B. DuBois at Harvard" (Wright),
148
The Wages of Whiteness (Roediger), 256,
259
Walcott, Derek
Auden's influence on, 2
awards and honors, 5, 279
biographical info, 114–115, 278–279
Eliot's influence on, 116
Homer's influence on, 115–116
Joyce's influence on, 116
on poetry, 279
post-traditional stance of, 9
Stevens and, 2
Trinidad Theatre Workshop, 116–117
Walcott, Derek, style of
dialogues reveal characters, 118
heavily plotted contexts, 118–119
historical implications, 115, 118–119,
133
metaphors, 132, 134, 137–138
militancy in art, 119
mythic method, 116
slow lines underscore significance,
141
theatrical organization structures,
116–117
themes
alienation/isolation, 132–138,
141–142
colonialism, 114–115, 117,
119–121, 139
nature, 133, 136–137
political hierarchies, 120–121, 141

politics, 140–141
West Indian idioms, 134
Walcott, Derek, works of
"Allegre," 133
Another Life, 134–135
"The Bounty," 3
"The Castaway," 135
"Castiliane," 138
Cry for a Leader, 117–118
Dream on Monkey Mountain and Other Plays, 114–115, 119, 139–143, 279
"A Far Cry From Africa," 142
"Forest of Europe," 136–137
"Homecoming: Anse la Raye," 141
"In A Green Night," 5, 132–133
"Mass Man," 133–134
Omeros, 9, 114–121, 279
"Parades, Parades," 139–140
"Poetry—Enormously Complicated Art," 137–138, 143
"The Swamp," 140
"What the Twilight Says: An Overture," 114–115, 119, 139–143
Walcott, Ronald, 35–47, 285
Walker, Alice, 152, 177, 182, 189–191
Walton, Anthony, 33
Waniek, Marilyn Nelson, 258
Ward, Jerry D., 181, 191
Washington, Mary Helen, 179, 190–191
The Waste Land and Other Poems (Eliot), 33
"The Waste Land" (Eliot)
as end of modernism, 10
Hayden and, 11, 13, 16, 31
Jones/Amiri Baraka' jazz-poem compared to, 72–73
"Middle Passage" compared to, 19, 21–22
myth of Parsifal and, 24–25
"overcoming," 12, 14
"The Watershed" (Auden), 129
"Way Out West" (Jones/Amiri Baraka), 73
We, the Other People: Alternative Declarations of Independence by Labor Groups, Farmers, Women's Rights

Advocates, Socialists, and Blacks (Foner), 176
"We Real Cool" (Brooks), 56, 59
The Wealth of Nations (Smith, A.), 113–114
"Wednesday Night Prayer Meeting" (Wright), 146
"Wells, Fargo and Company" (Harlow), 221
Wells, Henry, 221
West, Cornel, 32, 34
Weston, Carol, 112
"What My Child Learns of the Sea" (Lorde), 188
"What the Twilight Says: An Overture" (Walcott), 114–115, 119, 139–143
Wheatley, Phillis, 50
"When State Magicians Fail: An Interview with Ishmael Reed" (Sheppard), 232, 243
"When We Dead Awaken: Writing as Re-Vision" (Rich), 258
White, Hayden, 177
White Buildings (Hart), 176
White Dove Review, 62–63
"White Man's Guilt" (Baldwin), 157, 175
"The White Negro" (Mailer), 61–62, 84
Whitman, Walt, 11–12, 156, 208–209, 227–228, 233
The Will to Change (Rich), 247–248
William Gibbs: American Genius (Rukeyser), 17–18, 34
"William Shakespeare in America" (Levine), 256, 259
Williams, Charles, 16
Williams, Martin, 217, 238
Williams, Pontheolla T., 6, 30–31, 34, 47, 63
Williams, William Carlos, 12, 64, 73
"Willie" (Angelou), 107
Wilmer, Valerie, 217, 238
The Wind Among the Reeds (Yeats), 219, 239
The Winding Stair and Other Poems (Yeats), 219, 239

"Wintering Out" (Heaney), 121
Wintering Out (Heaney), 121–122
Winters, Yvor, 243–244
"Witch Doctor" (Hayden), 39
*Witchcraft, Mysticism and Magic in the
	Black World* (Haskins), 211, 237
"Woman Work" (Angelou), 107
Women's Re-Visions of Shakespeare (Novy),
	258
"Words in the Mourning Time"
	(Hayden), 10, 30–31, 38–40
Wordsworth, William, 133, 233–234
A World Elsewhere (Poirier), 233, 243
"The Worms at Heaven's Gate"
	(Stevens, W.), 166
Worsham, Fabian Clements, 179–191,
	286
Wright, Jay
	antihistoricism of, 152–156, 159–160,
		162
	awards and honors, 145, 280
	on being black, 146–149, 163
	on Bicentennial celebration, 152
	biographical info, 147–150, 280
	Chapultepec and, 165
	Hayden's influence on, 8, 28, 31
	on "Middle Passage," 14
	Stevens' influence on, 153–154
	as Sublime, 4
Wright, Jay, style of
	"binary-resistant structural integrity,"
		156
	discontinuous narrative, 154–155
	evolving aesthetic structures of
		history, 163
	ironic, solipsistic imperative, 173
	metaphysical and mythical, 158–159,
		161–162
	multiple rhyme and syllabic schemes,
		149
	spiritual resonance, 155
	as "tangle of black traditions," 28
	themes
		autobiographical, 148, 162, 280
		death, 146, 163–165, 172–173
		parodies of pastoral, 169

	transfigurations, 147, 168–169, 172
Wright, Jay, works of. *see also Soothsayers
	and Omens*
	"The Albuquerque Graveyard," 146,
		163–165, 172
	"Beginning," 170
	"Benjamin Banneker Helps to Build a
		City," 147, 158
	"Benjamin Banneker Sends His
		'Almanac' to Thomas Jefferson,"
		157–162, 172, 176
	"The Birthday," 165–166
	Boleros, 146
	"The Charge," 155–156, 158, 162
	"Coda V," 149
	"Coda VI," 149
	"Crispus Attucks," 148
	"The Dead," 172–173
	"Death as History," 167, 177
	"Desire's Design, Vision's Resonance:
		Black Poetry's Ritual and Historical
		Voice," 14, 34, 147
	Dimensions of History, 28, 149,
		151–152, 167
	The Double Invention of Komo, 28,
		146–147
	Elaine's Book, 146
	"Entering New Mexico," 162
	"The Faithful One," 147–148
	"Family Reunion," 163–164
	"The First Word," 171
	"The Fisherman's Fiesta," 148
	"The Healing Improvisation of Hair,"
		149
	"The Hieroglyph of Irrrational
		Force," 149
	"Homecoming: Guadalajara—New
		York, 1965," 166–167
	"The Homecoming Singer," 164
	The Homecoming Singer, 146–148,
		164–165, 170
	"The Hunting Trip Cook," 147–148
	"Intuition: Figure and Act," 149
	"Jason Visits His Gypsy," 166
	"Jason's One Command," 148
	"The Master of Names," 162

"The Museums of Chapultepec," 165
"The Navigation of Absences: An
    Ode on Method," 149
"Nocturnal upon St. Lucy's Day," 149
"A Non-Birthday Poem for my
    Father," 148
"Second Conversations with
    Ogotemmêli," 155, 167–169,
    171–172
"Sketch for an Aesthetic Project," 148
"Sources," 157
Transfigurations: Collected Poems, 4,
    145–150
Transformations, 146
"Two House Painters Take Stock of
    the Fog," 148
"Villancico," 149
"W. E. B. DuBois at Harvard," 148
"Wednesday Night Prayer Meeting,"
    146
"Writers Converge at Fisk University"
    (Llorens), 6–7, 33
*Writing Between the Lines: Race and
    Intertextuality* (Nielsen), 177

Yale Literary Review (periodical), 63
"The Year of the Child" (Hayden), 42,
    45
*The Years of Our Friendship: Robert Lowell
    and Allen Tate* (Doreski), 176
Yeats: The Man and the Masks (Ellmann),
    226, 240
Yeats, William Butler
    activist temperament, 80
    Anglo-Ireland heritage, 9
    belief in multiple self, 233–234
    conflict as agent of renewal, 223
    Harper influenced by, 200
    impending social disruption, 27
    kind old nun of, 212
    passionate caring of, 11–12
    reconstructions of his heritage, 10
    Reed compared to, 206, 210,
        212–214, 219, 221, 230

    symbolism of, 223
    terror of change, 213
Yeats, William Butler, works of
    "Among School Children," 212–214
    The Circus Animal's Desertion," 9
    "Crazy Jane," 75
    "Cuchulain Comforted," 9
    "The Double Vision of Michael
        Robartes," 223, 240
    "Leda and the Swan," 206
    "Sailing to Byzantium," 213
    "A Second Coming," 213
    "The Second Coming," 206
    "The Song of the Happy Shepherd,"
        223, 240
    "Under the Round Tower," 223
    A Vision, 206–207, 230, 234
    The Wind Among the Reeds, 219, 239
    The Winding Stair and Other Poems,
        219, 239
*Yeats and American Poetry: The Tradition
    of the Self* (Diggory), 233–235,
    243–244
"Yeats and the Language of Symbolism"
    (Frye), 207, 235
Yeats Golden Dawn (Harper), 230, 242
Yellow-Back Radio Broke Down (Reed),
    210–211, 227, 229–230, 236
Your Native Land, Your Life (Rich), 9
Yugen magazine, 61–62, 70

Zamir, Shamoon
    biographical info, 287
    on free jazz, 214–220
    on Reed, 205–244
"Zinnias," 40
Zorn, Marilyn, 50, 58